# NEXT-GENERATION
## HOMELAND SECURITY

# NEXT-GENERATION HOMELAND SECURITY

Network Federalism and the Course to National Preparedness

## John Fass Morton

NAVAL INSTITUTE PRESS

ANNAPOLIS, MARYLAND

Naval Institute Press
291 Wood Road
Annapolis, MD 21402

Library of Congress Cataloging-in-Publication Data
Morton, John Fass, 1947–
  Next-generation homeland security : network federalism and the course to
national preparedness / John Fass Morton.
     p. cm.
  Includes bibliographical references and index.
  ISBN 978-1-61251-088-0 (hbk. : alk. paper) — ISBN 978-1-61251-089-7
(ebook) 1. United States. Dept. of Homeland Security. 2. National security—
United States. 3. Terrorism—United States—Prevention. 4. Emergency
management—United States. I. Title.
  HV6432.4.M67 2012
  363.325'160973—dc23
                        2012026504

  ⊗ This paper meets the requirements of ANSI/NISO z39.48-1992
(Permanence of Paper).
Printed in the United States of America.

20  19  18  17  16  15  14  13  12      9 8 7 6 5 4 3 2 1
First printing

Book design and composition: David Alcorn, Alcorn Publication Design

*For those of the next generation*

*who are called to be*

*homeland security professionals*

# Contents

# Foreword

In late March 2011 my friend and colleague Lisa Gordon-Hagerty came to my office with two fellow members of a homeland security study team. They were there to brief me on some of their recommendations for getting more unity of effort into what folks are now calling the Homeland Security Enterprise. With her were Dennis Schrader, who had served as the Federal Emergency Management Agency's (FEMA) first deputy administrator for national preparedness, and John Morton, who had assembled and was leading this sixty-member homeland security team for Jim Locher's Project on National Security Reform. What followed was a good political science discussion that seemed to align with my own thinking.

Wanting to cut to the chase, I turned to John and asked, "So what's the elevator speech?"

"Governor," he replied, "this federal-centric homeland security system we have right now is a single point of failure."

"I get it."

For almost all my time in public service, from serving in the Army in Vietnam, to my years as assistant district attorney for Erie County, Pennsylvania, my six terms representing northwestern Pennsylvania in the U.S. Congress, and my two terms as governor of the Keystone State, national security was something decided in Washington and executed beyond our nation's borders, on the front lines so to speak—not on the home front. Our national security system came to be just after World War II, and with it we won the Cold War. Today we would say it was a federal effort. State and local governments did not play a part.

The terrorist attacks of 9/11 changed all that. And I can tell you, so did the anthrax attacks. When the White House Office of Homeland Security, the Homeland Security Council, and eventually the Department of Homeland Security were constructed, we were in the midst of fighting an asymmetric enemy. We were wired and prepared for the other shoe to drop, as we weren't completely sure whether that enemy had more weapons of mass destruction (WMD) ready to spring on our people.

"Uneasy lies the head that wears the crown," wrote Shakespeare. The same was true in those months after 9/11 when we mere public servants wrestled with trying to put together an entirely different unity of effort to deal with these kinds of asymmetric threats that abruptly and cruelly made obvious how the strategic environment had changed. This book records, from the inside, much of that struggle, as well as how my successors grappled with the lessons learned from the Hurricane Katrina response and partnered with Congress to make the necessary changes that have given us the Homeland Security Enterprise we have today. It was a heroic effort. We were all having to sail the ship of state while we were re-designing it.

At the time most of Washington thought of national security as a borders-out thing on the federal plane. For them the focus was on a one-dimensional interagency reorganization for departments and agencies that had what we now called homeland security missions. Like President George W. Bush, I came to my post at the White House as a chief executive of a state. As governors both of us appreciated the strengths of our federal system of government and well understood that our federal republic is one of sovereign states and a sovereign people. War had been brought to the home front, even to the farm fields of southwestern Pennsylvania. For the foreseeable future homeland security would engage co-equally all levels of government—federal, state, and local—and for that matter the private sector, non-governmental organizations (NGOs), faith-based organizations, and all that form what today's FEMA administrator Craig Fugate calls community resilience networks.

In my view Craig has it absolutely right. At a 2004 symposium on public preparedness that the Department of Homeland Security (DHS) co-sponsored with the American Red Cross, the Council for Excellence in Government, and George Washington University's Homeland Security Policy Institute, I and Red Cross president and CEO Marsha "Marty" Evans stressed personal preparedness as the strongest element of homeland security. The reality is that the national-level security and resilience aggregate from the bottom up. Marty and I went on record, calling for a national preparedness system that would include recommendations and guidance to support preparedness planning for businesses, communities, families, and individuals.

Pennsylvania has always seen itself as an industrial and agricultural state. Yet the whole world has advanced from the Industrial Age into an Information Age. So when we are talking about intergovernmental dimensions, "network" is a good term. We don't get unity of effort today from outmoded organizational structures and processes working top-down via command and control. To make the point: Erie fire chief Tony Pol is not in the president's chain of command; neither is he in Pennsylvania governor Tom Corbett's. We recognized this truth when we decentralized PEMA, the Pennsylvania Emergency Management Agency, to facilitate lateral mutual aid across all counties and townships in the Commonwealth. In this Information Age, unity of effort is all about cross-jurisdictional, cross-disciplinary coordination. The means is what the fire service calls Unified Command, enshrined in ICS, the Incident Command System. Any firefighter, emergency manager, law enforcement officer, or public health official will tell you the keystone of our national response doctrine is "all disasters are local." But in times of catastrophe a disaster is something more, something regional.

When I represented Erie and Pennsylvania's 21st congressional district in Washington, before I became governor, I was distressed by how the federal government was failing to step up in support of local communities in time of need. The tipping point for me came in May 1985. It was the last day of the school year in northwestern Pennsylvania, when twenty-one tornadoes tracked across the region. One was an F5; another six were F4s, making for the deadliest day of tornadoes ever recorded in the Commonwealth. The F5 destroyed nearly all of Wheatland; one of the F4s leveled Albion, and another virtually razed Atlantic. All three towns were in my district, near the Ohio border, smack dab in what is historically northwestern Pennsylvania's tornado alley. By the time I arrived in Atlantic, a regional center for the Amish, neighboring communities and Amish volunteers from Ohio were already active in the response. The Feds were minor players. To my mind, the federal partnership was clearly not working and had failed to serve the people of my district. This heart-wrenching experience compelled me to act.

For the next three years, I worked hard on drafting and pushing legislative language that finally resulted in the Robert T. Stafford Disaster Relief and Emergency Assistance Act of 1988. My intent, however, was not to centralize disaster response in Washington. Far from it. Rather, I wanted to enhance an intergovernmental preparedness and response partnership and develop it into a national preparedness system. I was determined to help make FEMA what Craig Fugate's predecessor Dave Paulison would later call "forward-leaning." I had a mind to build this national system on something like the system of state and local partnerships we had developed via PEMA in Pennsylvania.

Similarly, fifteen years later, when I left the White House to become the first secretary of homeland security, I had the idea that this new DHS should disperse itself across the nation along with FEMA and its other component agencies to put ourselves as close as possible to the communities we were going to serve. With my chief of staff, Bruce Lawlor, and later Bob Stephan (at the time the head of the DHS I-Staff, the Integration Staff), I aimed to put in place a network of ten regional offices, or "mini-mes," as I called them. This book traces some of what we tried to do with our regional plan to the time I left government in late 2004. But we were proposing to break too many rice bowls. And so, as one of my key staffers, Chris Furlow, still says of the effort, it died a death of a thousand cuts. In hindsight I now realize Washington perceived us as taking power away from the agencies, and beyond-the-beltway saw us federal bureaucrats inflicting another layer of bureaucracy on the states while making the federal government yet more intrusive. The truth is that this book's term, "Network Federalism," is a more accurate description of the twenty-first-century intergovernmental partnership we had in mind.

Much later on, you'll read a quote from the House of Representatives' *Failure of Initiative* report on Hurricane Katrina. "The preparation and response to Hurricane Katrina show we are still an analog government in a digital age." Digital, yes, but as John says in his introduction, it is still operationally a Newtonian universe when it comes to logistics and span of control. To whatever degree some might think, the federal government in Washington cannot manage a response to a regional catastrophe. If it tried, it would have to become Big Brother, an un-American idea recalling twentieth-century totalitarianism. Twenty-first-century network theory tells us something else more counterintuitive: we make America less resilient, less secure, if we allow Washington to remain her single point of failure.

For both policy-makers and students alike, this book is one among very few seminal works in the yet-to-be-established homeland security canon. It is not a book on policy. It is a book on structure and process. John approached his task with the intent to give voice to the collective wisdom of the hands-on operators and practitioners from all levels of government and the broadest range of disciplines who execute homeland security missions. Many of them I know. They are my colleagues who sailed our ship of state before, after, and with me, at times in harm's way, and took the time to work with John to develop the case and the recommendations for a follow-on redesign.

Though an Army guy, I characterize our work using sea-service terms purposely. John Morton comes from a family with a long Navy line. Five generations are U.S. Naval Academy graduates, with the fifth, his daughter, a member of the class of 2010 and currently at sea with the fleet. As one might expect from this kind of legacy, John takes the long view, and his book looks beyond the National Security Act of 1947 to the Continental Congress and the earliest days of the federal partnership between the national government and the states.

We can't return America to an agrarian democracy or an industrial age. But we can restore a classical American bottom-up resilience for the Information Age. Networks empower people. A nation with a self-reliant citizenry makes not for a single point of failure but rather competitive advantage and continued global engagement.

This book does not claim to be the last word. Its proposal for a network of ten regional nodes, each with a staff drawn from intergovernmental detailees, offers a glimpse of what a future Network Federal governance would look like. This proposition should be a basis for much further discussion toward a homeland security governance. The Pennsylvanian in me would have that discussion take place via some latter-day continental congress in Philadelphia's Independence Hall. For our task is no less than to perfect the means for ensuring that the Homeland Security Enterprise fully expresses a new security and resilience partnership that will help make every region—every community in America—sustainable, safe, and globally competitive and engaged.

Governor Tom Ridge

# Introduction:
## Toward a Resilience Paradigm for American Security Governance

**N**ational security governance in the second decade of the twenty-first century is ill-serving the American people—if left uncorrected, civic life and national continuity will remain increasingly at risk. At stake also, well beyond our shores, is the stability and future direction of an international political and economic system dependent on robust and continued U.S. engagement. We need to be clear: changes in policy alone will not bring resolution.

The problem is one of structure and process—still-fragmented national security and homeland security structures and processes within and between all levels of government. These outdated Cold War–era structures and processes fail to require and empower systematic collaboration, coordination, and integration of security strategy and policy development, resourcing, and aligned operational execution, both in steady-state or crises.

The preamble to the U.S. Constitution enshrines the people's intent that constituted government among other things will "insure domestic tranquility, provide for the common defense, promote the general welfare." Elected officials and security practitioners thus have a duty to set aside partisanship and self-interest to come together for a comprehensive updating of governance for developing and executing security policy to honor the constitutionally guaranteed expectations of our citizens. To be fully effective, this necessary transformation must accurately reflect twenty-first century political, economic, and social realities, better to address strategic challenges and opportunities, better to provide for a resilient America that is stable, secure, and sustainable—come what may.

In 1945, a vibrant and expansive United States became the guarantor of an international political and economic system that by the end of the Cold War was global. Today, America owes its continued position primarily to two elements of its national power: its peerless military and its dollar currency, upon which the international monetary and economic system for the most part is based. Behind these was a third element, which in the forties initially enabled that hegemony: the U.S. national economy—that is its industrial might. Much of that element is no longer present today.[1]

Taking the long view, academics debate the idea that America's hegemonic role has been roughly analogous to Great Britain's in the nineteenth and early twentieth centuries by virtue of its Royal Navy and pound sterling. Parallels are striking. Yet oft overlooked in the colloquy is an important distinction. Whereas Britain was an imperial hegemon *before* it was an industrial power, U.S. military and monetary hegemony in the American Century was *based* on its industrial power. British institutions of governance—feudal, monarchical, and commercial—long preceded industrialization. In America—initially an agrarian and commercial republic—industrialization preceded its global role and establishment of its present system of security governance, institutionalized by the National Security Act of 1947. Regardless of contemporary challenges and opportunities, we are left with at least one question: Does America have the institutions of governance to manage the strategic environment in what may prove to be her "post-industrial" twenty-first century?

The post–World War II establishment of the U.S. national security system in 1947 reflected three strategic preconditions specific *only* to that time:

1.  America's singular and expansive industrial preeminence, undamaged by war, and the means through which she was able to apply transformational, technological advances for military use (e.g., atomic science) effectively enabled the United States and its wartime allies to win World War II. Thereupon, the United States was able to provide the leadership to reconstruct a postwar international political system and economy.

2.  Notwithstanding American preeminence, America and her postwar allies immediately had to focus on a geo-strategic threat from an ideologically driven, continental-sized Soviet Union. Moreover, by the 1950s, this single geo-strategic adversary had acquired a nuclear-weapons capability to threaten the survivability of the American homeland—effectively concentrating the national mind.

3. Fortunately though, mid-twentieth-century America was a time and place when and where a community of interest had arrived at the apex of national power in the political, economic, social, and cultural spheres. Notwithstanding the manifest tensions of the century, this established community of interest at bottom shared a common history and as such was able to sustain a workable cohesion and continuity at the top in New York and in Washington, where strategic consensus was generally expressed with the term "bipartisanship."

Today, however, all three of these strategic preconditions are absent. No longer a nation in surplus with an unrivaled, expansionist techno-industrial economic base, America is in debt and arguably becoming post-industrialized—or, as some would have it, de-industrialized. No longer faced with a single geo-strategic adversary, U.S. security governance attempts to manage strategic challenges that neither generate consensus on prioritization nor lend themselves to military solutions. Diverse events and situations like 9/11, Katrina, the ongoing debt crisis, uncontrollable immigration, the BP oil spill, the WikiLeaks revelations, and the potential domestic impacts of a Eurozone monetary collapse evidence the new and more complex, multi-dimensional strategic vulnerability—"borders-in." No longer a nation with an established community of interest providing cohesive leadership across all spheres of national discourse, America has become an unbounded space with multiple communities of interest. At the federal level these communities often reflect conflicting borders-in and borders-out priorities, and possess the means to effect them through favored executive branch departments and agencies and congressional committees with budgetary oversight—the interagency dimension of governance. Oft overlooked is how these communities also leverage conflicting local, state, national, and international priorities—the intergovernmental dimension.

Since the end of the Cold War, neither the U.S. policy-making community nor the nation has been able to define or communicate a vision or grand strategy for the long term. Absent has been broad agreement on the nation's geo-strategic goals, threats, and opportunities. With the demise of the Soviet military threat to our homeland, post–Cold War priorities shifted to align with notions of a New World Order. From the late eighties into the nineties, policy emphasis went from national security to international economic coordination via supra-national regimes, succinctly translated for the 1992 electorate via the campaign slogan "It's the economy, stupid." In the wake of this shift came a theoretical construct that characterized movement toward an international system of what Anne-Marie Slaughter, the former State Department director for policy planning, has called disaggregated states.[2] Anticipating the decay of the territorial nation-state, this disaggregation construct has implications borders-out, with respect to state sovereignty, and borders-in, as regard to representative government remaining fully accountable to its electorate.

A twenty-first-century system of American governance has to address developments and players by now quite familiar: global jihadism; stateless corporations; transnational criminal networks; rogue, failed, and failing states; China and other expansionist regional hegemons; sovereign wealth funds; cyberspace vulnerabilities; peak oil; national and international debt crises; perceived de-industrialization; complex and catastrophic natural, technological, and environmental disasters; and so on. Policy-makers don't necessarily see these forces returning the world in the medium term to an era of global, interstate military conflict. They are rather anticipating inter-communal conflicts, like those threatening Mexico, to be more the norm. The once optimistic assumptions put forth to justify monetary, trade, and investment policies serving a new world order of a single, globalized economy seem now naïve. The commercial and financial world, for example, no longer bases globalization strategies on simple 1990s-vintage return on investment (RoI) calculations. Private-sector assessments increasingly prioritize risk, safety, and security. Alas, once again the world has become a desperately dangerous place, far different than what the somewhat sophomoric "end of history" believers assumed in the nineties. Today, the conjured idea of an end of history harkens not to Hegel but rather a millenarian Mayan calendar.

Today's national security analyses stubbornly derive from a canon whose origins are in the academic work of the forties and into the Cold War. In the post–Cold War era, those who have made their careers through knowledge and application of this canon are attempting to transform governance structures and processes with inspired recommendations for so-called whole-of-government, system-of-systems approaches. Their emphasis is on optimizing the effectiveness and efficiency of federal-level interagency policy development, decision-making, and issue management. Their problem analyses have illuminated the less-than-optimal executive branch efforts to employ either lead federal agency approaches or the use of "czars"—now some thirty-seven—to overcome interagency bureaucratic turfs.

Along these lines, the Project on National Security Reform (PNSR), for example, made recommendations for institutionalizing mission-focused management using cross-functional teams (CFTs), initially hoping in 2007 to lay the groundwork for an "interagency Goldwater-Nichols" through a rewrite of the National Security Act of 1947.[3] PNSR was primarily recommending structure and process solutions to empower interagency integration and better alignment of strategy and resources to improve governance of the borders-out *horizontal* dimension. The Obama administration and Secretary of State Hillary Clinton chose to build a strategy on their vaunted 3Ds—defense, diplomacy, and development—an interagency approach for international engagement deriving from work applied during the Carter and Clinton administrations by Harvard's Joseph Nye, a PNSR guiding coalition member and one of the originators of the school of neoliberalism and complex interdependence. Nye's term of art today is the familiar "smart power."

Academically, insufficient emphasis has gone to examining a security governance that aligns the interagency, horizontal dimension with the intergovernmental, *vertical* dimension. To be sure, from 1947 to 9/11, national security was primarily a federal, interagency mission/function with very limited intergovernmental input. The 1947 national security system was built and continues to build on federal-centric governance mechanisms that have been ever expanding since the Progressive era prior to World War I. As such, they reflect industrial-age governance geared to industrial-age threats and opportunities. Beyond presenting America with a strategic capability, the rapidly advancing aerospace and nuclear technologies of the forties enabled a strategic threat to her homeland that together required a policy response and structuring of a centralized, top-down national security state replete with security classifications and command-and-control operational hierarchies consonant with that high-industrial era.

If it has been hard enough to redefine national security in the post–Cold War era, it has been harder still to define and bound homeland security. The field of homeland security has no canon comparable to that for national security. Yet, few would disagree: governance in the twenty-first century can no longer bifurcate borders-out and borders-in national security. The nature of the contemporary strategic environment is such that federal, state, and local governments have co-equal roles and responsibilities borders-in. Today's advancing technologies, strategic threats and opportunities, and political, economic, and social realities require structures and processes that are completely the reverse of those for industrial-era national security. Not just whole-of-government, twenty-first-century governance must entertain the idea of whole-of-nation, whole-of-society.

In order to proceed, we must first accept a truth that is fundamental, axiomatic: the structures and processes of a homeland security system have to account for the polity freely imposed by the American federal system of governance. This system is intergovernmental with three layers of shared sovereignty—federal, state, and local—over a common people in a common territory. We need to state the obvious for the borders-out national security community: state and local governmental organizations and personnel are not in the president's chain of command. This fact alone means the traditional defense and national security structures—top-down, hierarchical, and industrial—do not, will not, and moreover cannot apply to homeland security.

Secondly, homeland security structures and processes must accurately reflect the management law of weighting in terms of issue and incident management. The federal government alone does not have the weight to lead a response to a catastrophic event. Nor can it lead organizing the protection of national critical infrastructure. The oft-cited statistic bandied in discussions on critical infrastructure protection makes the point: the private sector owns and operates 85 percent of national critical infrastructure. The federal government hence does not "own" the problem; it thus cannot own the solution. This economic and political reality leads to one conclusion: any structure and process for homeland security must have up-front buy-in—systematically and comprehensively—from state and local authorities, the private sector, and nongovernmental organizations (NGOs), in other words, from the mission partners.

In a very basic sense, homeland security begins with a sovereign people, suggesting that its structures and processes are best driven from the bottom-up to serve resilience. Conveniently, this contention aligns with contemporary network theory.[4]

Network theory reflects how insights have moved from applications for the fast-paced innovations of the information technology (IT) world to theories of management and organization. The irony of networks is that their very vulnerability makes them most resilient.[5] This understanding informs recognition of the need to adopt a strategy of decentralized resilience,[6] with power devolving via regional processes to state and local governments, the private sector, communities, and ultimately individuals.[7] Structure and process for intergovernmental homeland security policy and execution must reflect this understanding of twenty-first-century socio-political reality.

To illustrate the point, in any high-end catastrophe like a WMD terrorist attack, attack on or failure of cyber-infrastructure, major natural disaster, or pandemic, response and short-term recovery will begin for individual Americans in the household, place of work, school, or wherever they may find themselves. From there, response and short-term recovery goes to a community level, to the local jurisdiction, state, region, and nation. There will be no federal cavalry. Pandemic preparedness policy, for example, posits this truth in an acronym: YOYO—"You're On Your Own."

It is an uncomfortable truth, a truth that has dramatic policy implications: the federal government will never be fully able to resource, command, or control the national protection, response, or recovery missions. At best, it will be able to serve as one element providing support to a state or states. The notion of "federalizing" a response is a chimera.

Still, a number of otherwise thoughtful and well-informed quarters of the national security establishment have persisted in taking the inside-the-Beltway perspective. In a 2007 study, several of these experts looked at the national response mission to make an argument for a federal solution "for large disasters like a nuclear detonation." "The Federal government," they wrote, "needs a realistic response plan specific to the Day After scenario that marshals the resources of all agencies." According to these authors, "the Federal government should stop pretending that state and local officials will be able to control the situation on the Day After."[8] As such, an event of this magnitude requires "a lead Federal role in all aspects of response."

These types of solutions miss the point. The problem is not in the inability of state and local officials to "control" such catastrophic situations. The problem is in federal-level implementation of the federal government's own foundational homeland security and emergency management strategy under, for example, the National Response Framework (NRF), National Incident Management System (NIMS), and Emergency Support Function (ESF) Annexes that provide for structures and processes governing federal support to state and local incident management. Operationally, we still function in a Newtonian universe of time and space. In emergency management terms, "all disasters are local." They cannot be controlled by Washington. Borders-in, the federal government is therefore merely a network enabler, a partner, one element, one stakeholder among several.

Required then is a new borders-in governance paradigm whose strategic objective is national resilience in the face of contemporary complexities and uncertainties. Given the multiplicity of twenty-first-century threats and opportunities, anticipated and unanticipated, resilience must be capability-based, as opposed to the more traditional threat-based. A resilience paradigm should be built around two concepts: Network Federalism and Anticipatory Governance.

Network Federalism is a concept that addresses the intergovernmental, vertical axis of security governance. It is similar to the European Union's subsidiarity principle, which holds that the appropriate level for bottom-up governance over a matter is at the smallest, lowest, or least centralized competent unit. Drawing on network theory, it informs recognition of the need to adopt a strategy of decentralized resilience, with power devolved to regional network structures and processes to engender federal, state, and local government collaboration for resilience, economic competitiveness, and long-term community sustainability.

The second is Anticipatory Governance. This concept addresses the interagency, horizontal axis of security governance at all three levels of government. A phrase associated with Leon Fuerth, former Vice President Al Gore's national security advisor and member of the PNSR Guiding Coalition, Anticipatory Governance is a principle promoting the institutionalization of "foresight" in the development and execution of plans of action. Foresight structures and processes enable a government to sense and execute changes ahead of the cusp of major events or situations, often unexpected, "the better to blunt threats and harvest opportunities."

A homeland security model for Anticipatory Governance is the emergency management concept of the Incident Command System (ICS), the basis for the National Incident Management System and incident command at all levels of government. ICS enshrines management by objectives and provides for empowered, mission-focused, temporary hierarchical networks, somewhat analogous to the private sector's use of cross-functional teams. ICS generates collaboration and coordination through what is called Unified Command that differs from the military concept of command and control ($C^2$). It is uniquely effective for multi-disciplinary, interagency, multi-jurisdictional, and intergovernmental activities involving three layers of sovereignty. Coordination and consensus emerges via an ICS structure and process, seen as the norm rather than the exception for a twenty-first-century strategic environment increasingly complex, increasingly uncertain.

To restate the premise: U.S. security governance today requires transformation. The strategic environment has changed; the system has not. An obsolete system of the industrial era, configured in 1947, no longer best serves national security decision-making borders-out or management of homeland security borders-in. Others may argue the affordability and merits for and against maintaining an expansive borders-out posture for international engagement. Those of us in the new and evolving field of homeland security, however, must find the means to establish a structure and process for national resilience borders-in, thereby ensuring the constituted governability of the homeland upon which America's international role as guarantor ultimately depends.

# PART I

---

## THE HOMELAND SECURITY DISCIPLINE

### From National Security to
### National Preparedness

# CHAPTER ONE

# The Evolution of Emergency Management and Preparedness

The 9/11 attacks were calculated attacks on the most obvious symbols of American global preeminence: the Pentagon, the sprawling five-cornered seat of a globally dominant American military; the World Trade Center, two gigantically assertive structures—worthy of an Ozymandias—representing Wall Street, the financial hub of the globalized international economic system. The one violated, the other felled—in well-coordinated, asymmetric acts, engineered not by a state, but by an elusive, non-state network. Egregious acts executed, not with exotic weapons, but with familiar elements of our own infrastructure, hijacked for strategic purpose and turned into catastrophically deadly weapons against ourselves.

A new administration had drawn policy-makers from the national security establishment and had seated them on the west side of the White House in the French Second Empire Eisenhower Executive Office Building. Like the battleship admirals of the interwar twenties and thirties, these men and women still saw the world and national security through the lenses of past institutions. Just to the east of 1600 Pennsylvania Avenue, Northwest, in the oldest departmental building in Washington, the Greek Revival Treasury Building, the appointed representatives of the American financial establishment were holding fast to a post–Cold War, bipartisan vision of a new world order of international finance, unfettered by national boundaries.

After 9/11, both the national security and financial establishments would have to square their views of political reality with policy-makers and stakeholders claiming a new set of equities. Under the rubric of homeland security, these equities were not unfamiliar. For some time, the precursor homeland security communities had been developing their own governance requirements despite being somewhat marginalized by the mainstream national security and financial communities with their borders-out priorities. Homeland security governance in fact draws upon four functional disciplines that pre-date 9/11:

- Emergency Management (variously defined over many years)
- Civil Defense (a twentieth-century term, somewhat fallen into disuse)
- Resource Mobilization (partially effective only in wartime)
- Counterterrorism (whose interagency structure took root in the early 1970s)

These interrelated disciplines have encompassed both interagency and inter-governmental (federal/state/local) dimensions. With varying success, these disciplines have generated a succession of structures and processes for policy, planning, resourcing, and execution. Although not always fully formalized or recognized, they have involved private sector and non-governmental organi-zation (NGO) participation.

In the 1990s, the four disciplines began to converge with calls for insti-tutionalizing them together into a single structural entity. Notable was the recommendation by the U.S. Commission on National Security/21st Century (the Hart-Rudman Commission), chartered in 1998, for a National Homeland Security Agency. At the same time, the Department of Defense began to use the term "homeland defense" for the mission to provide continental air and maritime defense against potential strategic and military adversaries.

Post-9/11, homeland security emphasized preparedness for and response to terrorist incidents. Immediately after Hurricane Katrina, the term assumed an all-hazards cast, in an effort to incorporate demands for preparedness for and response to natural, environmental, biological, accidental, and techno-logical disasters, the traditional realm of emergency management.

## Emergency Management to 9/11

A widely held expectation of our day holds that in times of extreme disaster, the federal government will provide primary emergency management support to communities when they are overwhelmed. This popular assumption reflects an overall trend from World War I, through the Depression, World War II, and the Great Society toward an expectation of a big government solution to societal problems. Notwithstanding this popular expectation, the federal government historically has regarded emergency management as a locally managed function. To this day, Washington continues to produce doctrinal statements supporting management of disaster response at the lowest level feasible.

Nevertheless, in 1992, the last year of the George H. W. Bush administration, just as the presidential campaign commenced, a Category 5 hurricane, Andrew by name, hit South Florida, crossed the Gulf of Mexico and made a second landfall in eastern Louisiana, leveling entire neighborhoods and prompting desperate calls for the Feds. "Where the hell is the cavalry on this one?" the exasperated Miami-Dade director of emergency management, Kate Hale, notoriously cried at a day-three press conference following Andrew's coming ashore and savaging her Florida jurisdiction. Endeavoring to manage a worsening crisis resulting from the fourth most powerful hurricane ever to hit the United States, Hale chose to signal angry frustration with her accusation of a delayed federal response. "They keep saying we're going to get supplies. For God's sake, where are they?"

The media purveyed Hale's emotional outburst into a legend that persists. In actual fact, the real delays were the result of the initial refusal by Florida's Democratic governor, Lawton Chiles, to ask for federal assistance. The impasse continued while his office and the White House wrangled over cost-sharing. In the meantime, federal officials were asking Hale what she needed. Her reply was, in effect, "Send everything!" In the end, Hale lost her job over her poor management of the Andrew preparedness and response.

The damage from the hurricane was undeniably catastrophic for many local communities including Hale's. Notwithstanding the storm's economic impact, the casualty figure was mercifully low—generally reckoned at twenty-three, a number disputed by many who claim the actual death toll was much higher. Thirteen years later, Hurricane Katrina unleashed utter devastation over an entire region, inflicting damages whose estimated worth was double that of Andrew. Hurricane Katrina was an epically catastrophic disaster. In terms of geographic size, this tempest was exceptionally big. By some reckonings, 300,000 homes were destroyed or made unlivable. In terms of mortality, somewhere approaching two thousand persons died. Perhaps as many as another one thousand are still missing.

As horrific as these relatively recent events were, they were not the worst ever to befall this nation. In terms of fatalities, the greatest natural disaster in U.S. history was arguably the September 1900 Galveston Island hurricane and surge in which at least six thousand people died in the city alone. Totals for the city and outlying region were 12,000 deaths, while well over 3,500 structures were destroyed. Other noteworthy pre–World War I disasters include the Chicago fire of 1871. While the death toll of three hundred was comparatively small, the fire burned nearly five square miles of the city, incinerated almost 25,000 buildings, and rendered homeless more than 100,000 persons. In the 1889 Johnstown flood in Pennsylvania, over 2,200 people died. The 1906 San Francisco earthquake and fire killed over three thousand, destroyed over 28,000 structures, and burned an area twice the size of the Chicago fire (three-quarters of the developed area of the city). In the interwar years, the Great Mississippi Flood of 1927 killed some 250 and left 700,000 homeless across seven states, and the Okeechobee Hurricane of 1928 took the lives of over 2,500.

Notwithstanding the scale of these nineteenth- and twentieth-century disasters, the principle of locally managed emergencies remained sacrosanct. These disasters were deemed local incidents requiring primarily a local responsibility for management of the response and recovery. Moreover, in the cases of Galveston and San Francisco, the private sector took the lead in managing the recovery.

The Federal Emergency Management Agency (FEMA) dates 1803 as the official beginning of federal support to state and local jurisdictions in times of extreme disasters.[1] That year produced the first Congressional Fire Disaster Act, which provided ad hoc assistance to fire-ravaged Portsmouth, New Hampshire. At the time, the city was a major port, one among many that constituted the national critical infrastructure of their day. Portsmouth was the cradle of American shipbuilding, and like all ports of the time its commerce contributed customs revenues to the federal government. The legislation was the first of many in response to devastating fires in Atlantic ports in the early part of the nineteenth century. Until passage of the Federal Disaster Act of 1950, lawmakers enacted some 125 incident-specific bills to give federal aid to jurisdictions overwhelmed by hurricanes, earthquakes, floods, and other natural disasters. Yet the ad hoc nature of disaster legislation resulted in inconsistent levels of support. Some Congresses could be miserly with their aid.

The modern trend toward a more proactive, presidentially led, federal role in emergency management began in the Depression when public works projects were seen to provide employment. In 1932, President Herbert Hoover established as an independent government agency the Reconstruction Finance Corporation (RFC), modeled after the War Finance Corporation of World War I.[2] Among its loan-making activities, the RFC had presidential authority to make loans for repair and reconstruction of disaster-stricken public facilities. Later in the decade, President Franklin Roosevelt gave authority to the Department of Agriculture's Bureau of Public Roads to provide funding for damaged highways and bridges and to the Army Corps of Engineers via the Flood Control Act to implement flood control projects.

Notwithstanding, Washington's approach to disaster assistance continued to be ad hoc and prompted legislation for greater federal-level cooperation among agencies and authorization for the president to coordinate their activities. State and local stakeholders, notably governors, came to believe that emergency management should be conjoined with wartime civil defense functions, which were assuming renewed urgency with the onset of the Cold War and Soviet development of atomic weapons. They brought pressure to bear on the federal government to apply civil defense funds and equipment toward natural disaster preparedness and response. The milestone Federal Disaster Act of 1950 authorized a presidential disaster relief program to be directed in the Executive Office of the President. It replaced once and for all the congressionally driven, single-incident, federal response that had previously assisted state and local governments.

Over the course of two decades into the postwar era, more general federal relief extended to communities, that is, beyond state and local governments. In the 1960s, a succession of major disasters generated significant federal response and recovery operations. Examples included such disasters as the 1964 Anchorage, Alaska, and 1971 San Fernando Valley, California, earthquakes and Hurricanes Carla (1961), Betsy (1965), Camille (1969), and Agnes (1972).

The year 1969 saw twenty-nine major disaster declarations—including that for the Category 5 Hurricane Camille—the largest number in any year since 1950. The Disaster Relief Act of 1969 was in part an attempt to formalize coordination of federal response during a major incident by creating the position of the federal coordinating officer (FCO), Washington's on-scene integrator of federal response and liaison with state and local authorities.

In the 1970s, President Richard Nixon proffered the idea of a "New Federalism" with the intent to shift power from Washington's federal bureaucracy to the state and local governments. As part of his effort to reduce the power of the departments and agencies, he consolidated some functions related to emergency management in the White House. The Nixon administration's April 1970 Reorganization Plan 1 transferred from the Federal Communications Commission (FCC) the responsibility for the ubiquitous public alerts system "Conelrad" to the Office of Telecommunications Policy (OTP) within the Executive Office of the President (EOP) and renamed it the Emergency Broadcast System (EBS). In 1978, OTP would become the Office of Science and Technology Policy, also in EOP.

In 1972, the Nixon administration reorganized the federal-level responsibility for civil defense. The Office of Civil Defense (OCD), which had been in the Department of the Army since 1964, went to the Pentagon's Office of the Secretary of Defense (OSD) and became the Defense Civil Preparedness Agency (DCPA). In civil defense terms, DCPA had the responsibility for population protection and continuity of operations in the event of a nuclear attack. From an emergency management standpoint, the agency provided 50/50 matching funds for civil defense to state and local levels, which they could now apply to general emergency preparedness. Further, DCPA personnel would also assist state and local governments in developing plans for natural disasters in addition to nuclear attacks.

Following Tropical Storm Agnes and its devastation in Pennsylvania's Lycoming Valley, the Nixon administration's July 1973 Reorganization Plan 1 reassigned a number of federal disaster and emergency preparedness functions across several agencies. Coordination of immediate federal *response* to major disasters went to the newly created Office of Preparedness, later the Federal Preparedness Agency (FPA), in the General Services Administration (GSA), which also launched several other internal divisions to manage other emergency preparedness–related activities. FPA was also responsible for preparing the federal government to mobilize in the event of war and assuring that it could continue to operate in the event of a nuclear attack. Coordination of long-term federal disaster *relief* to recompense victims went to the Federal Disaster Assistance Administration (FDAA) in the Department of Housing and Urban Development (HUD). Also in HUD was the Federal Insurance Administration (FIA) established in 1968. FIA provided flood insurance and management of efforts to mitigate flood damage, prompted by a number of studies generated after Hurricane Betsy. The agency also extended riot and crime insurance. This service emerged via the report of the President's

National Advisory Panel on Insurance in Riot-Affected Areas (The Hughes Panel), *Meeting the Insurance Crisis in Our Cities,* which addressed the collapse of the insurance market in the riot-ravaged ghettos of the late sixties.

The period 1973–75 witnessed extensive severe weather damage from tornados and flooding in the Midwest. Six Midwest tornadoes in April 1974 led to passage of the Disaster Relief Act of 1974 that established a process for presidential disaster declarations and expanded federal emergency and disaster activities. President Nixon tagged his approach "a New Federalism to our disaster preparedness and assistance activities." The legislation notably extended assistance beyond state and local governments to include aid to individuals and households and to nonprofit organizations providing community services. Also in 1974, the Federal Fire Prevention and Control Act created two more emergency preparedness agencies, housing them in the Department of Commerce: the National Fire Prevention and Control Administration (NFPCA) and the National Academy of Fire Prevention and Control (NAFPC). NFPCA assisted states and localities in developing fire prevention and control programs. NAFPC developed model training programs for fire service personnel. In 1978, NFPCA became the U.S. Fire Administration, and NAFPC, the National Fire Academy. A noteworthy intergovernmental entity, the U.S. Fire Administration coordinated and supported local government fire prevention and response and local emergency medical services.

Notwithstanding these efforts by the Nixon administration, emergency management in the seventies remained fragmented at all levels of government. The decade continued to see a number of incidents and natural disasters take their toll at the state and local levels. In addition, major hazardous materials (hazmat) incidents during the period made the nation aware of a growing threat to local communities and transportation corridors.

While the Nixon administration had allowed states to prioritize the application of civil defense funds to natural disaster preparedness, the Ford administration reversed the policy. Debates over strategic doctrine and nuclear deterrence were weighing the merits of nuclear warfighting versus "Assured Destruction." The federal government now required states to prioritize civil defense funding for planning for nuclear attack. This revision prompted an intergovernmental reaction. When the Carter administration came to Washington in 1977, states began to lobby their position that preparedness for hazmat and natural disasters should take priority over population relocations and sheltering surveys traditionally associated with civil defense. This intergovernmental issue would return in our current day with debates over preparedness and differing prioritization of risk across the federal, state, and local levels of government.

Phrasing the argument in terms of the dual-use emergency management application for civil defense funding and assets, the National Governors Association pushed President Jimmy Carter to simplify federal liaison with state and local mechanisms by centralizing federal emergency functions. At the outset of his administration, Carter had created a Reorganization Project for Emergency Management, and in May 1978 after a year of study he sent his Reorganization Plan No. 3 to Congress. With lawmakers voicing no opposition to the plan, the administration issued two executive orders in 1979, Executive Order (EO) 12127 and EO 12148, establishing the Federal Emergency Management Agency as an independent agency, thus inaugurating the modern era of emergency management.[3]

These executive orders established a single independent agency to prepare for and respond to the full range of emergencies including wars, terrorism, and natural disasters. Reporting directly to the president, FEMA became the primary agency for Cold War national security emergency preparedness. As such, it was responsible for policy formulation for and program oversight and coordination of national emergency mobilization preparedness and execution, working with state, local, tribal, and territorial governments and the private sector organizations.

The Carter plan consolidated the Pentagon's Defense Civil Preparedness Agency civil defense responsibilities, HUD's Federal Disaster Assistance Administration activities and its Federal Insurance Administration disaster-related responsibilities, the Department of Commerce's National Fire Prevention and Control Administration, and GSA's Federal Preparedness Agency all into FEMA. Four other disaster entities/functions came from the Executive Office of the President, including a function in the White House Military Office (WHMO) that had supported continuity of government (COG) planning in GSA's Federal Preparedness Agency.

FEMA would operate with regional offices inherited from the Eisenhower-era Office of Civil and Defense Mobilization (OCDM) and HUD. The new agency had operational entities in ten GSA-recommended regions. Six federal relocation centers had been established in 1958 with an OCDM regional office structure of six regions that had continued during the Kennedy/Johnson years under EOP's Office of Emergency Planning in 1961 (which became the Office of Emergency Preparedness in 1968). In 1972, the Nixon administration expanded the regional system to ten, which have remained to this day as the FEMA Regions.

John W. Macy Jr. became FEMA's first Senate-confirmed director. Macy had been Eisenhower's executive director of the Civil Service Commission (CSC) and during the Kennedy and Johnson administrations served as CSC chairman. When Macy and FEMA began their work, the Cold War was still the overarching strategic reality. Nineteen seventy-nine was the year that the Soviet Union intervened militarily in Afghanistan. Throughout the decade, many U.S. policy-makers had argued that the Soviet had gamed loopholes in the first Strategic Arms Limitation Treaty (1972) to gain advantage for their offensive nuclear strike capability. As the two nuclear superpowers continued negotiations for a follow-on SALT II, Washington embroiled itself in heightened debates over modernizing America's own strategic forces and the degree to which modernization should move beyond deterrence to support to a nuclear war-fighting doctrine.

From the outset, this strategic environment informed a FEMA mission-division along two lines. One focus was on national security emergency preparedness: civil defense and protection of populations and critical industrial infrastructure; planning for such war-related matters as nuclear and terrorist attacks; national mobilization; and stewardship of the National Defense Stockpile of strategic and critical materials. The other was on domestic planning and management of natural disasters, that is, pure emergency management. Although the FEMA goal was development of an all-hazards capability, the two mission foci did not mesh, particularly when the emergency management emphasis shifted from immediate response to disasters to recompensing victims with monetary handouts.

Nevertheless, Macy endeavored to arrive at an emergency management model that would marry civil defense activities with natural hazards preparedness and response. During his tenure, FEMA began adoption and development of a National Governors Association concept called Comprehensive Emergency Management (CEM), which divided incidents/events into phases—at the time, four: mitigation, preparedness, response, and recovery.[4]

These phases of the emergency management cycle have a mission set of actions that occur both sequentially and simultaneously:

- Mitigation—reducing the adverse consequences of an emergency
- Preparedness—readying people, equipment, and supplies for response and recovery operations and mitigation programs
- Response—saving lives and minimizing disruption during and immediately after the incident
- Recovery—restoring the status quo ante or better after an emergency has occurred.[5]

From the start, the response mission presented FEMA with two major problem sets. The first were the horizontal, interagency relationships of the federal agencies with FEMA and among themselves. The second were the vertical, intergovernmental relationships among local, state, and federal agencies. Pre-9/11, FEMA's major thrust was on the horizontal coordination of the activities of federal agencies that have roles to play in emergency response. FEMA was and remains a small agency that has few resources to manage an emergency and does its work by coordinating the efforts of other federal departments and agencies and contracting with private sector organizations.

On the vertical, intergovernmental side, as the Hurricane Andrew example indicated, federal support of emergency response is entirely reactive, as per law and policy: the federal government can only provide resources following a state government's formal request for assistance. Federal resources are intended to augment but not supplant the resources of state and local governments, which have the initial and primary responsibility for emergency management in their respective jurisdictions.

In its first decade, FEMA led the way for developing a coordinated plan to govern the conduct of emergency response operations. The agency approached coordination as a means to meet the special requirements presented by each type of emergency. It established a top-level coordination committee. Each department and agency with emergency management functions appointed an emergency coordinator to serve on the body. At its headquarters, FEMA stood up an operations center. It put in place programs to hire temporary workers and purchase emergency supplies. In 1980, it established the National Emergency Training Center (NETC) in

Emmitsburg, Maryland, for teaching courses on the conduct of response operations and for hosting exercises to practice newly acquired operational skills.[6]

The plan relied on department and agency voluntary collaboration, which according to Col. John Brinkerhoff, USA (Ret.), FEMA's acting associate director for national preparedness in the 1980s, was "for the most part provided willingly." FEMA was responsible for incremental federal support and funding in response to requests for assistance from the states. "During this period, despite ups and downs in budgets and leadership, the prevailing rule," says Brinkerhoff, "was that the Federal government could do nothing until and unless the governor of a state asked for help."

Congress had been unhappy with the Carter administration's use of the Disaster Relief Act to help manage non-natural disasters like the 1980 Cuban refugee crisis (the Mariel boatlift to Florida, engineered by Fidel Castro to rid himself of some 125,000 "undesirables") and the Three Mile Island nuclear-power plant meltdown (at one point six counties were planning mass evacuations of 650,000 people). After lengthy congressional review through the two Reagan administrations, lawmakers decided not to limit presidential discretion and passed the 1988 Robert T. Stafford Disaster Relief and Emergency Assistance Act. That statute amended in part, repealed in part, and supplemented in part the Disaster Relief Act of 1974.

All along, FEMA continued to improve the federal doctrine and practice of emergency response. In 1964, the White House Office of Emergency Planning had produced a National Plan for Emergency Preparedness outlining the assignment of emergency preparedness and civil defense functions to federal departments and agencies. The outline was later made specific in the Nixon administration's 1969 Executive Order 11490 that addressed continuity of government in the event of a nuclear attack. The federal government issued no new significant plan until it adopted the Federal Response Plan (FRP) in May 1992. The FRP adoption process began in 1983, when FEMA put into place the Integrated Emergency Management System (IEMS), an all-hazards approach for planning. IEMS included, quoting FEMA, "direction, control, and warning systems which are common to the full range of emergencies from small isolated events to the ultimate emergency—war." IEMS was a forerunner to FEMA's work on a Federal Response Plan for a Catastrophic Earthquake in California, which ultimately would become a national plan as the FRP, finally implemented less than 120 days before Hurricane Andrew made landfall in Florida and Louisiana.

The Federal Response Plan formalized federal response and twelve Emergency Support Functions (ESFs) that assigned lead and supporting agencies by function. Later in 1997, a revision would add a Terrorism Incident Annex to the FRP to implement President Bill Clinton's Presidential Decision Directive 39 (PDD-39), The U.S. Policy on Counterterrorism. In January 2001, seven departments and agencies would release the federal government's interagency concept of operations plan (CONPLAN) for response to domestic terrorist threats or attacks.

The Federal Response Plan was thus the first plan for the coordination of the federal government's response to natural, accidental, or terrorist disasters and emergency incidents/situations requiring federal assistance under the Stafford Act. It described the basic mechanisms and structures through which the federal government mobilizes the resources and conducts activities to augment state and local response efforts. The FRP both facilitated the provisions of federal assistance and used the twelve Emergency Support Functions as its functional approach to group the types of assistance that a state is most likely to need. FEMA's Grant Peterson, who served for six years as the Reagan and George H. W. Bush administrations' associate director for state and local programs and support, was key to the federal adoption of the plan. Peterson and a number of his FEMA colleagues successfully pushed department and agency heads to sign the document—thus obligating their subordinates to respect the plan.

Unfortunately, all-of-nation FRP implementation did not come in time for testing during the response to Hurricane Andrew. FEMA endured much criticism for its role in the Andrew response. Although its efforts were substantial, the public assessment was that the agency met neither the needs nor the expectations of the devastated communities and thus was unable to do its job properly. As would be the case in the Hurricane Katrina response, the partisan politics between a Democratic governor and federal officials in a Republican administration considerably impeded collaboration. Nevertheless, capitalizing on the perceived federal failings in the Andrew response, the Clinton administration came to Washington determined to change that perception. It resolved to transform FEMA into what, post-Katrina, would be called a forward-leaning agency.

From the state and local perspectives, FEMA had failed to bridge the divide between civil defense/national security planning and assistance for disaster preparedness and response. Now in a world freed from the fears of the Cold War, FEMA could afford to shift priority from its national security emergency preparedness and civil defense functions. Over the course of the nineties, it would progressively eliminate those functions altogether. Under James Lee Witt, Clinton's proactive FEMA director, the first with experience as a state emergency manager, the agency redirected its attention to all-hazards emergency management programs. To be sure, FEMA management of natural disasters, particularly hurricanes, greatly improved, generating deserved acclaim. Clinton and Witt relaxed established federalism policy that limited federal intervention in disasters to instances where a state governor makes a formal request. The experience of the Hurricane Andrew response illustrated the political pitfalls of waiting for the request, particularly if a governor is reluctant to make the call for federal assistance.

At the beginning of his second term, the president made Witt an ex officio member of his cabinet. Witt, however, did not believe that preparedness for terrorism should be included in all-hazards preparedness, with the consequence that in the late 1990s the FBI and the Department of Defense (DoD) undertook the mission to support state and local authorities. In 1997, when Witt came to accept that terrorism was part of the risk in the all-hazards environment, he established FEMA's Terrorism Coordination Unit. By this time, FEMA was without its original national security emergency preparedness functions and thus was unable, even reluctant, to undertake effectively the roles and responsibilities for executing domestic policies related to the terrorist threat. As such, post-9/11 the executive branch had a gap that would eventually be filled by the formation of the Department of Homeland Security.

The Federal Response Plan provided for a FEMA Catastrophic Disaster Response Group (CDRG), composed of assistant secretary–level officials or their designees, to referee interagency disputes and dilemmas that arose from catastrophic events. Any issues that the CDRG could not resolve went to the White House's Domestic Policy Council for resolution. President Clinton and FEMA director James Lee Witt rarely used the Catastrophic Disaster Response Group. Given his emergency management background, Witt was confident that, as a cabinet-level official in a declared disaster, he could handle the flow of decisions coming to the White House in any catastrophe. As a result, his largely personalized system was effective in the numerous smaller-scale disasters that the Clinton administration had to face.

Throughout the Clinton administration, FEMA also shifted emphasis from augmenting local first responders to recompensing victims of natural disasters. Critics claimed that FEMA in effect was becoming a "check-writing agency" where Clinton and Witt were using disaster declarations to "hand out checks" as political payoffs to, in their view, worthy state and local constituencies. In 1993, his first year in office, for example, Clinton declared a record fifty-eight disasters. Whatever the validity of this assessment, the net result of the Witt tenure was further, if not conclusive, institutionalization of federalized disaster response and assistance.

It must be said, the executive branch was not wholly responsible for the upward trend in disaster monies going for state/local disaster relief. Major disasters routinely generate supplemental congressional appropriations. As well, the Stafford Act had established the Disaster Relief Fund (DRF), a revolving fund without fiscal-year limitation, having a FEMA budget line for average annual disaster outlays for annual budget requests. It is thus more meaningful to conclude that when it comes to federal response to disasters, executive branch requests and congressional appropriations have been generally in sync.

### Civil Defense—Not Exactly Defense, or Civil

What we now regard as protection of physical and cyberspace national critical infrastructure has its origin in civil defense. Organizing for non-military, civil defense did not really arrive until World War I. At that time, the perceived threat was foreign sabotage, especially with respect to defense industries. Despite the growing awareness in the interwar years that airpower had the potential for offensive strategic bombardment, civil defense continued to be regarded as the organized non-military effort to prepare American civilians for saboteurs whose targets were industrial. When war in Europe finally came in 1939, President Roosevelt issued a statement on espionage requesting all citizens, including state and local officials, to pass relevant information to the FBI. For its part, the Bureau initiated surveillance of plants under contract to manufacture defense materials. It also prepared a plant protection manual for use by local police chiefs.

In May 1941, Roosevelt issued an executive order establishing the Office of Civilian Defense (OCD) in the EOP Office of Emergency Management, itself established just after Europe went to war. New York Mayor Fiorello La Guardia, who was at the time president of the U.S. Conference of Mayors, had pushed for an OCD. He thus served as OCD director on a volunteer basis without compensation until February 1942. OCD provided a federal government liaison with state and local governments to coordinate civil defense activities and volunteers. The office thereby assumed the responsibilities of the Division of State and Local Cooperation under the Advisory Commission to the Council of National Defense (CND). While the World War I–era CND had become active the previous August after having suspended its operations in 1921, the OCD stand-up with a national staff of twenty-five meant the final abolition of CND.

Aerial bombardment was now a palpable threat exemplified by the air war being waged on European cities by the German Luftwaffe, specifically London. OCD's functions were to coordinate federal, state, and local defense programs for the protection of civilian populations in emergencies, most particularly those in major metropolitan areas. As well, OCD facilitated civilian participation in various war programs like First Lady Eleanor Roosevelt's network of volunteer women to staff nursing and clerical positions.

Both CND and the Office of Civil Defense had a noteworthy state/local dimension in their links to a nationwide network of state and local defense councils. OCD's network would grow to forty-four state and one thousand local councils. A July 1941 OCD administrative order established nine autonomous Regional Civilian Defense Areas, geographically coterminous with the War Department Corps Areas. These bodies coordinated civilian defense activities and provided the liaison with state and local agencies, other federal agencies, and the military. Although they were abolished in 1944, these regional offices anticipated the concept of a FEMA regional structure. La Guardia left his post in early 1942, and his executive assistant, the former chairman of the Securities Exchange Commission and FDR brain truster James M. Landis, fleeted up to OCD director. Landis resigned in late 1943, recommending OCD's abolition owing to the diminished threat of air raids. In June 1945, the office was stood down.

The federal government always deemed civil defense more of a civilian responsibility of individuals and governments at the local level. The forties, however, saw the coming of age of strategic airpower during the war—from the London Blitz, to the strategic bombing campaigns of the Eighth Air Force, to the climactic atomic air bursts over Hiroshima and Nagasaki. Once the Truman administration engaged America in the Cold War struggle against the Soviet Union in the late forties, a greater potential federal role in organized civil defense against the threat of strategic bombing had sudden relevance for the American homeland.

While the War Department considered postwar planning for civil defense as an appropriate Army function, it did not want the responsibility for civil defense. It saw it as a broader national responsibility involving other federal agencies and state and local organizations. The 1947 stand-up of the National Military Establishment and soon thereafter the Department of Defense enabled the military to undertake a civil defense role without it being the responsibility of a military department. The responsibility would only be temporary, when in 1948, civil defense shifted from OCD in the Executive Office of the President to the Pentagon Office of Civil Defense Planning (OCDP). Directed by Russell J. Hopley, the former president of Northwestern Bell Telephone Company, OCDP lasted only for a year until it became the DoD Office of Civil Defense Liaison. That office in turn lasted just a year until its civil defense functions returned to EOP's Office of Emergency Management with the stand-up of the Federal Civil Defense Administration (FCDA). The FCDA acting director was James J. "Jerry" Wadsworth, from the influential New York Republican family, who had been acting director of the Civil Defense Office in the National Security Resources Board (NSRB), the independent mobilization body established by the National Security Act of 1947 and intended to be on a par with the National Security Council (NSC). At that time, NSRB was recommending that the Federal Works Agency, forerunner of GSA, assume responsibility for "wartime disaster relief planning," and that the Office of Civil Defense Planning be responsible for planning civilian participation in active defense.

Additional urgency had come with the August 1949 Soviet test of its first atomic bomb. When war came to Korea the following year, Congress passed the Federal Civil Defense Act of 1950, which provided FCDA with statutory authority as an independent agency. Recognizing the importance of state equities in civil defense, the Truman administration chose to appoint a former Democratic governor of Florida, Millard F. Caldwell Jr., as FCDA director. Caldwell had gravitas among the nation's governors. He had chaired the National Governors' Conference from 1946 to 1947 and was president of the Council of State Governments from 1947 to 1948.

The year 1951 heralded the birth of civil defense as we remember it. That year, FCDA began exercising authority for planning, sheltering, evacuation, and support to states and localities. Support came in the form of planning, technical guidance and assistance, training, and 50/50 matching grants for equipment. Olney, Maryland, became the site for FCDA's National Civil Defense Training Center. Both the center and FCDA moved to Battle Creek, Michigan, in mid-1954. The concept of civil defense that took shape included: planning for evacuations and continuity of government; municipal establishment of emergency operations centers (EOCs) and fallout shelters; architectural design protocols for survival; and the Conelrad emergency broadcast system. By the mid-fifties, some states were instituting civil defense ordinances to develop emergency procedures for nuclear threats or attacks. Congress, however, did not support large budget requests for FCDA. Indeed, agency leadership was in any case inexperienced in civil defense. As such, the agency never got priority.

In 1957, the Soviet launch of their Sputnik satellite graphically demonstrated that the strategic nuclear threat was maturing from delivery by aircraft to that by ballistic missile. Sputnik galvanized the nation and prompted President Eisenhower to effect a governmental reorganization the following year. As part of the shuffle, FCDA closed its doors and transferred its civil defense and mobilization activities to what EOP now called the Office of Defense and Civilian Mobilization (ODCM), the first of a series of alphabet-soup-like renamings. Before the end of the year, ODCM was renamed the Office of Civil and Defense Mobilization (OCDM) in an effort to reinforce the civil defense theme.

The Eisenhower administration had followed protocol when appointing its first civil defense chieftain. In 1953, the nod had gone to a former Republican governor of Nebraska, Val Peterson. The chairman of the State Governors Conference, Peterson presided over the Council of State Governments in 1952 and had been a vocal proponent for civil defense. In 1957, the OCDM helm went to Leo A. Hoegh, a one-term Republican governor of Iowa, prematurely tipped by *Time* magazine as a rising star two weeks before defeat in a run for a second term. Hoegh had been a dynamic Army officer during the war, known to Eisenhower.

President Kennedy continued the tradition in 1961, appointing former Louisiana governor Frank Burton Ellis, a liberal southern Democrat, as his

OCDM director. Ellis proved to be a runaway bureaucrat in his espousal of a vast fallout shelter program. Ellis was an embarrassment who among other things revealed carryover plans for a shadow emergency government of mainly private citizens, tagged the Eisenhower Ten, with authority over key aspects of the economy and government in the event of a nuclear attack and declaration of a national emergency. After four months, Kennedy shifted a few OCDM functions to the Office of Emergency Planning, leaving Ellis with fewer responsibilities: authority for strategic stockpiling, minor civil defense preparations and planning for the continuity of local and state governments, and finally natural disaster relief programs.

As noted above, the more important civil defense functions returned to the Pentagon Office of the Secretary of Defense as the Office of Civil Defense (OCD), which had the brief during the Cuban Missile Crisis. Here Kennedy looked beyond the governors to appoint Steuart L. Pittman, an international investment and finance attorney, to head OCD.[7] In 1964, OCD transferred to the Department of the Army. In 1969, Melvin Laird, Nixon's secretary of defense, returned to form and appointed a former one-term North Dakota governor, John E. Davis, to be the Army's director of civil defense. In 1972, OCD returned to OSD as the Defense Civil Preparedness Agency (DCPA). With the 1979 stand-up of FEMA, DCPA and its civil defense functions transferred from DoD into the new civilian agency.

Civil defense programs continued in the Reagan administration with three National Security Decision Directives (NSDDs). Two back-to-back 1982 NSDDs on civil defense (NSDD-23, U.S. Civil Defense Policy, and NSDD-26, U.S. Civil Defense Policy) gave FEMA responsibility for developing plans for population protection, industrial protection, and blast sheltering. The NSDD-23 and NSDD-26 directions to plan for industrial protection evolved into a 1990s discipline with a new name—critical infrastructure protection (CIP). The 1987 NSDD-259, U.S. Civil Defense, superseded NSDD-26 and in part gave FEMA additional responsibility to encourage mutual aid agreements— for example, jurisdiction-to-jurisdiction at the state and local levels.

In November 1988, just after George H. W. Bush's election to the presidency, and the same month that Congress passed the Stafford Act, the White House issued Executive Order 12656, Assignment of Emergency Preparedness Responsibilities. In defining national security emergency preparedness, the EO specified COG concerns, especially as the result of nuclear attack. It gave the

National Security Council responsibility for developing and administering a national security emergency preparedness policy and provided for the FEMA director to serve as an NSC advisor on "national security emergency preparedness, including mobilization preparedness, civil defense, continuity of government, technological disasters, and other issues, as appropriate." The FEMA head would also assist the NSC with implementing and managing the policy and in coordinating departments and agencies and with state and local governments.

Civil defense as a *resourced* discipline with program funding, as Burton Ellis discovered at a cost to his federal career, had lost impetus by the early sixties after years of such efforts. The oft-cited example is the widely derided "Duck and Cover" information campaign in the fifties that intended to prepare schoolchildren and the public at large to protect themselves against atomic blast. In reality, global thermonuclear war rendered civil defense a compromised concept. The alternative was strategic defense, embodied in concepts like Massive Retaliation, Mutual Assured Destruction (MAD), and later the Strategic Defense Initiative (SDI). They too had their own counterintuitive logic. While some would argue that civil defense still had a role protecting populations from missiles able to penetrate any missile shield SDI might deploy, civil defense offered no billion-dollar programs around which it could build a constituency. Strategic programs provided major acquisition opportunities for the defense industrial base. National resourcing of fallout shelters did not.

### Mobilization—Industrial Policy without a Name

As was discussed in the previous section, the idea of wartime mobilization of resources began with the Preparedness Movement prior to World War I and finally matured in the 1940s during World War II. The outbreak of war in Europe in September 1939 enabled President Franklin Roosevelt to implement a major executive reorganization, which would set the stage for a second war mobilization almost within a generation. It was something he had wanted to do for a couple of years to salvage his New Deal, which suffered a prolonged setback in the recession of 1937–38. Wall Street wizard Bernard Baruch had been chairing a Defense Coordination Board for industrial mobilization in an effort to revive Woodrow Wilson's World War I War Industries Board. FDR wanted his own stamp on an office that would provide him with mobilization advisors in the White House.

His 1939 Reorganization Act established the Executive Office of the President (EOP). Declaring a national emergency, he issued a September 1939 executive order that provided EOP with six principal divisions: (1) the White House Office, (2) Bureau of the Budget, forerunner of the Office of Management and Budget, (3) National Resources Planning Board, (4) Liaison Office for Personnel Management, (5) Office of Government Reports, and (6) "in the event of a national emergency, or threat of a national emergency, such office for emergency management as the President shall determine."

A follow-on administrative order of May 1940 created in the new Executive Office of the President the Office for Emergency Management (OEM). The term "emergency management" did not mean what it means today in relation to homeland security, however. Its meaning was behind Roosevelt's 1939 national emergency declaration and was expressed in a 1939 executive order that further defined the functions and duties of the soon-to-be OEM. Roosevelt proposed that the office would be the federal mechanism to (1) increase production for national defense through *national mobilization* of material resources and industrial facilities and (2) oversee national civil defense. As war spread throughout the world, he expanded OEM's coordination responsibilities into such far-flung mobilization areas as defense-related housing. Although dormant since 1950, OEM still exists today. The other EOP wartime entities like the Office of Production Management, War Production Board, and Office of War Mobilization closed their doors at the end of the war.

Mobilization figured prominently in defense advisor Ferdinand Eberstadt's plan for a postwar national security system. A Wall Street colleague of Navy Secretary James Forrestal, Eberstadt was the director of the wartime Army-Navy Munitions Board who oriented that agency toward ensuring a smooth shift to peacetime production and postwar national policy and organization. The 1945 Eberstadt plan provided the basis for the National Security Act of 1947. Oft-overlooked, this act established the National Security Resources Board as the federal mobilization entity. Initially housed in the Pentagon, the NSRB was vested with the responsibility for postwar emergency preparedness planning and advising the president on coordinating military, industrial, and civilian mobilization. In Eberstadt's words, it would be "kind of an economic and social general staff" for peacetime emergency preparedness that in time of war would assist the president in running the country. The position of NSRB chairman was a civilian appointment requiring Senate approval. Arthur M. Hill, the president of Greyhound, was the first NSRB chairman, albeit unconfirmed. Like Eberstadt, Hill was a wartime mobilization associate of former Navy secretary and now Secretary of Defense James Forrestal. As for the specifically military side of mobilization, the National Security Act also established another successor agency to the wartime Army-Navy Munitions Board, now titled simply the Munitions Board. Also a Pentagon entity, it was chaired by Thomas J. Hargrave, president of Eastman Kodak, and another Forrestal associate. Two bureaucracies now competed for postwar resourcing and called into question their respective raisons d'être. Never fully resolved were the questions as to whether the NSRB was a planning body or one also responsible for execution, and whether it or the Munitions Board should be the primary contact point for industry.

The NSRB commenced operations in November 1947. Like the NSC, its members were cabinet level: the secretaries of defense (and the non-cabinet-level military departments), interior, the treasury, commerce, labor, and agriculture, and later the secretary of state. From the outset, Hill worked aggressively to expand his and the NSRB's directive authority, generating hostile scrutiny and the suspicions of President Harry Truman and the New Dealers. Truman would not go so far as to make the NSRB into a War Production Board in line with the intent of its architects, Eberstadt and Baruch. He wanted merely a body to coordinate mobilization plans across government. Among the cabinet-level players and heads of military departments, Hill soon came to realize that as acting chairman he was more a convenor without the authority to direct resources. Frustrated by Truman's refusal to accept his and Eberstadt's revised plan to empower the board, he resigned in December 1948.

Not about to replace Hill with another Forrestal man, Truman nominated one of his poker-playing cronies from his Senate days, the former Democratic governor of Washington Mon Wallgren, who had been defeated running for his second term in 1948. Partisan state politics, however, followed Wallgren into the confirmation process, resulting in a succession of Republican-generated delays. In the meantime, the president turned to appoint one of his trusted lieutenants, John R. Steelman, to chair NSRB. An Arkansas specialist in labor-management conciliation, Steelman was far from expert in military matters, although in 1946 he had become chairman of the new Science

Research Board and thus a rival to FDR's lordly research and development (R&D) administrator, Vannevar Bush. While Steelman had been responsible for labor affairs, he was more Truman's de facto chief of staff, serving until 1953. As acting NSRB chairman, he retained his title as assistant to the president. After Forrestal died in office in May 1949, Steelman transferred the NSRB to the Executive Office of the President and shifted its mission toward industrial planning for emergencies, notably critical materials stockpiling. In early 1950, he downgraded the agency to an advisory body that was more a staff office reporting through him to the president.

In 1949, the Soviets detonated their first atomic bomb, and China fell to the communists. The Soviet bomb changed the game. No longer would the United States have a monopoly on atomic weapons. Strategic defense of the homeland suddenly entered the calculus of national security. The threat was not just to ports this time; it was potentially to the whole continent. The calculus immediately called for an offensive national security strategy. In the spring of 1950, the NSC released NSC-68, establishing a national security policy that would require massive expenditures for rearmament and mobilization.

Amid this new strategic environment of heightened and presumed global threat, Truman continued to look for a nominee to the NSRB chair who would have Senate support. He fixed on W. Stuart Symington, who had recently served as a too-forceful secretary of the air force. Symington had made a name as the head of Emerson Electric, the St. Louis small-motor manufacturer that was big in aviation, where he had been notoriously well disposed to labor and a strong proponent of collective bargaining. During the war and afterwards, Symington's reputation grew as a vigorous air power proponent who as air force secretary in the late forties butted heads with the administration and Louis Johnson, Forrestal's successor, over constraints on the Air Force budget. The ambitiously dynamic Symington resigned, but Truman sought to keep him safely in his corner. Symington had wanted to replace David Lilienthal, the outgoing chairman of the newly created Atomic Energy Commission (AEC), but the post was already going to a sitting AEC commissioner, Gordon Dean. Truman offered him the NSRB chair. Symington liked the idea of a seat on the NSC at the cabinet level. He thus accepted Truman's offer, gained Senate confirmation, and took charge in the spring of 1950.

Symington came to the NSRB just as the Truman administration changed course on defense spending to implement NSC-68, a document that reflected much of the argument he had espoused as secretary of the air force. Notwithstanding his predecessor's NSRB downgrade, the position of chairman got new life via a recommendation from the congressionally mandated first Hoover Commission to empower the post. Initially, Symington chose to emphasize the NSRB's role in civil defense, appointing the well-connected Jerry Wadsworth, who happened to be his brother-in-law, to lead those particular efforts.

The June 1950 North Korean invasion of South Korea gave a further boost to mobilization and its advocates. The press now touted Symington as the Truman administration's "mobilization czar." Three months later, Congress passed the Defense Production Act with the same urgency as the Federal Civil Defense Act. The act, pushed hard by Bernard Baruch and now even Truman, established a Korean War–inspired mobilization bureaucracy. The act had the potential to increase Symington's authority for coordinating department and agency civil defense and mobilization activities. For a time, it appeared that the NSRB—not the Pentagon's Munitions Board—would have the bureaucratic upper hand, particularly with regard to critical materials stockpiling. Symington had worked particularly closely with the big three aluminum companies, ALCOA, Kaiser, and Reynolds, given that material's importance for aviation. Yet other quarters of industry were suspicious of Symington's record at Emerson, which betrayed a coziness with labor. Moreover, influenced by Baruch, Symington was moving toward the use of wage and price controls to check inflation. The NSRB chairman was now getting ahead of a president who was irritated by Symington's increasingly apparent grabs for power.

In December, Truman declared a national emergency. Under the authority of the Defense Production Act, he created by executive order another agency in the Executive Office of the President, the Office of Defense Mobilization (ODM). The EO also created the Defense Production Administration, the Wage Stabilization Board, the Office of Price Administration, and other agencies that would control inflation and run mobilization, putting them under ODM. Truman appointed "Electric Charlie" Wilson, the General Electric president who had worked on mobilization in the war, to head ODM and direct federal mobilization activities. Whereas the business community had remained skeptical of Symington, it had long regarded Wilson as one of its own. The stand-up of ODM and the Wilson appointment marked the effective end of the NSRB and Symington's authority. In early 1951, Symington left his NSRB post and accepted Truman's consolation prize—again to keep Symington in his administration tent—to head the Reconstruction Finance Corporation.

The Defense Production Act also established the National Production Authority (NPA) under the Defense Production Administration, which was placed in the Department of Commerce and given operational responsibilities for general control of defense production. In addition to the National Production Authority, the Defense Production Administration had authority over a number of agencies; however, most remained organizationally within their respective departments, and the confused arrangements led to a lot of senior staff turnover.

In March 1951 the administration tried to address the mobilization disconnect by establishing the National Advisory Board on Mobilization Policy with representatives from business, labor, and agriculture. By now, industry itself had its problems with mobilization, as reflected by the readiness of the U.S. Chamber of Commerce, National Association of Manufacturers, and Republicans to oppose renewal of the Defense Production Act in 1951.

When Truman's successor, Dwight Eisenhower, issued a February 1953 executive order abolishing the NSRB, he transferred its functions to the Office of Defense Mobilization. As part of the Eisenhower reorganization, the 1953 EO also abolished the Defense Production Administration and similarly transferred its functions to ODM, what had been its parent agency. Now, under its acting chairman, Jack Gorrie, ODM engaged itself in the planning for the dispersal of industry, a key element of civil defense, which proved especially beneficial for the South and Southeast.

As discussed above with regard to civil defense, the Eisenhower administration later in the decade consolidated ODM and the Federal Civil Defense Administration to form the Office of Defense and Civilian Mobilization in the Reorganization Plan No. 1 of 1958. Housed in the EOP, ODCM had the responsibility for civil defense and emergency mobilization coordination. Immediately thereafter, ODCM was renamed by statute the Office of Civil and Defense Mobilization. By a 1961 executive order, the Kennedy administration transferred the civil defense functions of OCDM to the Office of the Secretary of Defense. Several months later, what remained of OCDM in the Executive Office of the President was re-designated by statute as the Office of Emergency Planning. OEP coordinated emergency preparedness activities, principally in areas of resource utilization, civil defense, economic stabilization, post-attack rehabilitation, and government organization and continuity.

As for other mobilization duties remaining with the White House, however, the Cuban Missile Crisis generated a September 1962 executive order prescribing Office of Emergency Planning preparedness responsibilities to support mobilization. Recognizing the entwining of national security and economic growth and prosperity, the EO directed effective coordination of emergency preparedness measures with national economic policies and objectives. It said that all federal departments and agencies have responsibilities for emergency preparedness and that the effective and efficient accomplishment is related to their established roles and capabilities for mobilization readiness and civil defense activities. But the EOP would serve as a central point of leadership and coordination, citing the authorities in the National Security Act of 1947, the Defense Production Act of 1950, the Federal Civil Defense Act of 1950, and other authorities under the Reorganization Plan No. 1 of 1958. In 1968, the Office of Emergency Planning was re-designated the Office of Emergency Preparedness.

Responsibilities went to successor agencies. In the EOP, these agencies were the Office of Telecommunications Policy (1970–78) and the Office of Science and Technology Policy (1978–79) with their successive responsibility for emergency telecommunications systems. GSA had the Office of Preparedness (1973–75)—later the Federal Preparedness Agency (1975–79)—for emergency preparedness planning.

The establishment of FEMA prompted the Carter administration to revisit mobilization coordination with its March 1980 Presidential Directive-57 (PD/NSC-57). The directive gave FEMA the authority to coordinate mobilization planning. In the Reagan years, mobilization policy came with the July 1982 NSDD-47 on emergency mobilization preparedness. Rescinding PD/NSC-57, NSDD-47 emphasized a mobilization partnership with state and local governments and the private sector. It spoke of the need for developing approaches to resource management and economic stabilization as well as standby plans and procedures for government intervention. Citing the need for earthquake preparedness (in California in particular), the directive put a primary focus on the threat of catastrophic natural disasters and management responsibility into FEMA's Emergency Management Preparedness Board. While the National Communications System (NCS) was first established by President Kennedy in a memorandum, a 1984 Reagan administration executive order, EO 12472, authorized NCS "to provide for the consolidation of assignment and responsibility for improved execution of national security and emergency preparedness telecommunications functions." In 2003, the Homeland Security Act transferred the NCS function to DHS.

# CHAPTER TWO

# Counterterrorism:
## An Overseas Tactic of Choice Comes Ashore on the Homeland

Terrorism is a tactic with a long history. Terrorist objectives have been political, criminal, or personal. Modern-day terrorism for political objectives began to sustain the attention of U.S. national security officials in the late sixties and early seventies.[1] Then, the perpetrators were overseas groups such as the Popular Front for the Liberation of Palestine, the Abu Nidal Organization, Hezbollah, Al Fatah, Black September, and the Provisional Irish Republican Army, who hit the headlines with their terrorist campaigns involving commercial airliner hijackings, kidnappings, murders, and bombings.

At the outset, three general principles guided U.S. counterterrorism policy when American interests were involved:

- Make no concessions to terrorists
- Define them as criminals, subject to the rule of law
- Determine their state sponsors in order to apply diplomatic and economic[2] pressure to effect a desired outcome

In 1977, the Carter administration sought to formalize a process for counterterrorism decision-making and incident management. Drawing on the ad hoc approaches of previous administrations, its Presidential Security Memorandum 30 (PSM-30) confirmed the Department of State as the lead agency for terrorist incidents overseas and the Justice Department as the lead for domestic incidents. The directive also provided for the Federal Aviation Administration (FAA) to serve as lead agency for incidents involving U.S.-registered airplanes. PSM-30 put oversight of the interagency process for counterterrorism in the NSC by establishing a Counterterrorism Working Group that reported to an Executive Committee on Combating Terrorism.[3] The working group had a primary oversight responsibility related to the simultaneously established U.S. Army direct action unit, the Delta Force, whose anticipated functions would include hostage rescue. Several years later, the unit attained unwanted notoriety as the result of the failed Operation Eagle Claw, the U.S. attempt to rescue embassy staff in Tehran who had been seized by Iranian revolutionaries in 1980. Revolutionary Islamists had overthrown the U.S.-supported shah in early 1979. In November, radical students stormed the American embassy and took hostage fifty-two diplomats. Over the course of a full year, the Iranian hostage crisis gave America a foretaste of threats that would not fit neatly into Cold War molds—threats we would come to define as asymmetric.

The fallout from the hostage crisis, which ended in January 1981 just after Ronald Reagan's presidential inauguration, must be seen in the strategic context of the time. The incoming administration had determined that its primary national security objective was to execute a Cold War–winning strategy vis-à-vis the Soviet Union. At the same time, the oil crises of 1973 and 1979 had made abundantly clear that the Persian Gulf and Iran were geographical areas strategically vital to the world oil supply. In light of the Soviet military intervention in Afghanistan in late 1979, U.S. policy-makers now worried that Iran, notwithstanding the extreme nature of its Islamic regime, might be next to fall into the Soviet sphere.

Before its first year was out, the administration had to contend with a series of terrorist actions in Europe that included two separate Marxist-Leninist groups taking aim at senior U.S. military personnel and their wives. In September, the Red Army Faction, also known as the Baader-Meinhof Gang, attempted the assassination of the U.S. Army Europe commander, Gen. Frederick Kroesen, and his wife in Heidelberg while the two were driving in their car. It was the tenth attack made on service personnel and installations in West Germany that year. Three months later, the Red Brigades, a violent Italian group responsible for numerous political abductions and murders, kidnapped the deputy chief of staff for NATO Southern Land Forces, Brig. Gen. James Dozier, USA, leaving his wife bound to a chair in their Verona apartment.

To address this evolving class of threats, the Reagan administration further solidified the interagency mechanisms, choosing—like the previous administration—to do so via presidential directive. Defining the need, the December 1981 National Security Decision Directive 3 (NSDD-3), Crisis

Management, said, "A national security matter for which Presidential decisions and implementing instructions are required more rapidly than routine interdepartmental NSC staff support provides may be considered in the context of crisis management." From there, it made a specific tasking: "Crisis management shall be the responsibility of the Special Situation Group (SSG), chaired by the Vice President," with support coming from the NSC staff.

Vice President George H. W. Bush came to his post having served as President Gerald Ford's director of central intelligence (DCI) in 1976, just as the post-Watergate Church and Pike congressional committees were completing their investigations into intelligence activities. With General Dozier still in captivity, the administration released NSDD-2, National Security Council Structure, in January 1982.[4] The directive detailed the authorities of the NSC and created Senior Interagency Groups (SIGs) for foreign policy (including arms control), defense policy, and intelligence to deal with issues that fell into the interagency realm. NSDD-2 provided each "IG" with a permanent secretariat and charged each to provide "full, prompt, and systemic consideration" and to "monitor the execution of approved policies and decisions." Going beyond NSDD-3, the directive stated: "To deal with specific contingencies the IGs will establish full-time working groups, which will provide support to the crisis management operations of the NSC." Notwithstanding, NSDD-2 further stated it did not limit the operational responsibilities or authorities of any secretary or agency head over their personnel serving on IGs. In other words, the administration was still seeing counterterrorism more in terms of lead federal agency responsibilities.

The year 1982 saw the beginning of the decadelong succession of hostage-takings in Lebanon that would total ninety-six cases, of which twenty-five were U.S. citizens. The April 1982 NSDD-30, Managing Terrorist Incidents, restated the Carter administration PSM-30's lead federal agency approach to managing terrorist incidents. The directive renamed the Executive Committee on Combating Terrorism as the Interdepartmental Group on Terrorism (IG/T) and further formalized the classification of terrorist incidents and their federal-level interagency response. The Department of State would have the lead responsibility for handling overseas incidents and response. The Department of Justice (DOJ) would have lead authority in domestic terrorism incidents. The FAA would have the lead in incidents involving the airlines. NSDD-30 added one more: anticipating that the management of some terrorist incidents might require more than just direct action, it provided authority to FEMA for the management of the health response.[5]

In April 1983, the U.S. embassy in Lebanon suffered a deadly attack in which fifty-three people died, seventeen of whom were Americans, including the entire seven-person staff of the CIA Beirut station. Events in Lebanon now shifted Reagan administration sense-making. It now saw terrorism not so much as a tactic employed by proxies of the Soviet Union or its allies, but rather one pursued by Iran via radical Shiites.[6] Later that year, the horrific Islamic Jihad/Hezbollah truck bombing of the Beirut Marine barracks killed 241 U.S. service personnel. With neither the concrete intelligence upon which to base a response nor a clear policy to satisfy its competing bureaucracies, the administration was incapable of a response—military or otherwise. In January 1984, Islamic Jihad murdered Malcolm Kerr, president of the American University of Beirut. The following month, an exasperated Secretary of State George Shultz officially labeled Iran as a state sponsor of terrorism.[7]

The manifest need to address the mechanism for counterterrorism policy development and the escalating terrorist violence in the Middle East region led to the March NSDD-138, Combating Terrorism. NSDD-138 took the view that the Beirut truck bombing, the hostage takings (particularly that month's Islamic Jihad/Hezbollah kidnapping of William Buckley, the CIA's Beirut station chief), and the persistent attacks on airlines were state-sponsored, for example, by Iran. A high-ranking Agency counterterrorism asset, Buckley was the third American kidnapped in 1984. The Buckley abduction and eventual murder raised the possibility that the United States would use the military to retaliate. NSDD-138 provided authority for preemptive and retaliatory military operations against terrorists. The January 1985 NSDD-159, Covert Action Policy Approval and Coordination Procedures, provided for the NSC in effect to "review fully and integrate covert and overt activities" and coordinate the process to allow for the president to decide "which purposes can be best be accomplished by covert action."

The department and agency bureaucracies, however, resisted this approach, forcing the administration to issue another directive in July, NSDD-179, Task Force on Combating Terrorism. NSDD-179 established Vice President George H. W. Bush's Task Force on Combating Terrorism, led by Adm. James L. Holloway III. For the rest of the year, this body of senior officials with counterterrorism experience would study the issue and report yet another set of findings and recommendations for formalizing interagency counterterrorism policy development and response. In the same month, NSDD-180, Civil Aviation Terrorism Program, broadened the use of air marshals and gave the lead to the Department of Transportation and the FAA. Additionally, the directive spoke of expanding Transportation's counterterrorism research and development efforts with the Interagency Working Group on Combating Terrorism and the Technical Support Working Group (TSWG). A DoD/DOJ-led interagency body, TSWG to this day generates counterterrorism program requirements, funds projects, and lends technical expertise to monitor program development.

Terrorists were active throughout 1985. In October, four Palestinians hijacked the cruise liner *Achille Lauro* in the Mediterranean, killing one American passenger. In December, the Palestinian terrorist Abu Nidal, with Libyan material support, bombed airports in Rome and Vienna—targets neither military nor diplomatic. While the Bush/Holloway task force continued its review, the U.S. Intelligence Community (IC) was actively gathering intelligence under the assumption that Libyan terrorist squads—never proven—were operating in America, raising the question of policy development for and management of incidents on domestic soil.

The Bush/Holloway report, released in January 1986, was the U.S. government's first in-depth study of counterterrorism strategy. Its findings appeared as NSDD-207, The National Program for Combating Terrorism. Restating U.S. counterterrorism policy, NSDD-207 made the state-sponsored assumption. Identifying terrorism as a potential threat to national security, it reiterated that it was U.S. policy not to negotiate with terrorists. Committing the government to work with foreign countries and use all means to apprehend terrorists, NSDD-207 affirmed the lead agencies established in 1982 by NSDD-30 and previously by PSM-30. As well, it gave authority to the president's national security advisor for resolving interagency responsibilities. The Bush/Holloway task force had actually wanted to create in the NSC a counterterrorism czar, but again the bureaucratic resistance from State, CIA, and the FBI was too intense to pursue implementation. State, in particular, was anxious to maintain its authority as lead federal agency for overseas terrorist incidents.[8]

Crucially for institutionalizing a future interagency counterterrorism structure, NSDD-207 established a Terrorist Incident Working Group (TIWG) in the NSC staff to support the vice president–led Special Situation

Group (SSG) for crisis management and agency coordination in terrorist incidents. The chairman of the TIWG became Lt. Col. Oliver North, USMC, who had been serving as director of the NSC Office of Politico-Military Affairs and was a participant in the Bush/Holloway review. Chaired by State's Ambassador-at-Large for Counterterrorism Robert B. Oakley, who had also served on Bush/Holloway, the Interdepartmental Group on Terrorism would lead counterterrorism policy development. TIWG also got an intelligence fusion center, an early attempt to connect the dots across the IC information-gathering stovepipes. Finally, NSDD-207 called for a review of a proposal to enhance federal jurisdiction over domestic terrorist incidents. Satisfied that Justice and the FBI had been very successful to that point in foiling terrorist operations in the American homeland, Ambassador Oakley continued to regard the overseas threat to Americans as the primary concern.[9] For the remainder of the decade, events would support his assessment.

The Beirut U.S. Embassy and Marine Barracks bombings, Buckley murder, and succession of abductions twice led Congress to expand FBI extraterritorial jurisdiction. The Comprehensive Crime Control Act of 1984 provided federal jurisdiction over hostage taking when Americans were victims or perpetrators, the United States was the target of demands, or the perpetrator was in the United States. The Omnibus Diplomatic Security and Antiterrorism Act of 1986 broadened U.S. territorial jurisdiction to include terrorist acts where Americans were killed or seriously injured. As such, the 1980s saw the FBI expand its overseas investigations into terrorism. Because of the focus on treating terrorism as a crime, the FBI Criminal Investigative Division, rather than the then–Intelligence Division, was managing the Terrorism Section, which oversaw all FBI domestic and international counterterrorism efforts. From 1985 to mid-1989, the FBI, supported by State and the CIA, conducted some fifty investigations into terrorist acts under these authorities.

Administration counterterrorism officials thus prepared to go on the offensive overseas with direct action. State used diplomacy and the labeling of state sponsors; CIA conducted intelligence operations abroad; the FBI went after terrorists in order to bring them to justice; and the military served as the option of last resort. As the Reagan DCI, William Casey was a Wall Street player and a crusty veteran of the wartime Office of Strategic Services (OSS). Seeking to restore the agency's capabilities, gutted as part of the fallout from the Church and Pike congressional investigations and subsequent Foreign

Intelligence Surveillance Act (FISA) and Attorney General Guideline constraints, Casey wanted an activist CIA. In late 1985, he established the DCI's Counterterrorism Center (CTC) in its demoralized and languishing Directorate of Operations (DO). To rebuild an operational capability, Casey relied on Dewey Clarridge, whose background included service as the Istanbul station chief. The CTC mission was to "preempt, disrupt, and defeat" terrorists and coordinate the IC's counterterrorism activities.[10] Clarridge and his successor, Fred Turco, expanded the CTC to go after terrorists who were attacking Americans. The IC and the CTC were targeting the major state sponsors, Iran, Syria, Libya, Iraq, and the PLO, as well as the "hostile" intelligence foes, North Korea and Cuba.

Over at State, the Bureau of Intelligence and Research (INR) and one political-military official, Richard Clarke, were taking a different view, informed inductively by what was happening on the ground in the Middle East. At the time, the use of the military for response to terrorism was still an issue between DoD and State. Defense Secretary Caspar Weinberger and the Pentagon were less inclined to the use of military force without conclusive intelligence/evidence establishing the perpetrators. Weinberger particularly worried about the risks of American servicemen being captured during counterterrorism operations. Informed by INR, George Shultz—the head of the lead federal agency for counterterrorism overseas—held that terrorism was "armed aggression" and thus justified a military response. NSDD-207 favored the Shultz position and the use of military force to preempt or retaliate for terrorist attacks.

The CTC view following the December 1985 Rome and Vienna airport bombings was that the United States should first target the Libyan-supported Abu Nidal Organization. A secret annex to NSDD-207 provided centralized operational authority for counterterrorism activities and operations via an Operations Sub-Group (OSG), an interagency NSC entity given directive authority over agencies.[11] Under the TIWG, the OSG was led by Lieutenant Colonel North, who now had the title coordinator of counterterrorism. His OSG staff included many of those who worked on the Bush/Holloway task force. OSG opted to emphasize the use of the military directly against the state sponsor, Libya, and its leader, Muammar al-Gaddafi.

The military operation against Libya was a key milestone in the counterterrorism timeline. In January 1986, the U.S. Navy began a provocative exercise in the Gulf of Sidra, international waters claimed by the Libyans as their territory. These naval operations continued into March. In April, a bomb detonated in the La Belle disco in West Berlin, injuring 230, including over fifty U.S. servicemen, two of whom died. Intercepted telex messages linked Libya to the bombing and now provided sufficient cause for a military retaliatory strike against a comparatively vulnerable state sponsor. With naval forces in position, the OSG dove into the planning for Operation El Dorado Canyon. Ten days after the La Belle bombing, U.S. air strikes rained on selected Libyan military facilities and the Gaddafi family compound. Unfortunately, the attack failed to put an end to Libyan terrorism against Americans. In December 1988, Pan Am 103 exploded over Lockerbie, Scotland, killing 243 passengers, sixteen crew members, and eleven persons on the ground as the result of falling debris. After a three-year investigation, Scottish law enforcement and the FBI determined that Libyan intelligence agents were behind the bombing. For some, the counterterrorism campaign against Libya illustrated the questionable effectiveness of a limited military response short of all-out war on a state sponsor.

When Frank Carlucci succeeded Vice Adm. John Poindexter as national security advisor at the height of the Iran-Contra affair in December 1986, he dismantled the NSC's presumed operational mechanisms that had competed with State and DoD. Titles changed accordingly. The deputies-level Crisis Pre-Planning Group (CPPG) became the Policy Review Group; North's Operations Sub-Group became the Coordination Sub-Group (CSG). For the remainder of the Reagan administration's second term, counterterrorism activity would continue with a much lower profile.

President George H. W. Bush's national security advisor, Lt. Gen. Brent Scowcroft, USAF, essentially continued the counterterrorism structures he inherited, except for changing the name of the Policy Review Group (the interagency entity for policy development) to the Deputies Committee. In late 1989, the administration had to deal with a crisis in Panama over strongman Manuel Noriega's voiding of electoral results, which led to U.S. intervention in December. The Deputies Committee handled Panama crisis management. As the United States prepared for war with Iraq during Operation Desert Shield in late 1990 and early 1991, the CSG anticipated the possibility of Iraqi terrorist attacks in the homeland. In particular, it addressed the need for protection of critical infrastructure. Subsequently, the FBI determined that unlike Iran or Libya, Iraq had no functional terrorist network operating in the United

States. With no domestic incidents to suggest otherwise, policy-makers went through the presidential transition after Bill Clinton's 1992 victory maintaining the view that terrorism was a tactic employed overseas by perpetrators serving as proxies for their state sponsors.

### Terrorism Hits the Homeland

In 1993, terrorism landed on domestic soil with a rapid-fire reality. In January, four days after Clinton's inauguration, Pakistani lone-wolf Islamist Mir Amal Kansi attacked CIA employees in a traffic queue waiting to enter Agency headquarters in Langley, Virginia, killing two and wounding three others. February saw the Bureau of Alcohol, Tobacco, and Firearms (ATF) siege and assault on the Branch Davidian cult in Waco, Texas, and the first World Trade Center (WTC) bombing. In April, it was the discovery abroad of the Iraqi plot to assassinate former President George Herbert Walker Bush during his visit to Kuwait. Now that terrorism had assumed a domestic dimension, the new president and his national security advisor thus were quick to embrace counterterrorism as a policy priority.

The consensus of the Clinton administration was to continue previous approaches—for example, those embodied in NSDD-207. The management of a domestic terrorist incident and counterterrorist response would remain primarily law enforcement responsibilities. While the priority was increasing, questions about who should be in charge resurfaced. Should it be Justice? Or the FBI? And what about the CIA or State?

The first WTC attack—a truck bombing that killed seven, including an unborn child, and wounded over a thousand—put fire under the CIA's Counterterrorism Center. CTC's initial suspect was Hezbollah, a supposition that the FBI did not share. The Bureau knew almost immediately that the perpetrators had connections throughout the Middle East and Pakistan when one of their number, Mohammad Salameh, returned to the truck rental office for a $400 deposit refund, information it shared with the CIA and CTC. Ramzi Yousef, the leader of the WTC operation, had escaped to Pakistan. A few years later, the FBI tracked and arrested him. The CIA had been focused on other groups associated with the Maghreb—that is, the Libyan-backed Abu Nidal Organization and Sunni extremists in Algeria. As a partner with the New York Police Department's investigation into the bombing, the FBI became aware of a network of Sunni conspirators not aligned with a state sponsor but rather manifesting a number of links to a Saudi terrorist financier, Osama bin Laden. FBI officials thereupon opened a file and made the information available both to the CIA and the NSC's Coordination Sub-Group, marking bin Laden's introduction to the U.S. counterterrorism community. At a time when the State Department's counterterrorism office was in disarray, FBI director Louis Freeh was ready for the Bureau to play a more global role via its legal attaché offices in the embassies. While the president and Freeh were not personally close, Clinton was disposed to the FBI taking the lead in cases where Americans were victims. It suited his conception of a less military and more legally principled foreign policy.

The Clinton administration attempted to finesse the counterterrorism coordination problem by drifting away from a lead-agency approach. Drawing upon the unimplemented Bush/Holloway recommendation for a counterterrorism czar, it put more authority in the NSC staff to coordinate counterterrorism via a national coordinator. The job went to State's Richard Clarke, a career civil servant whom Bush National Security Advisor Brent Scowcroft had transferred to the NSC staff in 1992. Clarke had made a name for himself in the mid-eighties for his efforts to supply Stinger missiles to the mujahideen fighting against the Soviets in Afghanistan. An NSC staff carryover from the previous administration, Clarke had impressed the new national security advisor, Anthony Lake, with his briefings in 1993 on the U.S. intervention in Somalia in support of the United Nations peacekeeping operation in Somalia. Lake made Clarke the chairman of the Coordination Sub-Group, whose title would change to Counterterrorism Security Group. Ill-disposed to bureaucratic reorganizations, Clarke felt that the NSC staff could serve as the appropriate entity for coordinating counterterrorism. Now that terrorists were striking the homeland, Justice and the FBI counterterrorism equities rose. Clarke benefitted from the convergence in the mid-nineties of a collaborative group of counterterrorism professionals from a number of agencies and departments who were prepared to make counterterrorism a team effort at the working level—that is, in the CSG.[12] Clarke had an excellent relationship with CSG members. An effective facilitator, he would only meet resistance when he appeared to be veering in the direction of attempting to exercise operational control of missions that were agency and departmental functions.

The persistence of terrorist plotting became evident in late 1994 with the discovery in the Philippines of Ramzi Yousef, wanted in connection with the first World Trade Center attack, in a conspiracy to bomb twelve airliners over the Pacific, which after two years finally led to his arrest and conviction. Yousef, it had been established, was a conspirator behind the first WTC bombing and one of the drivers of the Ryder van containing the bomb. The nature of Yousef's so-called Bojinka Plot in Manila was such that policy-makers had to address an entirely new question over how to characterize the terrorist threat. To what degree, if any, should terrorist plotters be regarded as state-sponsored? If they determined that terrorist "networks" existed independent of state sponsorship, then U.S. military retaliation to an incident—à la NSDD-207—could not be an appropriate response. Moreover, if such a network obtained what were now being called weapons of mass destruction (WMD), then the U.S. national security threat/response paradigm would correspondingly have to shift to include further consideration for managing the consequences as well as going after the perpetrators.

The March 1995 Aum Shinrikyo sarin gas attack on the Tokyo subway was followed by a terrorist horror that finally came to American soil in April with Timothy McVeigh's truck bombing of the Alfred P. Murrah Federal Building in Oklahoma City. This attack underscored the escalating borders-in trend line and prompted the administration to issue in June Presidential Decision Directive 39 (PDD-39), The U.S. Policy on Counterterrorism. In his original draft of the presidential directive, Clarke prepared to depart from his role as honest broker in the CSG interagency process and wrote into the document authority for him to exercise operational control for executing counterterrorism policy. Justice, the FBI, and the CIA forcefully resisted Clarke's language. The final PDD-39 built on Reagan's NSDD-207 and framed three basic management pillars for a new national counterterrorism strategy:

- Threat/Vulnerability Management—to reduce the vulnerability to terrorist attacks and prevent and deter them before they occur
- Crisis Response—for responding to terrorist acts that occur by denying terrorists their objectives or ending the crisis and apprehending/punishing the perpetrators
- Consequence Management—to manage the consequences of terrorist acts by restoring essential government services, providing emergency relief, and protecting public health and safety

The massive destruction of the Murrah complex and the horrendous loss of life, although geographically limited, required a response that was in some ways akin to that for a natural disaster or major hazmat incident. Coordination at the incident site had to meet somewhat conflicting priorities—for example, saving lives versus forensic collection. By including consequence management in this directive, a national counterterrorism strategy was thus moving into the realm of emergency management. Indeed, the threat and vulnerability management pillar was suggesting something akin to what had been an element of civil defense of infrastructure, advancing the thinking in 1982 behind the two Reagan directives on civil defense, NSDD-23, U.S. Civil Defense Policy, and NSDD-26, U.S. Civil Defense Policy. To that end, PDD-39 led to establishment of another NSC entity, the Critical Infrastructure Working Group (CIWG).

PDD-39 assigned agency roles and responsibilities and charged the NSC to take an interagency approach to coordinating terrorism policy issues, to ensure implementation of federal counterterrorism policy and strategy. To recap, prior to PDD-39 when a terrorist incident was an overseas event, most counterterrorism policy discussions had taken place in the State Department. With the onset of domestic terrorist incidents, these discussions shifted to the White House and Clarke's NSC Coordinating Sub-Group. While domestic incidents were under the purview of Attorney General Janet Reno, who shared information with Clarke and his group regarding matters under investigation, still, the FBI managed domestic terrorism incidents with little or no input from Clarke. Once terrorism had become a borders-in, domestic phenomenon, Clarke's sub-group was renamed the Counterterrorism Security Group (CSG). Although intelligence sharing issues remained, PDD-39 also resolved the distinction between two NSC communities, counterterrorism and nonproliferation. Terrorism and WMD became Clarke's issues. His clout came from the close relationship he had developed with Lake and Clinton who were now very aware of the palpable transnational terrorist threat. Clinton was evidently comfortable having Clarke take the lead for his counterterrorism strategy, an approach that also enjoyed support from Lake and Sandy Berger, who succeeded him as national security advisor in 1997. PDD-39 empowered Clarke as the CSG chair. He started with a 1995 cross-cutting federal counterterrorism budget at $5.7 billion, which he was able to double to over $11 billion by the end of the Clinton reign in 2000.

Meanwhile, the CIA was beginning to shift focus toward terrorist financier Osama bin Laden and his al Qaeda network, whose node was then in Sudan. The CIA Khartoum station had been seeing bin Laden as the money man behind the financing of Islamist extremists all across North Africa. The rise of the Taliban in 1994 among the Afghan Pashtuns provided Arab jihadists based in Afghanistan with an enhanced infrastructure to expand training. By early 1995, evidence was surfacing that they were experimenting with developing a range of WMD capabilities.

In November, a car bomb detonated at the Riyadh headquarters of the Saudi National Guard, killing five Americans and wounding another thirtyfour. The assumptions held that Iran was behind the bombing, but it was not yet clear. By the end of 1995, the CIA and FBI had pulled together enough intelligence to see a new pattern. Ramzi Yousef's Manila plot shed light on a new generation of Sunni terrorists who were planning strikes against the American homeland. One plan in particular was a plot to hijack a commercial airliner and crash it into CIA headquarters in Langley.[13] FBI and CIA analysts concluded that these Sunni extremists were not surrogates like an Iranian state-sponsored Hezbollah. They were "autonomous and indigenous."

As the decade advanced, focus shifted to Saudi Arabia where a controversial post–Gulf War U.S. military presence remained. The Riyadh bombing was followed by the June 1996 bombing of the Khobar Towers, a housing complex for U.S. Air Force personnel. The truck bomb killed nineteen servicemen and wounded close to four hundred personnel of many nationalities. Nineteen ninety-six was an election year, and the administration was compelled to respond to what was still presumed to have been an Iranian-supported attack as a follow-on to the Riyadh bombing. In the end, it was determined that the perpetrators were a Saudi Hezbollah group. In this case, overseeing the Khobar response in the NSC was Lake's so-called Small Group, which included Director of Central Intelligence (DCI) John Deutch, Defense Secretary Bill Perry, Secretary of State Warren Christopher, and Leon Fuerth, Vice President Gore's national security advisor. In the summer of 1996, counterproliferation leaders in Congress were also troubled by the prospect of WMD capabilities. The principal fear was clandestine transfers of nuclear and biological weapons capabilities from the former Soviet republics to terrorist networks. In their view, this potential WMD threat required a domestic WMD consequence management program. The Defense against

Weapons of Mass Destruction Act of 1996, contained in that year's DoD authorization legislation, established the Nunn-Lugar-Domenici Domestic Preparedness Program. Run by the Army's Directorate of Military Support (DOMS), Nunn-Lugar was an interagency program (including FBI, Energy, the Environmental Protection Agency [EPA], the Department of Health and Human Services [HHS], and FEMA) to provide training and equipment for better preparing 120 selected cities for WMD consequence management. The program ran to 2000 until President Clinton approved moving the so-called Nunn-Lugar-Domenici functions to the Justice Department's Office for State and Local Domestic Preparedness Support, a new DOJ organizational unit. Justice had been funding and training state and local officials since enactment of the Anti-Terrorism and Effective Death Penalty Act of 1996, with grants for training for the Fire Service run by FEMA's National Fire Academy at Emmitsburg, Maryland.

Congress authorized the Nunn-Lugar-Domenici Domestic Preparedness Program as part of the Defense Reauthorization Act of 1996. This domestic preparedness program focused on enhancing the ability of local and state governments to respond to a terrorist WMD incident. Elements of the program consisted of advanced training, equipment, and exercises for local first responders. While FEMA was the lead agency for consequence management in response to acts of terrorism, Nunn-Lugar-Domenici did not assign that agency as the lead agency for managing the program. James Lee Witt's FEMA was fixed on preparedness and response to natural disasters. Congress thus gave the task to DoD with the logic that it could apply its long-standing nuclear, biological, and chemical (NBC) warfare expertise to domestic consequence management. Nunn-Lugar-Domenici was the immediate legacy program of the homeland security preparedness grant programs of today. While the lead went to DoD, FEMA and other federal agencies also played a role—that is, the FBI, the Department of Health and Human Services, the Department of Energy (DOE), and the Environmental Protection Agency (EPA). At the time, FEMA chaired the Senior Interagency Coordination Group on Terrorism, established to improve coordination on policy issues and program activities concerning WMD response. Eventually, in the late 1990s, DOJ's Office of Justice Programs would manage the preparedness program through its Office for State and Local Domestic Preparedness Support, which later became the Office for Domestic Preparedness. The National Domestic Preparedness Office (NDPO), housed in the FBI, inherited oversight of the Nunn-Lugar-Domenici "train-the-trainer" programs for states and localities. At that time, FEMA declined the opportunity to assume the national preparedness mission. In addition, one of Dick Clarke's deputies in his NSC staff organization, Lisa Gordon-Hagerty, ran the state and local interface for NSC.

Following its institution via PDD-39, Clarke's Critical Infrastructure Working Group recommended forming a commission with the charge to develop a national policy and implementation strategy for protecting critical infrastructures from physical and cyber threats. That July 1996, an executive order established a public/private-sector study group officially titled the President's Commission on Critical Infrastructure Protection, or more colloquially the Marsh Commission, after its chairman Gen. Robert T. Marsh, the retired commander of the Air Force Systems Command. The CIWG identified for the commission eight infrastructures critical to the nation's "life support systems": telecommunications, electric power, oil and gas transportation and storage, banking and finance, transportation, water supply systems, emergency services (such as medical, police, fire, and rescue), and continuity of government services.

While CIWG's charge had extended across the nation's physical critical infrastructure, most attention went to the commission's subsequent output related to cyber security. The commission reported its findings in the early fall of 1997. Among them, the Marsh report identified computer-based infrastructure attacks as a new and serious threat and proposed a government-industry partnership to protect such key infrastructures.

In February 1998, two Sunni terrorist networks, Egyptian Islamic Jihad and al Qaeda, declared war on Egypt and the United States. The announcement put further urgency behind two PDDs released in the spring, which solidly addressed the consequence management piece of PDD-39 and the application of FEMA's Federal Response Plan to a terrorist attack.

PDD-62, Combating Terrorism, promoted interagency cooperation and coordination in counterterrorism planning and execution by delegating a shared lead-federal-agency designation among the FBI, Secret Service, and FEMA to resolve the "who's-in-charge" question and promote interagency communication. PDD-62 supported PDD-39 in designating the FBI as the lead federal agency for crisis response and intelligence related to terrorism during domestic special events. But the Secret Service became the lead agency for security design, planning, and implementation. FEMA got additional authorities for consequence management and coordination. PDD-62 also further defined and established special events as National Special Security Events (NSSEs) requiring enhanced federal planning and protection.

PDD-62 provided for a counterterrorism management structure based in the NSC: the Office of the National Coordinator for Security, Infrastructure Protection, and Counterterrorism. The so-called counterterrorism czar was Dick Clarke. Reporting to him were three senior executive working groups: (1) his Counterterrorism Security Group, which provided input on policy, budget, and programs; (2) the newly titled Critical Infrastructure Coordination Group (CICG); (3) the WMD Preparedness Group; and (4) the Continuity of Government Interagency Group. Clarke, as the national coordinator, chaired all four. Clarke's arrangement allayed agency refusals to allow any one department to have sole counterterrorism responsibility; however, his office did not have the authority to mandate procedures to agencies nor to direct authority over funds.

The second directive, PDD-63, Protecting America's Critical Infrastructures, effectively implemented the findings of the Marsh Commission, pending a National Infrastructure Assurance Plan. Clarke and his CICG were to coordinate the lead agencies for sector liaison and work any evaluations and recommendations with the Office of Management and Budget (OMB). PDD-63 also established in the FBI a National Infrastructure Protection Center (NIPC) for information sharing, which would include private-sector information sharing and analysis centers (ISACs), conforming to the Marsh Commission's identification of the eight national critical infrastructure sectors.

NIPC combined the elements of several federal agencies with roles in the defense of the national infrastructure: Transportation, Energy, and Defense, along with the National Security Agency (NSA), CIA, and FBI. NIPC intended to enable closer coordination between the intelligence and security operations of the FBI and the military. Most significantly, it attempted with modest success to build a partnership with the private sector, given the oft-cited statistic that 85 percent of the nation's critical infrastructure is privately owned and operated.[14]

Al Qaeda made good on its February fatwa. On August 7, the terrorist network simultaneously bombed U.S. embassies in Kenya and Tanzania. The paired incidents tested the interagency response under Clarke's counterterrorism structure. Unfortunately, his interagency coordination was not always successful in making bureaucratic priorities support each other and his counterterrorism brief. For example, he lost the bureaucratic battle with Treasury with respect to implementing a policy to disrupt terrorist financial networks. Treasury Secretary Robert Rubin opposed implementation of rules on money laundering, fearing that it would compromise the administration's primary strategic objective: advancing the U.S. role as the guarantor of the international financial system. Clarke maintained that Rubin's successor from 1999 to 2001, Lawrence Summers, however, proved to be more inclined toward terrorist finance tracking.[15]

In line with its focus on state threats, DoD resisted National Security Advisor Sandy Berger's desire to bring the department into active operations against the al Qaeda network. Burdened with the expense of an already increasing mission set that now included post–Cold War humanitarian, peacekeeping, peacemaking, and peace enforcement operations, specifically those supporting NATO in Bosnia and Kosovo, the Pentagon preferred to classify counterterrorism as a police, FBI, and intelligence matter. As such, it would not support Clarke in 2000 with his plan for the Air Force or CIA to use the Air Force's armed Predator drones to attack al Qaeda targets in Afghanistan. Since that time, armed Predators have been used successfully in many such operations.

The CIA itself could not agree on the threat posed by al Qaeda. The director of central intelligence, George Tenet, was supportive of Berger and Clarke on their desires for escalating CIA operations against al Qaeda. Yet Tenet's deputy director of operations, James Pavitt, remained skeptical, given the insufficient resourcing of his directorate. The CIA then and into the first months of the George W. Bush administration was resourcing analysis over ops as regard to terrorist networks and as such focused on intelligence collection rather than a proactive disruption mission.

The FBI and law enforcement community were similarly wrestling with priorities. The FBI reflected those at the city and county level—the foci of its field office work. In the nineties, amid a succession of structural and name changes, the FBI balanced those priorities between its National Security Division and its Criminal Investigative Division. The bureaucratic weight was in the latter, where the culture was all about evidence collection, the basis of investigation for prosecution, FBI's traditional core mission. In the former, the culture was more about intelligence gathering. Field offices in the nineties still dedicated resources to tracking Russian espionage, which competed with those needed to monitor terrorist network activities. Two agents in the mid-1990s who forcefully and successfully pushed for reallocations were Bob Blitzer, chief of the FBI's domestic terrorism/counterterrorism planning section, and John O'Neill, chief of its international terrorism operations section. Both sections were assigned to the National Security Division headed by Robert M. Bryant.

In August 1998, the FBI and Justice brought together leading members of the federal emergency response community to address federal WMD preparedness. The gathering concluded that the government needed a single office to coordinate all federal WMD preparedness assistance programs for state and local authorities. Attorney General Janet Reno placed the FBI in charge of the National Domestic Preparedness Office (NDPO) to manage a program to coordinate all federal efforts,[16] to assist state and local first responders with planning, training, equipment, exercises, and health and medical support for response to conventional or non-conventional WMD incidents. Bob Blitzer stood up NDPO in line with the Bureau's prevention and response mission and as an extension of its investigative programs. Grants management went to Butch Straub, the chief of the DOJ Office for State and Local Domestic Preparedness. In the end, major city police chiefs did not see much value in the training side of the NDPO programs. For the most part, the trainers came from the military whose WMD tactics, techniques, and procedures while effective in a combat environment were ill-suited to civilian consequence management applications. NDPO did not have a line item in the DOJ budget. When the office transferred to the newly created DHS in March 2003, it went with no staff and no funding.

Most troubled by terrorism, Sandy Berger was supportive of domestic preparedness and PDD-62's codification of a counterterrorism czar. In the summer of 1998, he ran another WMD tabletop exercise for senior federal-level officials at Blair House, the president's official state guest house across the street from the White House. Berger's tabletop, which Clarke facilitated, exposed a lack of preparedness throughout the federal government. Berger and Clarke now recognized that terrorists could use WMD, specifically an improvised nuclear device or an airplane-delivered aerosolized anthrax, to threaten U.S. constitutional government itself.

"This table top was a real awakening for many of these cabinet-level folks," recalled Bob Blitzer who was a participant. "It was a eureka moment." The preparedness gaps discovered during the tabletop generated the October 1998 PDD-67, Enduring Constitutional Government and Continuity of Government Operations. PDD-67 required federal departments and agencies to develop plans for COG and continuity of operations (COOP). PDD-67 superseded the Bush administration's NSD-69, Enduring Constitutional Government (June 1992)—which in turn had succeeded its NSD-37, also titled Enduring Constitutional Government (April 1990), and the Reagan administration's NSDD-55, Enduring National Leadership (September 1982).

Of course, COG and COOP policies pre-dated the WMD threat from terrorists. They essentially originated with the Eisenhower administration's recognition of the need for contingency plans in the event of a strategic nuclear strike on Washington. The initial document establishing continuity programs was the 1955 NSC-5521, NSC Relocation Plan. It was followed by a succession of directives and executive orders right through the 1980s. Beginning with the Kennedy administration, the responsibility for COG coordination resided in the Executive Office of the President with the director of the Office of Emergency Planning. Under a 1952 Truman administration executive order, that office already had the responsibility for COOP policies. COG and COOP planning intensified through the Reagan administration culminating with a November 1988 EO, Assignment of Emergency Preparedness Responsibilities, stating that the NSC had the responsibility for developing and administering national security emergency preparedness policy, including continuity of essential functions. The NSC was to assign emergency preparedness responsibilities to federal departments and agencies but would not have authority to implement plans. The FEMA administrator was to serve as an NSC advisor on national emergency preparedness, and FEMA was to coordinate and implement these plans.

By 2000, a number of quarters in Washington were active with studies and proposals for organizing counterterrorism preparedness.[17] One example was that year's congressionally driven legislation, opposed by OMB and the administration, to establish in the Executive Office of the President, the Office of Terrorism Preparedness. Patterned after the Office of the National Drug Control Policy (ONDCP), the office of the "drug czar," this initiative was another attempt to centralize leadership and coordination of federal programs to help state and local governments prepare for terrorist WMD incidents. In the eyes of lawmakers, agency administration of the various domestic preparedness grant programs had become duplicative and was generating wasteful pork. State and local jurisdictions were also complaining about the confused federal administration of programs and lobbying for their consolidation into a "one-stop shop." The Office of Terrorism Preparedness' duties themselves would have overlapped with those of the National Domestic Preparedness Office, whose funding had been strangled by congressional interests opposed to having such an entity in the FBI. Critics also deemed it too focused on WMD, as opposed to other conventional threats. The enabling legislation represented a familiar reorganization theme sung with lyrics from the counterterrorism book. A number of bills and related proposals now offered answers to the question of whether the structural focal point for counterterrorism should be in the EOP or a lead federal agency. Many candidate departments and agencies were now anticipating a federal feeding frenzy and identifying counterterrorism missions with proposals to establish program offices. As a result, OMB was increasingly facing a tracking and assessment challenge, characterized by the Center for the Strategic and International Studies (CSIS) in 2000 as a "definitional and statistical nightmare."[18] CSIS noted a lack of agency transparency for counterterrorism funding and, after citing a number of estimates on trends, settled with the OMB reckoning that federal counterterrorism expenditures increased by 55 percent from an FY98 (fiscal year 1998) total of $8.3 billion to $12.9 billion in FY00, across twenty-three major departments and agencies.[19]

## A Return to a Borders-out Conception of National Security

In terms of personalities, when the George W. Bush administration arrived in Washington in 2001, the nexus of national security decision-making was among the vice president, Dick Cheney, the secretary of defense, Donald Rumsfeld, and the national security advisor, Condoleezza Rice. Distinct from its predecessor, the Bush administration's strategic focus was less on coordinating the international monetary system and more on the military component of the unilateral national interest. Among other things, this strategic predisposition informed its approach to China, missile defense, and multilateral obligations—for example, the Anti-Ballistic Missile (ABM) Treaty.

It thus appeared that counterterrorism would be getting short shrift. Likewise, states and cities could expect to see cuts to federal programs supporting PDD-39's intergovernmental crisis response and consequence management capabilities.

Cheney had an unusually large national security staff in the Office of the Vice President (OVP). Via his chief of staff, Lewis Libby, he had a solid bridge to Rumsfeld, and his key OSD lieutenants, Paul Wolfowitz and Douglas Feith. As for Rice, her preference was to make the NSC less operational than it appeared to be with Dick Clarke and his enhanced role as national coordinator for security, infrastructure protection, and counterterrorism, as had been provided by PDD-62. She achieved her goal via an interagency restructuring that stressed NSC counterterrorism coordination rather than leadership. The Clinton NSC's interagency working groups were either abolished or rolled into supposedly empowered, functional policy coordinating committees (PCCs), which reported to the "deputies level," NSC-speak for the committee composed of the deputy secretaries of NSC-member departments and agencies. For Rice, the restructuring actually removed her and the NSC staff from any institutional power. In the case of her staff, it no longer had direct access to the president such as the Clinton administration had provided for the previous NSC staff. In actuality, this reorganization allowed the NSC "Principals," the committee of the statutory members of the Council (cabinet-level secretaries, specifically Defense Secretary Rumsfeld), free rein to bypass Rice and go directly to Bush. The consequences were acutely felt by State, which viewed the arrangement with some skepticism. Former Deputy Secretary of State Richard Armitage has been widely quoted as characterizing the NSC of the time as "dysfunctional."

In its first weeks in office, the Bush administration made it very clear that it was not going to give counterterrorism priority. Clarke was unsuccessful in getting Rice and her deputy Stephen Hadley to fit counterterrorism into broader foreign policy. During the transition, Clarke and Berger had alerted her to the terrorist threat. In their view, they were ignored. Rice insisted on aligning the focus of the NSC staff to supporting Cheney and Rumsfeld's national missile defense policy. The staff member with the missile defense brief was a Cheney man: Ambassador Robert Joseph, a government official expert in nuclear forces and arms control. Also the nonproliferation staff lead, Joseph was among a circle of counterproliferation advocates who were focused on rogue states with developing ballistic missile and nuclear programs—that is, they were oriented to state threats rather than terrorist networks. Joseph later attained notoriety for refusing the CIA request to remove from Bush's 2003 State of the Union address the reference to the questionably authenticated Iraqi quest to obtain yellowcake uranium from Niger.

Cheney's involvement in the NSC was at the Principals level. At the beginning of the administration, the Principals focused on three specific national security issues: withdrawal from the ABM and Kyoto international climate treaties and what to do about Iraq.[20] Counterterrorism was indeed getting short shrift. The Rice reorganization both removed the counterterrorism czar, Clarke, from the Principals committee and the assistant OMB director from the Counterterrorism Security Group. The latter removal effectively killed Clarke's mechanism for budget review. His brief was now the Office of Transnational Threats, which did not figure as strongly in the administration calculus as did Cheney's energy policy and Rumsfeld's national missile defense program. Further, counterterrorism and critical infrastructure protection merged into one Counterterrorism and National Preparedness Policy functional PCC, which like all PCCs reported to the Deputies.

The new administration was determined not to have an empowered NSC entity that could further increase department and agency budgets for counterterrorism—as Clarke had done in the second Clinton administration. In short, it would not allow counterterrorism to compete for funds for big-ticket DoD transformation and ballistic missile defense programs. The administration attitude on counterterrorism also mirrored its view on emergency management. The new team believed it saw in James Lee Witt's politicized FEMA bloated amounts of disaster relief going to favored jurisdictions. It was not having some interagency entity shunting counterterrorism funding to favored state and local law enforcement, especially under the guidance of a Clinton holdover like Clarke. Lastly, the new team was sensitive to leaving itself open to legacy comparisons between Clarke's activities and those of Ollie North and his Operations Sub-Group. The George W. Bush administration was not leaving itself vulnerable to partisan accusations of having secret White House operational entities functioning without congressional oversight.

At the oft-cited first deputies meeting of the Bush NSC, which didn't take place until late April 2001, Clarke (with some support from State's Armitage) attempted to focus attention on the al Qaeda threat. He was famously rebutted by Deputy Defense Secretary Paul Wolfowitz, who wanted to shift focus to Iraq as a state sponsor of terrorism. The widely reported colloquy also included a statement in support of Clarke by Deputy DCI John McLaughlin that no evidence existed on any Iraqi terrorist activity against the United States.

Beyond the NSC, the priority for counterterrorism was also apparently downgrading. At the FBI, the National Security Division re-emphasized monitoring of Russian and Chinese espionage. Conforming to Robert Rubin's views when he headed Treasury, neither the director of the National Economic Council, Lawrence Lindsey, nor Treasury Secretary Paul O'Neill embraced the urgency to explore terrorist financing. They resisted the European-led Organization for Economic Cooperation and Development (OECD) 2001 campaign against tax havens and money laundering via offshore banking.

From the benefit of hindsight, we can now appreciate how Dick Clarke, as the national counterterrorism coordinator, and his prescient and inter-agency-minded colleagues in the Counterterrorism Security Group, together epitomized the post–Cold War national security senior executive. Clarke had begun his service as an analyst in the Pentagon. He had gone to State, where he worked in political-military affairs and rose to become the director of the Bureau of Intelligence and Research. At the interagency level he had served successively three Republican and Democratic presidents in the transition from Cold War to New World Order. He had NSC crisis management experience that included policy development and management roles in the shadow conflicts in Afghanistan and Somalia, two failed states on the "new map of the world." Thanks to the international and domestic intelligence and criminal investigative work already done by the CIA and the FBI, Clarke was able to form his views on the threat then facing America. Between Sudan and Afghanistan, he and his CSG came to recognize the shadow of one man, Osama bin Laden, another figure who epitomized another model.

Clarke's career path, experience, and increasing responsibilities led him to conceptualize the coming national security threat, post Cold War, and conceive of flattened governance mechanisms to deal with it. Clarke knew his enemy, an enemy who was mastering his own networked governance and his own tactics, neither of which were dependent on state sponsors. In one respect, bin Laden's wealth, dispersed throughout the global financial commons, enabled al Qaeda to be self-financing. In another, al Qaeda had a murky, contradictory relationship with Saudi Arabia—a U.S. ally. Al Qaeda would employ what the Marines call fourth-generation warfare against the United States, the West, and authoritarian Arab regimes, leveraging our and their own technologies and vulnerable hierarchical, industrial-era infrastructures to wage war.[21] Beyond the CSG's analysis of al Qaeda capability, Clarke understood the compelling reality of his adversary's intent. His enemy's declaration of war on Egypt and the United States was starkly specific—unlike the United States' rhetorical "war on terrorism," which as Governor Tom Ridge has written was "mislabeled from the outset."[22]

Clarke's interagency governance model repeated the mobilization authorities of World War II, established by Franklin D. Roosevelt via executive orders. Clarke and his CSG team had sown the seeds of an operational counterterrorism framework that extended from the proactive "disrupt" mission through the "prevent, protect, respond, and recover" missions. It was a counterterrorism framework that aligned with emergency management and the Federal Response Plan. The Oklahoma City and African embassy bombings were also disasters with a first-responder dimension. Critical infrastructure protection repackaged civil defense elements for the post–Cold War era and paralleled FEMA's mitigation mission. For his part, Clarke had the foresight to put particular emphasis on protection of the nation's cyber-security infrastructure as the key resource that is the network that supports all other infrastructures in this post-industrial, information age. Here was an approach that presaged anticipatory governance, network federalism, and the coming of the integrated national security professional of the twenty-first century.

# CHAPTER THREE

# The Political Dynamics behind the Creation of the Department of Homeland Security

In his 1998 Naval Academy commencement address in Annapolis, President Bill Clinton announced PDD-62, Combating Terrorism, and PDD-63, Protecting America's Critical Infrastructures. These two presidential directives were the Clinton administration's attempt to refine configuration of NSC counterterrorism, infrastructure protection, and consequence management structures, and enhance NSC process linkages to state and local governments and the private sector. PDD-62 and PDD-63 further advanced a security governance approach to deal with the post–Cold War, asymmetric threats to the homeland, by that time so very evident.

Yet other quarters of the national security establishment—at that time not in office—remained intent on prioritizing the more familiar, traditional threats presented by advanced weapons development programs in nation-states. These policy-makers, who would return to office and serve in the Bush administration NSC system as principals, deputies, assistants, and directors, expressed the sense-making of what was left of the Cold War–era techno-industrial base. In their view, the national security system—properly focused on what they regarded as true strategic-level, existential threats to the homeland—required military transformation and specifically deployment of national missile defense.

Not two months after Clinton's 1998 Naval Academy address, Donald Rumsfeld's congressionally mandated Commission to Assess the Ballistic Missile Threat to the United States reported its findings. While addressing existing Russian and Chinese missile programs, this panel focused attention on newer, developing threats emerging in North Korea, Iran, and Iraq, which it claimed in a few years' time would enable these rogue states to launch missile attacks on the American homeland. This Rumsfeld Commission narrative directly informed the high-policy national security priorities of the incoming Bush administration. Central to these priorities was the administration intent to transform nuclear deterrence and bring into being a new strategic framework with Russia and China.

The Bush administration expressed this intent in two related directives: the February 2001 National Security Presidential Directive 4 (NSPD-4), Transforming Deterrence, and the subsequent NSPD-10, U.S. Strategic Nuclear Forces, issued in December, three months after the 9/11 attacks. Enunciating the high-policy thinking behind these two directives in a May 2001 speech at the National Defense University, Bush said:

> We need new concepts of deterrence that rely on both offensive and defensive forces. Deterrence can no longer be based solely on the threat of nuclear retaliation. Defenses can strengthen deterrence by reducing the incentive for proliferation. We need a new framework that allows us to build missile defenses to counter the different threats of today's world. To do so, we must move beyond the constraints of the 30-year-old ABM Treaty.[1]

Strategic-level institution of ballistic missile defense was at the heart of the Bush administration conception of national security. The author of NSPD-4 was the NSC's senior director for proliferation strategy, counterproliferation, and homeland defense, Robert Joseph. A Cheney man, Joseph was committed to deployment of a national missile defense against long-range ballistic missiles. As such, he espoused the need for a U.S. withdrawal from the ABM Treaty, which specifically forbade such defenses. His NSC staff ally was Franklin Miller, a special assistant to the president and Condoleezza Rice's senior director for defense policy and arms control. Miller came to the White House with an extensive DoD background in strategic nuclear policy and arms control, including a stint as chairman of NATO's Nuclear Policy and Counterproliferation Policy Committees. Working on a track parallel to Joseph, Miller's job was to oversee the Pentagon's nuclear posture review to determine the levels to which the United States could further reduce its strategic nuclear forces and thus inform NSPD-10. These combined efforts took place without a detailed NSC-led interagency policy review. "The process was tightly controlled by the NSC staff, ensuring that the decision [to withdraw from the ABM Treaty] was close-hold, shared with only a small, trusted group of people, and implemented in a short time."[2]

It was this big picture into which Condoleezza Rice had willingly fit herself as national security advisor—one that was in the mold of her mentor, Gen. Brent Scowcroft. In the minds of many, Scowcroft epitomizes the national security advisor as the honest broker of the national security system. The successor to Henry Kissinger in the Ford administration, he returned to serve as national security advisor a second time during the George H. W. Bush administration. Like Kissinger, his own mentor (though not model), Scowcroft bequeathed to the nation a substantial and gifted network of protégés. The Scowcroft legacy would continue in the George W. Bush administration with Rice and her deputy national security advisor, Stephen Hadley. A lawyer with the Scowcroft Group, Hadley had previously served on Scowcroft's NSC staff during the Ford administration. In the mid-eighties, he was a staff member supporting the general as one of the three commissioners on the Tower Commission that investigated the Iran-Contra Affair and assessed the workings of the national security system.

Scowcroft had met Rice in the mid-eighties while she was a Sovietologist at Stanford's Hoover Institution. Already a young academic who had done the rounds at the Council on Foreign Relations and in Washington, Rice was mentored earlier in her student career by political scientist Josef Korbels, father of Clinton's secretary of state, Madeleine Albright. In 1989, Scowcroft brought her to Washington to serve on his national security staff as an advisor on policies toward Eastern Europe during the disintegration of the Soviet empire. In the nineties, Rice returned to Stanford where George Shultz was also hanging his hat. Via Shultz, she was able to secure a seat on the board of Chevron. Parlaying her Soviet background, she assisted company negotiations with President Nursultan Nazarbayev of Kazakhstan to obtain oil rights in the Tengiz oil fields, thought to hold reserves that were potentially among the largest in the world. Through Shultz, she would also meet George W. Bush.

True to Scowcroft's example, Rice reflected his low-key approach to policymaking. National security advisors brokered but did not make policy, a point of view common in most Republican administrations, yet in practice one only honored in the exception. According to one account, Rice believed that her predecessor, Sandy Berger, had allowed the NSC staff to get too big, stating that on her watch the departments would lead.[3] Notwithstanding, Robert Joseph and Franklin Miller would proceed to manage the U.S. decision to withdraw from the ABM Treaty and effect reductions to strategic forces.

Two days before the release of Joseph's NSPD-4, the administration issued its NSPD-1, Organization of the National Security Council System, the directive outlining how Rice would configure interagency policy-making.

> Management of the development and implementation of national security policies by multiple agencies of the United States Government shall usually be accomplished by the NSC Policy Coordination Committees (NSC/PCCs). The NSC/PCCs shall be the main day-to-day fora for interagency coordination of national security policy. They shall provide policy analysis for consideration by the more senior committees of the NSC system and ensure timely responses to decisions made by the President. Each NSC/PCC shall include representatives from the executive departments, offices, and agencies represented in the NSC/DC.

NSPD-1 abolished all previous interagency working groups, except those established by statute. Replacing them were six regional PCCs and eleven functional PCCs. Rice herself would chair seven of these new functional PCCs, including the PCC for coordinating counterterrorism policy. This Counterterrorism and National Preparedness PCC absorbed the functions of Dick Clarke's Counterterrorism Security Group, Critical Infrastructure Coordination Group, and Weapons of Mass Destruction Preparedness, Consequences Management, and Protection Group, as well as the interagency working group on Enduring Constitutional Government. Rice and Hadley, however, continued to have Clarke develop counterterrorism policy that was primarily focused on al Qaeda in Afghanistan.[4]

To that end, five days after the inauguration, Clarke sent a memo to Rice advocating an offensive strategy with more focus on al Qaeda and covert support for the Afghan Northern Alliance in their armed struggle against the Taliban, the al Qaeda enablers. His interpretation was that al Qaeda presented a strategic threat to the nation. Its objective was to drive the United States from the Muslim world and replace comparatively moderate governments with Taliban-like regimes. From April to July, threat reports refocused

Clarke on "coordinating defensive reactions," with the anticipation that terrorist attacks were coming. At the time, the targets were assumed to be U.S. embassies, not the American homeland. At the deputies level, Clarke continued to develop the offensive strategy. The substance of the approach would find expression in the October 25, 2001, NSPD-9, Combating Terrorism. Clarke famously presented a mature draft of this directive to the NSC principals for decision at a September 4 meeting just seven days before the al Qaeda attacks on the U.S. homeland. With modifications to the draft reflecting the impact of 9/11, the final NSPD was dated and released on October 25.

In his statement to the eighth public hearing of the National Commission on Terrorist Attacks Upon the United States on March 23, 2004, Defense Secretary Donald Rumsfeld said that NSPD-9 called on him to plan for military options against al Qaeda and Taliban targets in Afghanistan, the new strategic objective being—eliminate the al Qaeda network, sanctuaries, and related terrorist networks.[5] To that point under the Bush administration, the Pentagon role in the counterterrorism mission had lapsed.[6] On their watch, Rumsfeld and Cheney would hence move to backfill counterterrorism policy development with the military.

Nine days after the 9/11 attacks, President Bush announced the appointment of Governor Tom Ridge (R-PA) to be his homeland security advisor. Ridge was the governor of the state where the fourth hijacked plane had crashed in a remote farm field, the result of valiant actions undertaken by passengers to thwart the hijackers' presumed intent to pilot the aircraft into either the U.S. Capitol or White House. Philadelphia had hosted the 2000 Republican Convention, and Ridge, having served six terms in the House of Representatives, had been on the short list as a potential vice presidential candidate.

On October 8, the day after the United States commenced retaliatory military operations against al Qaeda and their Taliban enablers in Afghanistan, Ridge assumed his post. His authority came from Executive Order 13228 that established the Office of Homeland Security (OHS) in the Executive Office of the President and a Homeland Security Council (HSC) chaired by Ridge. The HSC, read the EO, would be "responsible for advising and assisting the president with respect to all aspects of homeland security." It would serve "as the mechanism for ensuring coordination of homeland security-related activities of executive departments and agencies and effective development and implementation of homeland security policies." The October 2001 Homeland Security Presidential Directive 1 (HSPD-1), Organization and Operation of the Homeland Security Council, provided for an HSC structure parallel to NSC with its own eleven functional PCCs.

EO 13228 specified that the functions of Ridge's Homeland Security Office would be to coordinate "the executive branch's efforts to detect, prepare for, prevent, protect against, respond to, and recover from terrorist attacks within the United States." The office would provide interagency coordination in each of these functional areas and at the same time "work with Federal, State, and local agencies, and private entities." With the addition of "detect" and "prevent," the EO in effect was providing the basis for expanding proactive counterterrorism functions in the Federal Response Plan and its Terrorism Incident Annex, shifting the responsibility for FRP coordination from the FEMA administrator to the homeland security advisor. The EO essentially recreated the same authority in the White House that Dick Clarke had with his Office of the National Coordinator for Security, Infrastructure Protection, and Counterterrorism—with a significant difference. Whereas Clarke's office had been in the NSC system, Ridge's would be in a parallel HSC system with a staff that in many cases reported also to the NSC, thus serving two masters.

With regard to domestic incident management, the executive order said:

> The Assistant to the President for Homeland Security shall be the individual primarily responsible for coordinating the domestic response efforts of all departments and agencies in the event of an imminent terrorist threat and during and in the immediate aftermath of a terrorist attack within the United States, and shall be the principal point of contact for and to the President with respect to coordination of such efforts. The Assistant to the President for Homeland Security shall coordinate with the Assistant to the President for National Security Affairs.

In his remarks at the Ridge swearing-in, Bush made clear his borders-out priorities. "The best defense against terror," he said, "is a global offensive against terror," referencing the attacks on the Taliban the day before. Alluding to the interagency nature of the counterterrorism offensive, he added, "The first shot of the war was fired several weeks ago, as we began freezing bank accounts and cutting off funding of known terrorist organizations and front groups that support them. And I appreciate so very much the secretary of treasury's work, Paul O'Neill." Summarizing his borders-in charge, Bush said, "I've given Tom and the Office of Homeland Security a mission: to design a comprehensive, coordinated national strategy to fight terror here at home."

Notwithstanding the EO's language referencing her coordination role as national security advisor, Rice did not fully play in homeland security policy-making or management. Nor did she want that responsibility. Her priorities were borders-out, the strategic big picture, primarily with regard to the strategic dialogue with Russia. In the traumatic weeks after 9/11, Ridge was stepping into a high-profile role burdened with high expectations. He would be coordinating homeland security activities and policy development in a number of borders-in areas revealed by 9/11. First and foremost was intelligence and information sharing, followed by immigration, aviation security as a subset of critical infrastructure protection, and consequence management.

As a governor, Ridge appreciated the intergovernmental aspects of domestic preparedness and incident management. While in Congress, he was the driver behind the writing of the 1988 Stafford Act, having been dissatisfied with FEMA responses to disasters in his Northwestern Pennsylvania district. He came to his White House position attuned to the findings of Virginia Republican Governor Jim Gilmore's commission, the congressionally mandated Advisory Panel to Assess Domestic Response Capabilities for Terrorism Involving Weapons of Mass Destruction. In five annual reports starting in 1999, the Gilmore Commission was widely regarded as having produced the best and most comprehensive analysis of the borders-in, intergovernmental aspects of domestic preparedness, as homeland security was known in the late nineties.

Ridge particularly embraced the Commission's call for a better means for intergovernmental intelligence sharing, voicing the need for "uncommon openness."[7] In this regard, he found an ally in the newly appointed FBI director, Robert Mueller. Ridge felt Mueller was "eager" to open communication channels in ways that were congruent with his own determination to share as much information as possible with state and local officials. Ridge had committed himself to the idea of moving from a need-to-know to a need-to-share information culture. His watchwords were disclosure and transparency, and he "hoped to turn American citizens into partners of OHS, fully informed and prepared for anything."[8]

Upon assuming office, Ridge encountered an immediate disconnect. For the most part, the senior officials assigned to his OHS were not from the intergovernmental realm. While otherwise extremely well accomplished and proven professionals, they were principally personnel from Vice President Cheney's and Defense Secretary Rumsfeld's offices. To rectify this apparent deficiency, Ridge secured approval from Bush Chief of Staff Andrew Card to bring on board a number of aides with intergovernmental experience, including two staffers from Harrisburg: Mark Holman and Duncan Campbell.[9]

Holman, a seasoned Republican campaign official, was a protégé of the late Senator John Heinz (R-PA) and was well-versed in the ways of Washington policy-making and issues management and their critical relationship to campaign politics. In the early eighties, Holman worked for Heinz on Capitol Hill before returning to manage Tom Ridge's first congressional campaign. On the Hill, he became his administrative assistant. When Ridge ran for governor in the early nineties, Holman similarly managed that campaign before becoming his chief of staff in Harrisburg. At OHS, Holman served Ridge as a deputy assistant to the president for homeland security.

Duncan Campbell became deputy chief of staff, having had that position in Pennsylvania. Campbell had recent Washington experience as the executive director of the Republican Governors Association (RGA) when Ridge became association chairman in 2001. At OHS, Campbell served as senior director of intergovernmental affairs, Ridge's primary liaison to state and local public officials. Campbell extended the OHS reach to state and local officials during the autumn of 2001 when the office was able to bring on board Chris Furlow. A Capitol Hill veteran and former national field director of the Republican National Committee, Furlow was detailed from the Commerce Department where he had built relationships with state officials as deputy assistant secretary for intergovernmental affairs. As the OHS director for state affairs, he worked on policy initiatives and threat-level communications with governors and their handpicked homeland security liaisons to the White House. Campbell and Furlow drew from their expertise at the state level and established the network of state homeland security advisors. With limited resources, they launched an initial information-sharing exchange, hosting bi-weekly teleconferences that were organized according to the ten-region FEMA structure.

In early 2002, OHS got a further assist for outreach to local government from New York City's Josh Filler. Referred by Rudy Giuliani and detailed by Mayor Mike Bloomberg, Filler had been Giuliani's chief of staff in the office of the deputy mayor for operations and director of legislative and intergovernmental affairs. He had oversight of the New York Police Department, Fire Department, Office of Emergency Management, and numerous other city agencies. Following 9/11, he had been responsible for emergency operational issues and managing contacts with local, state, and federal officials. Filler came on board as the OHS director of local affairs and assumed the outreach to mayors.

A number of staff came from Cheney's task force on terrorist threats to the United States along with its staff director, Lt. Col. John Fenzel, who had also served as Rumsfeld's military assistant. A Green Beret who worked with the Kuwaitis during Operation Desert Storm and later commanded a Special Forces battalion operating in the U.S. and British sectors during the NATO intervention in Bosnia, Fenzel continued as Ridge's staff director for OHS. Leading the Cheney task force review had been Adm. Steve Abbot, USN (Ret.). An aviator, Rhodes scholar, and former deputy commander of U.S. European Command, Abbot was another who went to OHS from the Cheney staff to serve as Ridge's operational deputy.

Overseeing Abbot and the work of the task force had been Lewis "Scooter" Libby, Cheney's chief of staff. A D.C. lawyer from Columbia Law School, Libby had been mentored as a Yale undergrad by Paul Wolfowitz, Rumsfeld's deputy secretary, who was in the early seventies Libby's political science professor. Cheney's policy advisor, who had focused himself on nuclear and biological terrorist threats, Libby was later notorious for being disbarred and convicted on four felony counts related to leaking the identity of the CIA operative Valerie Plame Wilson.

Using the term "homeland defense," the Cheney task force was the White House's response to the Hart-Rudman Commission. Led by former Senators Gary Hart, the Colorado Democrat, and Warren Rudman, the Republican from New Hampshire, the U.S. Commission on National Security/21st Century had just recommended establishment of a National Homeland

Security Agency. The Cheney task force was supposed to study both the terrorist threats facing the nation and WMD consequence management in the event
of a successful attack on the homeland. Announced in May 2001, the task force
was very slow to get off the ground. In fact, its work did not get under way until
just before 9/11. With his and Rumsfeld's political capital ambitiously focused
on transforming deterrence, Cheney was said to oppose making any kind of
big-government recommendation with regard to any counterterrorism reorganization as Hart-Rudman had suggested. In any event, Abbot, Fenzel, and
other Cheney task force members on Ridge's senior staff were military who, by
virtue of their experience, brought to their posts a borders-out perspective to
counterterrorism.

At the same time, borders-out counterterrorism briefs remained with
the NSC staff. The day following the Ridge appointment, Wayne Downing, a
retired Army special operations commander general, became deputy national
security advisor and national director for combating terrorism in the NSC
chain. Ostensibly, Downing was brought on board to drive the "disrupt" component of the counterterrorism mission, in effect undertaking the borders-
out piece of what had been one of Dick Clarke's briefs. However, in addition to
staffing the NSC's Office of Combating Terrorism, Downing's charge was also
to organize and staff the OHS Intelligence and Detection Directorate, further
to the EO 13228 tasking for OHS/NSC coordination between Ridge and Rice
and their staffs.

It was a telling appointment. Whereas Clarke and his NSC staff had been
working the al Qaeda and Afghani briefs since the mid-nineties, Downing's
expertise had been elsewhere. At the time he was appointed, he was an NBC
television news analyst and a special operations legend. As the four-star commander of U.S. Special Operations Command, he was in charge of special
operations forces during the 1989 Panamanian operation to remove President
Manuel Noriega. Downing himself took Noriega's surrender in the middle of
a Panama City street. During Operation Desert Storm, he commanded a joint
special operations task force operating behind the Iraqi lines. His introduction to global terrorism was in 1996, following retirement, when he chaired
the Khobar Towers bombing investigation, which made recommendations for
better protection of U.S. personnel and facilities abroad. Downing also served
as a commissioner on a third congressionally mandated panel, Ambassador
Paul Bremer's National Commission on Terrorism, which reported in 2000.

Downing recognized that Islamic extremist groups were at war with the United States, yet his focus remained on Iraq. He was known for his support for arming the Iraqi National Congress, a rebel coalition based in London working to overthrow Saddam Hussein. Bremer, an assistant to Secretaries of State Henry Kissinger in the early seventies and Al Haig a decade later, had been Reagan's ambassador-at-large for counterterrorism in 1986, retiring from State in 1989 to work for Kissinger Associates. Later he would serve as the civil administrator of Coalition Provisional Authority in Iraq, 2003–4, overseeing the reconstruction and transition of limited sovereignty to the Iraqi Interim Government.

The Downing appointment eased Dick Clarke into the role of special advisor to the president for cyberspace security, always a priority for him. Nevertheless, Clarke was able to keep his hand in some al Qaeda discussions. He also co-chaired the Campaign Coordination Committee with Franklin Miller, the NSC staff's nuclear policy expert who was the co-author with Robert Joseph of NSPD-4. Although Miller's brief had been to develop Pentagon policy around strategic forces reductions, he was now co-chairman of this NSC group preparing the offensive strategy against al Qaeda. Clarke would not chair a second NSC group, however: the Domestic Preparedness Committee. That body would work on interagency and intergovernmental issues very familiar to him that addressed the internal security measures for vulnerable critical infrastructures prompted by the 9/11 attacks. Its chairman was Deputy Attorney General Larry Thompson, a conservative African-American associated with King & Spalding International, Atlanta's oldest law firm. Thompson was a Republican loyalist who had served in the Reagan administration as a U.S. attorney and had assisted Supreme Court nominee Clarence Thomas during his quest to secure Senate confirmation.

In his EO 13228 coordinator role, Ridge had a lot of responsibility, but frequently he found himself having to vet policy decisions with the Office of the White House chief of staff, Andrew Card. A Bush family loyalist from Massachusetts, Card had run the 2000 Republican National Convention as chairman of the convention's Bush-for-President operation. In the nineties, he was president and CEO of the American Automobile Manufacturers Association and later vice president of government relations for General Motors. In terms of homeland security, he could draw on some intergovernmental experience, having served in the Reagan White House as the director of intergovernmental affairs, where he was responsible for liaison with governors, state officials and state legislators, mayors, and other elected officers. In the George H. W. Bush administration, Card became Chief of Staff John Sununu's assistant and later transportation secretary. In that latter post, he coordinated the administration's disaster relief efforts in the wake of Hurricane Andrew. Sununu had asked FEMA director Wallace Stickney to undertake the mission. Stickney declined, pleading that he did not have sufficient expertise. Sununu gave the order to an equally reluctant Card who nonetheless saluted smartly.

EO 13228 had given Card the authority for personnel, funding, and administrative support to Ridge's Office of Homeland Security. As White House chief of staff, Card was at the apex of an inner circle of Bush family loyalists.[10] They were the campaign advisors who were awarded with the opportunity to determine policy, notwithstanding their lack of operational, line-authority experience in emergency management or counterterrorism. Card's two deputies were Josh Bolten, deputy chief of staff for policy, and Joe Hagin, deputy for operations. Bolten received his law degree from Stanford and had worked in the George H. W. Bush White House. In the mid-to-late nineties, he headed Goldman Sachs' legal and governmental affairs office in London.[11] In 1999, he left to be George Bush's policy director for the 2000 campaign.

Joe Hagin began his association with the Bush family during the elder Bush's 1980 campaign when he served as the candidate's personal aide. A native of Cincinnati who would be a longtime volunteer firefighter, Hagin went to Washington as a vice presidential aide in the Reagan administration and later worked in legislative affairs. In the nineties, he was a corporate vice president for Cincinnati's Chiquita Brands International. In the 2000 campaign, he was the deputy campaign manager and senior presidential advisor Karl Rove's deputy chief of staff. A consummate political operative, Hagin was a key player in the presidential transition.

Card would entrust two lawyers on his staff with the homeland security brief, despite their lack of any meaningful experience in the field. Both were very junior, in their thirties, but had worked on policy for the 2000 Bush campaign. One was Joel D. Kaplan, a Harvard lawyer, policy analyst, and Bolten protégé. The second was another Harvard lawyer, Brad Berenson, a White House associate counsel.

A third Harvard policy-maker, Richard Falkenrath, was somewhat more versed in homeland security. Although still in his twenties, with no operational expertise, Falkenrath had co-authored a 1998 book with two more senior academics, *America's Achilles' Heel: Nuclear, Biological, and Chemical Terrorism and Covert Attack*, sponsored by the newly named Belfer Center for Scientific and International Studies at Harvard's John F. Kennedy School of Government. This book was the result of Belfer's participation in a number of nonproliferation discussions involving the Cooperative Threat Reduction (CTR) program, better known as the Nunn-Lugar initiative. Nunn-Lugar was a 1992 law sponsored by Senator Sam Nunn (D-GA) and his colleague Richard Lugar (R-IN) to secure and dismantle weapons of mass destruction and their associated infrastructure in former Soviet Union republics. The Center for Science and International Affairs (CSIA), Belfer's forerunner, was especially interested in the threat posed by Soviet WMD stockpiles making their way into the hands of non-state actors. The 1998 book specifically mentioned Osama bin Laden by name as a particularly threatening such actor. With this research in his pocket, Falkenrath had been able to provide input to the Gilmore Commission and ultimately come to the NSC staff in January 2001 as director for proliferation strategy. His issues were biological weapons proliferation and preparedness, missile defense, and Asian proliferation. After 9/11, he became special assistant to the president and Ridge's senior director in OHS for policy and plans.

Falkenrath was one example among many of Harvard placements on the NSC staff, a legacy pattern that dated from the Kennedy administration. Harvard sought this role, inspired by its neighboring rival, MIT, which had enjoyed such success during World War II and the first decade of the Cold War. A creative tension existed between these two institutional points of view in Cambridge. MIT under its president, Karl Compton, had positioned itself to win funding from defense policy-makers to do the research and development Washington wanted. Harvard had opted to reverse this model. Its president, James Conant—along with Compton, a longtime associate of FDR's R&D czar Vannevar Bush—wanted his institution to influence proactively the national security policy itself. In so doing, Harvard would become the epitome of the so-called Cold War University.

Responding to the sudden demands of the containment policy, Conant launched the Russian Research Center in 1948, staffing it with a number of former wartime Office of Strategic Services (OSS) intelligence analysts and operatives. Conant went about his business with another imperative in mind, which was socially progressive. A bastion of the Boston Brahmins, Harvard, like all the Ivy League colleges, had been exclusive. Yet in the forties, many were opening their doors to students who had not been to the New England prep schools, who were sons and grandsons of immigrants, Americans—whether Old Left or converts to anti-communism—who coincidentally better understood the nuances of Russia, Eastern Europe, and the Cold War battlefields. The beneficiaries included a number whose names would become prominent in the advancing field of nuclear strategy: Stanley Hoffmann, Henry Kissinger, and James Schlesinger, to name a few. These were the experts who would come into their own in the sixties and seventies. For the next two decades, these men and others would wrestle with strategic weapons modernization and arms control, attempting to weave both into a cohesive, systematic policy approach that ultimately would contribute to winning the Cold War.

When Kennedy, a Boston Democrat, came to the White House in 1961, he chose to break from past reliance on experienced corporate minds to shape national security policies. Instead, he peopled the executive branch with Harvard and MIT academics to advance a Democratic Party restoration after eight years of Eisenhower Republicanism. As such, the national security establishment transmuted from a military-industrial to a military-industrial-scientific-academic complex.

Jack Kennedy placed his academic coterie into his administration, notably on the NSC staff and in the Pentagon's Office of the Secretary of Defense. Under Kennedy, the NSC staff would elevate to house this new breed of presidential advisor tagged "policy analyst." The young president appointed the equally young McGeorge Bundy, dean of Harvard's Faculty of Arts and Sciences, as his national security advisor to ride herd over these analysts. With Bundy came Walt Rostow, the MIT professor of economic history. During the Kennedy campaign, Bundy and Rostow's colleagues at Harvard, MIT, and elsewhere in academe had provided input via the so-called Academic Advisory Group, conceived in 1958 and modeled on FDR's Brain Trust. Among their number was Harvard's Henry Kissinger. Although closely associated with his

CREATION OF DHS    77

sponsor, Republican presidential contender Nelson Rockefeller, Kissinger, like Bundy and Rostow, worked both sides of the partisan divide.

Henry Kissinger's academic power base was Harvard's Center for International Affairs (CFIA), founded in 1958 and chaired by Robert Bowie, who had just previously headed the Policy Planning Staff at State. CFIA didn't do case-specific research but rather drove a process that brought the right people together, nurtured discussion, and built consensus around a policy. In the late fifties, Harvard and MIT were at the center of arms control doctrine development. Bowie and CFIA hosted what was called the Arms Control Group that included Kissinger, Jerome Weisner, George Kistiakowsky, Thomas Schelling, Sidney Drell, Albert Wohlstetter, Arthur Schlesinger, Marshall Shulman, and one Paul Doty.

A biochemist who worked on isotope separation for the Manhattan Project, Paul Doty became chairman of the Federation of American Scientists in 1958. An invitee to the first Pugwash Conference in Nova Scotia to discuss the threat of nuclear weapons, Doty forged a partnership with counterpart nuclear scientists in the Soviet Union to lead two Pugwash gatherings in 1960–61 in the run-up to the 1963 Limited Test Ban Treaty. Thereafter, he was positioned to provide key support to Kissinger during the negotiations leading to the 1972 Anti-Ballistic Missile Treaty. A year later, Doty founded the Program for Science and International Affairs within Harvard's Faculty of Arts and Sciences. His original goal was to revive serious analysis of nuclear dangers and arms control. In 1978, Doty secured a major Ford Foundation grant to reconfigure his program as the Center for Science and International Affairs (CSIA), the first permanent research center at Harvard's newly fashioned John F. Kennedy School of Government. In 1990, the Center expanded to incorporate the Science, Technology, and Public Policy and the Environment and Natural Resources programs. Seven years later, the Center received an endowment from one Robert Belfer resulting in a new name: the Robert and Renée Belfer Center for Science and International Affairs.[12] Among Belfer's leading lights are such national security experts as Ashton Carter, Joseph Nye, and Graham Allison.

In the context of this background, Richard Falkenrath took Robert Bowie's consensus-building process model and helped found in the late nineties the Executive Session on Domestic Preparedness. This effort was a joint program between the Kennedy School's Belfer and its A. Alfred Taubman

Center for State and Local Governments. By 2001, it was functioning as a two-year-old standing task force on terrorism and emergency management that convened twice annually. After 9/11, the Executive Session hastily produced the "Memorandum on the Intergovernmental Dimensions of Domestic Preparedness" for Ridge and his office on November 2, 2001. Notwithstanding the very impressive list of participants who provided a measure of input to the seven-page consensus document, the result was far short of the executive summaries offered by the Gilmore, Hart-Rudman, or Bremer panels.

This brief case study is illustrative when compared to the two decades of research and analysis, for example, by the Council on Foreign Relations, and the real-world wartime Washington experience that informed the architects of the National Security Act of 1947. In the fifty years that followed, the Ivy League, Stanford, and other institutions of higher learning amassed a well-funded national security expertise with a library-sized canon of work. Yet in 2001–3, academe had contributed to producing no homeland security canon to inform policy-making. As such, post-9/11 governmental reorganization—unlike the effort in 1945–47—had precious little on the normative side to balance the raw dynamics of bureaucratic and partisan politics.

Four days before Ridge assumed his post, the White House got word from Boca Raton, Florida, of the suspiciously inexplicable death of a *National Enquirer* employee from anthrax inhalation, the first anthrax fatality in the United States in twenty-five years. The following week, authorities discovered powdered anthrax in the *Enquirer* offices. Before the week was out, an employee at NBC News headquarters in New York City tested positive for anthrax poisoning. Letters laced with weapons-grade anthrax were arriving at media offices in New York and congressional offices on Capitol Hill. Not a month after 9/11, the nation was once again under attack. This time the tactic was bioterrorism via the postal system. In the end, the anthrax mailings would kill five and sicken seventeen.

The initial lack of cooperation among the agencies amid the attacks, said Ridge, caused "not just perceived but actual problems."[13] Responding agencies had different mission priorities—be they forensic, public health, remediation, or the security of the U.S. mail. Ridge, Attorney General John Ashcroft, and Health and Human Services Secretary Tommy Thompson, along with the Environmental Protection Agency and U.S. Postal Service, presented an unnerved nation with a confused message as the cascade of consequences compounded. Early on, Ridge was able to secure agency agreement that his Office of Homeland Security would serve as the regular voice of the federal government, or as he put it the single "focal point for press conferences." Yet, behind the scenes, the bureaucratic push-back only deepened as agencies protected turf against OHS encroachment in the name of coordination. The anthrax attacks on top of 9/11 had given sudden impetus to all manner of calls for a far-reaching homeland security reorganization. Agencies were fearful and protective.

Beginning in the latter years of the Clinton administration, three successive congressionally mandated commissions had put forth counterterrorism restructuring proposals. Now, proposals for establishment of a cabinet-level domestic security agency were coming from both sides of the aisle. Six months prior to 9/11, Rep. Mac Thornberry (R-TX) introduced a bill to establish a National Homeland Security Agency, in line with a recommendation by one of these panels. The Hart-Rudman Commission had presented its final report a month after the Bush team took office. In making its recommendation, the Hart-Rudman report recommended that this agency be chartered by statute to provide a focal point for federal response in "all natural and man-made crisis and emergency planning scenarios." The Commission envisaged that the core of such an agency would consist of FEMA, the Customs Service, Coast Guard, and the Immigration and Naturalization Service (INS), of which the Border Patrol was a part.

Shortly after the 9/11 attacks, the Commission co-chairman and one-time Democratic presidential candidate, Gary Hart, went political, saying of the Bush administration's response to the recommendations, "The White House shut it down." Four days after Ridge took his oath, the chairman of the Senate Governmental Affairs Committee, Senator Joe Lieberman, introduced his own bill to establish a Department of Homeland Security, similarly inspired by Hart-Rudman. Lieberman then proceeded to hold hearings to solicit additional input to consolidate the restructuring proposals into one piece of legislation.

As a fraught-ridden autumn advanced, at the other end of Pennsylvania Avenue Ridge and his deputy, Steve Abbot, who chaired the HSC deputies committee, came to the view that OHS would not have the clout—nor indeed the full White House backing—sufficient to manage homeland security effectively. A staff of one hundred with a budget of $25 million, both perhaps large by NSC/EOP standards, was inadequate to the task.

Looking for a means to begin a restructuring, Ridge opted to start with a proposal to create what he called a "mini Federal agency" to execute the border security mission. He tasked Abbot to work on a proposal to merge into one agency the three separate FY03 appropriations accounts of the Coast Guard, Border Patrol, INS' enforcement functions, and the Department of Agriculture's food inspection program. Ridge was able to secure support from OMB director Mitch Daniels, which led to development of a second, more detailed plan, drafted with great care by Falkenrath, to establish a Federal Border Administration. In late December, Ridge presented his plan to the HSC principals. There he met strong opposition. Department secretaries and their deputies were unwilling to entertain any bureaucratic poaching. Particularly vocal resistance came from Secretary of State Colin Powell. Ridge's one ally was the administration's free spirit, Treasury Secretary Paul O'Neill, an evident believer in the need for a twenty-first century governmental reorganization.[14] The hasty stand-up of OHS had been an exception to the rule. It did not compromise the Bush administration's resolute commitment to the principle that the federal government conduct its business through the departments and agencies.

Beyond border security, EO 13228 had charged Ridge and OHS with the coordination of federal counterterrorism efforts borders-in. As the president's homeland security advisor, it was his responsibility to coordinate the federal domestic response to an act or threat of terrorism. This borders-in responsibility involved those areas of consequence management, civil defense, and national security preparedness and mobilization that had been FEMA roles until the nineties, when FEMA director James Lee Witt had allowed the non-natural disaster agency's capabilities to atrophy or be transferred to Justice and DoD.

Much of the main action had gone to the Army and the National Guard. The Army Directorate of Military Support (DOMS) had gotten the Nunn-Lugar-Domenici "train the trainers" program to equip and train state and local trainers in chemical, biological, radiological, nuclear, or high-yield explosive (CBRNE) response. The DOMS director was dual-hatted and fell under the Army Department's assistant secretary for logistics and installations and the chief of staff's director of operations, readiness, and mobilization. In 1998, DOMS organized and stood up the initial ten Weapons of Mass Destruction–Civil Support Teams (WMD-CSTs), one for each FEMA region, as announced by President Clinton along with PDD-62 and PDD-63 in his Naval Academy commencement address.

In charge of this stand-up was Brig. Gen. Bruce Lawlor, an Army National Guardsman from Vermont. A lawyer and Harvard national security fellow, Lawlor had served in naval intelligence in Vietnam. A year later when DoD stood up the Joint Task Force–Civil Support (JTF-CS) under the U.S. Joint Forces Command, Lawlor got another star and became its first commanding general. As the JTF-CS commander, he was responsible for planning and integrating DoD military support to civil authorities—FEMA or the lead federal agency—following a domestic CBRNE incident. If necessary, Lawlor would be the one to deploy to a CBRNE incident site to provide command and control of responding DoD forces. JTF-CS was, however, a standing military headquarters. It had no assigned forces. Only when the secretary of defense issued an execute order to a warfighting commander in chief to provide support would JTF-CS have forces with the detection, decontamination, and medical and logistical assets to accomplish the mission.

Though JTF-CS was a creature of the Clinton administration, two months into the Bush administration, Deputy Defense Secretary Wolfowitz signed interim policy guidance for operationally integrated DoD consequence management support in domestic CBRNE incidents. JTF-CS would provide such support under the Federal Response Plan in Stafford Act events, when the lead federal agency would be called to assist state and local governments if a major disaster or emergency overwhelmed their ability to respond effectively.

In mid-October 2001, the White House asked the Pentagon to assign a general officer immediately to OHS. The Department of the Army, as the executive agent for military support, referred the request to Gen. Eric Shinseki, the Army chief of staff. Shinseki picked Lawlor, gave him verbal orders, assigned him to one of his general officer holding billets, and sent him to the White House. Defense Secretary Rumsfeld opposed the assignment, and for a moment, Lawlor was enmeshed in a bureaucratic tug of war between OSD and the White House. After Andy Card intervened, the Army detailed Lawlor to OHS where he would serve as the senior director for protection and prevention. Lawlor would later join Ridge in DHS where he served as his chief of staff until October 2003. With the Lawlor appointment to OHS, Ridge and Abbot finally had a senior subject-matter expert with operational line authority experience in consequence management and who knew his way around the intergovernmental nuances of the federal, state, and local relationships.

Lawlor was fortunate to have staff support from Mike Byrne, a FEMA detailee with a solid operational background in emergency management. Byrne served as the OHS senior director for preparedness, response, and recovery. At FEMA, he had been the division director for response and recovery. Immediately after 9/11, he went to the field as the agency's deputy federal coordinating officer (DFCO) for operations at Ground Zero, coordinating and managing all federal response assets and recovery operations. For two decades, he had served in the New York City Fire Department variously as a captain, chief information officer (CIO), and director of strategic planning. Byrne capped his municipal government career as the first deputy director of the New York City Office of Emergency Management.

In Col. Joe Rozek, USA, Lawlor had another official with a solid operational background in counterterrorism. A most able Special Forces veteran, Rozek had been serving as deputy assistant to the secretary of defense for civil support and director for combating terrorism and sensitive activities. Immediately following the 9/11 attacks, he was in charge of Rumsfeld's Pentagon Crisis Coordination Center to synchronize response efforts. He then served as a subject matter expert for combating terrorism on the Cheney terrorism task force with Steve Abbot. In October, he had moved to OHS as the senior director for threat countermeasures and incident management. Rozek's response expertise derived from his experience in the late nineties in DoD's office of the assistant secretary of defense for special operations and low-intensity conflict (SO/LIC). He led SO/LIC's efforts to provide classified military support to state and local law enforcement alongside DOMS under the Nunn-Lugar-Domenici program. Rozek's contact with law enforcement further deepened through his occasional interagency work supporting drug enforcement.

Over the course of the winter, Ridge took inputs from the Gilmore Commission's executive director, RAND's Mike Wermuth, and others. Into the mix had also come a November 2001 study, *Defending the American Homeland*, via a Heritage Foundation Homeland Security Task Force. Its chairmen, former Reagan administration Attorney General Edwin Meese and Ambassador L. Paul Bremer, strongly advocated for an intergovernmental approach to deal with what they called "catastrophic terrorism." By now, Ridge could see that a case could be made for a homeland security department. Recognizing his work on the initial border agency proposal, he tasked Falkenrath to secure approval for a review of homeland security organization. In the early spring of 2002, Falkenrath engaged two of Andy Card's mid-level staffers, his policy analyst, Joel Kaplan, and his operations deputy, Joe Hagin. The trio met with Josh Bolten, Card's policy deputy, and persuaded Bolten to represent the idea of a review to Card.

In the mind of Andy Card, the proposal had tactical value to the extent that it could protect the president's vulnerable political flank. Though Bush and Cheney had been against the idea of a homeland security department, Card understood the political necessity for reversing their position. An administration reorganization would pre-empt credit going to Lieberman and congressional Democrats who had seized the initiative while the bureaucracies in the executive branch continued to resist OHS coordination and defend turf. Card, Rove, and the mid-level campaign advisors on the White House staff had lingering sensitivity toward Lieberman. A Connecticut senator closely aligned with New York City interests, Lieberman had been Al Gore's running mate in the 2000 elections. The Gore-Lieberman ticket had won the popular vote by 48.4 to 47.9 percent in the closest election since 1876. Owing to the final Supreme Court decisions on recounting the popular votes in Florida, the vote in the Electoral College gave Bush and Cheney the win. The tally was 271–266.

The Florida recount was contentious, and the stakes were high. Representing the Bush-Cheney interests on-site and reporting to Card in the Florida recount were precisely those campaign advisors—Hagin, Bolten, and Kaplan. At issue was the award of Florida's twenty-five electoral votes to the Republican ticket by a state whose Republican governor was Jeb Bush, the president's younger brother. The issue was rancorously partisan and did not resolve until mid-December 2000, when the Supreme Court voted in two 5-4 decisions not to reverse the Florida Supreme Court decision to order a number of recounts. The decisions were controversial: the justices had voted along party lines according to whether they had been appointed by a Republican or Democratic president.

In sum, the spring of 2002 was a time for campaigning. The November congressional elections would serve as a referendum on the performance of the Bush administration in its first two years in office. While the United States and Britain with NATO support had defeated the Taliban in December and installed the interim Hamid Karzai government, they had failed to capture Osama bin Laden. As policy-makers worked to build their case against Iraq as a state sponsor of terrorism, the nation was struggling to maintain the initiative in what President Bush had called the global war on terror. In his homeland security department bill, Lieberman had an issue with traction, an election-year issue the Democrats could use to question a Republican administration's ability to lead in a post-9/11 world.

In April, Card thus decided to put a small group together to develop a White House plan for a Department of Homeland Security. Given his own political and bureaucratic priorities, which he had to weigh and with which he had to contend, Card chose not to people this group with subject-matter experts from the Gilmore, Hart-Rudman or Bremer commissions. Nor did he call on anybody from Richard Clarke's team who had been working on counterterrorism, critical infrastructure and domestic preparedness policy development, and interagency coordination for almost a decade. Instead, he chose to empower a mid-level staff of five. Two were from his own staff: lawyers Joel Kaplan and Brad Berenson. As one administration official put it, Kaplan served as Card's "eyes and ears" and Berenson, a White House counsel, "was there to provide legal structure." A third member was Mark Everson, OMB's deputy director for management. A Mitch Daniels protégé who had served as a Reagan administration deputy INS commissioner at the Justice Department, Everson chaired the President's Management Council, a panel of department and major agency chief operating officers (COOs). His function was to provide the group with "OMB organizational and budgetary information about any agency it wanted to know about." The last two members were Richard Falkenrath and Bruce Lawlor—the only two representatives from Ridge's OHS. Falkenrath, according to the official, "wrote up the group's deliberations for presentation to the HSC Principals." Lawlor, a two-star general, certainly more than mid-level, the only member with operational experience in homeland security, "worked to focus the group on creating a framework of homeland security functions upon which to build the new department." In the opinion of this well-placed official, "Card was the real driving force behind the creation of DHS."

Andy Card charged his operations deputy, Joe Hagin, to ensure the review was done in great secrecy. The administration did not need department heads leaking to the press or congressional staffs its intent to transfer agencies to a new department in the hopes that they could prevent such action. Hagin arranged for the team to meet in the White House bunker. Card relied entirely on Josh Bolten via his protégé, Joel Kaplan, to monitor progress. For the almost two months it met, the five-man review team would report several times a week to an oversight group of Card, Bolten, Ridge, Cheney Chief of Staff Scooter Libby, and OMB director Mitch Daniels. According to the administration official, "The fact that some folks were not 'in the know' caused a kerfuffle later. Condoleezza Rice and Karen Hughes were particularly miffed that they were not part of this oversight group."

This month-and-a-half process to reorganize security governance aimed to accomplish what the drivers of the National Security Act of 1947, Secretary of the Navy James Forrestal, his former Army-Navy Munitions Board director, Ferdinand Eberstadt, and his team achieved in two years of grueling give-and-take with Congress and the military departments and services. In an equally fraught process that indeed killed Forrestal, those architects nevertheless had the advantage of demonstrable success and political continuity. They served in an administration that had brought the nation through a decadelong depression, won a world war and was enjoying its fourth consecutive term. Though Roosevelt had died in office, his successor Harry Truman inherited his wartime national security team and as a relative national security naïf wholly depended on them. By contrast, in 2001 the circumstances were very different. Burdened with an uncertain mandate, the Bush administration had only completed its first year. Moreover, its strategic plan and its implementers had come into office completely oriented to another agenda that gave little thought to homeland security—until 9/11, a discipline without a name.

When Card's group briefed its reorganization plan at a June 6 meeting of the HSC, the reaction among the principals was hostile. Yet his close-hold strategy was a tactical success. His review team had presented the executive branch bureaucracy with a fait accompli, leaving it with no choice but to close ranks behind the chief executive. That evening, President Bush addressed the nation to announce his proposal for "a permanent cabinet-level Department of Homeland Security to unite essential agencies that must work more closely together" and to "ask the Congress to join [him] in creating a single, permanent department with an overriding and urgent mission: securing the homeland of America, and protecting the American people." The president characterized the effort as "the most extensive reorganization of the federal government since the 1940s."

The legacy of the National Security Act of 1947 has long revealed a truth that reorganizations on such a scale will remain a work-in-progress. DHS was soon to be a department in name, but it was questionable whether it would prove to be one in fact. In 1947, the contentiously received National Military Establishment, the forerunner to the Department of Defense, was able to usurp the War Department's newly completed Pentagon.[15] The Department of Homeland Security in 2003 was offered no such building to inhabit. Instead, it would find itself with twenty-two agencies, offices, and programs, each with its unique culture, some proud and fractious, scattered all over Washington. Compounding the governance challenge of coordinating all the federal departments and agencies with homeland security missions, DHS would have to face an additional, internal challenge—that of coordinating itself.

# CHAPTER FOUR

# DHS and the Politics of National Preparedness

In July 2002, the White House Office of Homeland Security released the first National Strategy for Homeland Security. Touted as a national as opposed to a federal strategy, the document ranked three strategic objectives in order of priority: prevent terrorist attacks; reduce vulnerability; minimize damage and recover from any attacks that may occur. These objectives later appeared in the document as the administration's stated definition of homeland security.

The strategy conceptualized homeland security in terms of functions falling into six critical mission areas. These six missions would inform how the twenty-two legacy agencies, offices, and programs consolidating as DHS would fit into its initial directorate structure:

- Intelligence and warning
- Border and transportation security
- Domestic counterterrorism
- Protecting critical infrastructure
- Defending against catastrophic terrorism
- Emergency preparedness and response

These six areas constituted the homeland security mission continuum—prevention, protection, response, and recovery—a new iteration of the emergency management mission continuum previously covered by the Federal Response Plan and its Terrorism Incident Annex. Referring to its three strategic objectives, the strategy noted that the first three mission areas dealt with prevention. The next two addressed vulnerability, that is, protection. The last addressed minimizing damage—the response and recovery missions. In time the more military-minded practitioners of homeland security would speak of a continuum divided in the middle by the "event": "left of the boom" was the realm of prevention and protection; "right of the boom," response and recovery.

The Department of Homeland Security would have to struggle with the proud cultures of the legacy law enforcement agencies whose missions were left of the boom. Their issues were primarily an interagency challenge, analogous to what the Department of Defense faced in its infancy and first four decades vis-à-vis the military services. However, it was the last critical mission area, emergency preparedness and response—the right of the boom—that would bedevil the new department as the abiding and interrelated interdepartmental and intergovernmental challenge. Read the strategy: "Our structure of overlapping federal, state, and local governance—our country has more than 87,000 different jurisdictions—provides unique opportunity and challenges for our homeland security efforts." Preparedness and response was a conjoined area where the Federal Emergency Management Agency felt it had the core departmental equities that were at the heart of the intergovernmental dimension of homeland security. The lifeblood of that dimension would be the national preparedness system of preparedness grants and disaster assistance—in other words, money.

With national security, it had been all about DoD acquisition—the Pentagon monopsony. The United States had won the Cold War with strategic and conventional military policies, enabled by Defense Department acquisition of big systems: missile, aircraft, ship, and land systems. These weapon system programs were multi-billion-dollar big-ticket items researched, developed, and produced by the big defense contractors with constituencies and workforces in every state. By contrast, homeland security would be about little ticket items like personal protection equipment, CBRNE sensors, and training to develop and sustain local and state preparedness capabilities. Procurement authority would be in many of those 87,000 different jurisdictions that have diverse and modest means to buy these thousand-dollar items in the dozens, scores, and hundreds. For the most part, they could only pay for them with help from preparedness grants that since the nineties had been administered by the Justice Department. What deterrence had been to national security and the Pentagon, preparedness would be to homeland security and DHS.

When it came to ballistic-missile defense systems, policy-makers were able to use deterrence to support multi-billion-dollar programs that would—hopefully—never be used in war. As history had demonstrated with civil defense, the case for preparedness, on the other hand, would not be as effective, though the dollar amounts by comparison were trivial. Dollars would go not to R&D and procurement programs in federal departments and agencies. They would go into preparedness grants to be spent by state and local governments that had no constituency comparable to the Pentagon's military-industrial complex. The manufacturers were generally small- and medium-sized niche technology providers struggling to make a buck. The grants process would become a convoluted system of departmental, OMB, and congressional oversight and reporting requirements with problematic criteria for measuring performance and outcomes. It would be a process destructive of unity of effort throughout the federal, state, and local levels of government. Persistent use of the conjoined phrase "preparedness and response" suggested erroneously that both were missions. In truth, preparedness was an activity that undergirded all missions in the homeland security mission continuum. This confusion contributed to the mutual misperceptions that arose between FEMA and other components in DHS.

The first National Strategy for Homeland Security expressed the need for a comprehensive national preparedness system incorporating the multiple plans in place for response to incidents of national significance. "Under the President's proposal," read the document, "the Department of Homeland Security will consolidate federal response plans and build a national system for incident management in cooperation with state and local government." Among twelve major initiatives it listed for emergency preparedness and response, the strategy identified the intent to "integrate separate response plans into a single all-discipline incident management plan." Three years later, this single plan would emerge as the National Response Plan (NRP). The process would include simultaneous development of a National Incident Management System (NIMS) and National Preparedness Goal (NPG). This comprehensive vision was ambitious.

> We will build, for example, a national incident management system that is better able to manage not just terrorism but other hazards such as natural disasters and industrial accidents. We will build a medical system that is not simply better able to cope with bioterrorism but with all diseases and all manner of mass-casualty incidents.

We will build a border management system that will not only stop terrorist penetration but will also facilitate the efficient flow of legitimate commerce and people.[1]

The strategy listed a number of other, more specific strategies subsumed within the twin concepts of national security and homeland security.

The *National Strategy for Combating Terrorism* will define the U.S. war plan against international terrorism. The *National Strategy to Combat Weapons of Mass Destruction* coordinates America's many efforts to deny terrorists and states the materials, technology, and expertise to make and deliver weapons of mass destruction. The *National Strategy to Secure Cyberspace* will describe our initiatives to secure our information systems against deliberate, malicious disruption. The *National Money Laundering Strategy* aims to undercut the illegal flows of money that support terrorism and international criminal activity. The *National Defense Strategy* sets priorities for our most powerful national security instrument. The *National Drug Control Strategy* lays out a comprehensive U.S. effort to combat drug smuggling and consumption. All of these documents fit into the framework established by the *National Security Strategy of the United States* and *National Strategy for Homeland Security,* which together take precedence over all other national strategies, programs, and plans.[2]

With this strategic guidance in place, the Department of Homeland Security came into being when President Bush signed the Homeland Security Act of 2002 into law on November 25, 2002. The legislation had passed the House in July. Mired in issues over collective bargaining rights for government employee unions, the Senate had not passed the bill until November.

In late June 2002, Andy Card had stood up the DHS Transition Office, which convened at offices on G Street, Northwest, several blocks from the White House. Since Congress had modified Card's reorganization plan in committee, the law was somewhat different to what OHS and the agencies had anticipated. The Transition Office thus had to review the authorities and mechanics of the new department that the statute now provided. Setting the terms of the DHS stand-up were the White House personnel chief, Clay Johnson, supported by Card's deputy, Joe Hagin. OMB had a presence as well and with Johnson pursued the objective of building new capability in a way that was "budget neutral" and required no new hires.

In December 2002 and into January 2003, the Transition Office ramped up its efforts. At the end of January, the office, re-titled the Transition Planning Office (TPO), relocated to the Nebraska Avenue Complex—the NAC—in a far corner of northwest Washington. Sally Canfield, Ridge's deputy chief of staff for policy in OHS, ran TPO administration and later became his chief of staff for policy when DHS stood up. Ridge's deputy chief of staff, Duncan Campbell, served as the TPO's deputy for operations. The line leadership of the TPO was John Gannon on the intelligence side, Mike Brown for FEMA, and Rear Adm. Harvey Johnson, USCG, who reported to Ridge. A Navy captain and Vietnam vet, John Gannon came from the CIA, where he had been its deputy director for intelligence (DDI). As DDI, he had been the chairman of the National Intelligence Council and assistant director of central intelligence for analysis and production. At the TPO he led the team that stood up the DHS Information Analysis and Infrastructure Protection Directorate.

Whatever may have been his faults later in his FEMA career, Mike Brown was a good advocate in the TPO process for his agency. He was supported by Brooks Altshuler, his deputy chief of staff, who had come to FEMA via the White House Office of National Advance Operations; Eric Tolbert, deputy director of FEMA's Office of National Preparedness (ONP) that focused on WMD consequence management; Dave Paulison, the administrator of the U.S. Fire Administration; and Marko Bourne, Paulison's executive officer and assistant director. Tolbert's role was particularly key in terms of intergovernmental emergency management experience at the federal, state, and local levels. He came to FEMA in 2002 as the director of the North Carolina Emergency Management Division, the year he was president of the National Emergency Managers Association. Tolbert represented FEMA's ONP, working closely with OHS in coordinating federal terrorism preparedness and WMD consequence management programs. Ridge took his oath on January 24, 2003. On March 1, DHS opened for business.

In its original form, DHS had five directorates, each led by an undersecretary. Three—Information Analysis and Infrastructure Protection, Border and

Transportation Security, and Emergency Preparedness and Response—were mission-focused, respectively on prevention, protection, and response/recovery. The Management Directorate was responsible for the back-office administrative functions including budgeting, procurement, and personnel. The Science and Technology (S&T) Directorate would serve as the DHS research and development entity. Not wanting the Coast Guard or Secret Service to fall under the directorate structure, Congress provided for these legacy agencies to report directly to the DHS secretary.

Unlike DoD, acquisition in DHS was not a system. DHS R&D was with the S&T Directorate. While the department did have a chief procurement officer, his was a back-office as opposed to mission function. The main action was in the components, which had their own procurement shops. By DoD standards, procurements were small potatoes—with three noteworthy and notorious exceptions. The biggest acquisition entity was the Coast Guard, by virtue of its existing $24 billion Deepwater program to replace its fleet of aging cutters. Deepwater was meant to be a model program. The Coast Guard had outsourced it in its entirety to Integrated Coast Guard Systems, a joint venture of Lockheed Martin and Northrop Grumman, formed specifically for Deepwater to do construction and day-to-day contract management. Similarly, when the newly established Transportation Security Administration moved to DHS, it brought along a 2002 $1 billion IT managed-services contract with Unisys for airport security and communications equipment. The third was Customs and Border Protection's Smart Border Initiative (SBI) for a virtual fence along the southwest border with Mexico, a 2006 award with an estimated value of $2 billion that went to Boeing. By 2009, the value of the SBI task order to date was $1.1 billion, but in January 2011 the program was cancelled. In fact, all three programs came unstuck. All used performance-based contract mechanisms where the private-sector lead system integrators both managed and provided oversight. The practice invited cost and schedule overruns, lent itself to conflicts of interest and abuses in self-certification, provided insufficient transparency, and worked against re-competition for the lead system integrator role and successor programs.[3]

The Homeland Security Act did not provide DHS with a policy shop to guide integration. Policy direction came from the Homeland Security Council, now empowered with statutory authority via the 2003 legislation. With the creation of DHS, the HSC assumed the responsibilities of what had been the Office of Homeland Security. This arrangement would remain throughout the Ridge tenure. Absent an undersecretary for policy, DHS was thus in a mother-may-I mode. Director-level DHS officials would find they had to defer making decisions to their director-level counterparts on the HSC staff.

When Ridge took his oath as secretary of the new department in January 2003, Steve Abbot briefly became acting homeland security advisor. Richard Falkenrath, who had overseen the drafting of the homeland security strategy document, was promoted to serve as his deputy. In April, Gen. John A. Gordon, USAF (Ret.), relieved Abbot, becoming also national director and deputy national security advisor for combating terrorism on the NSC staff. A pattern was emerging in the course of HSC business. The homeland security advisor would primarily focus on borders-out homeland security—for example, the interface with the NSC staff and the military and intelligence community's execution of counterterrorism functions overseas. The deputy homeland security advisor's duties would be more borders-in—for example, focusing on homeland security and emergency management intergovernmental and interagency issues.

Gordon was an accomplished general officer with an all-around strategic and planning background. As homeland security advisor, his primary function was to coordinate homeland security policy with DHS, DoD, and the intelligence community. He had transferred from the Department of Energy where he had been undersecretary for nuclear security and the first administrator of the National Nuclear Security Administration (NNSA). Established by Congress in 2000 as a separate agency within DOE, NNSA assumed responsibility for managing and securing the nation's nuclear weapons, nuclear nonproliferation, and naval reactor programs. Gordon had previously been deputy director of central intelligence, rising from the associate director of central intelligence for military support. A senior intelligence officer and nuclear physicist, he had served as the Air Force chief of staff's strategic planner. A onetime director of operations at the Air Force Space Command and a long-range planner at Strategic Air Command, Gordon also had State Department and prior NSC experience. During the elder Bush's administration, he was the NSC's senior director for defense policy and arms control and a special assistant to the president for national security affairs, responsible for the oversight and completion of the START II negotiations.

Gordon and Falkenrath held their posts until the spring of 2004, whereupon Frances Fragos Townsend transferred from the NSC staff, where she had been the deputy assistant to the president and deputy national security advisor for combating terrorism. She was the first of two homeland security advisors to represent Justice Department equities from a New York City perspective. Townsend started her career in the mid-eighties as a no-nonsense prosecutor, serving as a Brooklyn assistant district attorney. From there, she moved to the U.S. Attorney's Office for the Southern District of New York. In 1988, she went to the Office of the Attorney General in Washington to help establish the Office of International Programs, the predecessor to the Executive Office for National Security. In the early nineties, she joined the DOJ Criminal Division where she served as chief of staff to the assistant attorney general, playing a critical part in the stand-up of the division's international training and rule of law programs. She completed her Justice career as counsel to the attorney general for intelligence policy before moving to Coast Guard Headquarters as the assistant commandant of Coast Guard intelligence.

Townsend was characterized as a national security lawyer who started her career in New York, like Chertoff, as a prosecutor in organized crime and narcotics cases, mentored by Rudy Giuliani and also by Louis Freeh, when he was another top prosecutor who became a federal judge. While Freeh was FBI director, she came to Justice where she rose to serve as director of its Office of Intelligence Policy and Review, a DOJ entity with responsibility for administering domestic electronic eavesdropping laws in espionage and terrorism cases. She was chief of staff to Jo Ann Harris, the assistant attorney general for the criminal division. One of the few senior carryovers from the Clinton administration, she relieved Dick Clarke on the NSC staff as Condoleezza Rice's deputy for counterterrorism in 2003.

Townsend would remain homeland security advisor until January 2008. Two months later, Kenneth L. Wainstein, Justice's first assistant attorney general (AAG) for national security, succeeded her. Like Townsend, Wainstein began his career in the late 1980s in the U.S. Attorney's Office in the Southern District of New York. From there, he went to the U.S. Attorney's Office for the District of Columbia before becoming director of the Executive Office of U.S. Attorneys. He also served with the FBI as general counsel as well as chief of staff to the director.

## FEMA: The First among Tribes

The HSC staff and the department leadership were orienting themselves to the left of the boom. One component agency was feeling left off the DHS reservation: FEMA. "The biggest danger in the department was tribalism," observed Ridge's first chief of staff, Bruce Lawlor, in retrospect, "and FEMA was the number one tribe."[4]

FEMA was not in sync with the law enforcement culture in the rest of DHS. It saw itself as the department's odd man out, at war with a White House that wanted to force upon it a forgotten Reagan-era function. In the 1980s, the Republican administrations had bolstered FEMA's national security emergency preparedness function that was resident in its National Preparedness Directorate. They had done so in the context of a strategic doctrine that had evolved toward a nuclear warfighting strategy, replete with modernization of offensive nuclear weapons and strategic defense. The United States was signaling to the Soviet Union its readiness to fight and survive a nuclear war.

The Clinton administration, however, came to town at the Cold War's end, riding on the electorate and agency expectations of a peace dividend. FEMA's national security emergency preparedness function no longer had a rationale. Clinton's FEMA director, James Lee Witt, thus immediately abolished the National Preparedness Directorate, starved its civil defense and continuity of government programs, and refocused the agency on disasters. The poster-child program of his tenure was his Project Impact, a FEMA-funded, community-based, pre-disaster mitigation program initiated in 1997. By 2000, the program had reached into 249 jurisdictions nationwide and almost one thousand communities. Project Impact had over 2,500 corporate partners and cooperative agreements with the U.S. Chamber of Commerce, the U.S. Humane Society, and a number of federal agencies. When Witt left office, FEMA was touting its intergovernmental role as "the central point of contact within the federal government responsible for a wide variety of emergency preparedness and planning, mitigation, and disaster response and recovery activities"—no mention of any national security function.[5]

Witt came to Washington having served as Clinton's head of the Arkansas Office of Emergency Services. Not a career emergency management professional, he was rather an owner of a construction firm and county judge who had been elected for six terms. Nevertheless, he was celebrated as an activist FEMA director who declared some 350 disasters, a record for an eight-year period. Conservative Republicans chose to take the view that Witt's FEMA was a check-writing agency important too as a vehicle for patronage. Certainly, all levels of government had emergency managers who were appointed as much on the basis of their service to political campaigns as on their professional qualifications. As often as not, in the minds of conservative Republicans, fire chiefs were legendary as captains of Democratic wards and precincts who excelled in getting out the vote. As such, their rewards were retirement positions in emergency management, where they could dispense disaster assistance monies.

Both Republicans and Democrats recognized FEMA's important role in serving intergovernmental relationships. The most senior political advisors, like Bush's first FEMA director, Joe Allbaugh, came to Washington with state and local relationships developed from his time in the Texas governor's office. Allbaugh had been in the running for a senior political post in the White House. A Bush family loyalist, he had run Bush's 2000 presidential campaign but had failed to win a coveted White House appointment, having lost a three-way power struggle to political consultant Karl Rove and communications strategist Karen Hughes, rivals from their time together in Austin on Bush's gubernatorial staff. An Oklahoman who was somewhat of an oil-and-gas man with Republican connections, Allbaugh worked for state campaigns for the elder Bush. In the nineties, he had managed George W. Bush's campaign for governor and served as Bush's chief of staff. Unable to continue that role in Washington when Andy Card won that honor, Allbaugh went to FEMA. As Bush's chief of staff in Austin, he had overseen nine presidential disaster declarations and more than twenty state-level emergencies.

In February 2001, the Bush administration announced FY02 budget cuts that included Witt's prized Project Impact pre-disaster mitigation program.[6] The announcement came just prior to the Nisqually Earthquake in Washington State. Occurring in an area that had been one of the Project Impact beneficiaries, the event proved the worth of the program. Nevertheless, the administration was determined: on its watch, FEMA priorities were going to change, if not revert.

In his May 2001 announcement of Vice President Cheney's counterterrorism task force and review, Bush also gave notice of the stand-up of a new FEMA entity, the Office of National Preparedness (ONP). Its responsibility, said the president, would be implementation of the Cheney task force findings.

ONP was to coordinate all federal WMD consequence management programs in DoD, HHS, Justice, Energy, and EPA, among others. The foremost preparedness grant program was Nunn-Lugar-Domenici that specifically educated and trained first responders in WMD consequence management. At the time, Justice's Office of Domestic Preparedness (ODP) was administering Nunn-Lugar-Domenici grants. It had not been a FEMA function in the nineties, because James Lee Witt did not want his agency to be in the counterterrorism business, a preparedness tasking that would compete for funds with its mitigation and disaster assistance functions. In 2001, Cheney was eager to orient FEMA to the contemporary version of civil defense and call it "homeland defense." The newly established Office of National Preparedness thus was a restoration of FEMA's Reagan-era National Preparedness Directorate.

To head ONP, Allbaugh named John Magaw, who had been serving as acting FEMA director until Allbaugh took his oath in March. Magaw had been with FEMA since 1999 as the head of its domestic terrorism preparedness activities. The post involved no programs, but rather Magaw's representing Witt in various interagency meetings on terrorism preparedness. Witt had accepted Magaw because he was well suited to handling law enforcement and national security liaison duties. He came to the agency from the Secret Service where he had been director, having previously run ATF, sorely in need of restoration after its disastrous February 1993 raid on the Branch Davidian compound in Waco, Texas, that resulted in the deaths of eighty-five people.

Magaw was not happy in his posting to ONP. The office had yet no line item appropriation or established staffing. After 9/11, he jumped at the opportunity presented to him by the administration to transfer to the Department of Transportation where he could run the newly created Transportation Security Administration (TSA). When he left in January 2002, FEMA career man Bruce Baughman assumed the ONP directorship, moving from his post as director of the planning and readiness division of FEMA's Readiness, Response, and Recovery Directorate.

The 9/11 attacks provided greater urgency for the consolidation of grant policy and grant management into one federal office. Cheney and Allbaugh had an idea to transfer Justice's Office of Domestic Preparedness (ODP) with its Nunn-Lugar-Domenici grants to FEMA's newly established Office of National Preparedness. The 9/11 and anthrax attacks focused attention on all of the federal intergovernmental resourcing of the federal government's domestic preparedness support to states. The primary grant-providing agencies were FEMA, Justice, and HHS. In advance of a final homeland security bill, FEMA and Justice in 2002 began collaborating on first-responder grants to states. The FEMA grants focused on planning; Justice, on equipment. HHS grants came in the wake of the anthrax attacks. In 2002, $1.1 billion in HHS bioterrorism grants went to the states for public health and hospitals.

The 2002 administration proposal for a Department of Homeland Security had called for DHS to absorb FEMA and transform it, along with several other components, into the Emergency Preparedness and Response Directorate. Ridge, a true believer in an empowered FEMA, had seen the transformation as an upgrade that would be reinforced by elevating the FEMA director with a new title: undersecretary for emergency preparedness and response. However, Allbaugh, the FEMA loyalists in Congress, the states, and local jurisdictions did not see the renaming as meaningful empowerment. In the end, Allbaugh's successor, Mike Brown, got the new title and retained the old title, FEMA director. FEMA thus kept its name while becoming a directorate.

With congressional oversight of preparedness grants at stake in the homeland security reorganization, lawmakers had formed two competing camps reflecting law enforcement and emergency management equities as would relate to the intergovernmental funding of DHS missions. Among the principal authorization committees were the House Transportation and Infrastructure Committee (T&I) that held the emergency management brief, and Senate and House Judiciary Committees responsive to law enforcement.[7] Notwithstanding any intent for FEMA's Office of National Preparedness to acquire Justice's Office of Domestic Preparedness, from its inception to 2003 ONP had only been performing an interagency preparedness program coordination function with the White House Office of Homeland Security. From the Justice side, most ODP officials had not wanted to go to FEMA. In their view, it was a response agency with no experience in integrated training with law enforcement in what was then called crisis as opposed to consequence management. To the dismay of FEMA, ODP and its law enforcement allies lobbied Congress to support putting the office in the DHS Border and Transportation Directorate. This entity would house two legacy law enforcement agencies, the Federal Protective Service and Border Patrol, and the newly created TSA and Immigration and Customs Enforcement (ICE).

Ridge had supported linking ODP and FEMA. Yet even in the pre-proposal stage in the spring of 2002, law enforcement had been intent on killing the idea. The action officers representing the legacy law enforcement agencies and TSA who were going to be putting Border and Transportation Security together in fact did not want FEMA in the directorate. Inside ODP, Andy Mitchell, the deputy director, and Corey Gruber may have been willing to work with putting their office into the Emergency Preparedness and Response Directorate, but their boss, ODP director Butch Straub, a career Justice official, was another who lobbied against the idea on Capitol Hill. The judiciary committees, eager to protect their grant-approval turf, were responsive to Straub's and the law enforcement case and were not about to let FEMA be in charge of law enforcement grants. In the end, the House Judiciary Committee, in particular, and Senator Judd Gregg (R-NH), a major law enforcement ally on the Hill, succeeded in putting language in the final bill providing for ODP to go into Border and Transportation Security, thus protecting the judiciary committees' turf.

Joe Allbaugh chose to leave the administration when FEMA rolled into DHS. His successor, Mike Brown, was Allbaugh's protégé, another Oklahoman with a vague background in the oil business. Starting him as his FEMA general counsel, Allbaugh had groomed Brown to succeed him. When John Magaw left for TSA, Allbaugh promoted Brown to deputy director. With Allbaugh's departure, Brown fleeted up to FEMA administrator and found himself walking the agency point against Ridge over a number of intra-DHS bureaucratic battles, in particular the fallout over this very transfer of Justice's ODP and its grant programs to DHS.

Section 872 of the Homeland Security Act, from language originally proposed by Andy Card's five-man review group, gave Ridge the authority to reorganize DHS. He could "allocate or reallocate functions among the officers of the Department, and [could] establish, consolidate, alter, or discontinue organizational units within the Department." Exercising his prerogative, Ridge decided to consolidate preparedness grants in his office, causing further FEMA upset. As director, Brown now joined battle with what would become the familiar FEMA line: grants management must take place in an office where preparedness and response functions were conjoined. Ridge's answer to Brown was simple: Ridge and his senior team had lost the battle with lawmakers and the law enforcement lobby, so get on board and help make preparedness grants and grant management into a one-stop shop as state and local officials had long been requesting. It was Ridge's way of removing the Office of Domestic Preparedness from the Border and Transportation Directorate and putting it into his office while not antagonizing the law enforcement community by transferring it to the Emergency Preparedness and Response Directorate, aka FEMA. As was becoming his routine tactic in these intra-DHS tussles, Brown went over Ridge's head to his political allies in the Bush White House inner circle, Deputy Chief of Staff Joe Hagin and Director of Presidential Personnel Clay Johnson. Hagin and Johnson, however, did not always support him. In September 2003, Ridge appointed Suzanne Mencer, a career FBI veteran in counterintelligence and counterterrorism and a Colorado public safety director, to head ODP. In protecting the turf of her office, Mencer found a kindred spirit and ally in the U.S. fire administrator, Dave Paulison, one senior official in the FEMA chain who was not supporting Brown in his effort to derail Ridge's plan for ODP. A month later, Ridge merged ODP with the Office of State and Local Government Coordination to become the DHS Office of State and Local Government Coordination and Preparedness, with Mencer as its executive director. Mencer served until January 2005. In October 2005 under Mike Chertoff, Ridge's successor, Mencer's office was renamed the Office of Grants and Training.

Brown's efforts on behalf of his agency didn't just fail to secure the transfer of preparedness functions to FEMA; they further irritated Ridge and his front office. The FEMA administrator had pushed too many head-office buttons. Also poisoning the well of intra-departmental goodwill was a canard that started floating around in emergency management quarters that FEMA budget lines were "getting taxed" to fund those for DHS functions. In truth, the same could be said for all the legacy agencies, although some—for example, the U.S. Secret Service—were more successful than others in making the case for keeping their monies. In truth, the tax—as it were—was the result of the budget neutral requirement imposed on the stand-up of the department. The DHS budget top-line was not to be more than the sum of its twenty-two parts.

### The National Response Plan: Balancing Both Sides of the Boom

In the midst of its 2003 preparations for war in Iraq, the administration released Homeland Security Presidential Directive 5 (HSPD-5), Management of Domestic Incidents. Its authors were Richard Falkenrath and David Howe, a special assistant to the president and the HSC senior director for emergency preparedness and response. Howe was a policy coordinator for counterterrorism, WMD defense, and disaster preparedness and response. A Harvard undergrad with an MBA from the University of Pennsylvania's Wharton School, he had been a Navy special warfare officer during Operations Desert Storm and Provide Comfort, the follow-on operation to defend Iraqi Kurds. Later a McKinsey consultant and California-based software entrepreneur, he would also serve as the chief of staff to the President's Critical Infrastructure Protection Board, where he helped draft the National Strategy for Cyber Security.

HSPD-5 directed the secretary of homeland security to undertake two key tasks that addressed structures and processes for interagency and intergovernmental coordination. The first tasking was for Ridge to "develop, submit for review to the Homeland Security Council, and administer a National Incident Management System (NIMS). This system will provide a consistent nationwide approach for Federal, State, and local governments to work effectively and efficiently together to prepare for, respond to, and recover from domestic incidents, regardless of cause, size, or complexity."[8] NIMS would derive from the well-established protocols of the incident command system (ICS), which state and local authorities had been developing and using since 1970 when California initiated, with support from the U.S. Forest Service, a concept of a temporary hierarchical network approach to fight cross-jurisdictional wildfires.[9] NIMS implementation would require establishment of standardized training, organization, and communications procedures for multi-jurisdictional interaction, and identified authority and leadership responsibilities. Similarly, the second HSPD-5 tasking called for Ridge to craft and administer a National Response Plan (NRP). "This plan shall integrate Federal Government domestic prevention, preparedness, response, and recovery plans into one all-discipline, all-hazards plan."

Ridge brought on board Jim Loy, a retired Coast Guard admiral, to lead these tasks. Loy had been Coast Guard commandant before relieving John Magaw as TSA administrator in June 2002. The transfer of TSA to DHS put him in Ridge's chain of command, where in October 2003 he would later fleet up to become Ridge's deputy. Both Pennsylvanians, Loy and Ridge had a good personal relationship that began while Ridge was governor. Having served in the Army in Vietnam, Ridge valued the military planning culture. He recognized the Coast Guard as uniquely versed in intergovernmental collaboration. "Emergency management was a particular Coast Guard strength," recalled

Loy. "He [Ridge] had been advised that the Coast Guard and the fire service guys really understood the guts of what a new NIMS and NRP should contain since we were the 'first responders' who used the current version and would use the new one."

Unlike the regular military, the Coast Guard has law enforcement author-ity. At the same time, unlike law enforcement, which is more tactically ori-ented, the Coast Guard is a military institution with a long-standing planning culture. Ridge's direction to Loy was another bone of contention with FEMA, other federal agencies, and state and local governments. They regarded the NRP as the next iteration of the Federal Response Plan, an emergency man-agement document for interagency/intergovernmental coordination. In their view, NRP development should be more appropriately a FEMA responsibil-ity. Given the DHS emphasis on counterterrorism—the prevention and pro-tection side of the mission continuum—Ridge made the decision to put the first phase of NIMS and NRP development in Loy's hands. Work began in March with contract support from Mike Wermuth and his RAND team, who leveraged their considerable expertise drawn from their involvement with the Gilmore Commission.

HSPD-5 specified that the NRP was to be a single "all-discipline, all-hazards" plan encompassing all homeland security functions. The initial ver-sion asserted the right of the secretary of homeland security to designate the duties and direct the activities of the other departments and agencies having roles and responsibilities to play in homeland security. In its initial version, the NRP identified ten homeland security functions:

- Information/Intelligence, and Warning
- International Coordination
- Terrorism Preparedness
- Domestic Counter terrorism
- Border and Transportation Security
- Infrastructure Protection
- Military Defense
- Emergency Management
- Law Enforcement
- CBRNE Hazards

In May 2003, DHS held the Top Officials 2 (TopOff 2) national counter-terrorism exercise that included terrorist use of a radiological dispersal device (RDD) in Seattle and biological agent releases in several locations in Chicago. TopOff 2 introduced the position of principal federal official (PFO), which would find its way into the NRP. The PFO, designated by the DHS secretary for an incident requiring extraordinary coordination, would promote federal collaboration in the Joint Field Office (JFO), the on-scene unified command structure managing the federal response. The PFO essentially provided the secretary of homeland security with situational awareness. A PFO did not have directive authority over the senior FEMA, federal law enforcement, or military officials on site for the incident. The PFO concept aroused FEMA, which saw it as introducing another layer of federal incident management bureaucracy that would rival the authority of the agency's federal coordinating officer (FCO). The Federal Response Plan had provided for the FCO to be the senior federal official responsible for coordination of Stafford Act events.

The same month, DHS circulated the initial version of the NRP for interagency coordination. It provoked fierce opposition from the Pentagon, Justice, and other agencies which were unwilling to cede directive authority over their organizations to the secretary of homeland security. DoD was particularly insistent that the NRP's military defense function was its responsibility. It would participate in other NRP functions only when directed by the president and as long as such participation did not interfere with other military operations. Faced with near unanimous non-concurrence from the executive branch, DHS returned to the drawing board.

At the time, the National Incident Management System was yet unde-fined, with many contending models. One was the National Interagency Integrated Management System (NIIMS), a preferred alternative at the federal level. NIIMS was more of a logistics, emergency support function-based system that was better suited for resource providers. It was not as operational as the original iteration of the Incident Command System, California's FIRESCOPE (FIrefighting RESources of California Organized for Potential Emergencies). FIRESCOPE developers were the U.S. Forest Service, the California Department of Forestry and Fire Protection, the Governor's Office of Emergency Services, the Los Angeles City Fire Department, and the Los Angeles, Ventura, and Santa Barbara County Fire Departments—a genuine intergovernmental collaboration of equals.

FIRESCOPE/ICS was the most-used system in the country. Its primary advocates in the final NIMS development were U.S. Fire Administrator Dave Paulison, dual-hatted as the director of the National Preparedness Division of the DHS Emergency Preparedness and Response Directorate, and his division deputy, Marko Bourne, whom he sent to be acting director of the division's new NIMS Integration Center. As a fire-service professional from Florida, a hurricane state, Paulison had firsthand experience with FIRESCOPE/ICS' operational effectiveness and its advantages as the most expandable system for a disaster that morphs into a major multi-site, multi-jurisdictional disaster. Paulison wanted an ICS-based system that enabled operations to be the lever point to control resources, and as the nation's senior fire services educator he was adamant that FIRESCOPE/ICS serve as the foundation for NIMS. Ridge supported him. Beyond applications for emergency management and into homeland security, NIMS development thereupon built on ICS, adding the required intelligence and information-sharing components. Once the NIMS Integration Center had vetted and completed NIMS development, Bourne undertook the driving of nationwide NIMS implementation at all levels of government.

For the next phase of development, Loy handed coordination of NIMS and NRP development in late August to Col. Bob Stephan, USAF (Ret.), a special operations expert and another well-accomplished planner. Stephan had been senior director for critical infrastructure protection in the Executive Office of the President. His Air Force background had prepared him well. He was a master in the planning and execution of complex operations. During Operation Desert Storm, he was a joint battle staff planner and mission commander supporting the Joint Special Operations Task Force's strategic interdiction operations in Iraq. In the nineties, as an Air Force Special Tactics Squadron commander, he organized, trained, and equipped forces for contingency operations in Somalia, Haiti, Bosnia, Croatia, Liberia, Colombia, and Kosovo.

Building on Jim Loy's work with RAND, Stephan drew on an interagency writing team of over a dozen principal representatives from DHS, FEMA, and other key federal agencies. The process involved coordinating a wide array of federal, state, and local government and private-sector partners. At the same time, he had lead responsibility for developing, with FEMA's Emergency Management Institute in Emmitsburg, Maryland, an initial program of NIMS and NRP education, training, and awareness.

## EMERGENCY SUPPORT FUNCTIONS (ESFs)

The Incident Command System provides for the flexibility to assign ESF and other stakeholder resources according to their capabilities, taskings and requirements to augment and support the other sections of the Joint Field Office (JFO)/Regional Response Coordination Center (RRCC) or National Response Coordination Center (NRCC) in order to respond to incidents in a more collaborative and cross-cutting manner.

While ESFs are typically assigned to a specific section at the NRCC or in the JFO/RRCC for management purposes, resources may be assigned anywhere within the Unified Coordination structure. Regardless of the section in which an ESF may reside, that entity works in conjunction with other JFO sections to ensure that appropriate planning and execution of missions occur.

### ROLES AND RESPONSIBILITIES OF THE ESFs

| ESF | Scope |
| --- | --- |
| ESF #1 – Transportation | Aviation/airspace management and control; Transportation safety; Restoration/recovery of transportation infrastructure; Movement restrictions; Damage and impact assessment |
| ESF #2 – Communications | Coordination with telecommunications and information technology industries; Restoration and repair of telecommunications infrastructure; Protection, restoration, and sustainment of national cyber and information technology resources; Oversight of communications within the Federal incident management and response structures |
| ESF #3 – Public Works and Engineering | Infrastructure protection and emergency repair; Infrastructure restoration; Engineering services and construction management; Emergency contracting support for life-saving and life-sustaining services |
| ESF #4 – Firefighting | Coordination of federal firefighting activities; Support to wildland, rural, and urban firefighting operations |
| ESF #5 – Emergency Management | Coordination of incident management and response efforts; Issuance of mission assignments; Resource and human capital; Incident action planning; Financial management |

## ROLES AND RESPONSIBILITIES OF THE ESFs *(CONT.)*

| ESF | Scope |
| --- | --- |
| ESF #6 – Mass Care, Emergency Assistance, Housing, and Human Services | Coordination of incident management and response efforts; Issuance of mission assignments; Resource and human capital; Incident action planning; Financial management |
| ESF #7 – Logistics Management and Resource Support | Comprehensive, national incident logistics planning, management, and sustainment capability; Resource support (facility space, office equipment and supplies, contracting services, etc.) |
| ESF #8 – Public Health and Medical Services | Public health; Medical; Mental health services; Mass fatality management |
| ESF #9 – Search and Rescue | Life-saving assistance; Search-and-rescue operations |
| ESF #10 – Oil and Hazardous Materials Response | Oil and hazardous materials (chemical, biological, radiological, etc.) response; Environmental short- and long-term cleanup |
| ESF #11 – Agriculture and Natural Resources | Nutrition assistance; Animal and plant disease and pest response; Food safety and security; Natural and cultural resources and historic properties protection and restoration; Safety and well-being of household pets |
| ESF #12 – Energy | Energy infrastructure assessment, repair, and restoration; Energy industry utilities coordination; Energy forecast |
| ESF #13 – Public Safety and Security | Facility and resource security; Security planning and technical resource assistance; Public safety and security support; Support to access, traffic, and crowd control |
| ESF #14 – Long-Term Community Recovery | Social and economic community impact assessment; Long-term community recovery assistance to states, local governments, and the private sector; Analysis and review of mitigation program implementation |
| ESF #15 – External Affairs | Emergency public information and protective action guidance; Media and community relations; Congressional and international affairs; Tribal and insular affairs |

Ridge announced the elements of an initial NRP at the end of September 2003.[10] The plan was going to supersede the Federal Response Plan, Domestic Terrorism Concept of Operations Plan (CONPLAN), and Federal Radiological Emergency Response Plan. The core NRP also linked to an array of national-level, hazard-specific contingency plans—for example, the National Oil and Hazardous Substances Pollution Contingency Plan (NCP). These plans could be used independently for localized incidents or concurrently with the NRP for those that rose to the level of incidents of national significance. The NRP also incorporated many concepts and mechanisms associated with these plans—for example, the FRP's Emergency Support Functions.

The National Response Plan included a base plan and supporting annexes and appendices. The base plan outlined the coordinating structures and the processes for national incident management. It covered the concept of operations, roles and responsibilities, specific incident management activities, and plan management and maintenance. Inherited from the FRP, the ESF Annexes grouped capabilities and resources into functions required during an incident. They also described the responsibilities of primary and support agencies involved in providing support to a state or to other federal agencies during incidents of national significance. Support Annexes provided the procedures and administrative requirements—for example, public affairs, financial management, and worker safety and health. Finally, the Incident Annexes described the procedures and roles and responsibilities for specific contingencies, such as bioterrorism, radiological response, and catastrophic events. In many cases, more detailed supporting plans in turn supported these annexes.

The initial NRP introduced: (1) the newly created PFO and Joint Field Office, (2) the Homeland Security Operations Center (HSOC), and (3) the Interagency Incident Management Group (IIMG). Loy established a PFO curriculum at FEMA's Emergency Management Institute to train a cadre of predesignated PFOs for incidents of national significance. DHS used the PFO system to manage the 2004 Republican National Convention in New York, where a Secret Service PFO supported an FBI special agent in charge (SAC) as incident commander.[11]

Ridge stood up the HSOC in July 2004 at DHS Headquarters, the Nebraska Avenue Complex (NAC), the site of the Navy's Security Station, on a ridgeline of hills overlooking northwest Washington. He was able to staff it with extremely capable Coast Guard officers: from the outset, it was

Coast Guard policy to detail its high-performing people to DHS positions. The HSOC stand-up was another provocation to FEMA, which already had its National Response Coordination Center (NRCC) in its southwest Washington headquarters. The NRCC is FEMA's hub that links to its Regional Response Coordination Centers (RRCCs), each directed by a FEMA regional administrator.[12]

While Brown may have resisted the DHS effort to establish its own operations center, the HSOC and the NRCC were not duplicative. Ridge described the HSOC as "the primary national-level hub for operational communications and information pertaining to domestic incident management."[13] The NRCC is a functional response component of the HSOC (now titled the NOC, the National Operations Center) to support incident management operations. The HSOC's protection component is the DHS Office of Infrastructure Protection's National Infrastructure Coordinating Center (NICC) that coordinates the now eighteen critical infrastructure/key resources (CI/KR) sectors and information sharing via the Information Sharing and Analysis Councils (ISACs) and Sector Coordinating Councils (SCCs). Additional HSOC components are DoD's National Military Command Center (NMCC), the Office of the Director of National Intelligence's (ODNI's) National Counterterrorism Center (NCTC), the FBI's Strategic Intelligence and Operations Center (SIOC) with its liaison with the National Joint Terrorism Task Force (NJTTF), and the CBP (Customs and Border Protection), TSA, Coast Guard, and Secret Service operations centers.

The Interagency Incident Management Group was the facilitator of national-level domestic incident management coordination in an incident of national significance. The IIMG received its situational awareness from the HSOC.[14] Ridge's IIMG director was Bob Stephan. A multi-agency federal coordination entity composed of senior representatives from nearly forty different agencies, the IIMG reported directly to the secretary of homeland security to facilitate the strategic response to a domestic incident. In terms of division of labor, the IIMG was intended to focus on strategic-level issues and medium-term courses of action for secretary-level consideration, while the HSOC and its component centers maintained situational awareness and resolved operational- and tactical-level issues.

As Stephan and his team pressed forward with NIMS and NRP development into the autumn of 2003, in December the administration released

HSPD-8, National Preparedness. Authored by David Howe, this directive introduced the National Preparedness Goal (NPG), later expressed as the National Preparedness "Guidelines." Howe was responsible for developing the NPG's controversial fifteen national planning scenarios depicting a diverse set of high-consequence threat scenarios for both potential terrorist attacks and natural disasters. Twelve of the fifteen were attack scenarios, involving CBRNE devices or agents—for example, a 10-kiloton improvised nuclear device and aerosolized anthrax. Only three were naturally occurring: an influenza pandemic, major earthquake, and major hurricane. The fifteen scenarios were to focus homeland security contingency planning for all levels of government and the private sector. They formed the basis for coordinated federal planning, training, exercises, and—most particularly—grant investments.

Suzanne Mencer's DHS Office of State and Local Government Coordination and Preparedness used Howe's scenarios to arrive at the Universal Task List (UTL) and Target Capabilities List (TCL), components of the NPG. The UTL listed the two hundred critical common tasks for the federal, state, and local levels that in turn informed the thirty-six (later thirty-seven) interim TCL capabilities. In preparing the Interim NPG with its UTL and TCL, Mencer's office conducted an extensive review process that engaged over 170 stakeholder representatives in working groups and conferences and received comment from over 112 state agencies, 398 municipal bodies, and 94 national associations. The process dated from 1998 when the office was in Justice as the Office of Domestic Preparedness. "ODP was constantly engaging the stakeholder community for input into the grant programs and yearly made significant changes as a result," recalled one senior grants official. "The size of the homeland security stakeholder community, well beyond one discipline, means that consensus—much less agreement—on anything is very difficult at best."

Mencer released the Interim Goal in March 2005 with the aim to have the final completed in October. The NPG and seven national planning scenario priorities identified later that year formed the basis of DHS preparedness grant guidance.[15] Critics, notably Iowa's Sam Clovis, saw the initial NPG effort with its national planning scenarios as imposing federal priorities and detailed, prescriptive grant requirements on state and local governments.[16] To others, like National Academy of Public Administration (NAPA) fellow Paul Posner, the National Preparedness Goal and its Universal Task List and Target Capabilities List represented a centralization of federal standard-setting.[17]

## CRITICAL INFRASTRUCTURE AND KEY RESOURCES SECTORS
## AND THEIR SECTOR-SPECIFIC AGENCIES

A sector is a logical collection of assets, systems, or networks that provide a common function to the economy, government, or society. Criteria set forth in Homeland Security Presidential Directive 7 (HSPD-7) identified eighteen critical infrastructure sectors. HSPD-7 established U.S. policy for enhancing critical infrastructure protection by establishing a framework for National Infrastructure Protection Plan (NIPP) partners to identify, prioritize, and protect national critical infrastructure from terrorist attacks.

HSPD-7 designates a Federal Sector-Specific Agency (SSA) to lead critical infrastructure protection efforts in each sector. The directive allows for the Department of Homeland Security to identify gaps in existing critical infrastructure sectors and establish new sectors to fill these gaps. Each SSA developed a Sector-Specific Plan that details the application of the NIPP framework to the unique characteristics of their sector.

| Sector-Specific Agency | Critical Infrastructure and Key Resources Sector |
|---|---|
| Department of Agriculture Department of Health and Human Services | Food and Agriculture |
| Department of Defense | Defense Industrial Base |
| Department of Energy | Energy |
| Department of Health and Human Services | Healthcare and Public Health |
| Department of the Interior | National Monuments and Icons |
| Department of the Treasury | Banking and Finance |
| Environmental Protection Agency | Water |
| Department of Homeland Security *Office of Infrastructure Protection* | Chemical Commercial Facilities Critical Manufacturing Dams Emergency Services Nuclear Reactors, Materials, and Waste |
| *Office of Cybersecurity and Communications* | Information Technology Communications |
| *Transportation Security Administration* | Postal and Shipping |
| *Transportation Security Administration, United States Coast Guard* | Transportation Systems |
| *Immigration and Customs Enforcement, Federal Protective Service* | Government Facilities |

## THE FIFTEEN NATIONAL PLANNING SCENARIOS

| | |
|---|---|
| **Scenario 1** | Nuclear Detonation—10-Kiloton Improvised Nuclear Device |
| **Scenario 2** | Biological Attack—Aerosol Anthrax |
| **Scenario 3** | Biological Disease Outbreak—Pandemic Influenza |
| **Scenario 4** | Biological Attack—Plague |
| **Scenario 5** | Chemical Attack—Blister Agent |
| **Scenario 6** | Chemical Attack—Toxic Industrial Chemicals |
| **Scenario 7** | Chemical Attack—Nerve Agent |
| **Scenario 8** | Chemical Attack—Chlorine Tank Explosion |
| **Scenario 9** | Natural Disaster—Major Earthquake |
| **Scenario 10** | Natural Disaster—Major Hurricane |
| **Scenario 11** | Radiological Attack—Radiological Dispersal Devices |
| **Scenario 12** | Explosives Attack—Bombing Using Improvised Explosive Device |
| **Scenario 13** | Biological Attack—Food Contamination |
| **Scenario 14** | Biological Attack—Foreign Animal Disease (Foot and Mouth Disease) |
| **Scenario 15** | Cyber Attack |

Posner would cite other, more collaborative intergovernmental approaches for arriving at performance standards and goals, such as the Environmental Protection Agency's use of negotiated rulemaking, voluntary state agreements like the Streamlined Sales Tax Project (SSTP), and cooperative standard-setting regimes like those established by the National Fire Protection Association (NFPA).

HSPD-8 implementation was less than satisfactory. In the view of one senior grants official, "Everyone thought that once the NPG had gone out to the states and locals there was nothing else they needed to do. They never came up with a plan or any actions for DHS to take to promote implementation. No one looked across policy, grants, training, and exercises to see how to use those tools to implement HSPD-8 and measure its effectiveness."

Part of the problem DHS had with HSPD-8 implementation was the result of its not having its own policy shop. DHS preparedness officials continually had to vet HSPD-8 implementation and numerous preparedness policy matters with the HSC and OMB staffs in the White House. OMB budgetary oversight came from Doug Pitkin, an analyst who had developed an expertise in state and local law enforcement assistance programs. On the HSC policy side, oversight came from Howe and his lawyer, Kirstjen Nielsen, a special assistant to the president and the HSC's senior director for prevention, preparedness, and response. Nielsen had come to the HSC staff from TSA, where she had stood up and managed its offices of legislative policy and government affairs, developed transportation security–related policy, and drafted legislation. Beyond transportation, she was not a homeland security or intergovernmental subject matter expert; nevertheless, she worked with Howe on policy development and coordination, particularly in the area of infrastructure, and was responsible for language in a number of policy documents. Nielsen was an attorney with Haynes and Boone, the Dallas international corporate law firm, where she had specialized in corporate transactional law. She had come into government via her time with Senator Connie Mack (R-FL), in the 1990s the influential chairman of the Senate Republican Conference and a name mentioned as Bob Dole's running mate in the 1996 presidential campaign.

Several years on, the Washington think tanks were looking at ways to make the preparedness grant process more collaborative. One 2008 report embraced a regional approach. The Center for Strategic and International Studies (CSIS) proposed to empower FEMA regional offices to be the "front line" of the grants process. CSIS wanted grant guidance for all major DHS grant programs to "focus proposed state investment in the target capabilities."[18] To that end, it recommended revising the DHS Target Capabilities List to set an agreed basis for assessing capability development.[19] According to CSIS, "a baseline survey of state capabilities, followed by the development of a database to track state capabilities, would facilitate operational planning at all levels."[20] Evidently confident that previous grant programs by 2008 had brought state efforts to a level sufficient for building incident management,

CSIS proposed shifting the risk-based grant strategies based on the NPG's fifteen national planning scenarios toward strategies for sustaining capabilities. CSIS also recommended that "the National Exercise Program should be designed explicitly to verify federal, state, and local acquisition of target capabilities."[21]

In March 2004, DHS issued NIMS. The following January, it released the NRP with the provision for a 120-day implementation period that included use of the National Exercise Program to test both NIMS and the NRP. Just prior to final implementation, the April 2005 TopOff 3 tested the NRP in complex mass-casualty scenarios in two state venues. New Jersey hosted two simulated bio attacks. The other, Connecticut's chemical attack exercise, generated a national interagency and international response that included Canada and the United Kingdom. Later that month, the heads of thirty-two federal departments and agencies and national-level private volunteer organizations signed the NRP, making it fully effective.

### Regional Empowerment: Toward a National Network of Security

CSIS' embrace of regional empowerment reflected some of Tom Ridge's governance-changing vision for the DHS and homeland security. It was a de-centralized, network approach whereby DHS would build upon regional departmental and component hubs to forge a "national network of security."[22] "Integrating all emergency plans," said Ridge, "and the development of mutual aid pacts as well as building a seamless information-sharing network would result in the type of collaborative environment necessary to meet the national goals of the department."[23]

In his 2009 book *The Test of Our Times*, he noted the considered thinking of others, specifically the National Academy of Public Administration, which had released a report in 2004 recommending modernization of the "federal field machinery."[24] "Much of our effort at DHS was to incorporate FEMA and other agencies into a new plan that would spread the federal presence around the nation. In my view, we needed to be much closer to the communities we served. An exclusive inside-the-beltway presence couldn't possibly develop the kinds of partnerships we needed. From the early days of DHS, we worked on a plan to establish regional offices."[25] Ridge said he wanted to create a DHS network of "Mini-mes"—regional DHS directors with authorities and integrated staffs.

In the spring of 2003, Ridge assigned his chief of staff, Bruce Lawlor, to develop a concept for such a plan. Lawlor engaged an action officer, Sam Roudebush, and together they presented Ridge with a proposal to decentralize DHS. "The idea was to adopt the advantages of Goldwater Nichols while avoiding the pitfalls," said Lawlor. "The Governor believed in the concept and gave us the green light to proceed."

A major challenge would be finding agreement on a common departmental mapping. For a start, the ten FEMA regions would have to align with the Secret Service and its four designated areas, TSA and its five areas, Customs and Border Protection and its twenty patrol sectors and seventeen management centers, the five districts of the Coast Guard, and the three districts of the Bureau of Immigration and Citizenship Services. In each region, Ridge wanted a "single, unified regional structure."[26]

Lawlor started drafting the plan by attempting to fit all DHS components into alignment with the FEMA regions, allowing exceptions for component missions. The common mapping would be no mean achievement. "Of course, none of the regional boundaries matched," said Lawlor. In the end, Lawlor settled on eight new regions with regional DHS headquarters in New York, Philadelphia, Chicago, Miami, New Orleans, Houston, San Francisco, and Seattle, with smaller units in Juneau, Alaska, and Honolulu, Hawaii. The department would reorganize the regional boundaries of all agencies to conform to the new boundaries, a major challenge since each agency had administrative and overhead personnel in their own regions, representing enormous overhead duplication. "In one instance, we had an airfield with a Coast Guard admin and support office on one side of the airstrip," said Lawlor, "and an admin and support office for Customs on the other side of the same airstrip." The plan proposed to consolidate all duplicative administration and overhead into a single regional office managed by a very powerful regional director. A planning, budget, and execution system would provide national strategic guidance and require regional plans to implement the strategy. "In effect, we demilitarized the system used to run the combatant commands and adapted it to domestic homeland security operations," Lawlor recalled. By so doing, DHS would be able to set goals for all preparedness money flowing to the states. The simple process of having the regional director sign off on all grants would have enabled the department to concentrate funds on broad national objectives for implementation at the state level.

Lawlor's approach was informed by his National Guard background. "We ran models on what the homeland security 'forces' would look like in each region. We found that the manpower and equipment available to the regional director to implement DHS strategic guidance and support the states in a homeland security situation was roughly equivalent to that of a division in a military situation"—that is, some 10,000–15,000 departmental personnel. Said Ridge, Lawlor's first draft proposal "gave daily operational control of the assembled units to the regional director."[27]

Later that spring, Ridge saw the need to create a task force to respond to Caribbean migration incidents in line with his determination to put priority on securing the nation's borders. Intelligence had concluded that fluctuations in large-scale migrant flows from Haiti since the 1980s were influenced more by changes in U.S. policy than by deteriorating internal economic factors.[28] Ridge was thus resolved to send a signal by standing up a task force. The operation order establishing Homeland Security Task Force Southeast (HSTF-SE) was DHS' first such order. To write it, Lawlor assigned Bob Stephan in his capacity as the head of the DHS Crisis Action Team, the predecessor of the IIMG. With HSTF-SE, Lawlor and Stephan were in fact building Ridge's model for regional operational empowerment on what the Coast Guard and federal, state, and local law enforcement were doing in Miami at the headquarters of the Coast Guard's Seventh District. The Coast Guard was heavily engaged in the region, supporting counter-illicit trafficking with the DoD-led Joint Interagency Task Force-South. As such, they assigned the new District Seven two-star commander, Rear Adm. Harvey Johnson, to command HSTF-SE. The choice was purposeful, for Johnson had been a player in the developing mechanics of intra-DHS collaborations. He had just come from serving as the one-star executive director of the Coast Guard's transfer from the Department of Transportation to DHS.

From the earliest years of the Republic, the Coast Guard had performed an illegal immigration mission authority when, as the Revenue Cutter Service, it enforced the laws against the transportation of slaves. In the sixties, this function became known as alien migrant interdiction operations (AMIO), notably with respect to Cuba and the 1965 Camarioca Boatlift of 2,979 Cubans seeking exile, and more familiarly following the 1980 Mariel Boatlift of some 125,000 migrants. AMIO had become a daily focus of the Coast Guard in South Florida and the Caribbean region.

During the summer of 1994, the Coast Guard had undertaken its largest peacetime maritime operation since Vietnam with Operation Able Manner and the follow-on Operation Able Vigil that addressed accelerating mass migration of Haitian and Cuban illegal migrants. The Coast Guard and Navy response in these operations was largely ad hoc, however. The services had no immediate holding facility. The Navy was unfamiliar with migrant processing. The numbers were overwhelming. Over 64,000 migrants attempted to make passage to Florida by boat.

In the threatened 2003 migration, Ridge and Lawlor immediately real-ized that the half-dozen or so agencies entering the newly created DHS had their own operational procedures for responding to migration incidents. Ridge intended that HSTF-SE be a joint task force to provide the framework for the coordination of a unified response under a single command and con-trol organization for all DHS agencies. This effort was thus to be a DHS proto-type strategic planning process, the model for standing up the regional offices and for unifying the field structure of its twenty-two agencies.

Drawing on his experience in DoD planning doctrine, Lawlor called for HSTF-SE to develop an integrated and comprehensive DHS mass-migration contingency response plan for interdiction, detention, screening, processing, and repatriation. Johnson led a process that involved Coast Guard coordina-tion with all DHS agencies in Florida: Immigration and Customs Enforcement (ICE), Customs and Border Protection with its U.S. Border Patrol and Citizen-ship and Immigration Services, FEMA, other federal partners—DoD, State, HHS, Justice, and the FBI—and various state and local representatives. By November, Johnson's team in Miami had arrived at Operations Plan Vigilant Sentry for contingency response and secured DHS and White House approval.

The objective of Vigilant Sentry was to protect the safety of life at sea and to deter and dissuade mass migration. HSTF-SE would execute Vigilant Sentry with organic DHS forces, supported by other federal assets and capa-bilities, maximizing "the operational factor of force." DoD would provide supporting maritime assets and the migrant processing facility support at Guantánamo Bay. Coordination of military support in the Caribbean would come from U.S. Southern Command. The Vigilant Sentry plan provided for the use of naval vessels embarked with Coast Guard law-enforcement detach-ments (LEDETs). U.S. Northern Command planning focused on the U.S. mainland issues associated with Operation Vigilant Sentry.

Johnson would serve as a regional operational director to manage this kind of temporary event. He would thus be Ridge's direct liaison in a crisis-state contingency. He would not oversee daily operations of the agencies, however. Steady-state day-to-day operational control would still be through the traditional agencies. In line with Ridge's ideas for regional empowerment, Vigilant Sentry was hoped to serve as the operational model for DHS management of future homeland security situations, events, and joint operations in the field. To minimize response time and improve command and control, HSTF-SE would serve as a standing core element in Miami at Coast Guard District Seven. In response to advance indicators of a spike in Caribbean migrations, agency officials would augment billets within the command and general staffs. Pre-designated officials would fill their positions as branch and section chiefs. The surge-staffing would conform to ICS, with the Coast Guard leading two of the five incident command sections—operations and intelligence. [29]

As HSTF-SE was finishing its work on the Vigilant Sentry plan, Lawlor would leave as Ridge's chief of staff in October 2003. Ridge had him pass the regions baton to Bob Stephan, who was still in the midst of his NIMS and NRP coordination duties. Advancing on Lawlor's work, Stephan attempted to craft a regional system patterned after the special operations commands. Drawing on his spec ops background, his was a mission-focused view. While the regional directors would not have command authority, they would have coordination authority. Moreover, they would have representational authority—that is, they would be empowered with the secretary's authority to act on his behalf in their areas of operations.

As IIMG director, Stephan was a proponent of integration and believed it could proceed in the regions in a coordinated and collaborative way. His best-practices example was Miami, where the Coast Guard, ICE, and CBP's regional collaborative effort was giving a boost to Ridge's regional department concept. Miami's organizational capability served the component mission areas well. Stephan saw that it could serve preparedness as well. He wanted to take the Miami example, fit it into FEMA's regional model, and extend it across the homeland security mission continuum from prevention, through protection and response to recovery.

In steady-state preparedness, the regional DHS headquarters would integrate a risk analysis from which to derive a gap analysis with regard to determining capabilities. In a crisis-state incident, event, or situation, a principal federal official, the PFO, would assume the lead to coordinate the federal response and, in the case of Stafford Act events, would liaise with the FEMA federal coordinating official, the FCO. The regional headquarters would provide a common operating picture across the region via a DHS operations center that would function as the regional HSOC.

The DHS regional director would be a senior executive service (SES) professional who would report directly to the secretary. Regional directors would have a concept of operations (CONOPS) to revalidate the regional missions, but "he would not be a CinC"—that is, analogous to a commander in chief in the sense of a military commander of a U.S. regional unified command. As such, Stephan thought that the components would accept the plan, given that command and control would remain with the components and not go to the DHS regional director. FEMA was hostile and in the final proposal succeeded in reducing the regional director to a GS-15-level position, akin to an FCO. When the plan had finally matured with a cost estimate, Stephan proposed a $50 million program line in the FY05 budget.

The necessary compromises notwithstanding, by late 2004, Ridge was confident that he enjoyed White House support. He was particularly pleased with the collaborative efforts and relationships formed in Florida during the 2004 hurricane season that in his view proved the value of the plan. In his October 2004 memo, Ridge said, "All existing Federal regional structures will continue to execute incident management responsibilities as detailed in current Federal incident management and emergency response plans, in coordination with the PFO, HSOC, and IIMG."[30] As his IIMG director, Bob Stephan had the responsibility for integrating DHS and interagency capabilities in response to domestic threats and incidents. Ridge thus assigned him in late 2004 to lead the so-called I-Staff, the DHS headquarters operational integration staff. His job was to integrate and coordinate under deputy secretary Jim Loy the headquarters-level, cross-organizational elements, the operational missions, activities, and programs, in military parlance the J3, J5, and J7 functions—operations, strategic plans and policy, and operational plans. When the White House signaled that it was going to approve Ridge's regional concept, DHS began to organize line-by-line a modification table for organization and equipment (MTOE) for the first region, not surprisingly, the southeast region with the Miami regional headquarters. Unfortunately, no action was ever taken on that decision.

In September, Ridge had met with White House officials, hoping to map a rollout strategy for his plan. However, they signaled a desire to delay announcement of any DHS regional plan until after the November elections. Political officials were unwilling to go public, fearing that in states not chosen to host regional headquarters GOP candidates might incur a political backlash for a Republican administration's failure to deliver. When Ridge finally met with Andy Card after the elections to coordinate the rollout, he "ran into a brick wall."[31] Card directed Ridge to shelve the plan for his successor—the kiss of an assured future death.

Two additional political considerations came into play in the White House decision to scuttle Ridge's regional plan, and both had to do with patronage. Karl Rove had wanted regional directors to be political appointees, not necessarily a problem for DHS. Rove, however, did not want any requirement for demonstrated experience or knowledge of operations—in other words, he was looking at the regional director positions as patronage opportunities. The second source of opposition came from Richard Falkenrath, who had risen to deputy homeland security advisor. According to one senior homeland security official, Falkenrath "opposed it because he had a habit of bypassing the secretary's office and giving orders directly to people within the agencies. He saw that regionalization of the department would remove his ability to continue that practice."

All along, unfortunately, Ridge's own deputies and component heads also had been resisting the regional empowerment effort. A number were appealing to Card's deputy, Joe Hagin, and Clay Johnson, the White House personnel director. Particular opposition came from the legacy law enforcement agencies, the Secret Service, CBP, and ICE. While DHS saw component heads as being responsible for building the strategy, capturing resources, implementing national policies, and manning, equipping, and training their forces, they saw themselves as operational commanders. Yet most had little experience in or knowledge of field operations. In addition to working the political side of the White House, they also worked Capitol Hill, where they lobbied their case that the new regional boundaries would either eliminate existing regional offices or transfer them from favored congressional districts. In the proposed consolidation to eight DHS regions, FEMA headquarters in Boston, Atlanta, Kansas City, and Denver, along with Denton for Houston in Texas and Oakland for San Francisco in California, would deactivate and only be retained as COOP sites.

FEMA administrator Mike Brown aggressively worked his personal relationship with Hagin. This time, Brown was in position to win this intra-DHS
battle. He had support from the law enforcement side of the DHS house—the
Secret Service, CBP, and ICE. Once Ridge was gone, Brown's effort would bear
fruit. When Mike Chertoff took the DHS helm in the spring of 2005, along
with him came Michael Jackson to serve as his deputy. Jackson was another
political operative, a Card man who had been his chief of staff when Card was
the elder Bush's secretary of transportation. Before that, Jackson was George
H. W. Bush's special assistant for cabinet liaison. Earlier in the George W. Bush
presidency, he had been deputy secretary of transportation.

The whole idea of integration did not sit well with Jackson—neither the
I-Staff, nor the IIMG, nor their replication in any integrated and empowered
regional structures. Integration was going to take place in his office. Jackson
was briefed on the DHS regional plan in the spring of 2005, and he rejected
it emphatically. Nevertheless, Ridge had left his relief with a number of reorganization ideas that would find their way into his successor's Second Stage
Review (2SR). Chertoff would accept Ridge's recommendations for an intelligence directorate, a chief medical officer, and most significantly a policy shop.
However, he questioned the regional plan proposal, based on his concern that
regional directors and regional offices would create regional silos. And so, based
on Jackson's recommendation, the plan was the one Ridge idea he summarily
dismissed. Today, the Ridge plan with its two-years' worth of analyses and documentation sits unimplemented, on a shelf in the DHS Office of Operations and
Coordination (OPS), a creation of Chertoff's Second Stage Review.

In his book *The Test of Our Times*, Ridge noted Mike Brown's characterization of the FEMA-DHS "clash of cultures," writing how Brown admitted that
"his loyalty and his line of communication went directly to the White House,
not to Secretary Chertoff or the department."[32] Ridge further questioned why,
during the coordination of the preparedness and response to Hurricane Katrina,
Deputy Secretary of Homeland Security Michael Jackson rejected appeals to
summon Bob Stephan's Integrated Interagency Management group to DHS
Headquarters.[33] (The NRP had provided for the secretary of homeland security
to activate the IIMG based upon a recommendation from the HSOC director.)
"Had the [New Orleans DHS] regional office been established," wrote Ridge,
"and had the National Response Plan . . . been used in the immediate aftermath
of the hurricane, rather than several days later, I believe the results would have
been different."[34]

# CHAPTER FIVE

# DHS Pre-Katrina:
## Moving Left of the Boom

"Welcome to the capital of the world!"

So began former New York Mayor Rudolph Giuliani in his first-night address to the 2004 Republican National Convention. It was the first time Republicans had ever decided to hold their convention in the city. A stridently partisan Giuliani told delegates crowding Manhattan's cavernous Madison Square Garden, "Above and beyond everything else, it's a statement, it's a strong statement that New York City and America are open for business, and we are stronger than ever."

In the aftermath of 9/11, Rudy Giuliani personified for Americans a resilient, defiant, and take-charge executive. By comparison to the conservatives in the Bush administration, he was a moderate Republican. Yet campaign strategist Karl Rove recognized the symbolic use of identifying the administration with Giuliani and his city, both to win a second term in the White House and to help sustain the momentum behind the Bush policy of global war on terrorism. Given his own presidential ambitions, it was also Giuliani's opportunity to seize the moment.

Since the mid-eighties, Giuliani had epitomized muscular law enforcement. As a Reagan appointee, he had made his name as the U.S. attorney for the Southern District of New York by using the 1970 Racketeer Influenced and Corrupt Organizations (RICO) statute both to prosecute the "Five Families" constituting the New York Mafia Commission and two high-profile Wall Street white-collar criminals, arbitrageur Ivan Boesky and junk-bond trader Michael Milken. During his time as mayor, Giuliani's tough approach to law enforcement resulted in record declines in the city's crime statistics. In the aftermath of 9/11, his prominent and unifying leadership won him *Time* magazine's Person of the Year for 2001.

Rudy Giuliani was also key to a larger Republican political strategy for 2004. Rove and his politicos saw an opportunity to leverage Giuliani and his identification with 9/11 to build on the power base of the current New York mayor, billionaire publisher Michael Bloomberg, and the conservative New York governor, George Pataki.[1] The object was to establish a Republican beachhead in the neoliberal tri-state, Wall Street–oriented region—as it were, the capital of the world.[2] In the U.S. Senate, the Democrats had a lock— Hillary Clinton and Charles Schumer representing New York; Joe Lieberman and Chris Dodd, Connecticut; and Frank Lautenberg and former Goldman Sachs CEO Jon Corzine, New Jersey. If New York was indeed the capital of the world, the Republicans didn't own it.

In the weeks after 9/11, frequently seen beside Giuliani at Ground Zero was his police commissioner, Bernard Bailey Kerik. At one time Giuliani's police chauffeur, Kerik ascended comet-like through the city's drug enforcement, police intelligence, and corrections organizations, and finally to commissioner in 2000. When Giuliani left office at the end of 2001 and formed Giuliani Partners with a number of senior officials from his administration, Kerik came with him. In 2003, Kerik, who had provided security services to the Saudi royals in the early eighties, would find himself in Baghdad helping the Coalition Provisional Authority reconstitute the Iraqi Ministry of Interior. Given a five-minute slot at the 2004 convention to make a Bush endorsement speech, Bernie Kerik identified himself as a Giuliani partner and assumed the role of a national player.

Although Bush miserably failed—and had not been expected—to carry New York in the 2004 elections, Giuliani's man got the appointment in December to succeed Tom Ridge to be the second secretary of homeland security. Unfortunately for Kerik, Giuliani, and the administration, it was not to be. Within a week of the nomination announcement, Kerik withdrew his name, ostensibly because he had unknowingly hired an undocumented immigrant as a nanny. Later allegations came to light on various ethics violations, ties to organized crime, and sexual harassment. Eventually, Kerik would go to prison in 2010 for tax fraud and making false statements to government officials during the 2004 vetting process.

The Kerik episode was a major embarrassment for the administration and Giuliani alike, and drove a wedge between the two Republican camps. Still, Rove was bound to Giuliani and a believer in his long-term New York strategy for the party—and the former mayor's potential as a presidential candidate for 2008. The administration likewise remained wedded to the on-the-offense brand of homeland security that Giuliani and Kerik represented—aggressive investigations, relentless prosecutions, and the primacy of law enforcement. In January 2005, it thus chose another, this time from across the Hudson River. Hailing from Elizabeth, New Jersey, the pick was prosecutor and jurist Michael Chertoff.

The son of a prominent rabbi, Chertoff had an equally remarkable mother. Press accounts characterized her as the Israeli airline El Al's first flight attendant. Notably, she participated in El Al's contribution, along with British and American transports, to the epic 1949–50 Operation Magic Carpet airlift that ferried some 47,000 Yemenite and 3,000 Habbanim Jews from Aden to Israel. Kerik had been a rough-hewn Russian- and Irish-American from Newark, whereas Chertoff, as a member of a distinguished family of Talmudic scholars, was nothing short of brilliant.

Honors came early. A graduate of both Harvard College and Harvard Law School, Chertoff capped his academic career as an editor of the prestigious *Harvard Law Review*. His legal career began when he clerked for Judge Murray Gurfein on the bench of the U.S. Second Circuit Court of Appeals in New York and later for Supreme Court Justice William J. Brennan, a Democrat appointed by Eisenhower. During the years of the first Reagan administration, he was a litigator in the Washington office of the Los Angeles Republican law firm Latham and Watkins. When Rudy Giuliani was an associate U.S. attorney, he hired Chertoff as an assistant attorney during the Mafia Commission trial and set him loose as his prosecutor. Later, Giuliani made him an assistant U.S. attorney in Manhattan. In 1987, Chertoff crossed the river to serve as a special assistant to the U.S. attorney in New Jersey. Three years later, the George H. W. Bush administration appointed him U.S. attorney for the District of New Jersey where he continued to prosecute organized crime. In 1993, Chertoff played a major role assisting the FBI and authorities in New York in their investigations into the terrorist networks behind the first World Trade Center bombing.

At the behest of New York Republican conservative Alfonse D'Amato, Chuck Schumer's predecessor, he returned to Washington in 1994 to serve as Republican special counsel for the Senate Whitewater Committee. D'Amato's Senate panel was investigating criminal allegations of real estate and bank

fraud against Bill and Hillary Clinton while the president was Arkansas governor. Much of the committee report reflected Chertoff's work and focused on
the first lady's role in the alleged fraud and conspiracy. Liberal Democrats like
Schumer, who may have been close to Giuliani but was no friend of D'Amato,
represented Chertoff as a Republican partisan for his role in Whitewater.
Chertoff's investigative zeal incurred Hillary Clinton's abiding enmity. In 1996,
he returned to Latham as a partner to head its national white-collar enforcement and internal investigations practice in New York. Subsequently, he
founded Latham's Newark office.

When the George W. Bush administration arrived in Washington,
Attorney General John Ashcroft picked Chertoff as a D'Amato man to head his
criminal division. Immediately following 9/11, Chertoff helped put in place,
with the FBI, a far-reaching dragnet designed to disrupt and prevent any further attacks from Islamic jihadists. Working closely with the Bureau and other
agencies, he crafted the nation's legal response to 9/11 and was directly engaged
in writing sections of the Uniting and Strengthening America by Providing
Appropriate Tools Required to Intercept and Obstruct Terrorism Act of 2001,
known more familiarly as the USA Patriot Act, that gave law enforcement
expanded surveillance powers. Chertoff increased FBI authority to conduct
domestic surveillance and use "material witness" warrants to detain persons of
Middle Eastern descent. As a consequence, the government interviewed thousands of Arab-American men who entered the United States before and after
the 9/11 attacks and aggressively prosecuted Zacarias Moussaoui, the French-
born Moroccan Arab, the so-called twentieth 9/11 hijacker. In his prosecution of the global war on terrorism, Chertoff asserted the government's right
to characterize suspects as "enemy combatants" and hold them indefinitely
without counsel. As the assistant attorney general for the criminal division,
Chertoff proved to be a skillful bureaucratic infighter on behalf of the Justice
Department. Toward the end of his service at Justice, he outmaneuvered DHS
to win FBI jurisdiction over terrorism-financing cases.[3]

In 2003, the administration appointed Chertoff to the bench of the Third
Circuit U.S. Court of Appeals in Philadelphia, whose authority covers New
Jersey, Pennsylvania, and Delaware. At his confirmation hearing before the
Senate Judiciary Committee, his work on the Patriot Act was fodder to
Democrats acutely sensitive to civil liberties issues. In the end, the Senate
approved the nomination with only one nay vote—from Hillary Clinton.

Politically, the Chertoff nomination sent a message to Democrats like Schumer and Clinton who could have capitalized on the Kerik imbroglio. Chertoff was a virtual New Yorker with connections to Giuliani and D'Amato. Despite their partisan differences, Schumer and Giuliani were close. As a Whitewater investigator possessing detailed knowledge of a time and place in her rise to power, Chertoff was not someone Clinton could challenge in 2005. Because he had won three previous Senate confirmations, politicos considered him a safe choice. Proponents hailed him as a federal prosecutor who helped craft the initial strategy for the domestic war on terror. Schumer had a whip hand in the confirmation process as a member of the Senate Judiciary Committee. When he and Chertoff spoke prior to the Senate vote, Schumer asked for assurances that New York would continue to receive its fair share of homeland security grant monies. He said Chertoff was receptive though non-committal.[4] In the end, Schumer endorsed him, "given his law enforcement background and understanding of New York's and America's neglected homeland security needs."[5] As for Hillary Clinton, she cast a yea, making for a unanimous Senate vote for confirmation of the second secretary of the Department of Homeland Security.

When Michael Chertoff succeeded Tom Ridge in mid-February 2005, the DHS culture at the top subtly changed. The one had come as an elected official with executive authority, a governor of a state. The other would enter as a lawyer with a career on the front lines as a criminal investigator and prosecuting attorney. Upon the president's announcement of his appointment, Fox News had quoted a Chertoff colleague, Harry "Skip" Brandon, the FBI's former deputy assistant director of counterintelligence and counterterrorism, as saying the new secretary "would 'absolutely demand' that DHS evolve from a newly formed department into a well-oiled terror-fighting agency."[6]

In his first policy address a month later, Chertoff outlined for a Washington audience at George Washington University what would be his signature risk-based approach to homeland security.

Risk management must guide our decision-making as we examine how we can best organize to prevent, respond, and recover from an attack. . . . Our strategy is, in essence, to manage risk in terms of these three variables—threat, vulnerability, consequence. We seek to prioritize according to these variables, to fashion a series of preventive and protective steps that increase security at multiple levels.[7]

In his 2009 book, *Homeland Security: Assessing the First Five Years*, Chertoff made the cost/benefit case for risk management, writing that reducing vulnerabilities and mitigating consequences are less costly than pouring money into risk reduction after disaster strikes in order to prevent a recurrence.[8] DHS, he wrote, was part of the government's decisive, post-9/11 effort to "remove some of the barriers between intelligence agencies, hunt al Qaeda leaders overseas, and institute measures to prevent or reduce vulnerability to further attacks."[9] Chertoff's risk management approach suggested DHS would shift further into a law enforcement, left-of-the-boom mode.

His embrace of the need to remove intelligence barriers precisely aligned with the thinking behind the 2004–5 Commission on the Intelligence Capabilities of the United States Regarding Weapons of Mass Destruction, established by a Bush executive order. This panel was more familiarly known as the Robb-Silberman Commission, after its co-chairmen, former Virginia Democratic governor and senator Chuck Robb and Laurence Silberman, the senior judge on the U.S. Court of Appeals for the District of Columbia Circuit. Its focus was on the intelligence failures in Iraq with regard to the Intelligence Community's assessment that Saddam Hussein had reconstituted his WMD programs, the justification for U.S. and British intervention. Yet one section of its report, titled "Intelligence at Home: the FBI, Justice, and Homeland Security," was noteworthy with respect to domestic intelligence and the interface with law enforcement. Robb-Silberman recommended making the FBI a full participant in the Intelligence Community.[10] It called for creating a separate National Security Service within the FBI that would include the Bureau's Counterintelligence and Counterterrorism Divisions, as well as its Directorate of Intelligence. "This separate National Security Service within the FBI would have full authority to manage, direct, and control all Headquarters and Field Office resources engaged in counterintelligence, counterterrorism, and foreign intelligence collection, investigations, operations, and analysis, thus ensuring better mechanisms for coordination and cooperation on foreign intelligence collection in the United States."[11]

A second recommendation called for reorienting the Department of Justice to overcome the "famous 'wall' between Intelligence and criminal law [that] still lingers, at least on the organization charts." Continued the report, "On one side is the Office of Intelligence Policy and Review, which handles Foreign Intelligence Surveillance Court orders—those court orders that permit wiretaps and physical searches for national security reasons. On the other side are two separate sections of the Criminal Division (Counterterrorism and Counterespionage)."[12] Robb-Silberman recommended a single office with responsibility for counterterrorism, counterintelligence, and intelligence investigations under the authority of an assistant attorney general (AAG) for national security. In September 2006, Ken Wainstein—a future homeland security advisor who would succeed Fran Townsend—would become the first national security AAG.

Thirdly, the panel proposed to strengthen the Department of Homeland Security's relationship with the Intelligence Community. The report characterized DHS as "the primary repository of information about what passes in and out of the country—a critical participant in safeguarding the United States from nuclear, biological, or chemical attack. Yet, since its inception, Homeland Security has faced immense challenges in collecting information effectively, making it available to analysts and users both inside and outside the Department, and bringing intelligence support to law enforcement and first responders who seek to act on such information."[13] The report specifically cited the legal hindrances on Immigration and Customs Enforcement that still operated under an order inherited from the Treasury Department in the 1980s. Said Robb-Silberman, "The order requires high-level approval for virtually all information sharing and assistance to the Intelligence Community. We think this order should be rescinded, and we believe the DNI [director of national intelligence] should carefully examine how Homeland Security works with the rest of the Intelligence Community."[14]

Not one month into the job, Chertoff announced to Congress that he was conducting a systematic evaluation of operations, policy, and structures to inform a DHS reorganization. What would come to be known as his Second Stage Review (2SR) would re-align organizational structure to support mission. Management was not, however, Chertoff's strong suit. The DHS management job would thus go to his incoming deputy, Michael Jackson. If Chertoff came to DHS representing Justice Department equities, Jackson brought with him those of the Department of Transportation—and more especially the power behind the establishment of the homeland security throne, White House Chief of Staff Andrew Card. Michael Jackson would be the driver of the Second Stage Review.

In July 2005, a week after the 7/7 bomb attacks on the London transportation system by homegrown al Qaeda sympathizers killed fifty-two and injured some seven hundred, Chertoff announced the Second Stage Review. In large measure, the reorganization was an effort to (1) strengthen border security and interior enforcement and (2) reform immigration processes. Jackson, the review's architect, saw his role as the department integrator. Hence, the 2SR recast DHS as a flatter organization whereby operational components would directly report to the secretary—that is, through Jackson. This approach was notable with regard to the former divisions of the Border and Transportation Security Directorate, which the 2SR eliminated. For Chertoff's well-oiled terror-fighting department, Jackson would now be integrating six law enforcement agencies—CBP, ICE, TSA, the Secret Service, the Coast Guard, and U.S. Citizenship and Immigration Services (USCIS).

Jackson's 2SR-structured DHS would now operate in line with the core functions and missions of the operating agencies, two reconfigured offices, and the two new undersecretary-level directorates—Policy and Preparedness—plus some two dozen support divisions. The new Office of Intelligence and Analysis (I&A) headed by an assistant secretary for information analysis, the DHS chief intelligence officer, and the Office of Operations and Coordination (OPS) would focus more on terrorist versus all-hazards threats. Both would report directly to Jackson and Chertoff. I&A succeeded the intelligence piece of the Directorate of Information Analysis and Infrastructure Protection that the 2SR abolished. The infrastructure protection portion became an office in the new Preparedness Directorate. The core of the new Office of Operations Coordination would be the HSOC, which the 2SR transferred from the abolished Directorate of Information Analysis and Infrastructure Protection (IAIP) and renamed the National Operations Center (NOC). Overseen by OPS, the NOC would have an operational and coordination role as essentially the national fusion center with intelligence and law enforcement components, including operations analysts. The National Response Framework, the successor to the National Response Plan, would later define the NOC as "the primary national hub for situational awareness and operations coordination across the Federal Government for incident management."[15] Brig. Gen.

Matthew Broderick, USMC (Ret.), who had been the HSOC and now was the NOC director, would become the first DHS director of operations.

The administration moved quickly in July to appoint attorney Stewart A. Baker to be the first head of the Policy Directorate, serving as an assistant secretary, although the position was and is an undersecretary-equivalent. It was a telling appointment. Following 9/11, Baker served as general counsel to the Robb-Silberman Commission and headed the team that drafted the report.

Baker was a Virginian, a lawyer with an intelligence background, having served in the George H. W. Bush administration as the National Security Agency's general counsel. Once described by the *Washington Post* as "one of the most techno-literate lawyers around," Baker had a legal mind and was thoroughly expert in technology and security issues. He started his career in the 1970s clerking for Republican- and Democratic-appointed judges, one of whom was Shirley Hufstedler who, as Jimmy Carter's education secretary, brought him to Washington in 1979 to serve as her deputy general counsel and special assistant. In 1981, Baker joined the Washington law firm Steptoe & Johnson. Originally a West Virginia firm dating from the state's turn-of-the-century oil and gas boom, it became a major Washington player in the late forties thanks to partner Louis A. Johnson. A founder of the American Legion and Roosevelt's prewar deputy secretary of war, Johnson opened the Washington office in 1945. A Truman loyalist, Johnson relieved the embattled James Forrestal to become the nation's second secretary of defense.[16] By the time, Baker joined the firm, it was prominent in regulatory, tax, and international trade law. When Baker returned as a partner in the 1990s, he helped launch Steptoe & Johnson's privacy, national security, computer security, electronic surveillance, and encryption practices. His additional focus was on the Committee of Foreign Investment in the United States (CFIUS).

The Robb-Silberman report was released in May. Two months later, Stewart Baker was on the job at DHS. Reflecting the report's desire to revisit the "wall" between intelligence and law enforcement, he had become one among those after 9/11 who advocated dismantling that wall. Baker fully embraced the idea that—like DoD—DHS should be an operational department serving an operational culture.

In law enforcement, a new operational approach called intelligence-led policing (ILP) was gaining currency, a concept whose origins were in the United Kingdom at the county level with the Kent Constabulary's policing model.[17]

ILP had taken root in the United States following the Justice Department Office of Justice Programs' October 2003 release of the National Criminal Intelligence Sharing Plan that recommended the adoption of minimum standards for ILP. Law enforcement's operational adoption of ILP processes meant "shifting from emphasizing post-event evidence collection to constantly gathering all relevant data and ensuring it is provided for entry into appropriate databases, as well as drawing from the intelligence analysts and relevant databases all the information that is needed to support ongoing operations."[18] In other words, law enforcement would be refocusing from an operational emphasis on evidence collection for prosecution in courts to intelligence collection supporting a range of counterterrorism activities—left-of-the-boom.

At the DHS policy level, Baker sought to remove intelligence sharing barriers between the IC and law enforcement with two major DHS initiatives to enhance border and transportation security—Chertoff priorities. Baker's technically informed view was that TSA, for example, needed to move from a weapons-focused air-security system to one that facilitated identifying potential terrorists—that is, taking the ILP approach. Baker wanted to use travel data and secure identification to shift to a more efficient, more flexible screening system. His views were thus completely in line with Chertoff, whose threefold emphasis was on information, biometrics, and secure documentation for travel.[19]

Baker was an advocate for better use of modern technology for tracking terrorists, including the use of electronic surveillance and better coordination with law enforcement officials. A supporter of DHS consolidation, he viewed it as serving his focus area, which was at the interface between intelligence and law enforcement and terrorist screening for border and transportation security. Prior to DHS, border enforcement had been scattered among Justice with its immigration authorities, Treasury with Customs, and Transportation with the Coast Guard. In each case, the agencies were then oriented to cultures focused on missions other than security—for example, prosecutions, revenue, and maritime safety, respectively. Once consolidated into DHS, these agencies could take full responsibility for border security in the global war on terrorism.

Baker's first initiative had an international dimension: a terrorist screening program called the Automated Targeting System (ATS). It led to his negotiating agreements between DHS and European governments over aligning European privacy laws with the U.S. legal requirement that airlines provide reservation data about American-bound passengers to the U.S. government's passenger name records (PNRs). Following the controversial 2007 PNR agreement with the European Union, the Bush administration proposed to exempt the ATS from the requirements of the 1974 Privacy Act for access to records and for an accounting of disclosures.[20]

His second initiative had a domestic focus and was the controversial REAL ID program. The 2004 Intelligence Reform and Terrorism Prevention Act established a committee of interested parties to study how to make state identification (ID) cards and licenses more secure. The belief was that the federal government needed to set standards for the issuance of birth certificates and other sources of identification, most especially driver's licenses. Congress responded with the REAL ID Act of 2005 that required the federal government to set standards for the identifications it accepts. REAL ID established security, authentication, and issuance procedures and standards for state driver's licenses and ID cards, as well as for various immigration issues related to terrorism. It also imposed a May 2008 deadline on the states for statutory compliance. Many states ignored and continue to ignore REAL ID compliance. A number have passed resolutions or legislation opposing its implementation. In March 2011, Homeland Security Secretary Janet Napolitano extended the deadline to January 2013. REAL ID thus remains a core intergovernmental issue, raising questions of its constitutionality, the principle of federalism, states' rights, and the applicability of the Tenth Amendment.[21]

Announcing the 2SR findings, Chertoff emphasized the DHS imperative to "increase preparedness with particular focus on catastrophic events." Restating his risk-based approach, he spoke of basing preparedness on "objective measures of risk and performance." DHS would apply the *National Preparedness Goal* and this risk-based planning approach to inform all preparedness grant allocations—particularly those addressing infrastructure protection.

Chertoff had a particular kind of catastrophic event in mind. Recall that the National Preparedness Goal incorporated fifteen National Planning Scenarios, the first of which was the scenario for a nuclear detonation of a 10-kiloton improvised nuclear device. Chertoff thus announced the establishment of the Domestic Nuclear Detection Office (DNDO) as an element of his 2SR preparedness imperative. DNDO would support development, acquisition, and deployment of a detection architecture that included sensor systems, port security systems, training, and intelligence sharing. This office would report directly to Chertoff—that is, independent of the DHS research and development entity, the S&T Directorate. For the most part, DNDO would pursue a portal strategy supporting the DHS protection mission. The linchpins were two billion-dollar development and deployment programs for detection and identification of nuclear materials at U.S. ports of entry. One was for an X-ray system called the Cargo Advanced Automated Radiography System (CAARS). The other was the Advanced Spectroscopic Portal (ASP) monitor program.

As for the linkage between preparedness and response, the 2SR abolished the DHS Emergency Preparedness and Response Directorate and replaced it with a Preparedness Directorate. FEMA—the response and recovery agency that had comprised the eliminated directorate and whose administrator had been the DHS undersecretary for preparedness and response—did not go into this new directorate, however. Instead, it became a stand-alone DHS agency. Like DHS' six law enforcement agencies, FEMA now reported directly to Chertoff and Jackson. The 2SR thus focused FEMA exclusively on its core missions, disaster response and recovery, and stripped the agency of its remaining preparedness functions. This 2SR restructuring generated a heated debate soon to be fueled by the uproar over the perceived failed response to Hurricane Katrina.

Chertoff's intent was to strengthen FEMA as an operational agency, a worthy goal, except that in the minds of many in the emergency management community FEMA needed preparedness functions to do that. This decision to separate preparedness and response met widespread resistance from the state and local emergency management communities, notably the National Emergency Management Association (NEMA), and their allies in Congress. FEMA morale plunged, as yet more senior-level emergency managers left the agency.

In Chertoff's view, FEMA's preoccupation with disaster response had resulted in a recent lack of agency capability for long-term catastrophic planning. Other than when it had done continuity planning during the Reagan era, planning generally had not been a FEMA strong suit—hence, the case for transferring FEMA's planning unit to the DHS Preparedness Directorate. The new directorate now had all DHS preparedness functions, notably grants and training that included authority for preparedness exercises for states and localities. The 2SR architect, Michael Jackson, opted to consolidate grants at the DHS Preparedness Directorate level to facilitate what he called subject matter owners and their relationships with their constituencies. Jackson was correct in that FEMA was not the only preparedness grant provider in DHS. While FEMA had the preparedness grants to support training for emergency managers, Coast Guard preparedness grants funded port security programs, while TSA grants went to subways, intercity rail, and transportation security generally.

In addition to grants and training, the 2SR transferred to the Preparedness Directorate the infrastructure protection half of the abolished IAIP Directorate—that is, the components of the Office of State and Local Government Coordination and Preparedness and the U.S. Fire Administration. The new directorate also oversaw the Office of Cyber Security and Telecommunications, which included the National Communications System and the National Cyber Security Division, the newly created chief medical officer position, the Office of National Capital Region Coordination, and the Center for Faith-Based and Community Initiatives.

Chertoff and Jackson's thinking behind the 2SR reorganization in part was informed by exchanges with state homeland security advisors and emergency management directors during the spring and summer of 2005. Frequently these meetings took place under the auspices of the National Homeland Security Consortium, a forum of a score of stakeholder professional associations administered by the National Emergency Management Association (NEMA) that provides policy input to the federal government. Over time, however, the 2SR messaging began to take an unfortunate turn from consensus-building. At an early-June DHS-organized meeting with state homeland security advisors in Annapolis, Maryland, it was apparent that these exchanges had become occasions for Chertoff to put forth the case for his 2SR changes. In one such meeting with homeland security advisors that took place in a downtown Washington hotel, Michael Jackson candidly conveyed his personal view from the podium that they were "at war" with the emergency management directors. Observed one homeland security advisor who was present: "He didn't seem to realize that in some states they were the same officials— dual-hatted." Moreover, throughout this 2SR socialization process, Chertoff did not seek nor was able to obtain wide-spread congressional support prior to implementation. The climax of this campaign occurred on August 22–23, just prior to Hurricane Katrina. For two days, Chertoff and his senior DHS staff hosted a national conference in Washington, DC, with all the state homeland security advisors and emergency management directors to roll out the 2SR reorganization to convey the rationale behind the 2SR. Recalled the same homeland security advisor who was also present at this meeting, "The conversation was a tad bit contentious."

Present for that conversation was George Foresman, Virginia's assistant to the governor for commonwealth preparedness, who was already slated to have responsibility for all these preparedness activities as DHS' first and only undersecretary for preparedness. The Foresman appointment wasn't announced until October, just over a month after Hurricane Katrina. A graduate of the Virginia Military Institute, Foresman was the youngest of four brothers who were VMI grads. His father had also been a distinguished VMI man who had served in the seventies as a special assistant to the superintendent. Early in his professional career, Foresman had been a volunteer firefighter. His notable expertise was in hazmat operations that early-on provided him hands-on experience with the Incident Command System, elemental to the emergency management and homeland security profession. As a state government official, he had served as the commonwealth preparedness assistant to Republican and Democratic governors, and was Republican Governor Jim Gilmore's executive director and ultimately vice chairman of the Gilmore Commission.

Foresman brought his ICS sensibility to his DHS post, and he sought to lead his directorate using a board-of-directors approach for preparedness activities. He would draw his unified command, as it were, from all seven of his lieutenants: the DHS chief medical officer, the assistant secretaries for cyber security and telecommunications and for infrastructure protection, the fire administrator, the directors of the offices of state and local government coordination and of National Capitol Region coordination, and finally the assistant secretary of grants and training. He was among many homeland security professionals who felt that planning was not just a FEMA function. Foresman recognized that while FEMA did planning in many areas—for example, in the Chemical Stockpile Emergency Preparedness Program (CSEPP) and Radiological Emergency Preparedness Program (REPP)—it had no common framework or doctrine. While the agency had the ostensible responsibility for facilitating federal interagency planning, it had no capability to do it. His and Chertoff's goal for the Preparedness Directorate was to ensure that DHS had a common focal point for operational- and tactical-level planning. An undersecretary-level function, planning throughout DHS supported training and exercises and had to integrate with planning under way across other departments and agencies as well as with state, local, tribal, territorial, and private-sector and NGO efforts.

With millions of dollars in grants at stake, the preparedness rubber hit the road in the DHS Office of State and Local Government Coordination and Preparedness, renamed by the 2SR the Office of Grants and Training. In July, the administration announced its intent to appoint Tracy Henke, another Justice Department official, to relieve the acting director, Matt Mayer, who had been covering for Suzanne Mencer after her January resignation and was then responsible for the rollout of the Interim National Preparedness Goal. Mayer would continue in the position until January 2006 when Henke assumed her post as assistant secretary for grants and training, a position that now required the advice and consent of the Senate.

Henke was a rising Republican official from Missouri, Attorney General John Ashcroft's state. Prior to DOJ, she had been a senior policy advisor for the Republican senator from Missouri, Kit Bond, having previously served on the staff of his Republican predecessor, John Danforth. At Justice, Henke had been principal and later acting deputy attorney general for the Office of Justice Programs. Her immediate boss was Deborah Daniels, the sister of OMB director Mitch Daniels. Chertoff announced her appointment on the same day in January 2006 as his announcement of another political appointment to head ICE: Julie Myers.[22] Henke and Myers were both recess appointments. As such, Democrats and some Republicans charged that it was a move by the administration to avoid a Senate floor fight over these and other confirmations put forth at the same time.

At Foresman and Henke's joint nomination hearing before the Senate Homeland Security and Governmental Affairs Committee, Senator Joe Lieberman, the ranking member, signaled his intent with regard to the effect that the left-of-the-boom priorities in DHS had been having on homeland security funding. "While debate has focused on the funding formula for homeland security grants," he commented, "less attention has been paid to the fact that funding for first responders has been dramatically reduced three years running. That is unacceptable and I hope we can turn it around."[23] Lieberman was looking for ways to restore grant funding across the board. "The admin-istration's FY06 DHS budget proposal," he continued, "would have slashed the key state homeland security grant programs by more than 30 percent. The appropriations bill approved by Congress cuts funds for the State Homeland Security Grant Program by half and the risk-based Urban Areas Security Initiative grants by 14 percent. This is unconscionable—tantamount to dis-arming in the middle of a war."

Like many, Lieberman was skeptical of the relationship between the Preparedness Directorate, with its Office of Grants and Training, and FEMA. Earlier in the day, he had heard testimony from FEMA operational profes-sionals during a hearing on the Katrina response. He said, "It spoke to a cry-ing need for more training" and prompted his "better understanding of the extent of the deprivation, for one, the denial of adequate funding to FEMA personnel for training to prepare them adequately for a Katrina-type disas-ter."[24] Foresman responded with a statement reflecting his own view of pre-paredness and its relationship to planning. "FEMA is but one component of the Nation's preparedness efforts," said the nominee, "albeit a very critical, and if not the most critical component, because of their responsibility for looking in an all-hazards approach. But FEMA, the Coast Guard, HHS, DoD, EPA, a host of Federal agencies, elements internal to the Department and external to the Department, we are going to have to make sure that we do a much stron-ger and better job in terms of our coordination for planning, our coordination on training and exercise activities, and I would just say everybody is going to have to be at the table to make us stronger."[25] In other words, preparedness was more than just about FEMA's right-of-the-boom response mission.

The 2SR preparedness restructuring was supposed to reflect Chertoff's risk-based approach for prioritizing and allocating grants. Yet within months, Henke's office generated a furor with the May announcement of the Urban Area Security Initiative (UASI) grants that resulted in 40 percent cuts to New York and Washington. Democrats and the two cities cried foul, especially in view of the increases that went to cities in her home state of Missouri, Dick Cheney's Wyoming, and Jeb Bush's Florida. Henke supporters countered that additional monies were going to UASIs like Jersey City, Newark, Los Angeles, and Long Beach—not all Republican bastions. Critics, however, persisted in their view that grants inexplicably had gone to Republican states that faced less apparent risk than Democratic metropolitan areas.

At a September press briefing, Chertoff and Foresman announced their objectives for the DHS infrastructure protection grants for fiscal year 2007.[26] Chertoff characterized the grant programs as "very much project oriented, where what we're interested in doing is funding particular projects that advance the kind of performance standards and security measures that add real value in reducing risk. This is not a block grant program; it is not an entitlement program." A reporter inferred a connection between the May uproar and the quadrupling of the 2007 port grant request for New York City, asking, "Is there any kind of cause and effect there?" "New York," Chertoff replied, "is in the highest risk category for infrastructure protection and ports, as it is for the Urban Area Security Initiative—that's true of Los Angeles and Long Beach, as well. What differs year to year are the particular projects that the communities are seeking to fund." Yet for all its vaunted mathematical and analytical objectivity, Chertoff's risk-based approach now seemed politicized.

The contentiousness over the allocation of preparedness grants and whether that allocation should have been determined by the DHS Preparedness Directorate or FEMA had assumed surmounting importance in the wake of Hurricane Katrina, with its perceived failed federal response amid DHS' increasing left-of-the-boom orientation. In mid-September 2005, immediately after this catastrophic disaster, the Senate Homeland Security and Governmental Affairs Committee held the first of almost five months of congressional hearings on the response. DHS had stood up its Preparedness Directorate in November, while these hearings were under way. In December, George Foresman and Tracy Henke had their joint nomination hearing. In his written statement, Lieberman announced how he had asked Chertoff to "hold off on his reorganization of DHS' emergency preparedness and response structure until our Committee completes its investigation into the total lack of preparedness at all levels of government exposed by Hurricane Katrina."[27]

Lieberman was preparing the ground for a homeland security restructuring—denied him in 2002 when Andy Card did his about-face, and the Bush administration pushed its own DHS proposal through Congress. The Section 872 provision of the Homeland Security Act had enabled Chertoff and Jackson three years later to do their own 2SR restructuring without congressional input. This time, Lieberman would ensure that Hurricane Katrina provided Congress with the pivotal event to do the next DHS reorganization by statute: "The disarray surrounding that disaster has shaken the confidence of the American people in their government's ability to protect them, and I am hopeful that our investigation will produce recommendations that would be helpful to DHS' internal management structure. I have told the Secretary that this Committee may write legislative changes after we have thoroughly reviewed the record and are confident we know everything about what went wrong during the most devastating natural disaster in our nation's history."[28]

# CHAPTER SIX

# Right of the Boom:
## PKEMRA, the Backstory

Not yet a year into its first term, the Bush administration was blindsided by 9/11. Its national security leadership was otherwise focused on instituting a new strategic framework with Russia and the pursuit of ballistic missile defense. Hurricane Katrina was a second black swan event that similarly befell the administration before it could fully settle into its second term. Notwithstanding the administration's considerable pre-landfall preparations, for an instant, this catastrophic natural disaster all but paralyzed a White House whose homeland security sense-making was focused almost exclusively on counterterrorism and counterproliferation. The storm's political aftermath upended Michael Chertoff's Second Stage Review to advance homeland security governance better to deal with evolving post–Cold War asymmetric challenges and threats, giving birth to what was called the New FEMA.

Reacting firsthand to Katrina's biblical devastation, officials at all levels of government were in shock. "From the air," Karl Rove recalled, "it looked like the hand of God had wiped off the map the entire fifty-mile Mississippi coastline."[1] Surveying the horizon-to-horizon destruction, Governor Haley Barbour of Mississippi said, "I can only imagine that this is what Hiroshima looked like sixty years ago." Mayor A. J. Holloway of Biloxi compared the scene in his coastal town to the catastrophic disaster that befell South Asia the previous December, stating flatly, "This is our tsunami." At one point on her tour of St. Bernard Parish just east-southeast of New Orleans, Senator Mary Landrieu (D-LA), crossing herself, would utter, "The whole parish is gone."

A hurricane of huge proportions, Katrina savaged all five Gulf states. The catastrophic damage, however, was to the Mississippi coastal cities and communities, Louisiana's coastal parishes, and New Orleans. In the morning of August 29, 2005, the behemoth storm came ashore along the Gulf Coast at high tide with a 10–28-foot surge in places that went inland and up rivers as far as twelve miles.

In New Orleans, the Mississippi River levee system began to fail in the early hours of the morning—before the storm made landfall. In Plaquemines Parish southeast of the city, the surge reached twenty feet above sea level. In Lake Pontchartrain to the north, it was twelve. With an average elevation between one and two feet below sea level, New Orleans on that epic morning was victim to flood waters rising at a rate of a foot every ten minutes. Three days later, 80 percent of the city was underwater, in some neighborhoods to a depth of over ten feet. In the end, the storm surge had breached levees and flood walls or caused them to fail in more than fifty locations, damaging 169 miles of the 350-mile levee system. The storm and surge killed 1,118 and left 135 missing and presumed dead. More than 400,000 citizens fled the city, many never to return. Property damage reached tens of billions of dollars.

Hurricane Katrina, President Bush wrote in his *Decision Points* memoir, "was not a single disaster, but three—a storm that wiped away miles of the Gulf Coast, a flood caused by breaches in the New Orleans levees, and an outbreak of violence and lawlessness in the city."[2] "Katrina," he continued, "was an enormously powerful hurricane that struck a part of the country that lies largely below sea level. Even a flawless response would not have prevented catastrophic damage. . . . Just as Katrina was more than a hurricane, its impact was more than physical destruction. It eroded citizens' trust in their government. It exacerbated divisions in our society and politics. And it cast a cloud over my second term."

Hurricane Katrina was a for-real, most deadly test of the nation's preparedness system. Parsed in intergovernmental terms, the response to Hurricane Katrina was not a single response. It was at least three. The performance of the system in each state reflected both different geographies and levels of state and local preparedness. Comparatively speaking, the system did not fail in Mississippi and Alabama. But in Louisiana, the preparedness and response in New Orleans was undeniably the poster child of intergovernmental failure.

Said the *Los Angeles Times* in an op-ed, "The scenes of devastation and civil unrest in New Orleans have made Katrina and the ensuing floods more reminiscent of Third World disasters than anything we would expect to see on U.S. soil."[3] The failure of the Mississippi River levee system in New Orleans and the consequent flooding represented the first time in history that an engineering failure resulted in the near-destruction of a major American metropolis. Two months after the event, Homeland Security Advisor Fran Townsend offered her initial thoughts as to why the federal government had inadequately prepared. Townsend said that in the couple of days prior to landfall preparedness officials all thought that "we were appropriately positioned and we had the right mechanisms in place. It turned out we were all wrong. We had not adequately anticipated. . . . The thing that changed this was not Katrina, itself. The thing that was the catastrophic event was the failure of the levee."[4]

While Fran Townsend's informed opinion is but one, this hurricane catastrophe with the failure of the levee system as a cascading, second-order effect was an apocalyptic event that struck at the industrial-era heart of America. It recalled 9/11 and the second-order structural failures of the Twin Towers that produced their collapse. Since, we have witnessed equal engineering failures associated with the 2010 BP oil spill and Japan's third-order failure at the Fukushima Daiichi nuclear power plant following the 2011 earthquake and tsunami. Both these recent disasters revealed dire inadequacies in governmental and private-sector preparedness and response. Throughout her history, America has sustained herself in the belief that she is the exceptional expression of Enlightenment and Progressive-era optimism, where American ingenuity can extend all engineering tolerances to build the highest skyscrapers, tap the deepest oil reserves, harness the atom, and put a man on the moon.

Hurricane Katrina was a primal event that shook the ground of America's being and called into question our faith in her institutions built on systemic, industrial-era assumptions like the engineer-president Herbert Hoover's associationalism.[5] Unlike Pearl Harbor or 9/11, Hurricane Katrina was brought to our shores not by our enemies, but by Mother Nature. As for lessons learned from the human aspects to the catastrophe, we were left to assess not the savagery or cunning of others—only the failings of ourselves. It was human nature—and politics—that tempted most of us to expect all lessons learned studies to assign blame.

With respect to New Orleans in particular, Hurricane Katrina laid bare a dark worry, thought by many to have died with Cold War fears of global thermonuclear war: the prospect of America losing the continuity of her government, the continuity of her operations, or as is now preferred, her enduring constitutional government. In New Orleans, neither the local, state, or federal government could provide essential services for a dependent, urban, post-industrial population, marginally self-reliant. At the most basic level, the existing interagency and intergovernmental preparedness system was unable to overcome geography or its own bureaucracies to help this population in a fully coordinated manner—either to evacuate them or to provide them logistical support, notwithstanding innumerable heroic efforts by units and individuals. An uncomfortable and unfamiliar sense was felt all the way to the presidency. Noting the desperate thousands begging for water, stranded on overpasses and standing on rooftops holding signs saying "Help me," George Bush was one among millions of distressed and empathetic Americans who expressed in bewilderment, "I can't believe this is happening in the United States of America."[6]

On the morning of August 27, two days before Katrina's landfall on the Gulf Coast, FEMA's national headquarters and its Region IV and Region VI headquarters in Atlanta and Denton, Texas, went on full alert. The agency activated all emergency support functions under the National Response Plan and began pre-staging supplies, assigning the military's Northern Command (NorthCom) to provide Naval Air Station Meridian in Mississippi as the operational staging base. FEMA, Coast Guard, DoD, and other federal assets began converging to or redeploying in FEMA's two Gulf Coast regions whose demarcation is the Louisiana-Mississippi border. In Louisiana, FEMA's national emergency response team leader, William Lokey, deployed to Baton Rouge, the state capital, to liaise with the state as its federal coordinating officer. The Coast Guard prepositioned assets for airborne search and rescue.[7] Later in the day, Bush announced an emergency declaration for Louisiana. The following day, he did the same for Mississippi and Alabama. That evening, the night before landfall, FEMA director Mike Brown deployed to the field, opting to join Lokey in Baton Rouge.

On Tuesday August 30, the day after landfall, the extraordinary magnitude of the storm's destruction was apparent—as was its effect on intergovernmental situational awareness and incident management and the ability of state and local governments to provide each other with mutual aid. As the principal federal official for management of domestic incidents under HSPD-5, Secretary Chertoff declared Hurricane Katrina to be an incident of national significance. In so doing, he appointed Brown to serve as the PFO to coordinate the federal response and provide him with situational awareness for all states affected by the storm.

In previous disasters, Brown had performed well for the administration, notably the previous year in support of Florida Governor Jeb Bush during four serious, back-to-back hurricanes.[8] Comfortable with his appointment of his gubernatorial chief of staff, Joe Allbaugh, as FEMA director, President Bush had accepted Allbaugh's recommendation that Brown succeed him. Brown's modus operandi in past disasters had been to work through White House Director of Operations Joe Hagin and Chief of Staff Andy Card, with apparent success. As a former Ohio firefighter, Hagin was not solely a political operative: he was the founder of the Miami Valley's Ohio Task Force 1, the state's urban search and rescue team that became one of the twenty-eight task forces in FEMA's national urban search and rescue system. As for Card, his understanding derived from his experience as secretary of transportation in 1992, when George H. W. Bush had sent him to Florida to provide on-scene oversight of the federal support to Democratic governor Lawton Chiles during the Hurricane Andrew recovery. Card was especially aware of the importance of getting the response right in a presidential election year. The perceived slackness of the federal response to Andrew was deemed by many to have been a factor in the rout of Bush 41 several months later in the 1992 presidential election.

Having managed a number of natural disasters as Texas governor, George W. Bush grasped the issues associated with preparedness and response. He was directly experienced with the state management of the intergovernmental interfaces with the federal government and local jurisdictions. Intergovernmental liaison was working in Mississippi and Alabama, where Governors Hailey Barbour and Bob Riley were respectively communicating to his administration that the level of federal support was enabling their states to manage the response. Yet communications with Louisiana, most especially with and within New Orleans, were confused. Reports on the ground were contradictory. The media were not always making the situational awareness any clearer. Most egregious were the "dodge the bullet" reports that worked against the urgency of evacuations.[9] They were followed by the panic reports of the breakdown of law and order—for example, in the Superdome, the city's shelter of last resort.

On Wednesday August 31, NorthCom activated Joint Task Force (JTF) Katrina at Camp Shelby, Mississippi. In charge was a Louisiana native and self-described African-American Creole, Lt. Gen. Russel Honoré, the commanding general of the First Army garrisoned at Fort Gillem, Georgia. With him were some three thousand active-duty personnel to assist evacuations, provide logistics support, and potentially be available for public safety and security.

The same morning, Governor Kathleen Blanco of Louisiana called the White House, telling Fran Townsend to "send everything you've got!" Later in the day, she asked the president for 40,000 troops, saying that her biggest concern was public safety.[10] The pleas were reminiscent of Miami-Dade's emergency manager, Kate Hale, during the 1992 Andrew response. Faced with opposition within the administration from Defense Secretary Donald Rumsfeld to any such effort, Andy Card and his White House legal team proposed federalizing the response for Louisiana that would have included federalizing the Louisiana National Guard. Opposed to yielding her authority to the federal government, Blanco nixed the idea. Said Bush in his memoir, "That left me in a tough position. If I invoked the Insurrection Act against her wishes, the world would see a male Republican president usurping the authority of a female governor by declaring an insurrection in a largely African-American city. That would arouse controversy anywhere. To do so in the Deep South, where there had been centuries of states' rights tension, could unleash holy hell."[11]

Once his ship had moored on Sunday September 4 in downtown New Orleans to serve as a primary hub for airborne search and rescue, Lieutenant General Honoré broke his flag as the JTF Katrina commander on board the Navy's amphibious ship *Iwo Jima*. By this time, Honoré was in command of over 14,000 active-duty personnel. The following day, Secretary Chertoff assigned Vice Adm. Thad Allen, the Coast Guard chief of staff, to serve as Brown's deputy PFO. His responsibilities would be to lead federal recovery efforts and support Lieutenant General Honoré in search and rescue operations. On Wednesday, Allen stood up his PFO-Forward Headquarters on *Iwo Jima*.

One of the youngest officers ever to make admiral, Allen was the son of a Coast Guard chief petty officer. Chief of staff since 2002, Allen had been transforming the service's previous missions of drug and migrant interdiction to those of terrorism and border protection. He was also very savvy on how the Coast Guard fit into DHS and the interagency realm, serving as the Coast Guard representative on the DHS Joint Requirements Council, at one time rotating to chair this departmental acquisition review body. The commander of the Coast Guard Atlantic Area during 9/11, he had been in charge of the maritime response that involved a mobilization for port closures and patrols of territorial waters.

The take-charge demeanors of Honoré and Allen and the can-do performances of JTF Katrina and the Coast Guard were in stark contrast to the mounting perception in the media and Washington that FEMA's Mike Brown was not up to the task and reflected poorly on his agency. In any case, a frustrated Brown was readying himself to resign. In *Decision Points*, Bush wrote that Chertoff had finally lost confidence in Brown and that state and local officials were complaining about FEMA's slow response. Chertoff had felt that Brown "had frozen under the pressure and become insubordinate."[12] On Friday September 9, Chertoff, at the urging of the president, finally recalled Brown to Washington and appointed Allen to relieve him as PFO of the Katrina response.

Over the weekend, the administration began vetting Brown's replacement at FEMA. The choice was Dave Paulison, a bona fide and experienced emergency management professional who since 9/11 had been the head of the U.S. Fire Administration and FEMA's director of preparedness. A career firefighter from Florida, Paulison was a hands-on official with thirty years of operational experience. In 1992, he became Miami-Dade County's fire chief and four years later served a year as the president of the International Association of Fire Chiefs. The beneficiary of executive-level training, Paulison completed the program for senior executives in state and local government at Harvard's John F. Kennedy School of Government. Most significantly, although a Democrat, he had a professional association with Andy Card, dating from Hurricane Andrew when, as a freshly minted fire chief, Governor Chiles had made him responsible for the hurricane clean-up.

On Monday September 12, Bush and Chertoff accepted Brown's resignation and appointed Paulison acting director of FEMA and acting undersecretary for emergency preparedness and response. The appointment, however, did nothing to stop the partisan carping that swirled with full force around the administration. Four days after landfall, Senators Susan Collins (R-ME) and Joe Lieberman (D-CT) had announced their intent to hold hearings and conduct an oversight investigation into Katrina preparedness and response. Democrats in the House were calling for an independent, bipartisan commission with subpoena powers, comparable to the 9/11 Commission, to investigate response failures. To assert control over events amid what was now a crisis of confidence in the administration, Bush returned to the devastated region for the third time on September 15 to address the nation from New Orleans' Jackson Square. Taking responsibility for the failures, he said he was ordering every cabinet secretary to participate in a comprehensive review of the federal response. The president pledged, "This government will learn the lessons of Hurricane Katrina."

Determined to fix the problem, Bush and Card put their full weight behind what would become known as the White House lessons learned report. The next day, Card sent a memo to each cabinet agency to designate a senior point of contact for the study. On Monday, September 19, Bush chaired an HSC meeting to convey his resolve that the effort was to be a thorough and comprehensive review.

His pick to lead this effort was Fran Townsend. As per HSPD-5, Townsend was responsible for interagency policy coordination on domestic incident management and thus the obvious choice for this role. Earlier in the year, she had similarly led the White House review of the recommendations of the Robb-Silberman Commission on intelligence capabilities. This previous effort was more in her day-to-day swim lane and drew both on her experience at Justice in the nineties when she was head of the Office of Intelligence Policy and Review and her ongoing work for the NSC as Rice's deputy for combating terrorism. Like Chertoff and the primary focus of DHS to this point, Townsend had been concentrating on counterterrorism and counterproliferation. She also had an added expertise in terrorist financing, which, as with the rest of her portfolio, meant she was the White House's top-level counterterrorism liaison with allied governments and intelligence agencies, particularly the Saudis. In 2004, she had been active supporting one U.S. effort to dismantle the A. Q. Khan network and another to force Libya to abandon its nuclear program—both successful. Announcing the findings of her Robb-Silberman review in June, she iterated the president and vice president's commitment to her professional focus. Said Townsend, both men "have repeatedly told the American people that our greatest terrorism threat is a weapon of mass destruction in the hands of a terrorist in an American city."[13] The priority the administration had placed on these briefs in Townsend's portfolio was evident in the midst of the Katrina response. The same day Chertoff relieved Brown and appointed Vice Admiral Allen as PFO, Bush sent Townsend overseas on a previously scheduled five-day trip that included consultations with the heads of the Moroccan and Afghani intelligence services and the new Saudi king, Abdullah bin Abdulaziz, who had risen to the throne in early August. Bush was adamant that the trip go forward as planned to send a signal to terrorist networks that the hurricane response was not distracting the United States from its global war on terrorism.

Nevertheless, Bush was giving Townsend full authority to oversee the lessons learned review. An energetic and thoroughgoing professional who was a quick study, Townsend launched the review process a week later, chairing a meeting with the principals and getting them to assign the senior department and agency points of contact (POCs) to her team.[14] The administration still had a response and short-term recovery to run, and her HSC staff still had its job doing policy coordination. Townsend also requested full-time detailees from the departments and agencies who were experienced professionals. By mid-October, she had her initial staff of twelve who spoke not for academic theories or political equities but rather for operational imperatives. Given that DoD had "the most lessons learned expertise and experience in the federal government," said Townsend, the department provided one civilian and three active-duty detailees.[15] Three came from DHS, one Coast Guard and two civilians. Justice sent two, one of whom was FBI. HHS detailed one public health service officer, and the Department of Transportation, one. Townsend had "primacy over the process." In terms of "taking tasking," Townsend said these officials did not work for their home agency, "They're working for me."[16]

The twelfth staffer whom she would task to run the study day-to-day would be one of her own. Townsend wanted someone versed not only in response but, given the magnitude of the disaster, the interface with the military. Those criteria eliminated her deputy, Ken Rapuano, who had been the White House POC when Katrina came ashore and was in charge of HSC coordination while she was on travel overseas going into week three of the response. Rapuano was a counterterrorism and counterproliferation professional.[17] Townsend's choice, therefore, was Joel Bagnal. A South Carolinian and second-generation West Pointer, Bagnal was a military man who had long embraced the import of the homeland security mission. The son of Lt. Gen. Charles Bagnal, onetime commanding general of the 101st Airborne Division (Air Assault), he was an infantry officer who had risen to command and staff positions. During the 1998–99 Kosovo Air Campaign, Bagnal served in Tuzla, Bosnia-Herzegovina, as the chief of operations for Multinational Division

North and Task Force Eagle. But it was in 1999 when he cut his teeth on domestic WMD consequence management as a domestic preparedness officer training first responders under the Army's Nunn-Lugar-Domenici program.

A year later, Bagnal was in the Pentagon as senior advisor to the Army's deputy chief of staff for programs. After 9/11, he served as a special assistant to the director of OSD's Homeland Security Task Force with the responsibility for coordinating responses to terrorist threats and incidents. Bagnal was among those DoD personnel assigned in the weeks thereafter to Tom Ridge's White House staff in the Office of Homeland Security. He went as the special assistant to the president and senior director for domestic counterterrorism and as director of incident management and threat countermeasures. In 2003, he helped develop the *National Strategy for Homeland Security* and the HSPD-5 policy for domestic incident management. From mid-2004 to the spring of 2005, Bagnal was on temporary duty (TDY) in a NorthCom planning cell as a special assistant to the commander, Gen. Ralph Eberhart, USAF, and his successor, Adm. Tim Keating. When he returned to the HSC staff, Townsend made him her executive secretary.

Townsend's lead writer would be Michele Malvesti, since 2002, the NSC's senior director for combating terrorism strategy. An intelligence analyst from North Carolina, Malvesti had been the principal author of the 2006 *National Strategy for Combating Terrorism*. She had come from the Defense Intelligence Agency (DIA) where she had been since 1994, first working as a program manager in the Office for Special Technical Operations and later as a specialist on Middle East terrorism in the agency's Office of Counterterrorism Analysis. Prior to DIA, she had gone straight from university to begin her career at Fort Bragg's Joint Special Operations Command.

Congress was already moving ahead with investigations and calls for an independent commission like that for 9/11. With lawmakers positioning to reconfigure FEMA and DHS by legislation, Townsend had two tactical priorities. The first was to arrive at a plan to fix what was wrong with FEMA. The second was to see that the review's recommendations got implemented—meaning she needed smart, energetic, subject-matter experts who knew how to work with Capitol Hill. She wanted young up-and-comers like herself, whose experience of 9/11 had ignited in them a life commitment to serve.

From FEMA, Townsend grabbed Tom Bossert, who had been deputy director of FEMA's Office of Legislative Affairs since February 2004. As the lead contact for nine congressional committees having primary jurisdiction over the agency, Bossert knew his way around Capitol Hill, a knowledge that would prove useful when it came to implementing review recommendations via statute. During the Katrina response, he was in the field with Brown. When Brown resigned and Paulison replaced him, Bossert assisted as his virtual chief of staff, supporting acting deputy director Patrick Rhode for several weeks until Townsend asked him to come to the White House.

After finishing George Washington University Law School in 2003, Bossert had worked for a year in the Small Business Administration (SBA) where Rhode had been an associate administrator. Bossert's job as counselor to the SBA deputy administrator and special assistant to the general counsel was to advise on and coordinate special projects. His initial Capitol Hill experience came from the late nineties when he worked a couple of years as assistant to the chief counsel for the House Committee on Government Reform and Oversight, a period when the panel was very active in investigating allegations of misconduct in the Clinton administration and the Democratic Party. From there, Bossert went to the Office of the Independent Counsel as an evidence specialist and law clerk where he worked on the Madison Guaranty Savings and Loan investigation and drafted portions of the final reports on the Whitewater, FBI Files, and White House Travel Office investigations.

To deepen the Capitol Hill experience on her bench, Townsend secured Dan Kaniewski and Josh Dozor, two young players who got their starts via Rep. Curt Weldon's (R-PA) Congressional Fire Service Institute (CFSI) network. A committed volunteer firefighter and chief himself, Weldon was the key fire service player on the Hill. In 1987, his first year as congressman, he founded both CFSI and the Congressional Fire and Emergency Service Caucus (which he co-chaired), one of the largest caucuses in Congress. Weldon had developed a strong interest in national security policy. In the mid-nineties, he was the driver of a program of parliamentary exchanges between the United States and Russia and an original supporter of the Nunn-Lugar Cooperative Threat Reduction program. Later, he became known as a strong ballistic missile defense advocate. Foremost in Weldon's mind when he established CFSI was his intent to develop interagency and national security experience in the professional development of the nation's fire service leadership. Kaniewski and Dozor, along with Marko Bourne who advised Townsend's staff during the preparation of the Katrina report and who would become FEMA director of policy and program analysis in 2006, were thus Weldon products, representatives of a new generation of national and homeland security careerists with roots in or an orientation to the fire service.

Kaniewski was an energetic Minnesotan who had been on Townsend's HSC staff since July 2005. He had come to the White House from the George Washington University's Homeland Security Policy Institute (HSPI), which he co-founded in 2002. Still in his twenties, he was HSPI's first deputy director. Kaniewski epitomized this new generation whose commitment to homeland security was galvanized by the experience of 9/11 when he was on Capitol Hill, witness to the smoke rising from the Pentagon in the immediate aftermath of Flight 77's impact.

A nationally registered emergency medical technician-paramedic, Kaniewski worked as a firefighter during his GW college years while he was earning his undergraduate degree in emergency medical services management. On 9/11, he was halfway through his masters in national security studies at GW's Washington rival, Georgetown University. It was his simultaneous work on the Hill that had already wired Kaniewski into homeland security policy-making and the network of policy-makers. His introduction came as a freshman in the nineties when he met the politically connected Bill Webb, who had just become CFSI's executive director in 1995. The director of advance for the secretaries of education and labor in the Bush 41 administration, Webb brought Kaniewski on board as one of his first interns in CFSI's homeland security fellows program. Webb made Kaniewski his CFSI emergency medical services advisor to assist staffs and lawmakers who were beginning to make policy on domestic preparedness. Ultimately, he was able to place him in Weldon's office as a full-time legislative fellow. While conducting research on congressional coordination of domestic preparedness, Kaniewski served as Weldon's representative to the Gilmore Commission. At one point, he would serve as FEMA's congressional liaison for terrorism preparedness and consequence management. Kaniewski's association with CFSI and Webb would prove to be a most important career-builder. One of CFSI's key Bush 43 connections was with Joe Hagin, the former Ohio firefighter whom Webb regarded as invaluable to the fire service during his time as White House director of operations.

Townsend's third congressional liaison was Josh Dozor. A Pennsylvanian from Weldon's Delaware County district, Dozor graduated from Widener

Law School in 2001 and went to work for the lawmaker. The son of a practic-
ing attorney whom Tom Ridge as governor appointed to the bench of the Delaware County Court of Common Pleas, Dozor spent two years post-9/11 as
Weldon's legislative assistant. Through Weldon, he became part of Bill Webb's
CFSI network, leading the lawmaker's efforts to advance fire-service legislation. With the establishment of the House Select Committee on Homeland
Security in early 2003, Weldon got a seat on the panel. Dozor went with him
to become a majority professional staff member. Active on issues of federal-
state relations, Dozor served as a majority counsel for the panel in the two
months prior to coming to the White House to work for Townsend.

Bossert, Kaniewski, and Dozor joined Kirstjen Nielsen, who as the HSC's
senior director for prevention, preparedness, and response, played a key policy development role in the implementation of HSPD-8. Nielsen's congressional experience was on the Senate side working for Rep. Connie Mack (R-FL)
in the nineties, which she later used to stand up and manage TSA's offices of
legislative policy and government affairs. For the agency, she both developed
transportation security–related policy and drafted legislation.

This lessons learned research team of Bossert, Kaniewski, and Dozor all
got the title HSC policy director and would later prove themselves in the outreach and implementation phase of the lessons learned effort. Along with Joel
Bagnal, Kirstjen Nielsen was titled special assistant to the president for homeland security, while Michele Malvesti retained her NSC title, senior director.

To Bossert's mind, he and Nielsen, along with Kaniewski and Dozor who
came as Capitol Hill Republicans, represented a number of political-appointee,
mid-level staff during the administration's first term who were "witnesses
to what worked and what didn't. To its credit, after Katrina, the administration took a big risk and kept many of us and gave us the opportunity and the
authority to put things right."

In its first term—from 9/11 to the establishment of DHS through
Chertoff's Second Stage Review—administration attempts to organize homeland security suffered. The political questions of funding authorities had
distracted policy-makers from fully focusing on the mission and honoring
the maxim "form follows function." On principle, the Bush administration
had been determined to return authorities to the departments and agencies.
By the same token, department and agency detailees to the NSC and HSC
staffs saw themselves as protectors of their parents' equities. When it came

to FEMA, detailees with operational DoD backgrounds to the White House and DHS were often dismissive of the agency, thus reinforcing the left-of-the-boom orientation to DHS and homeland security generally. When it came time to establish a Department of Homeland Security, Andy Card—on behalf of the president—had to wrestle with the competing interests of bureaucratic politics as he shifted 180 degrees to embrace interagency verities previously deemed ideologically verboten.

For Card, it was the political appointees who could "get things done." Especially in the contemporary Washington environment, they instituted new policy by developing "legal instruments,"—that is, language for statutes, executive orders, and presidential directives—a lawyer's job. Joel Kaplan and Brad Berenson, the members of Card's White House legal team who helped put together the administration's 2002 proposal for a department of homeland security, were campaign lawyers with no department or agency experience. Post-Katrina, Bush and Card took a different approach. They empowered Fran Townsend—someone who had acquired the tag "national security lawyer" and who had executive-level DOJ experience—to make it so. In turn, Townsend relied on three legal minds with similar agency or equally valuable Capitol Hill backgrounds: Nielsen with her TSA and congressional experience, Bossert coming from FEMA and the SBA, and Dozor fresh from the Hill. With this legal team, informed by operationally grounded subject matter expertise, Townsend laid the groundwork for what lawmakers would eventually pass as the 2006 Post-Katrina Emergency Management Reform Act (PKEMRA).

## The Townsend Report

Amid the partisan frenzy in Congress and the outcries in the media were incessant calls for heads to roll. At her October 21 press conference on the initial progress of her review, Townsend faced reporters probing whether her team would examine "competent leadership at the top."[18] Responding with what would become an administration mantra, she said that the goal was to "quickly identify and fix problems and not play the blame game." Her intent was to deliver her report in the January/February time frame and then begin the congressional outreach to those on the Hill who would be crafting statutory language during the spring 2006 legislative session. Townsend wanted the structural and process changes to be "comfortably in place and exercised in advance of the next hurricane season."

As she had done in her Robb-Silberman review, she would honor the reporting lines of the national security system's regular policy coordination and development process. The review team would get input from the departments and agencies and in this case travel to the five governors of the affected states for their comments, while welcoming additional advice from any other governors wishing to engage. The final report would not be "a consensus document," she said. "Where there are differences of opinion, policy options will go up to the deputies level, and then the principals and, if necessary, to the president."[19]

Townsend did not presume any need to revise the Stafford or Insurrection Acts. Nor was she building a case for federalizing response. "The Federal government is never going to be the nation's first responder. We shouldn't be, we don't have the capability to be, and we won't be."[20] Her concern, shared by the president as a former governor, was the current legal authorities of the government, particularly those covering the appropriate use of the military. The issue was whether the next worst-case, catastrophic disasters might represent "a narrow band of cases where [the federal government would be] expected to come in fast. . . . It is an issue that will absolutely have to go through a deputies and principals process to better frame options for the President."[21]

Four months later, her review team reported in late February with a list of 125 recommendations that flowed from seventeen high-policy, planning, and operational lessons learned. The Hurricane Katrina preparedness and response, said the study, exposed systemic weaknesses in interagency coordination, planning, and training. The review thus purposed to lay the groundwork for a comprehensive and transformed "National Preparedness System" requiring "adjustments to policy, structure, and mindset" in order to build and integrate operational capability.[22] To effect this transformation, the federal government would need to develop common doctrine for aligning preparedness plans, budgets, grants, training, exercises, and equipment. The framework for this National Preparedness System already existed with the White House 2002 *National Homeland Security Strategy* and HSPD-8, upon which the DHS Interim National Preparedness Goal was basing its establishment of a readiness baseline for capabilities at the federal, state, and local levels.[23]

A useful model for this National Preparedness System, said the report, is the six-decade-old national security system established by the National Security Act of 1947. Operationally organized from the president to the commander in the field, the national security system is "built on deliberate planning that assesses threats and risks, develops policies and strategies to manage them, identifies specific missions and supporting tasks, and matches the forces or capabilities to execute them."[24] The report stressed the importance of the national security system's emphasis of feedback and periodic reassessment. "Programs and forces are assessed for readiness and the degree to which they support their assigned missions and strategies on a continuing basis. Top level decision-makers periodically revisit their assessments of threats and risks, review their strategies and guidance, and revise their missions, plans, and budgets accordingly."[25]

Over the previous five years, said the report, the current system for homeland security—the plans, policies, and guidelines such as the National Response Plan, National Incident Management System, Interim National Infrastructure Protection Plan, and Interim National Preparedness Goal—had not coalesced into an operational framework sufficient to manage the interagency process in homeland security response to twenty-first-century catastrophic threats. Pre-Katrina, the NIMS and NRP framework under which the federal government coordinated resources "[did] not address the conditions of a catastrophic event with large-scale competing needs, insufficient resources, and the absence of functioning local governments."[26] The report continued: "We must transform our approach for catastrophic incidents from one of bureaucratic *coordination* to proactive unified command that creates true unity of effort. As set forth in *NIMS*, 'In a [Unified Command] structure, the individuals designated by their jurisdictional authorities . . . must jointly determine objectives, strategies, plans, and priorities and work together to execute integrated incident operations and maximize the use of assigned resources.'"[27]

With more than just a passing nod to the emergency management community, the report said that the National Preparedness System must emphasize all-hazards preparedness. Most of the capabilities necessary for responding to natural disasters and terrorist incidents are not competing priorities but rather "two elements of the larger homeland security challenge."[28]

In an inspired and somewhat non-linear fashion, the Townsend report was addressing the president's concern over the appropriate use of the military in worst-case disasters by rendering the question moot. If this empowered National Preparedness System transformed those non-military agencies of government with homeland security missions and functions to be more operational, more expeditionary, and more attuned to a planning culture historically associated with the military, then the federal government would not need to default to use of the military in catastrophes when it is "expected to come in fast."

Fundamental, then, is the interagency and intergovernmental embrace of a planning culture further to achieving "the considerable operational capabilities" demonstrated by DoD and the Coast Guard in the Katrina response. Notwithstanding those capabilities, the report characterized the rest of the federal response as "at times slow and ineffective" in dealing with the "massive operational demands of the catastrophe." In a refrain of the findings of the House's *Failure of Initiative* report, the authors said, "Despite reforms that encourage a proactive, anticipatory approach to the management of incidents, the culture of our response community has a fundamental bias towards *reaction* rather than *initiative*. As a result, our national efforts too often emphasize response and clean-up efforts at the expense of potentially more cost-effective anticipatory actions that might prevent or mitigate damage. The need for anticipatory response is a pillar of the National Response Plan."[29]

The authors were making the case for a New FEMA. The pre-Katrina system had been too reactive, biased toward responding to requests for federal resources under the concept of "pull." Post-Katrina, the orientation was going to be toward taking anticipatory actions under a proactive "push" system. In future crises, FEMA was going to "lean forward." Anticipatory actions were going to flow from a deliberative, capabilities-based planning culture that would replace what had been a culture more tactically oriented. "There is a difference between a plan (saying 'this is what we need to do') and a trained, resourced set of defined missions (saying 'this is what we are going to do, and this is how we are going to organize, train, exercise, and equip to do it')."[30]

While the White House review focused purely on the performance of federal response and did not offer recommendations for the state and local levels, it recognized the significant institutional and intergovernmental challenges to "operational cooperation." "Although each State and territory certainly confronts unique challenges, without coordination this planning approach makes the identification of common or national solutions difficult. Furthermore, our current approach to response planning does not sufficiently acknowledge how adjoining communities and regions can and do support each other."[31]

Deliberative intergovernmental planning was failing due to the weakness of DHS/FEMA regional planning and coordination structures.

The solution offered by the study was a throwback to Tom Ridge and Bob Stephan's shelved plan to empower DHS regional and field elements. DHS had removed what planning and coordination capabilities and responsibilities FEMA had and spread them among the department's other offices and bureaus. Instead of moving in the direction that Ridge had intended, DHS transferred personnel, resources, and programs that had been based in FEMA's regional offices (e.g., the state and local liaison program and all grant programs) to DHS headquarters in Washington. Programs operating from regional offices, said the study, develop closer and stronger relationships among all levels of government. "[T]hese relationships are critical when a crisis situation develops, because individuals who have worked and trained together daily will work together more effectively during a crisis."[32]

The White House review thus recommended priority restoration of the DHS regional structures—that is, below the headquarters level in line with what had been the Ridge/Stephan plan:

[T]he integration of State and local strategies and capabilities on a regional basis is a homeland security priority. Homeland security regional offices should be the means to foster State, local, and private-sector integration. Furthermore, DHS regional structures are ideally positioned to pre-identify, organize, train, and exercise future Principal Federal Officials and Joint Field Office staffs. . . . Each DHS regional organization should possess the capacity to establish a self-sufficient, initial JFO on short notice anywhere in its region.[33]

It is important to recognize that the White House lessons learned report did not see regional empowerment as a structural priority in isolation. Neither was the case in its characterization of the National Preparedness System generally. Sustained success would depend on a solid foundation provided by institution of a national system for homeland security professional development. It would start with the growing operational capabilities via NIMS compliance in all federal departments and agencies. "We must require all incident management personnel to have a working knowledge of NIMS and ICS principles."[34]

The report then went much further toward development of an expeditionary culture. Homeland security training and certification programs must ensure that management and response personnel—especially those in the field—are fully trained, educated, and exercised in plans and doctrine *and* experienced in their functions and missions to a high, uniform standard. At all levels of government, the leadership corps must be "prepared to exhibit innovation and take the initiative during extremely trying circumstances."[35] The study said it was imperative that all federal departments and agencies develop operational command and control structures with "battle rosters" of trained personnel that deploy in support of a federal response to a catastrophic event.

Beyond then-current plans and doctrine, the review team wanted a more systematic and institutional program for homeland security professional development and education. The report mooted the idea of a DHS National Homeland Security University (NHSU), analogous to DoD's National Defense University, for senior homeland security personnel as the capstone for homeland security training and education opportunities.

Flowing from this analysis was a lesson learned whose generational impact would be potentially far-reaching and transformative: "The Department of Homeland Security should develop a comprehensive program for the professional development and education of the Nation's homeland security personnel, including Federal, State, and local employees as well as emergency management persons within the private sector, non-governmental organizations, as well as faith-based and community groups. This program should foster a 'joint' Federal Interagency, State, local, and civilian team."[36]

## PKEMRA

On February 15, as the White House was readying to issue its Townsend report later in the month, the House released *A Failure of Initiative*, its take on the Katrina response. The House report enumerated scores of failures without making any formal recommendations. Yet its executive summary yielded one unpresupposing gem of a 30,000-foot-level assessment that points the way to a conception of twenty-first-century network governance: "The preparation and response to Hurricane Katrina show we are still an analog government in a digital age."[37]

The Government Accountability Office (GAO) had already published the first of what would be almost fifty Katrina-related GAO reports and congressional testimonies. In late March, the DHS Office of the Inspector General (OIG) would release its performance review of FEMA's Katrina disaster management activities. OIG summarized the findings, saying that the widespread criticism of FEMA's slow and ineffective response was warranted. Numerous associations, think tanks, and nonprofit organizations would offer their own analyses. In May, Susan Collins and Joe Lieberman would release their Senate report that resulted from twenty-two hearings. Among its findings was the key recommendation to empower FEMA under a new name, the National Preparedness and Response Agency (NPRA), by returning its preparedness functions, including the responsibility for critical infrastructure protection.

The aftermath of Katrina confounded Mike Chertoff's plan for final October 2005 implementation of his Second Stage Review organizational changes for DHS. The political winds were now calling for a dramatic overhaul of FEMA that threatened to spin the 2SR weathervane 180 degrees. As he had with the 2SR, Chertoff assigned his deputy, Michael Jackson, to carry the spear for an internal DHS FEMA review in the hopes that process improvements could preserve his 2SR structures.

Into early 2006, Chertoff was starting to speak of a "forward-leaning FEMA," re-engineered with the introduction of industry processes like just-in-time freight-forwarding delivery systems to improve logistics operations. DHS, FEMA, and DoD were exploring opportunities for joint training and exercises. Recognizing the need to improve FEMA planning, DHS was securing NorthCom planners to work in the FEMA regions. As well, DHS was assigning preparedness officials to the regions further to establishing cells of trained and exercised officials working with state and local counterparts in advance of an incident. In an effort to keep FEMA in DHS, Chertoff was making the case that a re-engineered FEMA would be comparable to the Coast Guard—a highly regarded, high-performance agency with its own culture that is nevertheless in DHS.

The Townsend report was released in late February amid criticism that it was not an independent review. Yet it had its independent advocates. Responding to GAO reports and leaks of a then-forthcoming House report, Craig Fugate, then director of the Florida Division of Emergency Management (FDEM), recalled on national television the futility of the finger-pointing in the aftermath of Hurricane Andrew. "I think in finding out what went wrong last time," said Fugate, "I would be less concerned about identifying which individuals [were responsible] as much as what were the systemic issues that happened."[38]

The review recognized that Congress would be an essential partner for system transformation. In so doing, its authors compared their effort to the 1986 implementation of the Goldwater-Nichols defense reforms via statute. As the White House review team began to engage with Collins and Lieberman over their promised legislation, it became clear that the White House was shunting senior DHS officials out of the loop. The review team's implementation strategy was not to present Congress with a specific White House proposal as was done in 2002 with the Homeland Security Act. Since inevitable legislation was originating in Congress, the plan was to work with lawmakers, likely to be Collins and Lieberman once they began drafting their Senate measure. The two sides would thus amalgamate the findings of both the White House's and Senate's Katrina lessons learned reports. Less obvious to the outside world, the legislation would codify the HSC's foundational homeland security documents, the 2002 national strategy, HSPD-5 and HSPD-8.

Once the review was complete, Townsend handed it to the implementers and she and Rapuano returned to their routine focus, the foreign liaison over such perennial issues as terrorism financing and Iranian support for Hamas and Hezbollah as well as that spring's issue de jour, the Dubai Port World acquisition of Peninsular and Oriental Steam Navigation Company (P&O) and the implications for port security at its port management operations in six U.S. ports.

The key staffer leading implementation for Townsend was Tom Bossert. As the one who compiled the report's 125 recommendations, he oversaw the transformation of that list into action items, those that the executive branch could implement administratively and those that required congressional liaison for a statute. As chairman of the Deputies Committee, which met weekly to track the follow-through on implementation of the recommendations, Bossert was on top of the White House's internal processes. Working with Congress meant staffers going to the Hill for testimony and consultations with professional staff members and lawmakers.

By the end of May, lawmakers had introduced eleven bills addressing FEMA's future in DHS. Eight proposed to establish it as an independent agency. Three were for maintaining it in DHS. Two of these bills had been reported by House committees—one to remove, the other to retain. The bill to retain was introduced by Rep. David Reichert (R-WA) and Rep. Bill Pascrell (D-NJ). Into the summer, this bill was getting traction. The Senate took a sounding on the issue in mid-July, when Collins and Lieberman offered an amendment to the 2007 DHS appropriations act to keep FEMA in DHS. The Senate approved the measure by a vote of 87–11. At the same time, Hillary Clinton offered her amendment to remove FEMA from DHS. The Senate rejected this measure 32–66. Two weeks later, Collins and Lieberman introduced their Senate bill comparable to Reichert-Pascrell that would strengthen the all-hazards approach to preparedness, ensure FEMA development of a professional leadership experienced in crisis management, reunite disaster preparedness and response functions in the agency, and give the agency an autonomy within DHS akin to the Coast Guard's.

The Collins-Lieberman bill provided the specific measure for the White House to engage over the statutory changes for a National Preparedness System transformation. At the same time, developments in Lieberman's home state of Connecticut were affording the administration political leverage. A supporter of the war in Iraq, Lieberman was being challenged in the August 8 Democratic primary by Greenwich cable television entrepreneur Ned Lamont, who ran as an anti-war candidate.[39] The seat itself was considered safe for a Democratic incumbent, but Lieberman lost the primary contest, getting 48 percent of the vote to Lamont's 52. Conceding, Lieberman announced he would run in the November election as an independent. He had primary support from Senator Ken Salazar (D-CO), whose name would appear on the Collins-Lieberman bill as a co-sponsor. In the run-up to the general elections, Lieberman got Republican support from Collins, Rudi Giuliani, Alfonse D'Amato, and others vis-à-vis Lamont, expressed without directly undercutting Alan Schlesinger, a weak GOP candidate facing court action over gambling improprieties.[40] This time, Lieberman and the White House were on the same team, a key factor in the negotiations between White House and congressional staffers as they resolved differences in the language of the final bill.

In late September, the Collins-Lieberman and Reichert-Pascrell bills went into conference as language included in the 2007 DHS appropriations act. On September 29 the House approved the conference report 412–6, and the following day the Senate approved it on a voice vote. President Bush signed it into law on October 4. Title VI of the Act became known as the Post-Katrina Emergency Management Reform Act (PKEMRA). The headline was that FEMA would remain in DHS, empowered by a return of most of the DHS preparedness functions and grant management. Yet taking the long view, the most far-reaching impact would result from the sections on National Preparedness that represented the lessons learned review's codification of the 2002 *National Homeland Security Strategy* and the HSPDs. Authorities, crafted by the administration, were now in statute. What remained was the degree to which FEMA and DHS would implement them. A lot would depend on the team the administration put in place in the new, forward-leaning FEMA.

Townsend and Bagnal's writing, outreach, and implementation team was of a generation that matured and came into government service after—and in some cases well after—the end of the Cold War. They would continue to serve in the Bush administration and in two cases would find themselves in key positions in the Obama administration to provide policy continuity.

In 2006, Joel Bagnal replaced Ken Rapuano as deputy assistant to the president and deputy homeland security and counterterrorism advisor. As Townsend's HSC chief of staff, he led the drafting of presidential directives on cyber security, identity management, continuity of government, public health, and medical preparedness, and was the primary author of the administration's second *National Homeland Security Strategy*, released in 2007. When Townsend left government in early 2008, he again fleeted up to serve as the acting homeland security and counterterrorism advisor until Ken Wainstein got the official appointment in April.

As she had with the Katrina review, Michele Malvesti assisted Bagnal on the 2007 *National Strategy for Homeland Security*. With the change of administration in 2009, the incoming homeland security and counterterrorism advisor, John Brennan, tasked her to co-chair the Obama administration's Presidential Study Directive-1 (PSD-1) interagency review to reorganize the NSC, HSC, and staffs for counterterrorism and homeland security.

In March 2007, Dan Kaniewski became special assistant to the president for homeland security and HSC senior director of response policy. In the role, he chaired the White House Domestic Readiness Group, the HSC body that coordinated preparedness and response policy to arrive at agreement before presenting advice to the president. He oversaw development and approval of the National Response Framework (NRF), the successor to the NRP, and managed the presidential disaster declaration process.

Josh Dozor became HSC director for preparedness policy and in 2007 went to FEMA to serve as the agency's director of transformation management. In August 2008, he became the director of policy for FEMA's National Preparedness Directorate. Dozor served as a holdover in the Obama administration, becoming FEMA's deputy director for regional operations in March 2010.

Tom Bossert rose to be deputy assistant to the president for homeland security, managing the HSC staff for Joel Bagnal. After adding director of infrastructure protection policy to his portfolio, he worked with Bob Stephan, the head of the DHS Office of Infrastructure Protection, on the National Infrastructure Protection Plan. He was also the author of HSPD-19, Combating Terrorist Use of Explosives in the United States. Bossert was also active as the HSC point man for liaison with state and local government officials and private-industry executives.

The White House lessons learned review team compared the importance of their work to that which led to the Goldwater-Nichols defense reforms of 1986. Arguably, it was far more. The post-Katrina effort was historically more akin to the wartime work of the many naval reserve officers—in their civilian lives, Wall Street attorneys—who contributed to the Eberstadt report for FDR and Secretary of the Navy James Forrestal. For, two years later, it was this report that informed the language of the National Security Act of 1947. The Townsend report was the genesis of the National Preparedness System language in PKEMRA. And it might also be said: Fran Townsend was PKEMRA's Ferdinand Eberstadt.

# CHAPTER SEVEN

# The New FEMA:
## The DHS Executive Agent for Preparedness

On March 31, 2007, the New FEMA opened for business. The Post-Katrina Emergency Management Reform Act vested FEMA director Dave Paulison with a new title, FEMA administrator, and cabinet-level authority in a disaster to advise and report directly to the president in a manner analogous to the chairman of the Joint Chiefs of Staff in his role as the commander in chief's principal military advisor. Since PKEMRA's passage six months earlier, the headlines had been trumpeting how the legislation reunited preparedness and response in an empowered FEMA that would remain in DHS. Not fully appreciated was the PKEMRA language providing the statutory grounding for the National Preparedness System, which gave the agency the authority to serve as DHS and federal government's executive agent for national preparedness. Two questions remained, however: Whose concept of preparedness would be in play, and to what extent would FEMA be able to execute this authority?

With the PKEMRA-mandated transfer of its preparedness functions and activities to the New FEMA, George Foresman's DHS Preparedness Directorate reconfigured into the National Protection and Programs Directorate (NPPD).[1] The function of this newly titled DHS directorate was essentially to integrate efforts for analyzing, managing, and reducing risk—reflecting Secretary Chertoff's risk-based approach to homeland security. In this new form, NPPD included: the Office of Infrastructure Protection (OIP); the Office of Cyber Security and Communications (CS&C), which combined the Office of Cyber Security and Telecommunications and the Office of the Manager of the National Communications System with the new Office of Emergency Communications; the Office of Risk Management and Analysis (formerly within the Office of Infrastructure Protection); and the Office of Intergovernmental Programs. Although they faced some congressional opposition, Chertoff and his deputy, Michael Jackson, also administratively relocated the United States Visitor and Immigrant Status Indicator Technology (US-VISIT) office to NPPD. Viewed from another perspective, the newly configured NPPD would oversee all DHS protection programs addressing physical, cyber, and human risks via OIP, CS&C, and US-VISIT respectively.

George Foresman was to have remained as a DHS undersecretary, with the official title now undersecretary for the NPPD. The removal of his directorate's all-important preparedness grants function, however, meant that he would no longer have budget-line leverage to drive his concept of an empowered DHS preparedness board of directors consisting of representatives from each of the operational DHS agencies. In late March, just days before the PKEMRA mandates went into effect, Foresman tendered his resignation.[2] Assessing his abrupt departure, one unnamed DHS official observed, "The biggest problem was the definition of what the job was. . . . Nobody was ever really able to define 'Preparedness.'"[3]

The major national preparedness components and functions that transferred from Foresman's Preparedness Directorate landed in FEMA's newly created National Preparedness Directorate (NPD). This new entity would be the driving force behind the establishment of the National Preparedness System envisioned by the Townsend report as the means to build and integrate operational homeland security capability. Along with existing FEMA preparedness programs, NPD housed the all-important Office of Grants and Training along with the Office of National Capital Region Coordination, the Chemical Stockpile Emergency Preparedness Program (CSEPP), and the Radiological Emergency Preparedness Program (REPP). With respect to the latter two programs, the focus was on policy, contingency planning, exercise coordination and evaluation, emergency management training, and hazard mitigation. The REPP effort was integrated with the Nuclear Regulatory Commission's (NRC) on-site program, and both FEMA and NRC had implanting regulations. The CSEPP was the off-site effort jointly managed with the Department of the Army.

NPD also had two divisions, Readiness, Prevention, and Planning (RPP), FEMA's central office to handle preparedness policy and planning functions, and the National Integration Center (NIC). As the key NPD driver for the National Preparedness System in terms of doctrine, certifications, training, and exercises, the NIC had been responsible for developing and implementing the National Incident Management System and National Response Plan. The center supervised FEMA training and exercise programs at the Noble Training Center in Anniston, Alabama, and training and education programs at the Emergency Management Institute in Emmitsburg, Maryland, coordinating its activities there with the co-located U.S. Fire Administration. The NIC also oversaw the National Exercise Division at FEMA headquarters.

The National Preparedness System purposed to define target preparedness levels and priorities, and provided for a cycle of standard-setting, training, exercise, planning, assessment, technical assistance, grant-making, and reporting activities to build those capabilities. The follow-on to the Interim National Preparedness Goal, the National Preparedness Guidelines released in September 2007 was the foundation for accomplishing and implementing this charge. The NPG provided the doctrine for how to achieve and sustain coordinated intergovernmental, interagency, private-sector, and non-governmental organization capabilities presumed to balance risk with resources and need.

### Defining Preparedness and Instituting a DHS Preparedness Culture

Despite PKEMRA and its sections on the National Preparedness System, preparedness still remained a homeland security concept in need of clarification. While the legislation codified the principles of HSPD-5 and HSPD-8, a gap remained between the law on the books and the realities in the field. Later in the year, the December 2007 HSPD-8, Annex-1, National Planning, correctly drew a distinction between preparedness—a supporting activity—and operations. Dating from the early years of FEMA, Comprehensive Emergency Management (CEM) had characterized the emergency management mission continuum as "mitigation, preparedness, response, recovery." Based in part on CEM, official language in HSPD-8, National Preparedness, similarly had represented the homeland security mission continuum as "prevention, preparedness, response, recovery." The conforming amendments in HSPD-8, Annex-1 corrected this representation by removing "preparedness," "prepare for" or "preparing for" from HSPD-5, Management of Domestic Incidents, and inserting "protection," "protect against" or "protecting against," as the case may be. The conforming amendments thus more correctly defined the homeland security mission continuum as "prevention, protection, response, recovery." In DoD-speak, Annex-1 was distinguishing management of "readiness" processes from "operations." The former had to do with a condition; the latter, actions. Further, those actions could take place in a "steady-state" or "crisis-state"—two operational *modes* in a homeland security mission.

Neither a mission, function, nor operation, preparedness is a process that *supports* missions, functions, and operations.[4] Yet departments and agencies with homeland security functions or missions do not necessarily answer the question "Prepared for what?" the same way. The military, intelligence, law enforcement, and emergency management communities have their own legacy preparedness cultures that predate homeland security and are typically oriented to steady-state or crisis-state operations, but not both. The "battle of the badges" between the law enforcement and fire service communities provides the classic example of preparedness cultures in opposition.[5] How a preparedness culture orients determines (1) how its members train, exercise, and pursue career paths and (2) the degree to which it embraces planning.

The military epitomizes a planning culture. Classical military preparedness is oriented to the ultimate crisis state—war. In the second half of the twentieth century, the military as an institution prepared and planned for high-end war, or as the Pentagon termed it in the 1980s, global thermonuclear war.[6] The classical military view held that political reality existed in two modes, war and peace. While the Cold War soon became seen as a time of "neither war nor peace," our post-industrial, information-age era of asymmetric threats has prompted a military culture that now plans for the full spectrum of operations from the high-end to those "other-than-war"—for example, humanitarian operations and defense support to civil authorities.

Unlike the military, law enforcement is not a planning culture. It's tactical. Law enforcement preparedness readies its members for public safety activities and orients to the steady state. Crime happens all the time. Basic law enforcement is a *reactive* culture—making arrests and gathering evidence for prosecution. Yet since 9/11, law enforcement has been increasingly involved in counterterrorism and counterintelligence operations. With the consequent shift in emphasis from evidence-based to intelligence-led policing, law enforcement has adopted some of the *predictive* analytical culture of the intelligence community. Intergovernmental law enforcement collaborations with the IC have been occurring (with DHS grant assistance) in the information-sharing and analysis arena at the state and major urban area fusion centers, often co-located with emergency operations centers. Over time, collaborations with the IC and the military have been under way via an expanding network of Joint Terrorism Task Forces—a standing DOJ/FBI collaborative model distinct from the incident-specific fire services' ICS-based NIMS model. The former reflects a preparedness orientation to the prevention and protection missions and threats; the latter, to response and recovery missions and hazards—all presenting a challenge to the New FEMA and its National Preparedness Directorate in the struggle within DHS over who would ultimately characterize a comprehensive National Preparedness System.

Both PKEMRA and the Townsend report reiterated "all-hazards" preparedness. Within DHS, only one component agency had a preparedness culture that cut across military, intelligence, law enforcement, and emergency management functions. Its motto Semper Paratus, the Coast Guard had garnered wide acclaim for its exemplary response role during Hurricane Katrina. Its unique preparedness culture is a result of the service's history. Initially, the Coast Guard was a specifically-focused law enforcement agency, the Treasury Department's Revenue Cutter Service. As one of his efforts at pre–World War I preparedness, President Woodrow Wilson combined the cutter service with the coastal Life Saving Service in 1915 to form the Coast Guard. As such, its culture became a blend of law enforcement and marine safety. Subsequently, the Lighthouse Service and the Bureau of Marine Inspection (a combination of the Steamboat Inspection Service and the Bureau of Navigation) transferred to the agency, giving the Coast Guard an added regulatory dimension. Both Wilson and FDR transferred the service temporarily during wartime to the Department of the Navy. As a wartime agency in the Navy Department, the Coast Guard took part in joint coastal defense and convoy escort operations against submarines, among other missions, introducing it to the twentieth-century military planning culture and the postwar national security system. Post Cold War, the Coast Guard and Navy continued forward joint operations in maritime interdiction and force protection, notably in the First Gulf War.

The preparedness culture of the Coast Guard thus provides the bridge across DHS' various preparedness cultures. In recent decades, the Coast Guard has been involved in functions and activities that require the full embrace of interagency and intergovernmental collaboration—maritime drug enforcement, interdiction and repatriation of illegal immigrants, maritime environmental remediation, port security, and maritime domain awareness. Not surprisingly, the Coast Guard has long emphasized the value of interagency assignments in its professional development, detailing its high-performers to interagency assignments. In this context, the appointment of Adm. Jim Loy to the number-two DHS position of deputy secretary was foundational for the department. As Tom Ridge's chief operating officer, Admiral Loy prepared the ground for a department-wide preparedness culture. From his time as a flag commander, Loy had a custom of making "PEP Awards" to those personnel and components under his command who exemplified the truth "Preparedness Equals Performance," a custom he continued as Ridge's deputy secretary.

The visionary Loy was Coast Guard commandant during 9/11. Four months after the attacks, he promulgated the first version of Coast Guard Publication 1, *America's Maritime Guardian*, the military, multi-mission, maritime service's "first publication to synthesize who we are, what we do, and how we do things."[7] During the Hurricane Katrina response, the Coast Guard demonstrated how preparedness is at bottom an expeditionary mind-set. In after-action presentations, the service would emphasize how Publication 1's statement of the principle of on-scene initiative guided the response in what it calls "commander's intent": "The concept of allowing the person on scene to take the initiative—guided by a firm understanding of the desired tactical objectives and the national interests at stake—remains central to the Coast Guard's view of its command relationships."[8]

### The New FEMA Initiative and Its Leadership

Admiral Loy's vision in Pub 1 set the stage for the new forward-leaning FEMA. Pub 1 implicitly shaped the mind-set that informed the leadership team that would start implementation of the PKEMRA-mandated National Preparedness System. When this team left FEMA Headquarters in January 2009 at the change of administrations, its members left behind the basis of a department-wide DHS culture of preparedness and the framework of an expeditionary homeland security culture not just in Washington, but most crucially in the regions.

The PKEMRA implementation that began in April 2007 conferred some autonomy on FEMA. Secretary Chertoff's own pre-PKEMRA restructuring a year earlier had already moved the agency in that direction. He had made acting FEMA director Dave Paulison's position Senate-confirmed with the new title undersecretary of federal emergency management. A semi-autonomous

FEMA would make the agency comparable to the Coast Guard in the DHS organization chart. Chertoff facilitated FEMA adoption of the Coast Guard's expeditionary ethos by appointing Vice Adm. Harvey Johnson as Paulison's number two. He had previously interviewed Johnson to be Coast Guard commandant, but after Thad Allen's take-charge performance during the Katrina response, the latter candidate emerged as the obvious choice to relieve Tom Collins in 2006. A proven planning and management high performer, Johnson would be Paulison's chief operating officer for driving PKEMRA implementation, informed by the spirit of Loy's Pub 1.

Johnson came to FEMA directly from Alameda, just across the bay from San Francisco, where he was the commander of the Coast Guard Pacific Area, one of the service's two major operational commands. Because Paulison had decided not to fill the position of FEMA chief of staff, he would in effect be triple-hatted as his deputy director, COO, and chief of staff, making him a FEMA executive with uncommon authority to make things happen. It was a role to which Johnson had become well accustomed. In addition to his operational background as a Coast Guard aviator, Johnson was a management and planning expert, with a master of science degree in management from MIT's Sloan School of Management. Before making flag in 2001, he had served as Cmdt. Jim Loy's executive assistant. As the service prepared to transfer from the Department of Transportation to DHS, Johnson was simultaneously the one-star executive director of that transition, director of operations capability, and director of policy capability. Once DHS stood up, he got his second star and command of the Coast Guard's Seventh District. His third star came in June 2004 when he became Commander, Pacific Area, where he remained until his FEMA appointment.

The key assignment that prepared him for his transformational role at FEMA was his tour in Miami as commander of Coast Guard District Seven. Johnson was the operational lead in an area of intense joint, interagency and intergovernmental maritime activity involving counter-narcotics and immigration interdiction. He was also Tom Ridge's commander of Homeland Security Task Force-Southeast that stood up in June 2003 as he was arriving.

In early February 2004, civil unrest and violence hit Haiti and soon exploded into a rebellion against its president, Jean-Bertrand Aristide. Several months before, Johnson and HSTF-SE had completed Operation Plan Vigilant Sentry to respond to potential Caribbean mass migrations arising from such a scenario. An army coup ousted Aristide at the end of February, and U.S. Marines came ashore in advance of a United Nations–authorized intervention to restore Haitian security and stability. As the political situation was deteriorating, Ridge activated HSTF-SE, and Johnson and his interagency staff began developing a concept of operations to implement Vigilant Sentry. Within days, Johnson had a fifteen-page document, Operation Able Sentry, whereby HSTF-SE would "conduct fully integrated mass-migration operations to deter illegal or unsafe migrant departures, and interdict, repatriate, and detain populations as necessary and appropriate to protect the security of the United States."[9]

While the Able Sentry patrols in the Caribbean and the Florida Straits were primarily a Coast Guard operation with fifteen cutters and 1,550 personnel, they included units and personnel from five DHS agencies and seven Florida and local law enforcement agencies, including a special operations group from the Florida Wildlife Conservation Commission. Among the DHS assets were twelve aircraft from ICE, planning specialists from FEMA, and public affairs officials from TSA. The Bureau of Citizenship and Immigration Services put seventeen pre-screening officers on Coast Guard cutters for the purpose of determining whether any Haitians qualified for asylum. ICE detention and removal officials further developed plans for dealing with any Haitians who might make it to U.S. shores.[10]

To coordinate Johnson's assets, DHS introduced an operational command structure that included his deputy, Lynne Underdown, the U.S. Border Patrol's sector chief for agency operations in Florida, Georgia, and the Carolinas, its first-ever female sector chief. As HSTF-SE operational commanders, Johnson and Underdown directly reported to Ridge and DHS headquarters—not via their agencies. The task force's crisis-state operational chain of command was thus parallel to the agency chain of command, responsible for the routine, steady-state operations.[11] Johnson thus found himself executing Tom Ridge and Bruce Lawlor's DHS regional empowerment initiative. In the hands of Bob Stephan, the idea came forward that HSTF-SE could serve as the department model for a decentralized regional command and organization.

In Harvey Johnson, Dave Paulison thus had a deputy with leadership experience in a ground-breaking joint, interagency, and intergovernmental operation that could be brought to bear for transforming FEMA into an expeditionary organization. Johnson purposed to instill the Coast Guard culture of commander's intent into a New FEMA mind-set appropriate to the forward-leaning agency mandated by the post-Katrina legislation.

To support Johnson in this effort, Paulison secured a trusted colleague, Marko Bourne, a fire service and emergency management professional with a sure grasp of the strategic big picture. Bourne came on board in October 2006 as FEMA director of policy and program analysis. He had first worked for Paulison in 2001 as his executive officer and assistant director at the U.S. Fire Administration in Emmitsburg, Maryland. A Massachusetts firefighter, Bourne's initial exposure to Washington had been in 1990 when he arrived for a yearlong internship as the external affairs director for Rep. Curt Weldon of Pennsylvania and his Congressional Fire Service Institute. While at CFSI, Bourne absorbed how the upper reaches of a fire-service career were moving into the realm of national security. Recognizing Bourne's deepening interest in policy, Weldon sent him to Harrisburg to found and direct the Pennsylvania Fire Services Institute, a state-level organization modeled on CFSI. While there, he expanded his fire-service portfolio into broader emergency management to include governmental, legislative, and public affairs, rising to become press secretary for the Pennsylvania Emergency Management Agency. During this time, he also coordinated the state's emergency preparedness for several presidential disasters and Y2K. From there he went to join Paulison at the Fire Administration, two months prior to 9/11. The day after the attacks, FEMA director Joe Allbaugh ordered him to report to the Pentagon incident site to serve as the FEMA spokesperson, recognizing that Bourne's experience in both urban search and rescue and media uniquely qualified him for the task. Later in the month, he transferred to New York where he ran FEMA's Joint Information Center at Ground Zero.

When the administration came to the decision to create the Department of Homeland Security, Allbaugh and Paulison assigned him to Andy Card's White House–led Transition Planning Office. When DHS launched in March 2003, Paulison relocated to Washington as the dual-hatted director of the National Preparedness Division of the DHS Emergency Preparedness and Response Directorate (as FEMA was then officially known), bringing Bourne with him as his deputy director of preparedness. With Paulison's support, Ridge put Bourne in charge of the stand-up of the NIMS Integration Center as its acting director and gave him the responsibility for nationwide NIMS implementation at all levels of government.

In mid-2004, Bourne left FEMA for the private sector to become the director of business development for homeland security at Earth Tech, a unit of the engineering and security consulting firm Tyco International. Shortly thereafter, he led Tyco's homeland security integration efforts in its Washington office. In 2006, he assisted Fran Townsend's team by providing input to the Katrina lessons learned report and subsequently the House and Senate committees in drafting the language for PKEMRA.

Johnson and Bourne's implementer of national preparedness was Dennis R. Schrader, Maryland's first homeland security advisor. Schrader's collaborative style made him the ideal person to step on the FEMA train that had already started running. A naval reserve captain, he had many years of active-duty service in the Civil Engineer Corps.

When Republican Governor Bob Ehrlich had lost his gubernatorial reelection bid to Baltimore's Democratic mayor Martin O'Malley the previous November, Schrader was immediately recruited by George Foresman to succeed Tracy Henke, who had left her post in October as assistant DHS secretary for grants and training. When Foresman was Virginia's homeland security advisor, he had known Schrader as an assertive, take-charge, state-level counterpart on National Capital Region (NCR) matters. Although Foresman left government in March and Henke's position disappeared when DHS preparedness grant functions transferred to FEMA, Schrader had completed the vetting process and fortuitously secured administration support to lead NPD.

Nominated in April 2007 and confirmed in August, Schrader had the title of deputy administrator for national preparedness. Like Foresman, he came into federal service representing a pronounced state point of view. He also had the benefit of prior federal service with the Navy. In August 2003, he had led the team that developed Maryland's first homeland security program that balanced law enforcement and emergency management equities—both sides of the boom. Schrader worked closely with his law enforcement counterparts, including federal leads in the state like Harvey Eisenberg, the chief of the national security section of the U.S. Attorney's Office in Maryland. "Ehrlich had already determined his preferred structure, and his senior team had integrated with the U.S. Attorney–led Anti-Terrorism Advisory Council (ATAC). We interpreted and implemented the guidance in the National Strategy of July 2002 and the Homeland Security Advisory Council (HSAC) state template, and for the next two years we struggled to keep pace with the federally generated requirements."[12]

As a homeland security advisor, Schrader had set for himself two immediate goals: improve Maryland's public safety communications and advance its information-sharing capabilities. Among his most significant collaborative, interagency projects was the stand-up of the state's information-sharing fusion center, the Maryland Coordination and Analysis Center (MCAC), co-located with the Joint Terrorism Task Force (JTTF). In addition to prioritizing fusion center development, Schrader was a strong proponent of the FBI's Joint Terrorism Task Forces and endorsed the detailing and home agency funding of state and local law enforcement officers to the Maryland JTTF in Baltimore.[13] At the time, 60 percent of the JTTF was staffed by state and local officers. He was also supportive of developing collaborations with the public health community. Prior to his time in state government, he had been the University of Maryland Medical System's director of operations and vice president of project planning and development where, among other things, he developed medical preparedness plans for mass casualty incidents.

Schrader thus brought to the National Preparedness Directorate a varied career, grounded in systems engineering. Starting life as an industrial engineer with General Motors, he developed a systems engineering expertise and a skill set that included project management, operations research, and human factors. Schrader keenly appreciated how management of twenty-first-century complexities required structures and processes that fostered collaboration. With Schrader as the third member of his PKEMRA implementation team, Paulison was now in a strong position to weld FEMA in place inside DHS as the federal government's executive agent for national preparedness.

Notwithstanding the statutory PKEMRA restructuring, Paulison and his senior leadership were not certain that the legislation would be the last word on FEMA remaining in DHS. The congressional calls for removing the agency continued, led by Rep. James Oberstar (D-MN), chairman of the House Transportation and Infrastructure Committee, the House panel with long-standing oversight of FEMA. The Paulison team shared a persistent assumption that an incoming administration or Congress in 2009 might attempt yet another reorganization that would make FEMA independent as a cabinet-level agency. As it happened, the day after Obama was elected president in November 2008, Oberstar would introduce such legislation.[14]

The team hence felt that it was under the gun to produce. PKEMRA and the White House imposed a long list of action items with the expectation that Paulison, Johnson, Bourne, and Schrader would accomplish them immediately. Throughout the process, they would endure constant distractions in the form of inquiries from the Government Accountability Office and the Congressional Research Service, which were tracking various aspects of PKEMRA implementation. Hence, Paulison and his team took the approach that they had until the end of the Bush administration to execute the PKEMRA-mandated preparedness authority and demonstrate the wisdom of PKEMRA maintaining FEMA within DHS. In short, they had two years to get it right.

From the outset of his tenure, Paulison was determined to take PKEMRA authorities to distinguish himself from the FEMA directors of the past by instituting a new workforce culture that would bring career employees to the forefront alongside the political appointees. Senior headquarters and regional workforces were to function as one team. To that end, he introduced a team-building mechanism around a series of several-day, all-hands, senior leadership retreats in 2007 and 2008. While he held the first in Annapolis, the following three took place at what had been the U.S. Post Office's national training complex, the Bolger Center, just outside Washington in scenic Potomac, Maryland. There, FEMA headquarters and regional leaderships gathered to discuss progress on implementation and recalibrate transformation processes and objectives—how best to operationalize preparedness.

Paulison instilled in his team that people were key to driving the preparedness culture change. Schrader's National Preparedness Directorate was the sharp end of FEMA transformation. As such, he prioritized among his responsibilities both hiring and professional workforce development. FEMA had an elaborate twenty-six-step hiring process that Schrader and his staff documented and managed every day to get the right people in the right positions, not only at headquarters but in the regions.

In addition to requiring integration into DHS, PKEMRA mandated that FEMA build its ten regions into a decentralized, distributed capability for the department. Under the initiative, the agency strengthened the regions by providing them with more resources and new responsibilities. For a start, Paulison's team filled all ten regional administrator slots with officials having twenty-five to thirty years of experience in emergency management, and sent

them over 140 FEMA personnel as planners, logisticians, preparedness officers, grants managers, and management support staff. Schrader made a point
of locating NPD components in the regional offices. Two key new regional
NPD positions were the federal preparedness coordinator (FPC) and the preparedness analysis and planning officers (PAPOs). The FPCs would support
state and local planning, training, and exercising. The PAPOs would augment
regional planning capabilities. As well, FEMA's Grant Programs Directorate
(GPD), which Paulison made independent from NPD, provided the regions
with grant specialists to improve management of grant dollars.

Schrader and Bourne worked in tandem to support Paulison's priorities. Bourne developed preparedness policy; Schrader executed it, with key
staff support from Josh Dozor, who served as his point man to get the work
done. The realignment of the steady-state, DHS preparedness functions into
FEMA presented them with an opportunity to integrate a capabilities-based
preparedness framework and a national operational architecture for all four
missions of the homeland security mission continuum. A priority was to
find ways to put FEMA into protection and prevention, linking its Response
Directorate into DHS law enforcement and intelligence entities to improve
its engagement in the operational aspects of the DHS prevention and protection missions.

PKEMRA required that the agency establish a position that provided a
law enforcement perspective on agency plans and policies. The requirement
had strong support from the International Association of Chiefs of Police,
the National Sheriffs' Association, and the Fraternal Order of Police. Two
months after Schrader arrived, FEMA secured Salt Lake City's police chief,
Rick Dinse, to serve as Paulison's law enforcement advisor. In 2002, Dinse
had been vice chairman of the Utah Olympic Public Safety Command, where
he led development and implementation of the public safety plan for the Salt
Lake City 2002 Winter Olympic Games. Previously, he had been deputy chief
commanding officer of the Los Angeles Police Department.

Dinse provided FEMA with a credible voice to the law enforcement community that historically was neither trusting of the agency nor the fire service. Having oversight of FEMA's law enforcement programs, he supported
the agency's growing interaction with law enforcement associations, fusion
centers, and JTTFs. Dinse worked cooperation at FEMA Headquarters via
the National Response Coordination Center (NRCC), where he established

a secure section to the NRCC watch team. He also achieved cooperation in the field commands, notably in helping forge FEMA liaison with law enforcement during the spring 2008 Iowa floods, particularly when FEMA moved to support the efforts of Governor Chet Culver (D-IA) to protect Cedar Rapids. Similarly in 2008, he facilitated agency cooperation with law enforcement for the evacuation of New Orleans during Hurricane Gustav. He also played a critical role as the FEMA mediator between Justice and the ATF during the writing of the Public Safety and Security Annex (ESF-13) to the National Response Framework. In both 2007 and 2008, Dinse advanced law enforcement and FEMA agreement on grant priorities, traditionally a particular area of contention.

A second thrust was a less successful FEMA attempt to reach across to Bob Stephan's Office of Infrastructure Protection in the DHS National Protection and Programs Directorate. In June 2006, OIP had released its first National Infrastructure Protection Plan (NIPP). In terms of the protection mission space, the NIPP was comparable to the National Response Plan for the response mission. It set national priorities, goals, and requirements for funding, and resources for critical infrastructure/key resources (CI/KR) protection. The NIPP structure incorporated initially seventeen (now eighteen) supporting sector-specific plans (SSPs), issued in May 2007, to provide a coordinated approach for federal, state, local, tribal, and private-sector security partners to revise and update CI/KR protection roles, responsibilities, information sharing, and risk management. For FEMA, the protection mission was analogous to mitigation; however, the agency's Mitigation Division was exclusively focused on natural hazards and was especially preoccupied with managing flood insurance programs. As such, risk prioritization in the DHS protection mission space remained an issue.

NPD's National Integration Center provided a better means to bring the law enforcement and emergency management workforce cultures together through the NIC's education, training, and exercise programs. From having stood up the NIC in 2003, Bourne resolved to emphasize integration of training and exercises. Taking the Army's Training and Doctrine Command (TRADOC) at Fort Eustis, Virginia, as their model, he and Schrader merged FEMA's training, exercise, and doctrine development efforts into an expanded National Integration Center. Schrader's acting assistant NIC administrator was Jim Kish, a retired National Guardsman and Special Forces colonel who had served as the National Guard Bureau's chief of civil support. Before coming to FEMA, Kish had served in Ridge's Office of Homeland Security as the director of training and exercises.

Kish's responsibilities included ensuring that NIC activities supported the National Preparedness System equities in homeland security workforce professional development. When the former Office of Domestic Preparedness and DHS Preparedness staffs transferred to NPD, they brought with them the prevention and protection points of view that needed to meld with those of response and recovery. The previous stovepipe organizations presented a challenge for integrated training and exercises. Bourne, Schrader, and Kish forged relationships that were accepting of inputs from the Emergency Management Institute, the Center for Domestic Preparedness, and the DHS National Domestic Preparedness Consortium (NDPC). While the National Fire Academy was statutorily separate, Bourne set a policy that required it to participate in the combined entity. With its Corrective Action Program (CAP), NPD set training and exercise benchmarks to improve linkages. Further emphasis on training and exercise integration came from the National Exercise Division, NPD's coordinating body to provide curriculum review and ensure no duplication in training courses. Addressing stakeholder training and exercise needs, the division worked with outside training partners such as state training academies, the NDPC, and other institutions of higher learning to coordinate national, regional, state, and local exercises. The National Exercise Division worked to involve FEMA's National Exercise Program in more state and local exercises that were otherwise hamstrung by those levels' lack of resources.

Drawing on his experience as a health administrator, Schrader recognized HHS' work in building national capability and the need to integrate it more effectively into the FEMA-led national exercise program and operational planning generally. Schrader also forged additional linkages across training and exercises by directing NPD to re-conceive Oklahoma City's National Memorial Institute for the Prevention of Terrorism (MIPT), a congressionally grant-funded agency doing systems development, into a law enforcement training facility. His NPD continued funding for the Naval Postgraduate School's Center for Homeland Defense and Security in Monterey, California, for the homeland security master's degree and executive leaders programs. At what had been the Army's government-owned, contractor-operated (GOCO) facility in Anniston, Alabama, he recruited Todd Jones, a federal civil servant with broad experience in contract management and professional education and training in the field, as the superintendent of the Center for Domestic Preparedness for civilian WMD training. Jones strengthened contract management at the post-BRAC (Base Realignment and Closure) facility to enhance FEMA's oversight.

PKEMRA called for a FEMA National Exercise and Simulation Center (NESC) which finally opened in January 2009 at FEMA Headquarters. A strong proponent of planning, Schrader wanted NPD to use the center to support operational planning assessment, especially in the area of mass casualty preparedness. The NESC was placed above the NRCC to co-locate it with FEMA Operational Planning Branch in the Response Division and make it convenient and accessible to a location that was well known in the federal interagency world. Subsequent to Schrader's tenure, NPD launched a process to integrate training and exercises which was completed in 2011 by the center's director, Keith Holtermann, an emergency health services professional who transferred from the HHS Office of the Assistant Secretary for Preparedness and Response.

## The National Response Framework and Planning

FEMA was not alone in its efforts to operationalize preparedness. Other quarters of the federal government and the Department of Homeland Security also had their stakes in wanting to mature planning. In the spring of 2006—a year before the PKEMRA-mandated transfer of preparedness functions to FEMA—DHS issued a notice of change for the National Response Plan and announced the Homeland Security Council's formation of an assistant secretary-level policy coordinating committee. Along with the HSC Deputies Committee, this PCC would set homeland security planning priorities. A Townsend report recommendation had called for establishment of such a committee, which it called a Disaster Response Group, "a forum where strategic policy and interagency coordination and de-confliction can take place." "These decisions," the report continued, "would then be implemented through the NOC. This HSC-chaired group would address issues that cannot be resolved at lower levels, and either resolve them or develop decision recommendations for Deputies and Principals."[15] The HSC titled this interagency entity the Domestic Readiness Group (DRG), which replaced what had been its Domestic Threat Reduction and Incident Management (DTRIM) PCC. Among the DRG's taskings was the responsibility to develop and coordinate implementation of preparedness and response policy. As such, it was the interagency's primary instrument for federal vetting of the NRP review and revision and the related update to NIMS—as the first of its 125 recommendations, the Townsend report priority.

At the deputies level, Fran Townsend's deputy, Joel Bagnal, chaired the meetings on the NRP and NIMS review and revision process. Bagnal would play a key role in guiding the process and the priority development of a deliberative, integrated, federal planning and execution system to meet the requirements of a revised NRP. Having worked as an Army officer with state and local governments in the late nineties supporting the Nunn-Lugar-Domenici train-the-trainers WMD consequence management program, Bagnal was committed to ensuring that non-federal equities were somehow represented in interagency policy development. When DHS attempted to make Deputy Secretary Michael Jackson the sole department representative, Bagnal insisted that FEMA have a seat at the table as well, opening the door to FEMA deputy administrator Harvey Johnson. Equally committed to speak for his agency on behalf of state and local equities, Johnson would frequently attend DRG meetings as well. Chairing the DRG during the review and revision process until he left government in August 2008 was Dan Kaniewski, Bagnal's senior director for response—another interagency voice for the states and the frontline responder community. At the deputies level, Jackson nevertheless exercised somewhat of a controlling influence over the process. As one senior DHS official put it, "Most folks don't know that he was Andy Card's chief of staff during Hurricane Andrew in '92. He was reliving that experience in many ways post-Katrina." Throughout the 2006–7 interagency discussions, Jackson was looking for the means to strengthen his and Mike Chertoff's hands in the execution of their HSPD-5 authorities for management of domestic incidents. Impressed by the Coast Guard's Publication 1, Jackson wanted to embed into the revised NRP the Pub 1 spirit of on-scene command initiative.[16] Whereas his predecessor Jim Loy understood command initiative in the context of interagency and intergovernmental collaboration, Jackson's understanding was DHS Headquarters- and federal-centric and, from the state and local perspectives, very top-down.

Jackson relied on his undersecretary for preparedness, George Foresman, to drive the review process at the DRG level. Foresman had just completed a

Nationwide Plan Review and was standing up a follow-on National Preparedness Task Force to implement its recommendations. In his October 2005 national address from New Orleans' Jackson Square in the midst of the Hurricane Katrina response, President Bush had ordered DHS to review, with local counterparts, emergency plans in every major American city. In response to this presidential charge and two congressional statutory directives to review and assess the status of catastrophic and evacuation planning in all states and seventy-five of the largest urban areas, DHS launched the nationwide review. With cooperation from the Department of Transportation and support from DoD, this DHS effort was two-phased, with a self-assessment and follow-on peer review. The lead was George Foresman and his Preparedness Directorate, notably his grants and training assistant secretary Tracy Henke, and Tim Beres in her Preparedness Programs Division. The manager of Henke's state and local preparedness assistance program of grants and technical assistance, Beres developed and implemented the first DHS risk-based preparedness grant program—the Urban Areas Security Initiative (UASI).

The review's project director was Corey Gruber, a former Army Signal Corps lieutenant colonel who had extensive experience dealing with state and local governments. In the nineties, Gruber served as chief of plans for the Army's Directorate of Military Support (DOMS), where he was responsible for military support to civil authorities, including planning and response to major disasters and emergencies, and management of classified continuity of operations programs. After leaving the Army, he continued to support DOMS as the deputy director of the emergency management division for Research Planning, Inc., working on the DOMS-administered Nunn-Lugar-Domenici WMD preparedness and response planning, training, exercise, and continuity programs for the 120 major metropolitan areas. In 2001, he returned to government service working in the Office of Domestic Preparedness, then housed in the Justice Department. In 2003, he migrated with ODP to DHS and Suzanne Mencer's Office of State and Local Government Coordination and Preparedness (SLGCP), where he served variously as the assistant director of the National Programs Directorate and the director of the Office for Policy, Initiatives, and Assessments. With the 2005 Second Stage Review, SLGCP and Gruber went into Foresman's Preparedness Directorate.

By 2006, Gruber had already become a respected and major planning resource in the homeland security bureaucracy. In 2004, he had been detailed for six months to Bob Stephan's DHS Integration Staff to be its director of training and exercises. While on the I-Staff, he supported David Howe, the HSC senior director for response and planning and chairman of the Domestic Threat Reduction and Incident Management PCC's scenarios working group, the DRG predecessor entity responsible for developing the NPG's fifteen National Planning Scenarios.

Gruber's Nationwide Plan Review team released its findings in June 2006. "Current catastrophic planning is unsystematic and not linked within a national planning system," read the executive summary. "This is incompatible with 21st century homeland security challenges, and reflects a systemic problem: outmoded planning processes, products, and tools are primary contributors to the inadequacy of catastrophic planning."[17] While Gruber's team found that most areas of the country were well prepared to handle standard disaster situations, it reported that the majority of state and urban-area emergency operations plans and planning processes were not fully sufficient to manage catastrophic events as defined in the National Response Plan. Most fell into the review's "partially sufficient" category. Moreover, the review recorded that states and urban areas were not conducting adequate collaborative planning as an element of steady-state preparedness.

To address the team's findings, Chertoff charged Foresman with the responsibility to oversee planning modernization and translate its initial conclusions into specific recommendations for the federal government. To that end, Foresman established a National Preparedness Task Force to develop and act on specific recommendations and oversee DHS efforts to strengthen and systematize catastrophic planning among all levels of government. In framing the role of this task force for Chertoff and Foresman, the Nationwide Plan Review charged it to "fuse and focus DHS preparedness policy, planning, exercise, evaluation, and field management assets in order to provide comprehensive preparedness solutions for challenges identified by operations counterparts in DHS and the homeland security community."[18]

Not surprisingly, Foresman gave Gruber the task force lead—effectively giving him the lead for HSPD-8 implementation and the construction of the National Preparedness System. In a July 2006 Senate hearing, Gruber had explained how HSPD-8 set the requirement for developing "a systematic planning methodology using a capabilities-based framework," that resulted in the Interim National Preparedness Goal. The Interim NPG's fifteen

National Planning Scenarios, Target Capabilities List (TCL), and Universal Task List (UTL), he said, were planning tools to support the capabilities-based planning process. The TCL provided "a common reference system for inter-governmental, non-governmental, and private sector-preparedness," and the UTL was the comprehensive task library in a "common language."[19] At that same hearing, he was among the first to introduce the term "homeland security enterprise" to characterize his vision of effective unity of effort and oper-ational readiness. Gruber and his task force thus played a key role in the NRP review and revision. Gruber had an informed belief that a preparedness culture could be developed and sustained via an NRP with a solid planning chapter providing a basis for what he called a "community of planners."

In May 2006, DHS had released the elements of its interim NRP revision. Three months later, Foresman briefed the NRP review and revision work plan to the DRG. Once approved, the interagency work began in the autumn with Foresman, Dave Paulison, and the FEMA National Integration Center providing oversight, as per the work plan. In parallel, the NIC proceeded with the NIMS update. While Foresman and Paulison were the review and revision steering committee leads, day-to-day direction was in the hands of their action officers, Tina Gabbrielli and Robert Shea. Gabbrielli was in the DHS Office of Infrastructure Protection but had been detailed to serve as the senior director for contingency planning and field-based preparedness on Gruber's task force. Having come to DHS from Justice, she had been an assistant U.S. attorney in the Eastern District of Pennsylvania. Shea was career FEMA who had risen to acting director of operations and then Johnson's associate deputy administrator.

In November 2006, Gabbrielli and Shea began the NRP redrafting. As the process matured, Foresman continued to provide oversight and brief the DRG on Gabbrielli and Shea's efforts. On the FEMA side, Marko Bourne assumed the agency's oversight responsibilities, which often involved supporting Foresman in the DRG. Reporting to Gabbrielli and Shea was a twelve-person writing team composed entirely of federal officials, who in turn delegated work to twelve work groups addressing discrete issue areas—for example, catastrophic planning. The process received stakeholder input via a series of stakeholder meetings. Altogether, 709 participants took part, of which 224 were non-federal stakeholders—32 percent. Generally, non-federal stakeholders had regarded the NRP as a bureaucratic document that was internally repetitive and insufficiently national in its focus. They wanted the revised NRP to speak more clearly to the roles and responsibilities of all parties involved in response. A common criticism was that the NRP and its supporting documents did not constitute a true operational plan as understood by emergency managers. Since the NRP's release in 2004, operational planning on a national basis for specific types of incidents had matured, and the writing team was eager to make improvements in the new NRP's Incident Annexes.[20]

Gabbrielli and Shea completed the first draft of the revised NRP in March. It was met with Jackson's strong disapproval. He criticized the draft as too long, too bureaucratic in tone, and too much like the NRP and its predecessor Federal Response Plan. Jackson rightly wanted a simplified document in plain English, "conversational." However, he wanted to go further. Still smarting from the widely held perception of a failed federal response to Katrina, Jackson clung to his own belief that local government had failed and the federal government was unfairly blamed. As such, he sought language that addressed the trigger mechanism for the federal assumption of all state and local roles in catastrophic events. Rather than drafting a document that put forth a response doctrine for federal support of local government, Jackson wanted the NRP to emphasize a federal command role at the expense of local authorities. As such, he was preparing to overturn or excise a number of long-standing emergency management tenants. Equally problematic from an intra-DHS perspective, he was preparing to eliminate references to the role of the FEMA administrator and FEMA and increase the role of DHS OPS.

Notwithstanding his right-thinking as to what the NRF needed to be, Jackson had become understandably impatient with the interagency review process. March 2007 was a very uncertain period for DHS. It was the run-up to the transfer of DHS preparedness functions to FEMA, and it was unclear whether Foresman would opt to leave or stay. Fearing that FEMA would take full control of the NRP revision, Jackson assumed Foresman's oversight duties and sidelined Gabbrielli and Shea's effort. FEMA officials privately accused him of "hijacking" the document. While the work plan called for another comment period to run to September, Jackson restricted the release of the draft only to the DRG and the steering committee for an internal federal review that did not included participation by the non-federal stakeholders. Over the next two months, he worked mostly alone on the draft. On the FEMA side, Johnson and Bourne attempted to influence his writing and moderate his edits, all the while lobbying to reassert a measure of FEMA control. Their argument was essentially that any new draft would have to be vetted by state and local stakeholders as well as by the DRG. As the spring advanced, the non-federal stakeholders began to clamor for inclusion in the redrafting process, forcing Jackson to reopen the process in May to allow FEMA input. Over the next month, Johnson and Bourne, with help from Bob Shea, Joel Bagnal, and two of Bagnal's HSC staffers, gradually began to exert more influence over the drafting process.

With preparedness functions now in FEMA NPD, Harvey Johnson leveraged his authority at the deputies level and in the DRG to represent the NRP revision as more appropriately a FEMA product. During what the FEMA leadership would call the "Jackson black-out period," Johnson undertook to shepherd the NRP through the interagency process—including giving most of the DRG briefs. Toward the end of the process, Johnson tasked Bourne to provide the DRG updates. Johnson also assumed the FEMA co-chair with Jackson for Gabbrielli and Shea's interagency NRF steering committee. Jackson endured a further setback in late July, when someone in the administration leaked a draft of Jackson's version of the revised NRP. According to one senior DHS official, "The comments on it were brutal. The criticism was withering." From that point to September, Johnson and Bourne had full control of the editing, supported by the renewed involvement of Gabbrielli and Shea's working groups. Most of the final redrafting actually came from Johnson, Bourne, Shea, and a group of a half-dozen FEMA staff, the HSC and two contractor subject-matter experts. Dennis Schrader supported Johnson with a number of NPD officials to assist the revision effort. All joined the writing team. Key NPD players were Tracy Haynes, the acting NRF branch chief, and Marge DeBrot of the Army Corps of Engineers, the FEMA Headquarters ESF 3 (Public Works and Engineering) lead. Marko Bourne was able to get Laura McClure, who had served with Michael Jackson in his Department of Transportation days, detailed from the White House staff to "break down White House barriers." Contractor support came from Steve Sharro, a former Emergency Management Institute director, and Booz Allen Hamilton's Mary Anne Rodenhiser. Recalled Schrader, "It was an heroic commitment and effort on their parts. They managed thousands of comments via the *Federal Register* and turned around significant editing and redrafts with incredible speed and accuracy. Without them, there would be no NRF."

In October, the steering committee was able to validate the concepts of the revised NRP and NIMS in the TopOff 4 that exercised National Planning Scenario 11 (Radiological Attack—Radiological Dispersal Devices) in Oregon, Arizona, and Guam. That month, Jackson resigned, but not before his September release for comment of the revised NRP, which he had renamed the National Response Framework. This final two-round comment phase was not soon enough to placate the two emergency management associations, the National Emergency Management Association (NEMA) and the International Association of Emergency Managers (IAEM). Both accused DHS of excluding them from the process. Irritation also resulted from the failure to honor a PKEMRA provision for a newly established FEMA Headquarters-level National Advisory Council (NAC), composed of a range of non-federal emergency management stakeholders, to participate in the revision process. FEMA did not stand up the NAC until June 2007, and it was not able to convene its first meeting until October. The NAC was thus only able to provide its comments on the NRF in December, just a month before the final release. Throughout the comment phase, Dennis Schrader had the at-times-difficult job of selling the NRF to a suspicious state- and local-level emergency management community. Jim Kish and the NPD National Integration Center managed comments and discussion via the NIC Web site and greatly contributed to reversing much of the non-federal stakeholder alienation from the review and revision process. In the end, notwithstanding their criticisms, stakeholders favorably accepted the NRF as an advance on the NRP.

Final DRG vetting came in December. Johnson and Bourne sought to convince the DRG to eliminate the agency signature process and have the president release the NRF. Their goal was to make it truly national policy, not the whim of twenty-two department and agency secretaries as the Federal Response Plan and National Response Plan had been. The requirement was for a truly national document. Rather than trying to get signatures from fifty state governors, they felt it appropriate that the president sign for all. It would also be a clear notice to the federal interagency that the commander in chief had spoken: the NRF set the rules, and they could not "wiggle out of their respective roles." Bagnal, Dan Kaniewski, and Tom Bossert, the HSC's senior preparedness director, brought together support for the effort, including at the principals level, since Fran Townsend had already announced her resignation that would take effect in January 2008.

In the end, FEMA released the final NRF in January, and in March it officially replaced the NRP.

The National Response Framework stated clearly: "Response doctrine is rooted in America's Federal system and the Constitution's division of responsibilities between Federal and State governments."[21] It was Dave Paulison's fervent intent that the NRF's revised response doctrine replace the former response doctrine of sequential failure—where a state only responds when a local jurisdiction is overwhelmed and the federal government only responds when a state is overwhelmed and makes a formal request for assistance. To accelerate federal forward-leaning, the NRF eliminated the Incident of National Significance declaration as the formal trigger mechanism for initial coordination of federal incident assessment and response efforts. With regard to catastrophic preparedness, the NRF emphasized the concept of a readiness to act for no-notice events. Reflecting the spirit of the Coast Guard's Pub 1, the NRF stated, "The *Framework* incorporates standardized organizational structures that promote on-scene initiative, innovation, and sharing of essential resources drawn from all levels of government, NGOs, and the private sector. Response must be quickly scalable, flexible, and adaptable."[22]

# CHAPTER EIGHT

# DHS OPS, FEMA,
# and the Mandate for Operational Planning

The National Response Framework characterized planning as "the corner-stone of national preparedness." In a dedicated chapter titled "Planning: A Critical Element of Response," the NRF incorporated familiar language that spoke of a common doctrine for planning consisting of the National Preparedness Guidelines, HSPD-8, the National Infrastructure Protection Plan and its seventeen (now eighteen) sector-specific plans to protect critical infrastructure and key resources, NIMS, the national continuity policies and directives, a coordinated national exercise schedule, and a grants program. These documents, said the NRF, define "the essential architecture of our national preparedness system."[1]

Woven through the Townsend report and codified in PKEMRA had been a case for (1) enhancing the federal government's operational planning capability and (2) establishing a shared interagency planning culture. As plans, said the report, the National Response Plan and NIMS had operational gaps. "For any plan to work, it must first be broken down into its component parts. Next, the plan's requirements should be matched to the human and physical assets of each responsible department, agency, or organization."[2] With its third recommendation, the report called for DHS to "lead an interagency effort to develop and resource a deliberative, integrated and Federal planning and execution system to meet the requirements of the revised NRP."[3]

In 2007, the HSC's Joel Bagnal led a team that included Michele Malvesti, his lead writer on the Townsend report, to do a rewrite of the 2002 *National Strategy for Homeland Security*. Released in October, Bagnal's rewrite advanced the report's two interrelated planning priorities. To enhance operational planning, the 2007 *Strategy* called for establishment of a Homeland

Security Management System, a transformative national effort involving a continuous, mutually reinforcing, four-phased cycle of planning activity:

- Updated presidential policy directives and coordinated supporting strategies, doctrine, and planning guidance
- Strategic, operational, and tactical plan development
- Execution of these operational and tactical plans via actual operations or as part of an exercise—for example, through the National Exercise Program
- Continual assessment and evaluation of both operations and exercises

As for the second Townsend report planning imperative, establishing a shared interagency planning culture, the Strategy called for directly relating this four-phased Homeland Security Management System to instituting multidisciplinary homeland and national security professional education. Its purpose would be to enhance knowledge and learning, build trust and familiarity among diverse homeland security practitioners, dissolve organizational stovepipes, and further exchange ideas and best practices. The Strategy pointed to the May 2007 Executive Order 13434, "National Security Professional Development," and the resulting *National Strategy for the Development of Security Professionals*, saying that they were "essential steps forward in meeting these educational needs."[4] Most critically, it emphasized continued development of interagency and intergovernmental assignments and fellowship opportunities tied to promotions and professional advancement. If required for advancement in the homeland security profession, such assignments would be akin to DoD's mandatory joint duty requirement for any military officer wanting to advance to flag and general officer grade—that is, the requirement that put the teeth into the Defense Department's transformative 1986 Goldwater-Nichols reforms.

To further its operational planning goals, the Townsend report had specifically recommended replacement of the Interagency Incident Management Group. Established by the National Response Plan, the IIMG provided only operational coordination for management during an Incident of National Significance. The Townsend report proposed to reconfigure it into a new, standing interagency staff, resident the OPS National Operations Center that would provide a planning capability beyond just operational coordination. To fulfill the intent of the recommendation, Chertoff and Jackson thus stood up the Incident Management Planning Team (IMPT) in OPS in September 2006, as the NRP review and revision was getting under way. Oversight of this IMPT and its strategic-level planning actions went to Vice Adm. Roger Rufe, USCG (Ret.), the new OPS director who had relieved Brig. Gen. Matthew Broderick, USMC (Ret.), earlier that summer. Since Broderick's time, the NOC and its predecessor, the Homeland Security Operations Center, were primarily staffed with military and Coast Guard officials who were disposed to undertake an operational function for DHS Headquarters. Whereas Jackson had had trouble with Bob Stephan's IIMG and Integration Staff, he was more comfortable with OPS, recognizing that the OPS military and Coast Guard cultures could reinforce his and Chertoff's HSPD-5 domestic incident management authorities.

It was thus OPS and not FEMA that had the charge to meet the Townsend report's recommendation for a "Federal planning and execution system." Informed by the IMPT, OPS developed a formal, curriculum-based planning process it called the National Planning and Execution System (NPES). The DoD-oriented IMPT planners elected to base NPES on the Joint Operational Planning and Execution System (JOPES), the military's deliberate and crisis-action planning methodology for warfighting. In 2007, OPS field-tested NPES in a number of DoD and DHS exercises, notably the May Northern Command Ardent Sentry exercises, one of which exercised National Planning Scenario 1 (Nuclear Detonation—10-Kiloton Improvised Nuclear Device) in Illinois, Indiana, and Ohio, and the October TopOff 4 that exercised National Planning Scenario 11 (Radiological Attack—Radiological Dispersal Devices) in Oregon, Arizona, and Guam.

By December, OPS had progressed with NPES to the point that the HSC was ready to issue a planning annex to HSPD-8. The lead writer was Joel Bagnal's senior director for preparedness, Tom Bossert. Assisting him was the DHS Preparedness Directorate's planning lead, Corey Gruber. HSPD-8, Annex 1 (National Planning) required establishment of an Integrated Planning System (IPS) as *the* single, standardized national planning process and integration system for synchronizing and providing guidance to federal, state, local, and tribal planning.[5] IPS was to implement phase one of the Homeland Security Management System and horizontally and vertically integrate state, local, and tribal plans into federal plans. Bagnal intended this phase-one implementation to lead to the phase-two development of a National Homeland Security Plan, an overarching strategic plan to guide national efforts to execute the 2007 Strategy. He envisaged an operational framework that would encompass the prevention mission space with its National Implementation Plan for the War on Terrorism (NIP-WOT), protection with its National Infrastructure Protection Plan, and response with its revised National Response Plan. Having just worked on the NSC and HSC's May 2007 NSPD-51/HSPD-20, National Continuity Policy, that established eight National Essential Functions (NEFs)[6] and definitions for COG, COOP, and enduring constitutional government (ECG), Bagnal was the HSC point man for updating continuity policy to meet the governance challenge of catastrophic planning in the twenty-first century's new strategic environment. As FEMA continuity practitioners involved in national security emergency preparedness in the Reagan era well understood, it was not sufficient for government just to manage a catastrophic incident itself—for example, a nuclear detonation. In spite of the incident, it had to manage continuity well beyond a region physically affected—for example, with regard to maintaining a functioning financial system, food distribution, and so forth. Bagnal's all-hazards thinking, informed by Hurricane Katrina, was reflected in the Strategy:

> [C]ertain non-terrorist events that reach catastrophic levels can have significant implications for homeland security. The resulting national consequences and possible cascading effects from these events might present potential or perceived vulnerabilities that could be exploited, possibly eroding citizens' confidence in our Nation's government and ultimately increasing our vulnerability to attack. This *Strategy* therefore recognizes that effective preparation for catastrophic natural disasters and man-made disasters, while not homeland security per se, can nevertheless increase the security of the Homeland.[7]

While the Katrina response was in the forefront of such thinking in 2007, now many years later, the national continuity leadership appreciates the ECG issues associated with a wide range of catastrophic events. In the cyber realm, for example, attacks from malware like the Stuxnet computer worm or electromagnetic pulse (EMP) weapons could collapse one of the three major U.S. electricity grids. In such a scenario, management of the secondary effects on enduring constitutional government would be on a scale likened to Cold War scenarios. These cyber examples and others among the fifteen National Planning Scenarios suggest a need for a new security paradigm of national resilience undergirding twenty-first-century security governance, one that moves away from a federal-centric national security paradigm that in effect results in a single point of failure. With this realization already evident in 2007, Bagnal and the HSC thus revisited the national security preparedness and mobilization planning processes last addressed in the Reagan-era's 1988 EO 12656, Assignment of Emergency Preparedness Responsibilities. To assure continuity of government, at every level, in any national security emergency situation, EO 12656 had given FEMA the responsibility for assisting NSC implementation of national security emergency preparedness policy and planning by coordinating with the other federal departments and agencies and with state and local governments. Having this interagency and intergovernmental continuity planning legacy, FEMA in 2007 was now empowered by the PKEMRA-mandated transfer of preparedness functions. Bagnal thus saw the agency—as opposed to OPS and the National Operations Center—as the appropriate lead for the development of an overarching National Homeland Security Plan, if it were properly resourced.[8]

OPS, however, was able to argue that it should have the responsibility for the plan's development. According to one HSC senior staffer, Broderick, Rufe, and their OPS staffs with their military backgrounds "could be dismissive" of FEMA. When OPS got the lead on development of IPS and the National Homeland Security Plan, the stage was set for another round of intradepartmental DHS conflict—this time between OPS and FEMA. The struggle would spill into the interagency arena in the DRG. An intergovernmental problem arose as well with regard to IPS development. State and local emergency management and other non-federal stakeholders perceived IPS as a stalking horse for imposing on states and localities a scenario-based planning requirement. FEMA was thus caught in the middle.

### The Integrated Planning System and the Optics of Scenario-Based Planning

The JOPES-based NPES served as the structured IPS planning framework for all federal departments and agencies having a role in homeland security.

The Integrated Planning System was to guide how these departments and agencies coordinated deployment of the resources needed to support state and local operations.

The policy documents stated that IPS employed a mix of three planning approaches: scenario-based, functional, and capabilities-based planning. At the same time, IPS required that departments and agencies develop their plans using scenario-based planning based on the National Preparedness Guidelines' fifteen National Planning Scenarios. The National Response Framework identified IPS as "the national planning system used to develop interagency and intergovernmental plans based on the National Planning Scenarios." Yet nowhere did the NRF speak of a scenario-based planning methodology to build response capabilities. It spoke only of adopting a capabilities-based planning method.

The National Planning Scenarios collectively depict the broad range of natural and man-made threats facing the nation and were intended to guide overall homeland security planning efforts at all levels of government and with the private sector. They were not planning *methodologies* but rather planning *tools* intended to form the basis for national planning, training, investments, and exercises needed to prepare for all-hazard emergencies. Arguably, the scenarios were not even planning tools in the strict sense of the term. They were developed to help guide and quantify the Universal Task List and the Target Capabilities List and provide some background support to the early exercise program. Some FEMA officials maintain that they were never meant to serve as a planning proxy for operational plans. They only became so because some lawmakers and DHS officials thought they would make a great "deliverable."

The federal strategic plans to support the scenarios only drove indirectly the detailed planning required to identify specific federal capabilities that states might request. Observed a well-regarded 2008 Center for Strategic and International Studies (CSIS) report, "The NPS [National Planning Scenarios] were not originally intended to be the foundation of interagency deliberate planning, but rather were designed to be a planning and exercise tool for the federal, state, and local levels of government. . . . Because the NPS were not created at the outset to be the foundation of federal interagency planning, many argue they do not necessarily reflect the highest risk scenarios and are at best an imperfect starting point for detailed planning and identification of necessary requirements."[9] The semantic distinction between the terms "method" and "tool" contributed to a major flap over the National Planning Scenarios that was arguably more an issue of optics than substance.

In the seven years since 9/11, state emergency managers were increasingly doing a lot of planning, yet state-level planning was not comprehensive. State plans infrequently integrated vertically with federal plans and did not fully engage with all the state-level stakeholders. Nationwide, state interaction with local planning was uneven. State and local plans were frequently functionally based to identify common tasks to be performed under all-hazards planning. A second type of capabilities-based plans evaluated a mix of training, organizations, plans, personnel leadership and management, equipment, and facilities to perform generally required response tasks. A recent approach had come forward called "game planning" that combined elements of scenario-, functional-, and capability-based planning.[10] State and local planning was not usually scenario-based. In many cases, state and local authorities resisted the approach, because they did not accept the assumptions behind a federal focus limited to the fifteen specific scenarios.

The National Planning Scenarios immediately generated controversy when the Interim National Preparedness Goal first introduced them in 2005. They had been developed by the HSC counterterrorism policy coordinator, David Howe, with key input from the DRG's Scenario Working Group and Corey Gruber. Lawmakers were critical, reflecting the state and local perception that they were too focused on federal prioritization of risk to the detriment of "nonterrorism events." In April 2005 congressional testimony, Gruber addressed this issue by explaining that the Scenario Working Group selected a minimum number of scenarios to define specific tasks and develop capabilities to meet those tasks. The National Planning Scenarios, he said, focused mainly on WMD-type attacks because the nation was least prepared for them, whereas with the planning scenarios for natural hazards, "we have great experience and actuarial data."[11] Post-Katrina, many would argue that the hurricane response disproved that assumption, at least with regard to planning for a disaster of such catastrophic magnitude.[12]

Nevertheless, despite the seven years of effort, no mechanism existed to inform regional or federal capability requirements for response or to integrate mutually reinforcing comprehensive plans at the local, state, and federal levels into a credible operational national response plan. At the local level, authorities, particularly those in rural areas of the country, were looking to intra- and interstate regional collaborations where participating jurisdictions understood that individually they did not have the resources for prepared-ness. Such localities were attempting to forge regional planning approaches to deal with threats, hazards, and common concerns on the basis of what would work or had the potential to work. However, federal agencies were not facilitating coordination at the local level. Despite supporting language, fed-eral programs did not sustain development, testing/exercising, evaluation, and maintenance stages of such regional efforts. Regional initiatives suffered under the changing political circumstances, which appeared to local author-ities to be prompting federal officials to undercut their own programs and relapse into stove-piped business-as-usual attitudes.

While various analyses of the Hurricane Katrina preparedness and response revealed a multitude of homeland security and emergency manage-ment shortcomings at the state and local levels, the Townsend report chose only to focus on implementing correctives at the federal level. It followed that with respect to planning and national security professional development, the prevailing interagency sentiment in the DRG was that the federal government needed to get its own house in order before it could have a meaningful dia-logue on planning with the states and local governments. The interagency thus had priority over the intergovernmental. This mind-set had reinforced the DRG's development of the National Planning Scenarios that were so mis-understood by state and local homeland security stakeholders. So too did it seem to characterize the OPS-led development of the Integrated Planning System. The OPS planners with their military backgrounds conditioned by Goldwater-Nichols may have prided themselves on understanding well the horizontal, joint, interagency imperatives. Yet they were still somewhat prone to look at the vertical intergovernmental relationships through a command and control prism, when of course they are relationships of collaboration, coordination, and cooperation.

In the last two years of the Bush administration, the interagency policy development and implementation process worked well when departments and agencies had agreement at the principals and deputies levels. The process, though lengthy, was particularly successful in the NSC Counterterrorism Strat-egy Group's (CSG) development and implementation of the domain-specific presidential directives with their national strategies and supporting plans. At the

CSG and DRG level, agency and department representatives had the responsibility to manage conflicts. Problems only arose when a department itself had internal conflicts. For DHS, the assistant secretary–level representatives were at odds in a tussle between OPS and FEMA over the Integrated Planning System.

Tom Bossert, Joel Bagnal's senior director for preparedness, chaired the DRG meetings on IPS. Unlike Bagnal, Bossert was predisposed to having the White House drive use of the National Planning Scenarios. Bossert's predisposition suited the DHS position vis-à-vis FEMA. DHS lobbied hard for OPS and Rufe to be the department's sole representation in the DRG IPS development process. Supporting Rufe was his OPS deputy director, Wayne Parent, another Coast Guard veteran with a strong operations background, and Rich Burke, a retired Marine who was the director of the OPS plans division. All were proponents of the military's Joint Operational Planning and Exercise System methodology and use of the National Planning Scenarios to drive a centralized, top-down planning approach. Rufe and his team took the position that effective and efficient DHS management of domestic incidents as per HSPD-5 depended on OPS having an enhanced ability to plan and coordinate operations. The OPS approach got traction with Chertoff. In spring of 2008, he renamed OPS as the Office of Operations Coordination and Planning. The only authorizing language that existed for OPS was actually in PKEMRA. OPS did not and still does not have any authority for planning. In effect, the renaming was a reach attempted by Jackson and Rufe.

The apparent OPS empowerment presented a problem to state and local homeland security stakeholders. Representative was the view of Larry Gispert, the president of the International Association of Emergency Managers (IAEM), the body representing primarily local-level emergency management. Also the emergency management director for Florida's Hillsborough County, which includes the City of Tampa, Gispert told lawmakers in March 2008 congressional testimony that IAEM was focusing concern on OPS. "Subtitle C of the Post-Katrina Reform Act clearly assigned the FEMA Administrator responsibility for the National Preparedness System, including the National Planning Scenarios and the planning system," said Gispert, "yet these functions appear to have been placed under the authority of the Office of Operations Coordination."[13]

FEMA still wanted to develop and run the Integrated Planning System. The agency had an ally in Joel Bagnal, who had insisted that there be a seat

| Key Scenario Sets | National Planning Scenarios |
|---|---|
| 1. Explosives Attack – Bombing Using Improvised Explosive Device | Scenario 12: Explosives Attack – Bombing Using Improvised Explosive Device |
| 2. Nuclear Attack | Scenario 1: Nuclear Detonation – Improvised Nuclear Device |
| 3. Radiological Attack – Radiological Dispersal Device | Scenario 11: Radiological Attack – Radiological Dispersal Device |
| 4. Biological Attack – With annexes for different Pathogens | Scenario 2: Biological Attack – Aerosol Anthrax<br>Scenario 4: Biological Attack – Plague<br>Scenario 13: Biological Attack – Food Contamination<br>Scenario 14: Biological Attack – Foreign Animal Disease |
| 5. Chemical Attack – With annexes for different Agents | Scenario 5: Chemical Attack – Blister Agent<br>Scenario 6: Chemical Attack – Toxic Industrial Chemicals<br>Scenario 7: Chemical Attack – Nerve Agent<br>Scenario 8: Chemical Attack – Chlorine Tank Explosion |
| 6. Natural Disaster – With annexes for different Disasters | Scenario 9: Natural Disaster – Major Earthquake<br>Scenario 10: Natural Disaster – Major Hurricane |
| 7. Cyber Attack | Scenario 15: Cyber Attack |
| 8. Pandemic Influenza | Scenario 3: Biological Disease Outbreak – Pandemic Influenza |

at the table for Harvey Johnson in the deputies committee and another for Marko Bourne alongside Rufe and his OPS team in the DRG. Bourne subsequently gave the FEMA seat in the DRG to Dennis Schrader, who was actively working on the interagency and intergovernmental IPS/CPG-101 interfaces issues. Together, Johnson and Bourne thus began to put effort into taking ownership of IPS development on the basis of the FEMA authority for concept of operations (CONOPS) development. Rufe acknowledged in congressional testimony that the OPS planning focus was at the strategic level and that PKEMRA gave the operational-level planning focus to FEMA. The OPS-housed IMPT was focusing on long-term planning at the strategic level and considered itself more of a deliberative-planning entity for the structured development of operational plans. Yet in 2007, FEMA had launched its Operational Planning Unit (OPU) with some twelve to fifteen planners, also mostly former military. With a name change to the Operational Planning Branch (OPB), this planning entity became resident in the FEMA Disaster

Operations Directorate. OPB did engage in deliberate planning, but primarily it focused on near-term planning for six-months-out in a manner analogous to a military J-35 staff working on future operations. Schrader's National Preparedness Directorate provided funds for part of OPB's work, yet it was under-resourced compared to the IMPT at OPS. It was, nevertheless, a FEMA planning capability that would grow into maturity under Rich Kermond, the FEMA chief of operational planning. Kermond's efforts were precursors of FEMA Associate Administrator for Response and Recovery Bill Carwile's 2010–11 "whole of community" catastrophic planning approach.

Meanwhile, state and local emergency management continued to hold the perception that OPS was forcing them to plan against fifteen National Planning Scenarios. Fifteen was too many. In response to mounting criticism, the DRG agreed to compress the fifteen into eight scenario-set groupings in October 2007 and thus documented in the National Response Framework. The state and local pushback nevertheless continued into 2008. Particularly vocal was IAEM's Larry Gispert, who objected to what many emergency managers perceived as the IPS scenario-based, military planning model. Writing in his association's monthly bulletin, he said that the IPS planning model was difficult to reconcile with the more familiar risk-based models. These state and local models, he said, were based on comprehensive emergency management for all-hazards, functional-, and capability-based planning that had commonalities in all disasters. "Since [IPS] is scenario-based, it cannot be called all-hazards planning as it is limited to a few chosen scenarios.... How vertical integration will be performed remains a question mark in my mind."[14]

In his March congressional testimony, Gispert voiced the familiar perception that the national scenarios were top-down and too focused on terrorism:

> For example, none of the scenarios deal with flooding or tornadoes as a primary problem.... Flooding and tornadoes accounted for 130 of 295 Presidential declarations of disaster from 1988 through 1996.... As such, these national planning scenarios are self-limiting, rather than reflecting the actual full range of threats that exist and anticipating the formation of potential new threats to our nation. The bigger picture here, however, is not the specific number of scenarios, but that any scenarios developed are utilized to create one Emergency Operations Plan identifying the functions and capabilities common

to all emergencies as well as the roles and responsibilities of government. Deriving multiple plans from these scenarios seems to be an
adoption of a military-style planning process. This process is great—
if you are the military and funded and equipped with the resources of
the military. If you are a state or local government, this simply is not
the most efficient and effective way to utilize planning resources.[15]

The bottom line was indeed money. Gispert expressed the familiar fear
that with IPS, DHS would incorporate some kind of mandated scenario-
based planning in future grant guidance.

The progress of IPS and operational planning development and implementation would prove challenging even for the federal government. OPS
delivered IPS to the DRG in February 2008 on the heels of FEMA's release
of the National Response Framework. After several months of interagency
review, the DRG released the interim version of IPS in June. Further revisions
continued until the final IPS release in January 2009.

The DRG had set a goal for the development of incident management plans
correlated with the National Planning Scenarios: completion of five strategic
guidance statements and four strategic plans by January 20, 2009. It didn't happen. DHS had stretched its planning resources too far across follow-on work on
development and implementation of both the fifteen scenarios and IPS. Then in
early 2008, the DRG instructed the interagency community to redirect its planning resources to develop plans for the so-called Period of Heightened Alert
that ran from the national conventions through Election Day to the inauguration and transition—August 31, 2008 to July 1, 2009. It told the departments
and agencies to complete their plans by early July. As a result, the interagency
completed work on only five of the eight scenario sets by February 2010, when
the DHS Office of the Inspector General (OIG) released a progress report on
DHS federal incident management planning. At that time, the interagency had
completed a CONOPS and OPLAN (operational plan) for only one scenario,
Terrorist Use of Explosives. Four scenarios, Major Hurricane, Major Earthquake, Cyber Attack, and Pandemic Influenza, had as yet no strategic guidance
statement and thus no strategic plan.[16] In the case of the Major Hurricane scenario, however, the DRG directed FEMA to complete the CONOP in advance
of a strategic guidance statement or strategic plan to prepare for the 2009 hurricane season. Work commenced in December 2008.

With the change of administration in 2009, incoming Homeland Security Secretary Janet Napolitano announced in March the DHS Southwest Border Initiative that further delayed scenario development and IPS implementation. In July 2009 and into 2010, IMPT planning was on hold while the DRG and NSC conducted an HSPD-8 review that delayed scenario-set development of the Chemical Strategic Plan and the Natural Disaster Strategic Guidance Statement. When the DHS OIG released its report, IPS was into a review process addressing the need to require operational plans to incorporate performance and effectiveness measures. Notwithstanding these federal-level difficulties, it would be FEMA that would prove successful in facilitating state- and local-level vertical operational planning integration with its own internal planning guidance review.

### Bringing On Board the States and Locals with CPG-101

While FEMA had been fighting an uphill interagency battle with OPS over IPS development, it was also engaged in revision of its general guidelines for federal, state, and local development of emergency operations plans. Coincident with the launch of the interagency NRP review, this internal agency effort had been under way since late 2006. It was the latest of routine planning guideline revisions following major disasters. In the sixties—pre-FEMA—the Cuban Missile Crisis induced the federal government to produce emergency operations plans at the tactical and operational levels—for example, the Federal Civil Defense Guide. Following the FEMA stand-up, such guidance documents were re-titled civil preparedness guides. Hurricane Hugo and the Loma Prieta Earthquake, occurring a month apart in 1989, influenced the development of the 1990 Civil Preparedness Guide 1-8. Similarly, Hurricane Andrew and the Great Midwest Flood of 1993 shaped the 1996 State and Local Guide (SLG) 101, "Guide for All-Hazards Emergency Planning," that was still in effect ten years later, post-Katrina. Developed by Kay Goss, James Lee Witt's influential associate director for preparedness, training, and exercises, SLG-101 was in 2006 the FEMA document that provided guidance for preparedness, response, and short-term recovery planning elements in state and local emergency operations plans. Attachment G issued in April 2001 gave guidance on terrorism response and was interagency focused and interagency coordinated. Released prior to the September 1997 report by the President's Commission on Critical Infrastructure Protection (the Marsh Commission),

SLG-101 did not reflect Dick Clarke's development of critical infrastructure and key resources protection as an emergency management function as mandated in PDD-63 in February 1998. The PKEMRA now mandates that inclusion.

The focusing events that shaped the mid-decade emergency planning environment for what would be called the Comprehensive Preparedness Guidelines 101 (CPG-101) were of course the 9/11 attacks and Hurricanes Katrina and Rita. The action officer for CPG-101 development was Donald "Doc" Lumpkins, the branch chief for planning and assistance in the NPD Office of Preparedness Policy, Planning, and Assistance. Lumpkins had a solid state planning background. He came to FEMA from the DHS Preparedness Directorate's Programs Division where he had participated in Corey Gruber's Nationwide Plan Review. Prior to that, he had been with the Maryland Emergency Management Agency where he had been a planner working with Dennis Schrader. For CPG-101 development, Lumpkins led a team that included some thirty state and local emergency preparedness practitioners. He reported to Gruber, who had also come to FEMA. When Tracy Henke left her grants position in October 2006, Gruber had become the acting assistant secretary of grants and training. The following April, when the DHS preparedness functions transferred to FEMA, Gruber and Lumpkins both found themselves in the agency's NPD. Gruber was its acting deputy administrator until Schrader came on board in August.

The CPG-101 effort caught its stride that autumn. To solidify the developing planning culture in FEMA, Marko Bourne established an agency-wide Planning Working Group, eventually giving the lead to Josh Dozor. This working group consisted of the deputies of the FEMA Preparedness (Catastrophic Planning Grants), Response, Recovery, and Mitigation Directorates. This group coordinated agency planning activities, set the benchmarks for a national planning system, and assisted the drafting of CPG-101. Representing Schrader and the NPD was Corey Gruber.

In line with the PKEMRA mandates and the forward-leaning precepts of the New FEMA, Dave Paulison and Harvey Johnson expected CPG-101 to provide guidance for integrating prevention and protection planning efforts. CPG-101 would further cement FEMA in DHS by giving emergency management planning a stake in prevention and protection while at the same time introducing Secretary Chertoff's left-of-the-boom, risk reduction verities into the FEMA mind-set. To those ends, CPG-101 spoke of adaptive and non-adaptive risks. Adaptive risks were human threats whose behavior may change in response to a jurisdiction's actions. This class of risks thus required emergency operations planning to reflect inputs from law enforcement information or intelligence. Non-adaptive risks were natural hazards whose "disaster dimensions" were not shaped by a jurisdiction's level of preparedness. For this category of risk, emergency operations planning needed only to address coordination of traditional mitigation activities informed by fire prevention inspections, planning and zoning, land development regulation, storm water management, and so forth.

Prevention planning would inform courses of action to reduce or eliminate threats to people and critical infrastructure and key resources deemed vital to state and local jurisdictions, national security, public health and safety, or economic prosperity and competitiveness. Protection planning would inform courses of action to modify structures, secure facilities and people, and conserve the environment. The objectives of prevention and protection planning were, respectively, identification of threats and protection of potential targets. To accomplish these goals, prevention and protection planning would focus on information collection and threat detection; risk, vulnerability, and intelligence analysis; information sharing and collaboration; criminal investigations and intervention; critical infrastructure protection; and risk management.

This CPG-101 embrace of the prevention and protection missions reflected not just a proactive FEMA adoption of the preparedness cultures of law enforcement, fire prevention, and the military. It signaled equally a restoration of the agency's Cold War–era national preparedness and national continuity functions, in accord with Joel Bagnal's thinking in the HSC. Thus informed, CPG-101 would integrate concepts not only from the National Preparedness Guidelines, National Incident Management System, and National Response Framework, but from the *National Strategy for Information Sharing* and National Infrastructure Protection Plan as well.

In actual fact, Paulison and Johnson intended CPG-101 to be more than a guide. CPG-101 was to be the *foundation* for state and local planning. On the DHS side, however, Michael Jackson and Roger Rufe were not entirely supportive of this CPG-101 effort. It was a challenge to OPS and its planning program by virtue of its intent to incorporate planning guidance for a prevention and protection CONOPS. As Lumpkins completed their draft CPG-101 in the summer of 2008, Dennis Schrader thus found himself having to protect FEMA development of CPG-101 in the interagency IPS discussions in the DRG. Rufe and OPS were pushing hard for IPS to be the single planning system wholly reliant on scenario-based planning. While Schrader was responsible for shepherding CPG-101 in the interagency DRG process, he also had to sell it to the state and local stakeholders like Gispert and IAEM and the powerful National Emergency Management Association (NEMA), the state-level emergency managers' association. The optics perception that he had to overcome in the non-federal stakeholder community was the fear that scenario-based planning would become a requirement in preparedness grant guidance. With maximum effort, Schrader kept the states and local governments on board with CPG-101 and by extension IPS by offering a compromise solution to the problem of vertical integration of federal, state, and local planning. Schrader put forth a promise that FEMA would not force the states to do scenario-based planning in return for their agreement to accept FEMA doing it at the regional level. De-confliction would thus take place in the regions.

The Schrader compromise enabled the intergovernmental planning framework to proceed. CPG-101 thus became the companion document to IPS that described how the state and local planning process would integrate vertically and synchronize (i.e., in purpose, place, and time) with IPS-driven federal-level planning. CPG-101 recognized that many state and local jurisdictions had already developed their operations plans. CPG-101 and IPS acknowledged the use of three planning approaches: scenario-based, functional, and capabilities-based planning. From the states' perspective, integrated planning addressed the process of working with other organizations and obtaining resources. The CPG-101/IPS goal was to mesh state and local planning up and federal planning down the various levels of government to inform combined operations. During the planning process, a local or a state planning team would identify a support requirement for a higher jurisdictional level, and together the two levels would work on resolving the problem.

Unlike the National Response Plan review and revision process, Doc Lumpkins ensured that the state and local stakeholders were fully engaged throughout the CPG-101 process. While the non-federal stakeholders continued to have issues with IPS, he had induced in them a sense of ownership with regard to CPG-101. In August 2008, NPD released the interim CPG-101,

"Producing Emergency Plans: A Guide for All-Hazard Operations Planning for State, Territorial, Local, and Tribal Governments." He had managed the non-federal stakeholder vetting process so well that that language in the final was virtually the same. The final CPG-101 was released in March 2009, after the change of administration, with the modified title, "Developing and Maintaining State, Territorial, Tribal, and Local Government Emergency Plans." The Integrated Planning System was issued two months earlier in January.

IPS and CPG-101 shared the same planning language. Both documents referenced each other. IPS acknowledged in some measure the primacy of CPG-101 in the context of state and local planning. In addition to incorporating lessons learned from the OPS development of the National Planning and Execution System, IPS credited the Interim CPG-101 with providing "the planning process and doctrine elements," adding that DHS encouraged state, local, and tribal governments to use CPG-101 to comply with IPS.[17] CPG-101, it said, "meets the Annex I requirement that IPS include a 'guide for all-hazards planning.' . . . It is expected that State and local jurisdictions will, over a period of time, align their existing planning processes with those in CPG-101."[18]

The Integrated Planning System referenced the *National Strategy for the Development of National Security Professionals* and its framework for integrated education, training, and professional experience opportunities across organizations, levels of government, and incident management disciplines. IPS charged the secretary of homeland security to develop a program to provide federal, state, local, and tribal government officials with education in disaster preparedness, response and recovery plans and authorities, and training in crisis decision-making skills. The secretary was also to define, organize and offer IPS-related training throughout the various levels. Finally, the secretary was to integrate IPS- and CPG-101-related training with established training programs and through appropriate interagency collaboration, and establish certification standards and professional levels for planners.[19] The Obama administration's Presidential Policy Directive 8 (PPD-8), National Preparedness, which replaces the Bush administration's HSPD-8, discarded IPS in favor of developing a broader National Planning System. As outlined in PPD-8, this effort began under Doc Lumpkins, with primary development falling under FEMA Associate Administrator for Response and Recovery Bill Carwile and his director of national planning, Don Daigler, who had succeeded Rich Kermond.

### Addressing the Resourcing Challenge

Still, FEMA and DHS were faced with the question of how to resource development of state and local operational planning capability. One approach favored by Harvey Johnson aimed to assist state planners struggling to identify capability gaps to inform regional or federal capability requirements for response. In 2007, FEMA launched the Gap Analysis Tool as a resource for assessing capabilities and capability gaps. Developed initially by Joe Bruno, the commissioner of the New York City Office of Emergency Management, this resource tool was rolled out in the hurricane-prone states among state and local agencies to assist them in conducting their pre-hurricane assessments. Johnson pre-assigned federal coordinating officers to those states to build relationships. Regional planners used the tool to identify asset gaps at the local, state, and national levels. It identified and reviewed seven critical areas: debris removal, commodity distribution, evacuation, sheltering, interim housing, medical needs, and fuel capacity along evacuation routes. FEMA's intent was to continue the rollout nationwide, adapting it for hazards specific to other FEMA regions. In the end, while the Atlantic Coast states balked at having to do the extra work required to implement the gap tool, they appreciated the results. However, the tool failed to translate its application to the regions threatened by the New Madrid Fault, and officials responsible for it conceded that it was not yet ready for nationwide all-hazards applications. Rather than fixing the tool and the program, after the new administration came into office FEMA discarded it with no replacement.

Also in 2007, FEMA launched the Regional Catastrophic Preparedness Grant Program (RCPGP) to provide funding to advance catastrophic incident preparedness to Tier I and designated Tier II Urban Areas Security Initiative (UASI) metropolitan areas. Said FEMA, "The goal of RCPGP is to support an integrated planning system that enables regional all-hazard planning for catastrophic events and the development of necessary plans, protocols, and procedures to manage a catastrophic event."[20] The program ran until 2012 with $155 million going to jurisdictions for developing coordinated plans in areas that DHS determined were at the highest risk for a catastrophic event. Congress would only fund RCPGP to assist jurisdictions in developing plans. Lawmakers would not, however, agree to funding the capability to sustain them.

At the same time, the Pentagon saw an opportunity to employ its own planning expertise. The Center for Strategic and International Studies and others had long been observing how preparedness could benefit from the cross-fertilization of military planners and emergency management planners schooled only on the Incident Command System.[21] This resourcing scheme for planning was the DoD's intergovernmental initiative called Task Forces for Emergency Response (TFERs). Originating with Paul McHale, the assistant secretary of defense for homeland defense, TFERs would task military planners for homeland security planning, specifically deliberate planning, not a field thought by DoD to be where civilian federal agencies and state and local governments had much experience. As opposed to targeting UASIs, the concept was aimed to appeal to rural states. McHale reckoned that while the capabilities of states with large- and medium-sized metropolitan areas may have been robust, rural states with smaller populations needed help.

A TFER would integrate into a state planning entity to provide a state-level planning capability. It was to produce the state plan tailored to the unique strengths and vulnerabilities of the state. Facilitating integration and synchronization of local, state, regional, federal, and private-sector incident planning, it would serve as a state's focal point for catastrophic response planning and integration of the military capabilities into those of the public and private sectors. TFERs would leverage DoD planning capabilities resident in the National Guard and National Guard Bureau and embed them under governors in their emergency management agencies. They included National Guard planners and DoD emergency preparedness liaison officers teamed with FEMA federal preparedness coordinators and state planners. TFERs were a regional defense coordinating officer's (DCO's) responsibility that would fall under his/her J-5 (deliberate planning support). The DCO would liaise with regional adjutants general (TAGs) to use TFERs to backfill states' planning capabilities, if needed, and report TFER findings to the NorthCom J-5.

The TFER concept was thus McHale and DoD's competing attempt to merge bottom-up local and state planning with IPS. TFERs piloted in twelve states. States did not, however, embrace the concept, largely because TFERs based their planning approach on the fifteen National Planning Scenarios. While DoD proactively covered the costs of piloting the TFERs, it looked to FEMA to undertake the costs of the program. FEMA did not have the budget to continue the effort and had concerns that the process would "militarize" planning at the state and local level and would work against building full-time planning capacity within the state and local emergency management agencies. State emergency management agencies that were not part of the TAG's National Guard structures were also concerned that this would put their agencies at risk of being transferred to the Guard over time. As such, the concept died.

### Devolving Preparedness to the FEMA Regions

The Integrated Planning System document said of FEMA regional planning that:

> FEMA-developed regional plans address actions and activities taken by FEMA regional offices in coordination with Federal agencies and in consultation with States to support integrated and synchronized Federal, State, local, and Tribal operations. . . . The FEMA Region plays a critical role in enabling state-to-state cooperation, coordinating disparate capabilities across its region, and serving as the translator between national-level planning requirements and State planning requirements. FEMA Regions determine capability gaps, resource shortfalls, and State expectations for Federal assistance through the process of the gap analysis method that best fits the need.[22]

For its part, the Townsend report had detailed a recommendation for the stand-up of DHS homeland security regions, a fully staffed, trained, and equipped DHS regional structure for preparedness—also a PKEMRA mandate. Key would be a "preparedness group" whose goal would be to prepare for disasters, conduct training, coordinate and integrate planning, measure capability and preparedness, and respond to disasters. As well, this group would help to ensure that federal spending in the region bolstered capabilities outlined in the National Preparedness Goal. Regional DHS directors were to comprise a principal federal official (PFO) professional cadre. The report sought to have regional directors, with "significant expertise and experience" sufficient to act as PFOs, who would have the authority to make any operational decisions necessary within the law without having to obtain approval from DHS headquarters. Each homeland security region would be able to establish a self-sufficient, initial Joint Field Office (JFO) anywhere within the region to enhance the federal government's ability to maintain continuity of operations. In terms of professional development, incident management teams (IMTs) would be composed of experts in the Incident Command System who could establish a command for the federal response that would connect with state and local response structures during disasters and large-scale events. IMTs would maintain certification in all levels of ICS for each ICS command element.

Schrader and Bourne were of a mind to find ways for DHS to leverage FEMA's existing regional structure. As opposed to managing programs from Washington or re-creating regions, they wanted the existing FEMA regions to serve as the DHS regions for preparedness. The FEMA regional structure was best positioned to integrate programs at the regional level to engage the states as partners in developing and sustaining national preparedness. Schrader particularly wanted the FEMA regions to have budget authority that would allow them to continue growing their personnel strength and capabilities to support the states and facilitate their engagement with the private sector, non-governmental organizations, and universities to develop regional capabilities. For his part, Bourne was intent on the regions developing their own metrics to provide guidance to the regional administrators for setting priorities, establishing standard operating procedures, and making decisions based on the specifics of the region. As he had done with the Planning Working Group, Bourne secured Josh Dozor to lead the regional efforts. Working closely with Schrader and NPD's director of operations, Andy Mitchell, and the assistant administrator for grants programs, Ross Ashley, Dozor began his work as the FEMA federal preparedness coordinators deployed to the regions and started developing their preparedness plans. Dozor made it a priority to establish grant metrics for regionalizing grants management. He also prepared the documents that provided each regional preparedness officer with a yearly statement of work and measures that linked grants with preparedness, planning, training, and exercises. FEMA initially piloted its regional metrics development and reporting templates in Region X, the Pacific Northwest, and then Region I, New England. The effort continued into the new administration with Bob Farmer, who served as Bourne's deputy in the Office of Policy and Program Analysis, while NPD continued to use the approach to help the federal preparedness coordinators with their yearly work plans. Farmer became the lead for program analysis and sustained the outcomes-based metrics approach to programs. Led by Dozor, FEMA released its regional CONOPS in February 2008.

# CHAPTER NINE

# The Homeland Security Enterprise:
## Toward a Network Governance

W̶hen the Obama administration took office in January 2009, its mani-fest priority was the management of the multi-faceted financial crisis, whose effects had cascaded into the September 2008 investment banking insolven-cies, the October stock market crash, and intense economic policy debates that engulfed the presidential transition. The primary attention of the new administration was thus not on security issues, managed immediately to the west of 1600 Pennsylvania Avenue in the Eisenhower Executive Office Building. The Obama White House was necessarily focused on the monu-mental matters addressed just to its east in the Treasury Building. There, the compelling issues were how to proceed with the bank-bailout strategy of the Bush administration's Troubled Asset Relief Program (TARP) and the new administration's own inevitably controversial economic stimulus package of tax cuts and government spending projects. The dramatic impact of the ongo-ing debt crisis propelled to the fore a familiar partisan exchange over the role of the federal government. The headlines were about a perceived revisiting of FDR's big-government, New Deal policies of the Great Depression that had been informed by British economist John Maynard Keynes and his mac-roeconomic remedies based on deficit spending. The challenges to security governance once presented by 9/11 and Hurricane Katrina were now below the proverbial fold, if not consigned to the back pages. The new administra-tion hence came to office with no front-page driver for homeland security reorganization.

The Bush administration had bequeathed its 2003 HSPD-8, National Preparedness, conceived at the height of the Global War on Terrorism. HSPD-8 was the foundational document of the National Preparedness System with its requirement for DHS development of a National Preparedness Goal.

The Obama administration's March 2011 release of its rewrite of HSPD-8, Presidential Policy Directive 8 (PPD-8), National Preparedness, reflected a through-line running from the post-Katrina DHS Nationwide Planning Review of 2006 and follow-on National Preparedness Task Force. The 2006 review had concluded that interagency and intergovernmental catastrophic planning was neither sufficiently systematic nor interlinked within a national planning system. The charge to the task force was: implement HSPD-8, construct the National Preparedness System, and develop the National Preparedness Goal to provide a systematic planning methodology for homeland security. The outcome was a capabilities-based framework for all four homeland security missions: prevention, protection, response, and recovery. Those working in national preparedness largely ignored the mitigation mission of emergency management. The efforts of the planning review and the preparedness task force, both led by Corey Gruber, made their way into the response mission set during the interagency review process for the National Response Plan and its ultimate revision into the National Response Framework.

In 2009–10, the Obama administration similarly would use a task force—this time one primarily composed of non-federal stakeholders—to inform DHS development of the National Preparedness Goal in line with PPD-8 and the National Security Staff's development of integrated planning frameworks for *all* homeland missions. The descriptive that expressed the new administration's approach to the shared interagency and intergovernmental responsibility for building and sustaining National Preparedness System was the term "homeland security enterprise," officially introduced by DHS in its first *Quadrennial Homeland Security Review (QHSR)* that came out in 2010.[1]

### Planning and Professional Development as Cornerstones to the Homeland Security Enterprise

The administration review of security governance at the interagency level followed the late-February 2009 Presidential Study Directive-1 (PSD-1), Organizing for Homeland Security and Counterterrorism. PSD-1 directed John Brennan, assistant to the president for homeland security and counterterrorism, to lead an interagency review of ways to reform the White House organization for counterterrorism and homeland security. During the 2008 campaign, Brennan had advised Obama on national security issues. A career

CIA official, he had served as DCI George Tenet's chief of staff and later as his deputy director of central intelligence during the Clinton and Bush administrations. In 2003, he became the director of the CIA-housed Terrorist Threat Integration Center that in late 2004, via the Intelligence Reform and Terrorism Prevention Act, subsequently transmuted into ODNI's National Counterterrorism Center, where Brennan continued as NCTC director for another year. Brennan thus was a career intelligence professional—borders-out focused.

The borders-in expertise came via Brennan's PSD-1 action officers, Michele Malvesti and Randy Beardsworth, both veterans of the Bush administration. Malvesti had been the Bush NSC's senior director for combating terrorism strategy who assisted Joel Bagnal in writing the Townsend report on the Hurricane Katrina national preparedness and response. Beardsworth was a career Coast Guardsman who had served in both the Clinton and Bush administrations as the director for defense policy on the NSC staff. As a member of Tom Ridge's DHS Transition Team, he helped develop and integrate the functional structure of the DHS Border and Transportation Security Directorate. Once established, he became its director of operations and later acting undersecretary. In August 2005 following Chertoff and Jackson's Second Stage Review DHS reorganization, he became assistant secretary for strategic plans as head of the DHS Office of Policy. Beardsworth was heavily focused on departmental operations and planning integration and on counterterrorism strategic planning and its implementation. His enduring legacy to the department came from having led development of the DHS long-range strategic vision, expressed in the 2008 *One Team, One Mission: Securing Our Homeland*, its strategic plan for FY08–13.

Brennan, Malvesti, and Beardsworth reported out the PSD-1 review in late May 2009. The review opted to keep both the NSC and HSC. The Homeland Security Council, established by statute, would remain as the White House's "principal venue for interagency deliberations on issues that affect the security of the homeland such as terrorism, weapons of mass destruction, natural disasters, and pandemic influenza."[2] Also remaining would be Brennan's position of homeland security and counterterrorism advisor. Whereas the Bush administration had provided for two parallel staffs to support the NSC and the HSC, the review called for a single, fully integrated National Security Staff to support both national security and homeland security policy-making.[3]

The White House's May statement on the PSD-1 review said, "The establishment of the new National Security Staff, under the direction of the National Security Advisor, will end the artificial divide between White House staff who have been dealing with national security and homeland security issues." This new National Security Staff would develop a single *National Security Strategy* to address both national security and homeland security issues. DHS would assume the responsibility to update the *National Strategy for Homeland Security*, initially issued by the HSC staff in its first two iterations in 2002 and 2007.

The PSD-1 review established new directorates and positions within the National Security Staff, in particular the borders-in Resilience Policy Directorate. In announcing the review findings, Beardsworth described the stand-up of this directorate as possibly the "most significant aspect of the reorganization." As the federal government's homeland security focus group, this body returned to the White House the policy development clout that had gone to DHS with the stand-up of the Policy Directorate in 2005 under the Chertoff/Jackson Second Stage review. The establishment of the Resilience Policy Directorate was PSD-1's attempt to improve the integration of state, local, and tribal governments and private-sector and NGO communities into the borders-in security and resilience policy process. The directorate would serve as a venue for these non-federal homeland security stakeholders to provide direct and up-front input on policy development. With regard to the homeland security mission continuum, the review recommended the transfer of the responsibility for long-term recovery policy and coordination from the national security staff to the Domestic Policy Council. Long-term recovery thus would no longer be seen as a homeland security mission.

At the helm of the Resilience Policy Directorate was Richard Reed, the special assistant to the president for homeland security and the NSC's senior director for resilience and continuity policies. An Army Airborne Ranger who had worked for FEMA, the Department of Veterans Affairs, and the General Services Administration as its first chief emergency response and recovery officer, Reed came to the Bush White House in 2006 as the HSC's senior continuity policy director. He was Joel Bagnal's principal drafter and implementer of the all-hazards National Continuity Policy, NSPD-51/HSPD-20. Notwithstanding his military background, he—like Bagnal—appreciated the twenty-first-century all-hazards dimension of continuity.

Reed's directorate had two policy portfolios: preparedness and response. Heading response was Elizabeth Farr, an intelligence specialist with a legal background who served as the NSC's director for combating terrorism. In the Bush administration, she had been the NSC's director of international organized crime, working on the linkages between terrorist and international criminal networks. The preparedness portfolio went to Brian Kamoie, another official with a legal background who came to the White House in the summer of 2009. As the NSC's senior director for preparedness policy, Kamoie led development of national policy related to all-hazards preparedness, resilience, and national security professional development. He came with an immediate Health and Human Services background. In 2004, he was the HHS deputy assistant secretary for preparedness and response and director of the Office of Policy, Strategic Planning, and Communications. There he had driven the HHS' assistant secretary for preparedness and response's (ASPR) bioterrorism and public health emergency policy development, strategic planning, and communications. Kamoie specifically led development and implementation of the National Response Plan and NIMS, the National Strategy for Pandemic Influenza, the Pandemic and All-Hazards Preparedness Act, the Public Readiness and Emergency Preparedness Act, and such directives as HSPD-10, Biodefense for the 21st Century, HSPD-18, Medical Countermeasures against Weapons of Mass Destruction, and HSPD-21, Public Health and Medical Preparedness. Operationally, he also played key leadership roles in the HHS response in the 2005 TopOff 3 and 2007 TopOff 4 national exercises, as well as in hurricanes, floods, and the 2009 H1N1 influenza pandemic.

Kamoie's arrival to work with Reed came as the new administration was in the midst of grappling with the H1N1 epidemic that engaged virtually the entire Resilience Policy Directorate staff—right through the early months of 2010, when it had the additional issues management burden associated with the U.S. response to the Haitian Earthquake. Throughout this period, Reed and Kamoie were entrenched in brokering the interagency H1N1 preparedness process. Vaccine development was the critical issue: the country had no H1N1 vaccine. The paramount administration fear was that the epidemic would metastasize into a worldwide crisis on a scale of the 1918 influenza pandemic. If so, it would be Obama's Katrina. Immersed in running a six-member team working under his All-Hazards Medical Preparedness portfolio, Kamoie was not able to start any meaningful work on developing generic national preparedness policy, the rewrite of the Bush HSPD-8, until the spring of 2010.

Not until May 2010 was the National Security Staff able to issue the new administration's *National Security Strategy*. Buried in the document was a passage that expresses the national security strategy of the United States that arguably dates from Woodrow Wilson and the Great War: comprehensive engagement to "underpin a just and sustainable international order" that is "a rules-based international system."[4] Success, it said, requires a whole-of-government approach to strengthen the U.S. national capacity for global engagement, of which homeland security and national resilience plays a part.

Homeland security, said the strategy, "traces its roots to traditional and historic functions of government and society, such as civil defense, emergency response, law enforcement, customs, border patrol, and immigration. . . . It is not simply about government action alone, but rather about the collective strength of the entire country."[5] To improve the borders-in preparedness for effectively managing emergencies, the national strategy emphasized the integration of intergovernmental all-hazards planning with the private and nonprofit sectors to build key capabilities for emergency response. "We are encouraging domestic regional planning and integrated preparedness programs and will encourage government at all levels to engage in long-term recovery planning."[6]

Three months ahead of the White House release of the *National Security Strategy*, the Department of Homeland Security stepped forward to issue its iteration of borders-in homeland security strategy. As amended, the Homeland Security Act of 2002 required the secretary of homeland security to conduct a *Quadrennial Homeland Security Review* to delineate and update the national homeland security strategy.[7] In its first-ever *QHSR*, issued in February 2010, DHS defined and framed homeland security as "a widely distributed and diverse—but unmistakable—national enterprise."[8] The department's use of the term "homeland security enterprise" referred to "the collective efforts and shared responsibilities of Federal, State, local, tribal, territorial, nongovernmental, and private-sector partners—as well as individuals, families, and communities—to maintain critical homeland security capabilities."[9]

While DHS consulted widely and received extensive stakeholder comment during its drafting, the *QHSR* had its shortcomings. Most significantly, it did not identify DHS programs, functions and activities and how they contributed to homeland security. It thus did not meet the statutory mandate to provide detailed descriptions of federal, state, and local roles and responsibilities—for example, specifics on funding, staffing, logistics, training, surge capacity, and so forth. Within DHS, it did drive some decisions by the Office of Program Analysis and Evaluation and the Policy Directorate on budget priorities during the preparation of the FY13 budget submission. Yet unlike DoD's more influential Quadrennial Defense Review and the executive branch's other quadrennial reviews, it had limited impact and did not carry much weight among lawmakers.

Nevertheless, the QHSR was very helpful in framing the direction of DHS as it moved forward toward its second decade. Though short on the details, it set forth a comprehensive approach to all homeland security activities that "must be built upon a foundation of ensuring *security and resilience*, as well as facilitating the normal, daily activities of society and interchange with the world" [emphasis added].[10] The QHSR outlined the nation's five enterprise-wide homeland security missions:

- Preventing Terrorism and Enhancing Security
- Securing and Managing Our Borders
- Enforcing and Administering Our Immigration Laws
- Safeguarding and Securing Cyberspace
- Ensuring Resilience to Disasters

As regard to this fifth disaster reliance mission space—the preserve of FEMA—the QHSR charted a clear path for the agency to exercise its yet-to-be fully realized PKEMRA authorities. It validated FEMA as the preparedness lead in the interagency and intradepartmental DHS battles over the rewrite of HSPD-8, a validation that FEMA administrator Craig Fugate used very effectively. In the intergovernmental, whole-of-nation sense, the QHSR also recognized and described the work required for DHS to continue evolving, with the acknowledgment that the Homeland Security Enterprise was more than the department.

The 2002 homeland security statute also provided for a QHSR follow-on: a DHS Bottom-Up Review (BUR). This departmental review of programs, budgets, and organizational alignment got under way in November 2009 and reported out five months after the *QHSR* in July 2010. With respect to enhancing enterprise-wide homeland security partner capability and capacity, the BUR said, "Responsibilities for homeland security are broader than those of DHS and indeed broader than those of the Federal government. For that reason, there is a need to strengthen the ability of partners in the homeland security enterprise—in particular, State, local, tribal, and territorial governments, and the private sector—to execute important aspects of core homeland security mission activities."[11]

With respect to the *QHSR's* Ensuring Resilience in Disasters Mission and its associated goals, the BUR emphasized the importance of catastrophic planning. "The *QHSR* and BUR analyses show that DHS' responsibilities in disaster resilience require enhanced planning, management systems, resilience policies, and the promotion of individual, family, and community preparedness. Planning for catastrophic disasters must be more coordinated and predicated on nationally agreed-upon, risk-based preparedness standards."[12]

Perhaps most important among the *QHSR's* unity-of-effort enterprise objectives was its recommendation to "build a homeland security professional discipline" by developing "the homeland security community of interest at all levels of government as part of a cadre of national security professionals."[13] To mature and strengthen the homeland security enterprise, the *QHSR* envisaged a comprehensive homeland security professional development program fostering unity of effort across a broad national culture of cooperation and mutual aid. It specifically referred to the May 2007 Executive Order 13434, National Security Professional Development, which was inspired by the lessons learned in the Hurricane Katrina response. EO 13434 was the genesis of a program to develop national security professionals via an integrated framework of training, education, and professional experience opportunities and developmental assignments. The *QHSR* embraced the idea, speaking of "enterprise-wide approaches to enhancing homeland security professional development."[14] The BUR added to the *QHSR* recommendation giving FEMA directive language with regard to developmental assignments: "FEMA will implement personnel exchanges between headquarters and regional offices to enhance employee understanding of headquarters and regional perspectives, as well as personnel exchanges between FEMA and State governments through the Intergovernmental Personnel Act."[15]

## The Genesis of a Networked Preparedness Policy Advisory System

In May 2009, the Senate confirmed New Mexico's Tim Manning to succeed Dennis Schrader as the head of FEMA's National Preparedness Directorate. Since 2007, Manning had served as homeland security advisor to Governor Bill Richardson (D-NM) and the first secretary of the state's Department of Homeland Security and Emergency Management. An all-around emergency management professional, he was a former firefighter, emergency medical technician, rescue mountaineer, hazardous materials specialist, and hydrologist—and a graduate of the Executive Leaders Program (ELP) at the Naval Postgraduate School's Center for Homeland Defense and Security.

Among his responsibilities as FEMA's deputy administrator for protection and national preparedness, Manning oversaw the new administration's iteration of the National Preparedness Goal. The 2010 Homeland Security Appropriations Act set a requirement for NPD to cooperate with the DHS Office of Intergovernmental Affairs to lead and deliver to Congress a report on preparedness with recommendations for all levels of government for streamlining response and recovery governance.[16] Manning chose to use this requirement as a way to get non-federal stakeholder input for revising the National Preparedness Goal.

Working with Juliette Kayyem, the DHS assistant secretary for intergovernmental affairs, Manning handpicked state- and local-level, tribal, and territorial officials from around the country to participate on the thirty-six-member staff that became known as the Local, State, Tribal, and Federal Preparedness Task Force.[17] His executive director for this effort was Kathleen Fox, the deputy director of Washington, D.C.'s Homeland Security and Emergency Management Agency. Assisting Fox was a key staff member, Josh Dozor, the FEMA deputy director of regional operations. This task force focused its work on four main areas, three of which were explicitly specified in the congressional language—policy and guidance (the ends), capabilities and assessments (the ways), and grant administration (the means).[18]

The Fox task force released its report, *Perspective on Preparedness: Taking Stock Since 9/11*, in September 2010. Choosing to use throughout the term "homeland security and emergency management enterprise," the task force noted up front with respect to policy and guidance how all levels of government recognized their "mutual responsibility for national preparedness."[19] Yet, "despite the best efforts of local, State, Tribal, Territorial, and Federal officials—the preparedness policy process remains primarily a Federal endeavor."[20] Said the report, "There is no consistent, standardized way for local, State, Tribal, and Territorial governments to meaningfully influence the preparedness policy process."[21] Required is "a clear and consistent policy coordination process that balances DHS' need for policy-making flexibility with its need to engage broader stakeholders in homeland security and emergency management into the policy-making process."[22]

Indicating its preference for a bottom-up conceptual approach, the task force recommended that "planning-related policy and guidance should ensure that basic emergency plans match community demographics. . . . We firmly believe that basic emergency plans ought to differ substantially by community, based on the composition of that community. . . . Communities better understand and account for their unique requirements and plans reflect these realities."[23] A desired outcome, said the report, would be a "national, comprehensive mutual aid system," based on NIMS, at the interstate level—that is, in line with FEMA emphasis on regionally shared resources and Emergency Management Assistance Compacts (EMACs).[24] The task force was clearly conveying an intergovernmental imperative that is two-dimensional—vertical, in the sense of federal-state-local, and horizontal, in terms of state-to-state and local-to-local mutual aid collaborations. This understanding introduced an awareness of complexities that are beyond the comparatively easy interagency coordination challenges that nevertheless occur within a chain of command with a single executive at the organizational apex.

Although the task force stated its belief that the key to making significant reductions to system costs was through structural means, it chose to focus its efforts only on ways to use existing coordination mechanisms more effectively to enable mere coordination to evolve to a culture of collaboration.[25] It thus recommended that DHS and Congress transform the existing advisory bodies into a tightly coupled, networked preparedness policy advisory system.[26] To that end, it identified FEMA's PKEMRA-mandated National Advisory Council (NAC) as the intergovernmental focal point in the preparedness policy process.

Stood up in June 2007, FEMA's National Advisory Council draws its membership from a cross section of officials from emergency management and law enforcement, including homeland security directors, adjutants general, state, local, and tribal emergency responders, and private-sector and NGO officials. In the latter half of 2007, the NAC provided immediate input in the development and revision of the Bush administration National Preparedness Goal, the National Preparedness System, the National Incident Management System, the National Response Plan, and other related plans and strategies. Later in 2007, FEMA rolled out the ten Regional Advisory Councils (RACs) to provide broad advisory input to each regional office.

This DHS-sponsored preparedness policy advisory system around the NAC and RACs would serve as a policy coordination process that engages detailees from local, state, tribal, territorial, and other stakeholders.[27] Revitalized and networked RACs would become "regional nodes" for providing regional perspectives for national policy and guidance, affording non-federal officials the means for "policy initiation, policy review, and policy implementation and monitoring."[28] This network system would thus enable a "two-way informational exchange" between the NAC and the ten FEMA RACs whereby a Regional Advisory Council would serve as a "major conduit for regional participation."[29]

The task force's network vision was consistent with the PKEMRA mandate that FEMA regions become the decentralized, distributed capability for DHS for integrating preparedness programs and engaging states. Implicit in the thinking behind FEMA's November 2010 Comprehensive Preparedness Guide 101 Version 2.0 was the understanding that the FEMA regions are obviously closer to the states and localities than FEMA or DHS headquarters and therefore should serve as the translators of capabilities and requirements.

This task force conception of a networked policy advisory system for preparedness doctrine and strategy applied foremost to the response and recovery mission sets. Yet the report also spoke of a shift in the QHSR from all-hazards preparedness to resilience as a homeland security goal, which necessitated the addition of traditional emergency management's mitigation mission into the homeland security preparedness spectrum. In light of this broader resilience conception, the task force proposed the creation of a National Advisory Council "futures analysis working group" that—from a borders-in, intergovernmental perspective—would "identify emerging threats and opportunities, changing risks, and the systems to thwart them, and evolving hazards and how to mitigate them."[30]

Futures analysis would better inform an intergovernmental preparedness assessment framework. The task force advocated investing non-federal stakeholders in preparedness policies to ensure consistent approaches to risk assessment and operational planning. It urged all levels of government to support development and phased implementation of a national capabilities assessment framework that would inform grant programs. This preparedness assessment framework would define risks, describe capability outcomes, type and inventory assets, determine risk-based levels of capability, and establish more meaningful outcome-focused assessment measures.[31] Noting how FEMA is working to evolve the Target Capabilities List into NIMS-based Capability Level Guidance, the Task Force spoke of basing the TCL on existing standards like the Emergency Management Accreditation Program (EMAP) to drive preparedness assessment metrics.[32]

### Planning Frameworks: From PPD-8 to the National Preparedness Goal

The responsibility for developing the rewrite of HSPD-8 fell to the Resilience Policy Directorate and Brian Kamoie. His drafting lead was Ed Dolan, who had been the HSC's director of preparedness policy prior to the PSD-1 reorganization. A policy man with a fire service background, Dolan was a detailee from the DHS Office of Policy Development where he had been the director of emergency preparedness and response. Pre-PKEMRA, he had been at the DHS Preparedness Directorate working on HSPD-8 implementation and development of the Bush administration's National Preparedness Goal and the Target Capabilities List. Dolan had come to DHS with long state-level experience as a New York State emergency medical technician instructor and volunteer firefighter.

Dolan oversaw the detailed work of addressing the multitude of reviewer comments on what would be Presidential Policy Directive 8 (PPD-8), National Preparedness, and the tallying of the interagency votes. Participation came from Richard Reed, John Brennan and his deputy for homeland security, Heidi Avery, and the White House counsel, along with DHS Secretary Janet Napolitano, FEMA Administrator Craig Fugate, and NPD's Tim Manning on the DHS and FEMA side. Dolan's first draft of PPD-8 was initially too long. The White House, DHS, and FEMA, particularly NPD's planning authority Corey Gruber, were opposed to anything that smacked of a lengthy prescriptive document. FEMA did not share the detailed findings of the Preparedness Task Force that Manning was assembling alongside Dolan's drafting of PPD-8. Other than what Manning and Gruber brought to the interagency discussions in the Domestic Resilience Group, not much if anything of the task force influenced the draft.

The review process concluded at the end of March 2011, and Kamoie and Dolan publically unveiled PPD-8 in the first week of April at Dan Kaniewski's Homeland Security Policy Institute at George Washington University. Replacing both HSPD-8 and its Annex 1, National Planning, PPD-8 did not overturn previous preparedness policy but rather advanced the efforts of the Bush administration and the authorities of the PKEMRA legislation. The directive reinforced the National Preparedness System as a shared interagency and intergovernmental responsibility for building and sustaining the cycle of preparedness activities. Moving beyond the idea of whole-of-government and its otherwise limited federal-level interagency connotations, PPD-8 spoke of an "integrated, all-of-nation" approach to help guide preparedness activities at all levels of government and in the private and nonprofit sectors. In wording similar to HSPD-8, PPD-8 reiterated the DHS responsibility to develop the National Preparedness Goal by *coordinating* with the departments and agencies and *consulting* with state, local, tribal, and territorial governments, the private and nonprofit sectors, and the public.[33]

The National Preparedness System of PPD-8 was an integrated set of guidance, programs, and processes for mission-driven actions taken to plan, organize, equip, train, and exercise borders-in homeland security capabilities—in DHS parlance, "POETE." PPD-8 added a new mission to the homeland security mission continuum—mitigation[34]—making the preparedness spectrum prevention, protection, mitigation, response, and recovery. "The term 'mitigation,'" said the directive, "refers to those capabilities necessary to reduce loss of life and property by lessening the impact of disasters. Mitigation capabilities include, but are not limited to, community-wide risk reduction projects; efforts to improve the resilience of critical infrastructure and key resource lifelines; risk reduction for specific vulnerabilities from natural hazards or acts of terrorism; and initiatives to reduce future risks after a disaster has occurred."

In the homeland security context, mitigation is a mission both to the left and to the right of the boom, with capabilities that transcend the preparedness spectrum. Observed a 2011 Congressional Research Service (CRS) report, "The policies advocated in PPD-8 and [the National Preparedness] Goal appear to widen the scope of traditional hazard mitigation to include land use, environmental, infrastructure, and health policy."[35] CRS noted that FEMA's risk standard in floodplain management is "1%-annual-chance-of-flooding" and asked, "Will the 1%-annual-chance standard be applied to mitigating terrorist events, or earthquakes, or pandemics as well?"[36]

PPD-8 directed the National Security Staff to develop for these five missions an integrated series of National Planning Frameworks and associated interagency operational plans. The five National Planning Frameworks are the foundational elements of the National Preparedness System. As scalable, flexible, and adaptable coordinating structures, the frameworks assign key roles and responsibilities for the delivery of capabilities. They guide all-of-nation activities under a unified planning system that uses common terminology where each framework will coordinate with other frameworks across the preparedness spectrum. Further, each national planning framework includes guidance to support corresponding planning for state, local, tribal, and territorial governments.

The responsibility for interagency development of the five frameworks lay with the National Security Staff, where each framework was assigned to an assistant secretary–level Interagency Policy Committee. The Counterterrorism Security Group had the responsibility for developing the National Prevention Framework with Justice, DHS, and ODNI as the federal leads. The Transborder Security Group, with DHS as the lead, was responsible for the National Protection Framework.[37] The Domestic Resilience Group (the successor to the Bush administration's Domestic Readiness Group) had the charge for the National Mitigation Framework and National Response Framework, with DHS as the lead, and the National Disaster Recovery Framework (NDRF), with DHS and HUD sharing the lead.

With the exception of the NRF that was released in 2008, the National Security Staff IPC completed their development of the National Planning Frameworks through 2012. The White House issued the National Disaster Recovery Framework in September 2011 as the first framework released under PPD-8 guidance. As the interagency reviews got under way, the Congressional Research Service speculated that the Prevention Framework would draw upon the existing policies of ODNI's Information Sharing Environment and such established prevention resources as the National Counterterrorism Center and associated fusion centers.[38] CRS deemed that the support function model for each framework would follow that of the NRF, with its Emergency Support

Functions (ESFs), and the National Disaster Recovery Framework, with its Recovery Support Functions (RSFs), given that the ESF and RSF models are more applicable to capability-based planning.[39] CRS acknowledged an alternative model, however, based on the National Infrastructure Protection Plan's SSA (Sector Specific Agency) coordinating approach that aligns responsibilities by physical or subject area of expertise as opposed to capabilities.

Each framework informed development of an interagency CONOPS that is another element of the National Preparedness System. As per PPD-8, each interagency operational plan included: a more detailed concept of operations; description of critical tasks and responsibilities; detailed resource, personnel, and sourcing requirements; and specific provisions for the rapid integration of resources and personnel. PPD-8 directed all executive departments and agencies with roles in the national planning frameworks to develop department-level operational plans to support the interagency operational plans. These CONOPS were to be consistent with FEMA's Comprehensive Preparedness Guide 101, where practical—a significant nod to the intergovernmental equities of state and local governments and other non-federal stakeholder mission partners. All together, the five National Planning Frameworks and their CONOPS supplanted the federal-centric Integrated Planning System that in the last two years of the Bush administration had intensified bureaucratic jockeying between DHS and FEMA and antagonized state and local stakeholders.

PPD-8 called for strengthening security and resilience, repeating the phrase introduced and emphasized throughout the QHSR.[40] The directive defined both. "Security," it said, "refers to the protection of the Nation and its people, vital interests and way of life. . . . Resilience refers to the ability to adapt to changing conditions and withstand and rapidly recover from disruption due to emergencies." The phrase found its way into the final National Preparedness Goal of 2011 that spoke of risk and core capabilities and their relation to security and resilience.

Both PPD-8 and the National Preparedness Goal pushed further the regional equities of the homeland security enterprise. PPD-8 explicitly addressed them in terms of mechanisms for prioritizing risk—the intergovernmental sticking point for state and local jurisdictions and the National Planning Scenarios. "The national preparedness goal," read PPD-8, "shall be informed by the risk of specific threats and vulnerabilities—taking into account regional variations—and include concrete, measurable, and prioritized objectives to mitigate that risk."[41] The follow-on PPD-8 Implementation Plan, issued in the late spring of 2011, reiterated the point, saying that the National Preparedness Goal "will respect and leverage the Nation's Federal, State, local, tribal, and territorial governmental structures, maximizing preparedness through adaptability and decentralization. . . . The national risk assessment should build on and integrate current models and best practices to enable the national assessment to be applied regionally and on a local level, as appropriate and practicable."

PPD-8 cited specifically acts of terrorism, cyber attacks, pandemics, and catastrophic natural disasters as among the threats posing the greatest risks to the security of the nation. PPD-8 generated a shift from the use of HSPD-8's fifteen National Planning Scenarios or eight scenario sets to identify capabilities for the National Preparedness Goal. The evidence was in the draft National Preparedness Goal that DHS disseminated for stakeholder review in late August 2011. For the purposes of informing national-level response and recovery planning, the draft described a meta-scenario that did not appear, however, in the final version of the Goal.

There is a no-notice event impacting a population of seven million within a 25,000-square-mile area. The impacted area includes several states across multiple regions. Severe damage is projected to critical infrastructure including essential transportation infrastructure. Ingress and egress options are severely limited. The projected number of fatalities is 195,000 during the initial hours of the event. It is projected that 265,000 survivors will require emergency medical attention. At least 25 percent of the impacted population will require mass care, emergency sheltering, and housing assistance.[42]

In its 2011 report, the Congressional Research Service speculated that the meta-scenario was a template for the administration to develop the capability list in the final National Preparedness Goal.[43] The final Goal spoke of the core capabilities required for a response to and recovery from a "no-notice, cascading incident."[44] It said that DHS drew a set of planning factors from three hazards identified in the Strategic National Risk Assessment—a large-scale earthquake, major hurricane, and WMD attack—to mimic this incident and determine the required core capabilities. In coordination with other departments and agencies, the DHS Office of Risk Management and Analysis conducted the PPD-8-mandated Strategic National Risk Assessment only for natural hazards, pandemics, technological and accidental hazards, terrorist attacks, and cyber attacks.[45] The risk assessment and the draft National Preparedness Goal's meta-scenario helped identify capabilities—for example, those to manage the consequences of a cyber attack that initiated failures to the power grid or financial system.

CRS offered a definition of capability-based planning, quoting FEMA's CPG-101: "Planning, under uncertainty, to provide capabilities suitable for a wide range of threats and hazards while working within an economic framework that necessitates prioritization and choice." The CRS observed that PPD-8 was not applicable to "slow-onset" natural hazards better handled through traditional land-use, urban development, environmental, or economic policy, like extended droughts, famines, gradual sea-level rise, and desertification. Nor was it appropriate for human error or technological failures—for example, oil spills, electrical blackouts, train derailments, and dam collapses where government and private-sector regulatory and safety procedures apply for prevention and protection.[46]

In late August 2011, FEMA disseminated the draft National Preparedness Goal for a two-week national review and received over 2,300 comments, a third of which were from non-federal stakeholders. After making the revisions, FEMA submitted the final draft to the Domestic Resilience Group, chaired by Brian Kamoie. On October 7, FEMA Administrator Craig Fugate announced the National Preparedness Goal at the National Emergency Management Association annual conference in Austin, Texas.

In 2010 congressional testimony, Craig Fugate spoke of his vision of a new governance model that was bottom-up in the classical American tradition that both harkened back to the early years of the federal republic and looked ahead to this digital twenty-first century. He used the phrase "networks to build community resilience." He said it was his "core principle" based on his reading of the *QHSR*.

> We need to move away from the mindset that federal and state governments are always in the lead, and build upon the strengths of our

local communities and, more importantly, our citizens. We must treat individuals and communities as key assets rather than liabilities. . . . FEMA will foster an approach to emergency management nationally that is built upon a foundation of proactive engagement with neighborhood associations, businesses, schools, faith-based community groups, trade groups, fraternal organizations, and other civic-minded organizations that can mobilize their networks to build community resilience and support local emergency management needs.[47]

It is to this vision that this study now turns. Moving from an analog to a digital mind-set, we must talk of a vision of Network Federalism and Anticipatory Governance, whose integrated all-of-nation processes are those components of the continually evolving National Preparedness System and whose interagency and intergovernmental structures are ICS-based.

# PART II

## NETWORK FEDERAL GOVERNANCE AS THE SECURITY AND RESILIENCE ENABLER

# CHAPTER TEN

# The Intergovernmental Dimensions of the Homeland Security Enterprise

"We've played the game. We're done playing the game."

With those words from the chairman of the Okaloosa County Commission, unified command during the 2010 BP oil spill momentarily collapsed along one section of the Florida Panhandle's Emerald Coast. Interagency and intergovernmental coordination for the containment and clean-up along the Gulf Coast was provided by the Incident Command System/Unified Command (ICS/UC), the on-site tool of the National Response System for managing multi-jurisdictional responses to oil spills or hazardous substance releases. The use of ICS/UC for this mammoth emergency response operation came under authorities set forth in the 1968 National Contingency Plan and 1994 revisions to the Oil Pollution Act of 1990 introduced after the *Exxon Valdez* oil spill in Alaska's Prince William Sound.

Eight weeks after the April 20, 2010, explosion on board BP's Deepwater Horizon oil rig, residents of Okaloosa County and the town of Destin were in an uproar. An approaching oil slick with its legions of tar balls produced by the gushing and then still-uncapped wellhead threatened major damage to their coastal beaches and the bayous, habitat, and fishing in Choctawhatchee Bay. These vacation draws accounted for 50 percent of the county's local economy. Tourist bookings for the summer were down 30 percent.

On the night of June 14, Okaloosa county commissioners met in an emergency session alongside the Destin City Council and unanimously approved a decision to shut the East Pass, the channel from the Gulf of Mexico to the bay and the fishing docks of Destin. The commissioners acted without prior authorization from either the Florida state emergency operations center or the federal government's Area Incident Command Center in Mobile, Alabama. A defiant Okaloosa Commission chairman, Wayne Harris, said that he and his fellow commissioners were prepared to break the law and go to jail to protect their county's waterways.

Faced with a potentially catastrophic impact to their environment and livelihood, the commission and local citizens were angry and frustrated with the federal response to the spill and the bureaucratic delays in the Unified Command's permit approval process for clean-up and containment activities. For some fifty days, Harris and his emergency management officials had made numerous requests for equipment and support. In its efforts to secure permits for booming to prevent contamination to its beaches and waterways, the county had sent paperwork detailing its actions and proposed actions to the state and the Area Unified Command. The Florida Division of Emergency Management had no issue with the county's plans. Mobile, however, stymied the process, questioned the permitting, and failed to communicate expeditiously with the agencies having federal-level regulatory authority—for example, the Coast Guard, Army Corps of Engineers, and Environmental Protection Agency. From this local government's perspective, the breakdown in Unified Command had resulted from Mobile's inability to make the decisions or grant permit approvals, in part because federal agency decision-makers were not co-located in the regional command center.

"The ICS system works very well, but one has to remember span of control comes into play in regional catastrophes," said Ken Wolfe, the Okaloosa emergency management coordinator. "To be fair to the Unified Command, they had to coordinate with so many local government agencies that the scope and span of issues on their level had to be overwhelming. Based one hundred miles away, they had no idea what the Destin Pass was or what our shore line looked like, so they made decisions based on average shoreline predictions and tides."

Wolfe was not alone in his assessment of ICS span-of-control limitations in a regional catastrophe. In after-action discussions, the national incident commander for the Gulf oil spill, Thad Allen, a retired Coast Guard admiral and main hero of the Hurricane Katrina response, offered his opinion that ICS was not regionally scalable as a command system for a major theater operation requiring a larger-scale command structure.

The Mobile Area Incident Command Center's work-around reflected a federal-centric predisposition for trying to drive the process top-down that only magnified the intergovernmental disconnects. "We in Okaloosa County have highly trained and skilled personnel who have been seasoned by numerous responses, not only for hurricanes in our local area but for Katrina events and other disasters that have affected Florida," said Wolfe. "What did not go well for the Deepwater Horizon event was that agencies many miles away were making decisions and holding the locals responsible for what they dictated without locals having a say in the process."

By some accounts, Okaloosa was the first local government to flaunt openly the national incident response.[1] Harris said that Okaloosa County "decided to be our own Unified Command" to stop the oil slick before it got into the Choctawatchee Bay, the basis of its tourist economy.

The Okaloosa Commission's decision enabled the county's public safety director, Dino Villani, to take a number of actions to protect the Destin Pass without prior approval from either the state or the federal authorities—for example, Florida's EOC and Department of Environmental Protection in Tallahassee and the Mobile Area Incident Command Center, Coast Guard, and EPA—that had repeatedly opposed Okaloosa's plans for responding to the spill. Initial plans for a boom system of barges and air curtains to close all the inlets and bayous from incoming oil would have cost $9 million. In their June 14 vote, commissioners authorized $200,000 to fund an underwater "air curtain" and $16,500 a day to push the oil to the surface for collection. In the face of Coast Guard opposition, they voted to give Villani's team the go-ahead to (1) deploy weighted barges to block the entrance to the pass and (2) study employment of a so-called underwater "slip curtain" to catch additional oil. Despite the apparent lack of federal cooperation, Villani and the county administrator, Jim Curry, signaled their willingness to continue to secure approval from state and federal authorities for their plans. With regard to costs, the county financed the operation with credit cards and a reserve fund that could cover the system costs for a month.

Two days after the Okaloosa County Commission vote, Mobile acceded to the county thus restoring Unified Command and ending this momentary intergovernmental crisis of governance. It took several weeks, however, for the federal agencies to start working with local officials in the field. In the end, crews did not close the Destin Pass but rather deployed an "inverted V" to funnel the oil to the sides where skimmers could retrieve it. The county additionally set booms in environmental areas—for example, estuaries and nesting areas for birds and sea turtles. The operation continued for a number of months until BP was able to cap the wellhead and Okaloosa detected no oil sheens in its area waters. The county's public safety department requested just under $1.4 million in funding through the state EOC, Mobile Unified Command, and BP claims process to cover costs for contracting, personnel and equipment/supply, and for protective actions. Of the funds requested, the Okaloosa Public Safety Department received just under $1.3 million in total from all sources.

While this intergovernmental tussle resolved quickly and in retrospect was a blip along the timeline of the Deepwater Horizon response, it illustrates how the vertical dimension of homeland security governance has yet to be resolved. In their September 2011 report card on the status of the 9/11 Commission's recommendations, former Governor Tom Kean (R-NJ) and former Congressman Lee Hamilton (D-IN), the Commission chairman and vice chairman, observed:

> Management of the [Gulf Coast oil spill] crisis was an improvement over the often seriously fragmented approaches taken in response to previous disasters but the response was not without flaws. The Coast Guard Commandant was placed in overall command of the incident, but state and local officials, responding to political pressures, at times focused their efforts on what they judged to be priorities for their constituents. State and local authorities set up their own local command centers and were often at odds with the overall plan for strategic response and clean up, creating resource demands in conflict with the overarching program. The complexity of the problem highlights the difficulty of establishing strong central command and control, and integrating incident response across all levels of government.[2]

As opposed to the top-down predisposition of the Mobile Area Incident Command Center and the Unified Area Command in New Orleans, Okaloosa was responding to the crisis bottom-up. "On the local level," said Wolfe, "we operate under the Stafford Act which, in a nutshell, says that all emergencies start at the local level and proceed out from there." Acting in accord with established emergency management verities—well-proven and accepted by counties and municipalities throughout Florida—the county commissioners and the Destin City Council were exercising their fiduciary responsibilities to the sovereign peoples within their jurisdictions.

Security and resilience, the objective of the Homeland Security Enterprise as expressed in the *QHSR*, come not from centralization of authority and command and control, which in any case without amendment to the Constitution is not possible in this federal republic with its checks and balances. Kean and Hamilton's 9/11 Commission recognized this point in its recommendation for unity of command and effort, referenced and reiterated in the Bipartisan Policy Center's 9/11 tenth anniversary report card: "Emergency response agencies nationwide should adopt the Incident Command System (ICS). When multiple agencies or multiple jurisdictions are involved, they should adopt a unified command. Both are proven frameworks for emergency response."[3]

### Networks in the Context of the Three Layers of Sovereignty

In September 2003, the National League of Cities hosted a roundtable at Washington's National Press Club on what to do about America's unraveling federal relationship. "[T]he intergovernmental partnership that has defined American governance for most of the nation's history is unraveling," Henry Cisneros, former secretary of housing and urban development under Bill Clinton, told participants. "Our nation is unsettled. It has come through a series of transformations but hasn't settled on a model for intergovernmental relations."[4]

While not a homeland security thought-leader per se, Cisneros was reflecting whole-of-nation thinking with regard to sustainability and competitiveness. Before coming to HUD, he had served eight years as the Democratic mayor of San Antonio, coming to office in 1981 as the first Hispanic mayor of a major American city. As mayor, he helped rebuild San Antonio's economic base and created jobs through large-scale infrastructure and downtown improvements. The interface of his thinking with what we now call the Homeland Security Enterprise comes in the mitigation and recovery mission spaces. As HUD secretary, Cisneros took a high-profile role in the clean-up operation after the 1994 Los Angeles Northridge Earthquake, the costliest quake in the nation's history, successfully pushing Congress to provide major funding for temporary housing for displaced persons and redevelopment.[5] Post-Katrina, he continued the interface with recovery as a private citizen; in

2007 he became chairman of the technical advisory committee for the New Orleans Office of Recovery Development and Administration.[6]

The synergistic intergovernmental approach that Cisneros has represented in the sustainability and competitiveness realms converges with evolving conceptions applied to the QHSR iteration of the Homeland Security Enterprise and its collaborative security and resilience space. In a 2004 study, the National Academy of Public Administration (NAPA) said, "Intergovernmental relations structures should be viewed as overlapping networks serving diverse functions. Conceptualizing intergovernmental relations by using network theory means that the system should be based on linkages and interrelationships, rather than hierarchical layers. Network thinking, rather than the standard notions of federalism, will promote the Department of Homeland Security's flexibility and adaptability."[7]

Cisneros and NAPA's statements influenced an experienced frontline homeland security practitioner in Connecticut who quoted them in his 2006 thesis for the Naval Postgraduate School's Center for Homeland Defense and Security (CHDS) in Monterey, California. Then the fire chief for West Hartford, Bill Austin is now the homeland security coordinator for Hartford's Capitol Region Council of Governments (CRCOG). A network visionary with over forty years of operational experience, Austin worked for fire departments in three different states—Florida, Maryland, and Virginia—before coming to Connecticut from Tampa, where he had also served ten years as fire chief, and previously another two years as fire chief for Maryland's Howard County. Earning his master's degree in defense and homeland security from CHDS, he was the second fire chief to graduate from the program. Originally a Virginian, Austin is an Army veteran with thirty-four years of active and reserve service, retiring as a command sergeant major at the two-star division level.

"Networks vary in nature and purpose," wrote Austin, "but many are held together by a nonhierarchical self-organizing process accompanied by an evolving mutual obligation among the players. Networks by nature can work horizontally among peers and vertically among the various layers of government."[8] Quoting CHDS' Chris Bellavita, the second reader for his thesis, Austin relayed Bellavita's view that "networks are organizing homeland security, not hierarchies—and then cooperating with the reality of how things happen, rather than remaining faithful to an ideal about controlling complexity."[9]

The breeding ground for such "network federal" insights is not in the interagency policy development circles of Washington's National Security System, diplomatic or military service borders-out, or Cambridge academe; it is in the operationally informed nitty-gritty of state and local governments and their intergovernmental efforts, both internal to their states and in concert with other states to address cross-jurisdictional issues. Network Federalism accepts what Bill Austin and others have come to appreciate after decades of daily, in-your-face accountability to the citizens they serve. Rather than trying to bend federalism to fit to a policy, these homeland security practitioners are working with it. In this regard, then, the actions of the Okaloosa County Commissioners gave evidence to an elemental truth consonant with the earliest principles of this federal republic: *local government is the level of government that is most responsive to the will of a sovereign people in these United States.* Unity of command and effort must respect this foundational truth.

Internally sovereign, states have their own constitutions. Of the fifty states, four are commonwealths: Massachusetts, Pennsylvania, Virginia, and Kentucky. The territories Puerto Rico and the Northern Marianas also use the term. Massachusetts, Pennsylvania, and Virginia use dates from independence when the drafters of their state constitutions opted for commonwealth to reinforce the point that their states were political entities autonomously governed by a sovereign people and not by a tyrant. In English history, the term referred to Great Britain's revolutionary Commonwealth Period when the British had no monarch and were governed by Parliament and Oliver Cromwell as their lord protector in the 1650s. Before statehood, Kentucky was part of Virginia and thus kept the ascription when it became a state in 1792. Yet the difference between these commonwealths and the other forty-six states is in name alone. Whether or not a state is a commonwealth represents no practical difference.

Home-rule states, on the other hand, represent varying degrees of difference, both from the seven that are not such states as well as from each other. Home rule is the result of the state transferring legislative authority to local governments to act in local affairs. The legal basis came via amendment to the state constitution, an action of a state general assembly or local charter, adopted and amended by the voters. Of the forty-four home-rule states, thirty-six provided for municipal home rule in their state constitutions, and eight states enabled it by legislative statute. Only Alabama, Idaho, Indiana, Mississippi, Virginia, and Vermont do not allow for municipal home rule. For the majority that are home-rule states, the intergovernmental problem presented by federalism is compounded. In those states, a third level of shared sovereign governance of the same people in the same territory exists at the municipal level.

In some home-rule states, state law or the amended state constitution grants cities, municipalities, and counties the ability to pass laws—within the bounds of the U.S. Constitution and their state constitutions—to govern themselves. The responsibility for local governance thus resides in the local community, be it a county, borough, or township. Home rule applies only to governance relationships between states and local jurisdictions, as opposed to having anything to do with such relationships between localities and the federal government. It does not confer any enhanced authority to local jurisdictions with respect to the powers of Washington.

The home-rule concept took form after the Civil War in the late 1860s. Communities sought local decision-making in response to concentrated corporate powers—trusts—that were beginning to exercise inordinate influence in state and federal governments. Corporate control over state legislatures had been preventing popular majorities from enacting laws to protect local businesses, natural resources, workers' rights, and community values. Railroad and mining interests in particular were putting their corporate attorneys on the bench at all judicial levels, who would then decide against citizens who were opposed to their projects in local jurisdictions.

The legal precedent that supported the corporate position came in an 1868 case in Iowa involving the Cedar Rapids and Missouri Railroad, one of four Iowa land-grant railroads, and the first such railroad to reach the eastern terminus of the First Transcontinental Railroad. The controlling interest behind that railroad and one other Iowa land-grant railroad was the robber baron Thomas Clark Durant of the Union Pacific Railroad. Writing the decision in the case was Justice John Forrest Dillon of the Iowa Supreme Court, a Ulysses S. Grant appointee and noted nineteenth-century municipal law authority. Dillon expressed the view that a state has preeminence over local governments and as such, municipal corporations owe their origin to and derive their powers and rights wholly from a state legislature.

The so-called Dillon's Rule relegated municipalities to the status of append-
ages of the state legislatures. When the U.S. Supreme Court accepted the
rule as the legal standard for decisions with regard to municipal governance,
state legislators used it as the basis for municipal codes. Most non-home-rule
states thus apply Dillon's Rule to determine the bounds of a municipal government's legal authority.

The judicial reaction to Dillon's Rule came in an 1871 Michigan case,
*People v. Hurlbut*. Judge Thomas M. Cooley of the Michigan Supreme Court,
later a charter member and first chairman of the Interstate Commerce
Commission, took the position that local government was a matter of abso-
lute right that the state could not abrogate. In putting forth the view that local
self-determination was an inherent right, this so-called Cooley Doctrine thus
furthered the home-rule cause.

Missouri was the first state to adopt home rule in 1875, followed by
California in 1879 and later Minnesota and Washington. Home rule and other
municipal reforms caught fire during the Progressive Era when the social
problems and political corruption associated with industrialism in America
principally manifested themselves in the cities. Toward the end of the nineteenth century, cities, through extensive business ties and corporate investments, expanded into unwieldy monsters amid a nation presupposed to be an
agrarian democracy.

Disintegration, waste, and inefficiency reigned in many municipalities as
political bosses and their machines continued to exploit local communities.
The combination of industry, commerce, and immigration made for rampant
city corruption that extended to state governments, the result of the spoils system, the power of the national political parties in local elections, and the lack
of what the Efficiency Movement would later term scientific methods of public and private administration. Some historians regard home rule as not so
much a governance model for expanding citizen participation and increasing
local democracy but rather a means for applying corporate efficiency models,
an element of Progressivism, to government.

Progressivism spread the home-rule idea nationwide. The National Municipal League,[10] founded in 1894 New York City by local citizen reformist groups,
was a principal force during the Progressive Era for promoting home rule
and other municipal reforms, later extending to county and state government
reform as well. In 1900, the League published its first "Model City Charter" for

municipal government reform. The Model City Charter was based on incorporating provisions in state constitutions for municipal home rule.

State governmental structures are, of course, not uniformly the same. Sovereign states and territories also differ in how they have organized for homeland security and emergency management and how they are structured to receive federal preparedness grants. Governors have the prerogative to organize their homeland security offices and emergency management agencies as they may wish. A change of administration in the governor's mansion sometimes brings a reorganization. By a November 2011 National Governors Association reckoning for states and territories, nine had their homeland security organizations in the governor's office, nine were under the adjutant general or Department of Military Affairs, ten were stand-alone homeland security entities, fourteen were under public safety, eight were under emergency management, five were in state police, and one (Wisconsin) functioned through a homeland security council that meets at the state's Department of Military Affairs and is led by the adjutant general.

The National Emergency Management Association looked at the question of state and territorial organization from the emergency management perspective. Based on NEMA's 2011 state director survey, updated totals for state and territorial emergency management organizations indicate that twelve states and one territory have their emergency management agency organized under the governor's office, nineteen have it under adjutants general, four have it combined with homeland security, thirteen have it under public safety, and two are with the state police. In Colorado, the Division of Emergency Management is under the Department of Local Affairs. In West Virginia, the Division of Homeland Security and Emergency Management is under its Department of Military Affairs and Public Safety. Finally, American Samoa has a stand-alone Territorial Emergency Management Coordination Office (TEMCO).

With reduced funding and a cutback in grants, states have started to consolidate their homeland security and emergency management organizations. In July 2011, budget pressures prompted Connecticut to consolidate its homeland security office and emergency management agency into the Department of Emergency Services and Public Protection. Colorado and Pennsylvania are recent examples. In October, Colorado Democratic Governor John Hickenlooper by executive order disbanded his Office of Homeland Security and transferred its programs to a re-titled Division of Homeland Security in the Department of Public Safety. (Evidently, the Office of Homeland Security had not kept a complete computer database of how money had been disbursed.) In November, Pennsylvania Republican Governor Tom Corbett separated his state's homeland security and emergency management agencies. He ordered the transfer of the Office of Homeland Security from the Pennsylvania Emergency Management Agency to the Pennsylvania State Police. Placing the office at the state police headquarters, he said, would improve intelligence gathering and sharing via the state's fusion center, the Pennsylvania Criminal Intelligence Center (PACIC).[11] The state police commissioner now serves as the homeland security advisor. Pennsylvania opted to consolidate homeland security and criminal intelligence gathering and sharing under law enforcement with a focus on the prevention and protection missions. PEMA thus moved to focus on its response and recovery missions. PEMA, however, remained as the state administrative agency (SAA) to oversee administration of federal preparedness grants.

Each state and territory has designated an agency to serve as a state administrative agency for grant administration. In some states, the SAA is the public safety agency. In others, the emergency management agency serves as the SAA. Each type of agency understandably applies its own institutional bias in developing the state's grant strategy, making it difficult for DHS to integrate a cohesive grant strategy at the federal level. As a rule, if the state emergency management agency is its SAA, then grant priorities are in response; if the SAA is a public safety organization, then the funds tend to go to supporting prevention and protection missions. A rough breakdown of SAAs across states and territories indicates that fourteen have designated their emergency management agencies as the SAAs; seventeen, as public safety or state police; eleven, as the adjutant general or department of military affairs; and fourteen, as the homeland security agency.

### The Horizontal Intergovernmental Dimensions—Interstate, Intrastate

Throughout this discussion, we have stressed the vertical—federal, state, and local—axis of intergovernmental relationships. In actual fact, the horizontal intergovernmental axes—state-to-state and locality-to-locality—have become increasingly important. States and UASI regions are losing those capabilities underwritten by federal preparedness grants whose dollar amounts are declining as the result of continued budget cutting. Yet preparedness and operational mechanisms not necessarily driven by the federal government are serving as foundations for the horizontal axes of Network Federalism.

At the state level, the accepted mechanism is the interstate compact, otherwise known as the interstate cooperative agreement. Compacts between states are akin to treaties between nation-states and have had a long history in this country. Such compacts were in play among the colonies before the American Revolution. Between 1783 and 1920, states approved thirty-six compacts, most of which were used to settle boundary disputes. In the last seventy-five years, states have negotiated over 150 compacts—the majority since World War II.

Whether enacted by statute or by bilateral or multilateral agreement, interstate compacts have the force and effect of statutory law and take precedence over conflicting state laws. Violations of compact terms constitute a breach of contract and thus are subject to judicial remedy. As agreements between states, such cases come under the jurisdiction of the U.S. Supreme Court. Because Congress and the courts can compel compliance with their terms, compacts have proven to be an effective means of ensuring interstate cooperation.

Article I, Section 10 of the Constitution, the Interstate Compact Clause, reads that "no state shall, without the consent of Congress, enter into any agreement or compact with another state." Thus, a compact relating to a mutual state-federal issue that could compromise the doctrine of federal preemption might require the consent of Congress. However, not all compacts require congressional approval. Interstate compacts have established multistate regulatory bodies as an alternative to federal regulation, offering the states an effective and enforceable means of addressing common problems without ceding authorities to Congress. They have addressed such matters as conservation, resource management, law enforcement, transportation, taxes, education, energy, mental health, workers' compensation, and low-level radioactive waste. The most familiar interstate compact is the New York–New Jersey Port Authority. In 1921, New York and New Jersey entered into a cooperative agreement to establish an agency to coordinate funding, development, and operation of their two-state port district to improve commerce and trade.

Today, the Port Authority manages within that district bridges, tunnels, port terminals, airports, transit systems, and the World Trade Center.

Interstate compacts providing horizontal, mutual-aid mechanisms for civil defense and emergency management date from the early years of the Cold War and the Interstate Civil Defense and Disaster Compact of 1951. This cooperative agreement was a state-level response to the provisions of the Federal Civil Defense Act of 1950 and recognition of the need for municipal preparedness to defend against a Soviet strategic attack with atomic bombs. Forty years later, the 1951 compact served as the template for the current state-to-state Emergency Management Assistance Compact (EMAC) that emerged from the devastation in Florida and elsewhere in the South wrought by Hurricane Andrew in 1992.

The scale of Andrew's destruction made states very aware of the need for working together to supplement federal resources in extreme emergencies. Southern governors and emergency managers thus sought to formalize their own state-to-state relationships via a cooperative agreement for mutual aid. The principal driver was Florida's Democratic governor, Lawton Chiles, who led the effort along with the Southern Governors' Association and Virginia's Department of Emergency Services, the previous name for today's Virginia Department of Emergency Management. The first iteration was the 1993 Southern Regional Emergency Management Assistance Compact. Two years later, the southern governors voted to extend membership to any state or territory wishing to join, resulting in an expanded agreement, the Emergency Management Assistance Compact of today. In 1996, Congress ratified the EMAC as law, making it the first ratified national disaster cooperative agreement since the 1951 compact upon which the EMAC provisions were built. A state-driven emergency management construct, EMAC is administered by the National Emergency Management Association.

Following a state emergency declaration, states implement EMAC provisions, formal business protocols, and standard operating procedures to facilitate rapid sharing of equipment, personnel, and other resources. Under the provisions, Unified Command can coordinate state-to-state EMAC resources with Federal National Response Framework resources. EMAC covers many of the issues associated with deployed emergency response personnel operating outside their parent jurisdictions. Personnel provisions encompass credentialing— that is, interstate license, certificate and permit recognition, tort liability and immunity, workers' compensation, and death benefits. EMAC also has language covering reimbursement for the cost to provide personnel and services and for loss or damage to equipment. Nationwide NIMS implementation is improving the effectiveness of the EMAC processes, in particular through the use of NIMS resource typing to facilitate identification and inventorying of response assets. NIMS resource typing is the standardized formatting system for categorizing the capability and performance levels of response personnel and equipment commonly exchanged in disasters through mutual aid agreements.[12]

The first use of the EMAC was in April 1995, when Virginia's Republican Governor George Allen used it as the basis for his executive order to send Virginia National Guard personnel and helicopters to Kentucky to help fight a major forest fire. Whether via the National Guard Mutual Assistance Compact or by mutual agreement between states, the use of EMAC may include Guard units in a humanitarian capacity—that is, not in a law enforcement or military role. Guard units activated by a governor for mutual aid serve in a state active duty (SAD) status (as a full-time state force under the command of their governor, paid at their state rate). In a federally declared disaster, they provide mutual aid either under Title 32 (activated as a full-time state force under the command of the governor but federally paid) or Title 10 (activated as a full-time federal force, federally paid). Guard units that are WMD Civil Support Teams (CSTs) may deploy out-of-state under Title 32 authorities. Use of the Guard in state-to-state mutual aid, however, does not take precedence over use by the federal government if it elects to federalize the Guard under its Title 10 authorities to serve in a military role.

During the 2005 Katrina and Rita response, the majority of assistance requested through EMAC was for National Guard resources and law enforcement personnel. Other disciplines deployed in large numbers were teams of emergency management, fire/hazmat, search/rescue, and health/medical professionals. Via EMAC, states deployed a total of 65,929 personnel to the affected areas of Louisiana, Mississippi, Texas, Alabama, and Florida at an estimated cost of $830 million. EMAC operations involved all member states. As of March 2006, forty-eight states, the District of Columbia, the Virgin Islands, and Puerto Rico are party to EMAC. As of June 2007, states have used EMAC seventy-two times.

Intrastate mutual aid agreements for cross-jurisdictional disaster assistance between or among local jurisdictions have a long history, both as standing compacts and post-event documents based on verbal agreements arranged as an event unfolds. Over the course of the last two decades, states have worked with tribal and local governments as well as with the private sector and NGOs to develop standing mutual aid systems via statewide mutual aid agreements. These efforts enjoy FEMA support through its development of policies covering things like the criteria for reimbursement of costs for emergency work authorized under the Stafford Act when a statewide mutual-aid agreement is invoked. FEMA encourages states to participate in intrastate mutual-aid agreements and to establish them in a manner that can encompass all local jurisdictions. The agency's Incident Management Systems Division in NPD's National Integration Center is responsible for developing a NIMS-based national system of standards and guidelines for implementation.

Statewide mutual aid agreements vary by state. Generally, they provide for a statewide mutual aid system that covers a variety of local government entities.[13] In addition to counties and municipalities, the system may include school districts, emergency services districts, and so forth. Agreements have been generally effected by state emergency management agencies with local parties that include tribes and special districts. They may establish disaster districts that have disaster district coordination committees with representatives from district stakeholders. The statewide mutual-aid agreement covers those jurisdictions that do not have any preexisting written mutual aid agreements but does not supersede the terms of those that do. Mutual-aid systems are generally not mandatory and have been effected by states with either an opt-in or opt-out option.

### The Nonprofit Regional Network Approach

The private sector has driven multi-jurisdictional collaborations in a number of regions and metropolitan areas across the country. In 1991, several states in the Pacific Northwest joined with Canadian provinces and territories to form a statutory, nonprofit public/private organization to coordinate state and provincial policies and promote regional collaboration, known as the Pacific NorthWest Economic Region (PNWER). Ratified by the legislatures of Idaho, Montana, Oregon, Washington, and Alaska and those of the Canadian provinces Alberta, British Columbia, and Saskatchewan plus the Yukon and

Northwest Territories, PNWER is based in Seattle, Washington. The non-profit serves as a conduit to exchange information, enhances regional competitiveness in both domestic and international markets, leverages regional influence in Ottawa and Washington, D.C., and facilitates economic growth while maintaining the region's natural resources.

Two months after 9/11, PNWER launched its Regional Disaster Resilience and Homeland Security Program to improve the all-hazard protection of the Pacific Northwest's critical infrastructures. PNWER worked with regional stakeholders on a regional infrastructure security initiative, the Partnership for Regional Infrastructure Security. The result was a series of Blue Cascades Exercises, the first of which focused in 2002 on infrastructure interdependencies and cascading failures from a terrorist attack on the regional energy sector. Follow-on Blue Cascades exercises targeted infrastructure-related challenges associated with physical attacks and disruptions (2002), cyber threats, disruptions, and impacts (2004), a major subduction zone earthquake (2005), pandemic preparedness (2007), supply chain resilience (2008), and public-health and safety impacts of major flooding (2010). These exercises resulted in development of a regional action plan to address capability gaps. The action plan led to PNWER pilot projects with DHS, DoD, the Department of Energy, the Corps of Engineers, and other federal entities. One major project was the development of the Northwest Warning, Alert, and Response Network (NWWARN) to encourage cross-sector information sharing. Over 2,200 vetted users participate in NWWARN and routinely use the system. Other projects have included a regional energy vulnerability assessment and an interdependencies identification tool for stakeholders. PNWER initiated the coordination of regional critical infrastructure protection (CIP) managers from the states and provinces, as well as federal partners to share CIP plans and conduct cross-jurisdictional training and exercises.

In Chicago, the financial services sector took the lead in 2003 to develop the nonprofit ChicagoFIRST, a coalition of financial institutions to coordinate homeland security, emergency management, and business continuity policies. Its drivers were Louis Rosenthal, executive vice president at LaSalle Bank/ABN AMRO, and Rohit Kumar, chief technology officer at the Options Clearing Corporation. The pair secured start-up support from BITS, the technology policy division of the Financial Services Roundtable, the association representing one hundred of the nation's largest integrated financial services companies. Today, ChicagoFIRST has expanded beyond financial services to include a range of private-sector firms in the metropolitan area that collaborate with all three levels of government to promote the resilience of the business community. The association has three active working groups that address pandemic planning, business continuity planning, and physical and cyber security. ChicagoFIRST has worked with the city on evacuation planning, and has participated in a pilot credentialing program covering both the city and Illinois. Among its deliverables, it has helped produce information-sharing protocols with local and state emergency response agencies to ensure that ChicagoFIRST members receive access to trusted, real-time information.

In the Mid-Atlantic region, a 2004 National Capital Region UASI grant provided initial funding for the All Hazards Consortium (AHC), a state-sanctioned nonprofit regional organization guided by North Carolina, the District of Columbia, Maryland, Virginia, West Virginia, Delaware, Pennsylvania, New Jersey, and New York. The AHC board of directors and its working groups include active state or local government homeland security directors, emergency management directors, and senior leadership from the eight member states and the District of Columbia, along with the three UASI regions, the NCR, New York City/Newark, and Philadelphia. The consortium supports member states in their regional collaboration efforts among government, private sector, higher education, and nonprofit/volunteer organization stakeholders.

On the infrastructure protection and resiliency side, it helps facilitate the integration of regional intergovernmental and private sector CIP planning efforts in the power, transportation, telecommunications, medical/food/water, banking/finance, information technology, housing/commercial, facilities, and chemical sectors. Other regional strategic planning areas are catastrophic event preparedness planning and information sharing. AHC-hosted workshops on various topics have resulted in production of "regional consensus" white papers that document needs, issues, best practices, lessons learned, and recommendations.

The Tennessee-based Community and Regional Resilience Institute (CARRI) has been developing a common national framework for community and regional resilience. Begun as a 2007 collaborative effort among the DHS Science and Technology Directorate, Oak Ridge National Laboratory, and a number of academic institutions,[14] CARRI forms collaborative, bottom-up networks as opposed to constructs driven top-down by the federal govern-ment. The institute has been developing its common framework with pro-cesses and tools that communities and regions can use to assess their resilience, determine a resilience vision, and take concrete actions. CARRI advised pilot resilience efforts in Memphis and in Gulfport, Mississippi. In South Carolina, it is assisting the Charleston/Tri-County Council of Government with a three-jurisdiction activity that is developing "hard" and "soft" networks for region-wide communications and information sharing.[15]

A unique four-state, county-to-county, city-to-city effort was the Shenan-doah Valley's Quad State Emergency Management Task Force initiative covering local jurisdictions in Virginia, West Virginia, Maryland, and Penn-sylvania. Quad State was a cross-border cooperative preparedness model for a suburban/rural region adjacent to a major metropolitan area, in this case the Washington National Capital Region, one hundred miles to the east. The initiative served to enhance the delivery of emergency response and man-agement within the jurisdictions bordering the I-81 corridor through the Shenandoah Valley from Chambersburg, Pennsylvania, to Harrisonburg, Vir-ginia. The goal was to facilitate, within seventy-two hours after the onset of a disaster, a regional response in advance of a state-to-state EMAC activation.

While jurisdictions already had cooperative agreements in place along the valley's interstate corridor, the effort began as a project at Shenandoah University's John O. Marsh Institute for Government and Public Policy, now known as the Institute for Government and Public Service. Promoting the idea was the institute's executive director, Dr. William Shendow, who had previously served eight years as a councilman for Winchester, the regional hub. In 2003, Shendow was able to secure a congressionally directed FY04 Department of Education grant to launch the Quad State Emergency Preparedness Program and serve as the institute's grant administrator. With a two-year performance period, the grant provided Marsh with funds to "expand and enhance its pro-gramming activities"; lawmakers designated most of the $250,000 appropri-ation for development of emergency preparedness training programs for the Quad State region.

Coordinating the participating jurisdictions was Lynn Miller, Winchester's retired fire chief who was serving as the city's emergency man-agement coordinator. Miller liaised with local and state agency representa-tives to develop the regional work plan. Key to Quad State's success was the support from governors and county and city elected officials, as well as buy-in from all the response agencies—law enforcement, public health, public works, and so forth. The program objectives were to provide for the sharing, coordination, and use of information and other resources to prepare for a regional emergency incident, and train elected and administrative officials responsible for emergency management and preparedness. A key grant requirement was for development of a directory, the *Quad State Emergency Preparedness Handbook*, and database that identified emergency services, resources, officials, and providers in the region. Another deliverable was establishment of a Quad State Emergency Preparedness Web site to enhance timely information sharing.

Quad State aimed to be a catalyst for an ongoing regional effort to coordinate preparedness for a catastrophic incident in the four-state area. A priority driver was the need to plan for a regional response to a national event in the NCR, specifically provision of medical assistance and sheltering during any mass evacuation westward from Washington. The planning leveraged the Winchester Medical Center, the regional referral center, and related facilities and services, most of which are adjacent to Shenandoah University's own Medical Center Campus. To these ends, Quad State formed operational-level task forces to conduct training and exercises, mock exercises, meetings, and summits. It provided regular reports to localities and states in the region on the status of emergency preparedness as well as disseminating preparedness information to citizens. Over the course of its work, Quad State highlighted communications interoperability and agreement on equipment standards and facilitated regional coordination on procurements, development of incident command, regional grant applications, and NIMS-based cross-training. In 2006, a Quad State task force capped its work with a summit on pandemic flu preparedness to build personal relationships for cross-border collaboration in that unique class of catastrophic emergencies. Following the grant's performance period, Quad State continued as a project of the individual jurisdictions.

Through the program, officials were able to get free emergency services training from the Institute for Government and Public Service and upon completion receive a certificate of emergency preparedness. This aspect of Quad State illustrates how the Marsh Institute and Shenandoah University served as regional academic centers for regional homeland security workforces.

Quad State, the All Hazards Consortium, and CARRI demonstrated how regional academe can provide an alternative to costly analytical support from contractors or remote federal entities. Shenandoah University represented local training and analytical support specifically focused on the region's own conception of its unique preparedness needs. Models for this kind of approach are DoD's use of University Affiliated Research Centers (UARCs) and the federal government's use of Federally Funded Research and Development Centers (FFRDCs).

DoD formally established its system of UARCs in 1996 during the defense downsizing to maintain essential engineering and technology capabilities. These not-for-profit organizations maintain essential research, development, and engineering core capabilities and thus keep alive the long-term strategic relationships with their DoD sponsors. UARCs operate in the public interest, free from real or perceived conflicts of interest, and may compete for science and technology work, unless specifically prevented by their DoD contracts. The system consists of over a dozen DoD UARCs, yet some notable centers date from World War II. The prime example was the first: Johns Hopkins University's Applied Physics Laboratory (APL) in Laurel, Maryland. APL developed the proximity fuse, at the time cutting-edge air defense ordnance, under a contract with Vannevar Bush's White House Office of Scientific Research and Development. In the postwar period, APL made the transition to missile development and for several decades has been a mainstay in the Navy's Aegis air and ballistic missile defense programs as the designer of the Aegis combat system.

Similarly, FFRDCs are independent entities sponsored and funded by the federal government to meet long-term technical needs beyond the capabilities of existing government or contractor resources. Typically, FFRDCs provide scientific research and analysis, systems development, and systems acquisition. Serving as an honest broker and managed by a university or nonprofit parent organization under regulatory guidelines, they bring together government, industry, and academe to solve a program's complex technical problems. Like the UARC model, FFRDCs arrived in World War II and are most associated with defense and DoD. Familiar such FFRDCs are Mitre (originally managed by MIT), Caltech's Jet Propulsion Laboratory, and the National Labs that supported the Manhattan Project. Today, some thirty-six FFRDCs now function in the defense, energy, aviation, space, health and human services, and tax administration sectors.

## Conceptualizing a Planning Region: Top-Down or Bottom-Up?

Hartford's Bill Austin and another Naval Postgraduate School thesis author[16] writing on regionalization cited the March 2005 *Interim National Preparedness Goal* for its definition of a homeland security region as a "designated planning radius of a core high-threat urban area."[17] This federal definition reflected the need to address planning for the pre-Katrina homeland security threat, specifically terrorist attacks employing WMD. By determining the bounds of the UASI regions according to *its* risk priorities, the federal government undermined the authority of states and local jurisdictions to determine and resource sub-state homeland security regions according to *their* priorities. It compounded the effect on sovereign authority by both imposing on state administrative agencies the requirement to distribute 80 percent of the value of homeland security grants to local jurisdictions (the so-called 80/20 rule) and developing a complicated risk formula for distribution of those funds.[18] With the 2011 elimination of thirty-three of the sixty-four UASI regions and deep cuts to many of those remaining Tier II UASIs, the maintenance of fully realized planning capabilities for UASIs past and present is problematic. As one of those eliminated Tier II UASIs, the Hartford metropolitan area is addressing this very problem today.

Austin represented the perspective of a widely experienced local government fire-service professional, expert in sub-state regional collaborative networks. To his mind, a self-defined community of interest was what drives an empowered, horizontal and vertical intergovernmental homeland security planning region—from the bottom-up.[19] In developing his 2006 case for regional networks, he both reflected Henry Cisneros' approach toward intergovernmental partnerships for sustainability and competitiveness and anticipated FEMA administrator Craig Fugate's vision of "networks to build community resilience." Early in his thesis, he cited one active federal-state partnership as a useful conceptual model: the Appalachian Regional Commission (ARC), a thirteen-state regional entity for sustainable community and economic development that has strong buy-in from local jurisdictions. Established by Congress in 1965, governance is provided by fourteen commissioners, thirteen of whom are the governors of the thirteen Appalachian states with the fourteenth a federal co-chair appointed by the president and subject to Senate confirmation. A state co-chair is annually elected from and by the governors of the thirteen. Bottom-up input to

ARC processes comes from local development districts, multi-county agencies with boards of elected officials, and private-sector leaders.

Austin noted the work of two bodies, like the ARC established by legislation, that were moving to address homeland security regionalization. One was the National Association of Regional Councils (NARC). Founded by the National League of Cities and National Association of Counties, NARC represents regional planning agencies, development districts, and councils of governments to further sub-state regional cooperation. NARC's allied organization in its homeland security work was the National Association of Development Organizations (NADO), serving small metropolitan and rural areas. In a 2005 survey, NADO concluded that regional planning was in need of formal decision-making structures to coordinate local government and first-responder groups. Addressing this challenge, NARC issued a 2006 policy brief to Congress saying, according to Austin, that the organization's regional councils of government were "fully prepared to provide the structure and support to accomplish the goal of enhanced regionalization."[20]

In a 2005 study, NADO similarly offered: "The nation's network of 520 regional development organizations and regional councils of government provide forums for local elected officials and other key community stakeholders to explore and address issues of regional significance. As organizations formed and governed primarily by local officials, these regional organizations have credibility with local governments, years of experience in coordinating local efforts across political boundaries, and the capacity to provide regional forums for dialogue, coordination, and strategic planning."[21]

Austin was satisfied that regional development organizations were uniquely positioned and qualified to coordinate, plan, and implement essential homeland security efforts. "These activities range from coordinating the integration of first-responder communication systems, to managing the GIS [geographic information system] data and tools necessary to enhance local decision making, to developing comprehensive response plans, to conducting regional forums."[22]

The West Hartford fire chief was recommending utilization of the national system of regional councils of governments that build on extant, bottom-up-driven networks—a nation of homeland security regions where various networks collaborate based on how they have been interrelating on a daily basis. Having credibility among local governments with respect to coordination and planning, these networks engender local buy-in. Because these bodies existed before the arrival of federal funding—for example, UASI monies— they see themselves remaining after Washington funds are reduced or eliminated altogether.

"Regionalization by any definition should include the benefits of decentralization of power, placement of power in a definite area, and greater efficiency."[23] For Austin, regionalization ought to be a by-product of state efforts to enhance local power rather than limit it.[24] While accepting that regionalization is somewhat at odds with home rule and local control, his thesis noted that regionalization successes had come in Missouri, Kentucky, and Texas. "The State of Missouri in partnership with the Missouri Association of Councils of Government (MACOG) forged an agreement whereby regional planning councils provide the operational structure to determine grant allocations and also handle the local administrative processing of the grant funds."[25]

Intrastate regionalization is not without its challenges, notably the problem of liability and workers' compensation in a regional incident not declared as a state or federal emergency. Some regional networks are only informational and never make a decision. Others are supposed to be empowered, yet the bottom-up approach to project ideas from the local level and further substate regional collaboration does not always translate to decision-making on those project ideas.[26]

Indiana University's Robert Agranoff, a specialist in public administration, intergovernmental relations/management, and public network studies, has written of regions that are "action networks" involving partners who formally adopt collaborative courses of action or deliver services.[27] Representing for Austin "the cutting edge of true regionalization" are action networks like the National Capital Region, the Dallas-Fort Worth Regional Emergency Managers Group, and his own Capitol Region Council of Governments for the Hartford, Connecticut, metropolitan area.

CRCOG is guided by the elected officials of the thirty municipalities in the Hartford metropolitan area. The mayors, first selectmen, and town council chairmen constitute its governing policy board and have been collaborating for over thirty years on a wide range of projects. After 9/11, CRCOG established its Capitol Region Emergency Planning Committee as a committee of its Public Safety Council. Chaired by Austin until the end of 2008, the planning committee covers the over 125 organizations and forty-one municipalities in the Capitol Region. In its first two years, the committee received no federal grants yet was able to develop a governance mechanism, policy options, operational capability, and interagency collaboration for the region. During Austin's tenure as committee chairman, networks started operating among officials in public health, fire, police, emergency medical, emergency management, and communications, despite the funding and liability challenges.

At the working level, the homeland security practitioners in all these disciplines are thoroughly versed in conducting interagency and intergovernmental planning and operational decision-making according to the principles of the Incident Command System, the basis of the National Incident Management System. It is the ICS-based NIMS that correctly informs the use of interagency and intergovernmental preparedness structures and processes—the network federal mechanisms better suited for this post-industrial, digital information age.

### ICS as the Management Model for Network Federalism

From the foregoing and brief characterization of some of the non-federal aspects of the intergovernmental dimensions of the Homeland Security Enterprise, it should be clear that analog, industrial paradigms do not efficiently and effectively produce unity of effort at the operational level.

Top-down application of military command and control models are not workable for domestic management of catastrophic events or situations. Presidential authority does not extend to directive authority over sovereign state or local components. The Incident Command System provides the more appropriate model for management of complex, multi-site incidents involving multiple jurisdictions and levels of government. ICS governance principles can thus serve as another cornerstone in the foundation for Network Federalism.

Management of a disaster or crisis requires a mix of skills and capacities beyond a single hierarchy and therefore calls for a network of responders. It also demands rapid decision-making and decisive, coordinated action, which are otherwise associated with command and control hierarchies. Because disasters and crises frequently involve jurisdictional and functional agency overlaps, the purely hierarchical military command and control model does not work. Civil authorities thus have come to rely on ICS, initially developed by the fire services in the 1970s, to manage complex incidents.

The Incident Command System blends hierarchical and network organizational models. A hierarchical network "is a form of social coordination that uses hierarchical control, in the form of unified and centralized command, to help manage a network of organizations pursuing a shared goal."[28] ICS is a temporary hierarchical authority that establishes in an incident certainty and clarity about the chain of command in order to coordinate a responder network.

The National Incident Management System, promulgated by FEMA, is based on ICS-derived principles for modular organization of the Incident Command Post (ICP). Under NIMS, when an incident falls within a single jurisdiction, it is managed at the ICP by a single incident commander (IC)—for example, a fire chief, police chief, or public health officer, depending on the nature of the incident. "The IC is responsible (within the confines of his or her authority) for establishing incident objectives and strategies. The IC is directly responsible for ensuring that all functional area activities are directed toward accomplishment of the strategy."[29]

Complex multi-jurisdictional or multi-agency incidents may require ICP management by a Unified Command (UC). NIMS provides that under Unified Command "[t]he individuals designated by their jurisdictional or organizational authorities (or by departments within a single jurisdiction) must jointly determine objectives, strategies, plans, resource allocations, and priorities, and work together to execute integrated incident operations and maximize the use of assigned resources."[30] Unified Command allows officials/responders who have authorities/responsibilities under an appropriate law, ordinance, or agreement to work together effectively without affecting individual agency authority. The UC provides direct, on-scene control of tactical operations.

ICS is structured to facilitate activities by section chiefs in five major functional areas—command, operations, planning, logistics, and finance/administration. In the case of a terrorist event, an ICS structure would include a chief for a sixth functional area, intelligence/investigation. Resident at the ICP, these section chiefs serve as the "general staff" for incident management and report to the Incident Command or in a multi-jurisdictional event the Unified Command. The IC or UC exercises tactical control via one operations section chief who directs all tactical efforts. This operations chief normally comes from the organization with the greatest jurisdictional involvement. (Agencies that are heavily involved in the incident but lack jurisdictional responsibility are defined as supporting or assisting agencies.)

ICS thus is a predefined hierarchy. It includes a chain of command and delineated responsibilities for every position, uniform terminology for identifying resources, and organizational functions. ICS provides for the updating of incident action plans for each operational period. Perhaps most importantly, it allows for the IC or UC to expand or contract the modular organizational structure, as needed, to ensure a manageable span of control.

Under ICS, the concepts of command and unity of command have legal and cultural meanings that are distinct from military forces and operations. In the military context, command runs from the president to the secretary of defense to the commander of the combatant command to the commander of military forces. With ICS, chain of command refers to the orderly line of authority only within the ranks of the incident management organization. Unity of command means that all individuals have a designated supervisor to whom they report at the scene of the incident. These principles clarify reporting relationships and eliminate the confusion caused by multiple, conflicting directives. Incident managers at all levels must be able to direct the actions of all personnel under their supervision.[31] (NB: Military forces do not operate under the command of the IC or the Unified Command structure.)

Crucially, ICS depends on personal relationships that build on network norms of trust and reciprocity. In a steady state, network hub members (i.e., those having capacity) work together on preparedness and planning and thereby develop trust and an ICS culture. As the military says, "Train as you fight." "Key related aspects of network management are time and stability, both of which are needed to allow network actors to interact with each other repeatedly—which in turn helps to foster agreements, establish shared norms, and build trust toward one another."[32] Also vital is the importance of centralizing information in one place to allow Incident Commanders comprehensive information to make operational decisions.

The National Response Framework response doctrine holds that "incidents must be managed at the lowest possible jurisdictional level and supported by additional capabilities when needed."[33] Responsibility for the establishment and expansion of the ICS modular organization ultimately rests with the incident commander. "As incident complexity increases, the organization expands from the top down as functional responsibilities are delegated."[34]

For complex, multi-site incidents, an Area Command oversees management coordination of the incident(s) and separate ICS organizations with multiple incident management teams. In addition, a multi-agency coordination system (MACS) element—for example, a communications/dispatch center, emergency operations center (EOC), or MAC Group—coordinates support activities above the field level and prioritizes the incident demands for critical or competing resources. The EOC, hence, is not synonymous with the Incident Command Post, although it applies NIMS standardized structures and tools to its organizational model. Standing EOCs are usually led by an emergency manager. State-level response would have state EOC over the local EOC, which directly supports the IC or UC at the Incident Command Post.

Under principles of unified command, a Unified Coordination Group (UCG) at the FEMA Regional Response Coordination Center (RRCC) coordinates federal support. The UCG includes a FEMA official, the federal coordinating officer, and a state coordinating officer (SCO) appointed by the governor, along with senior officials from the state and key federal departments and agencies. Should the incident intensify, the UCG shifts from the RRCC to a Joint Field Office (JFO). (In a multi-state incident, UCGs and JFOs are established in each state.) At the JFO, the UCG exercises unified command and relays all requests for support from the governor to the federal government. The JFO is thus a support entity for coordinating federal support and does not exercise tactical control over any ICS organizations.

As American history has amply demonstrated in the past, the Constitution's separation of powers, with its checks and balances, will impede a unified national—and not simply federal—development of the Homeland Security Enterprise in pursuit of the security and resilience of the nation. Designed to frustrate centralization of power in a national government, these constitutional provisions exacerbate fragmentation within and between levels of government with regard to security policy development and operational execution. In a truly national domestic crisis—one which by perception or fact constitutes a threat to enduring constitutional government—Congress and the American people will expect unity of command and effort among all responsible federal and non-federal entities.

The schematic for the Homeland Security Enterprise reveals:

- Horizontal interagency relationships at the federal, state, tribal, territorial, and local levels, needing further formalized extension to the private sector and NGOs
- Vertical intergovernmental relationships, stressed by two (and in home-rule states three) levels of shared sovereign governance of the same people in the same territory
- Preparedness and operational hierarchical (though merely temporary in crisis) collaborative networks for prevention, protection, mitigation, response, and recovery, based on or derived from the Incident Command System

"Homeland security is thus far more than a technical issue. It is more than a national security issue or a puzzle of federalism. It is, at its core, a problem of governance. And it is one that demands strong and effective political leadership to make the necessary decisions and to shape the necessary trade-offs."[35]

In their 9/11 report card ten years on, Tom Kean and Lee Hamilton, well-tested political leaders, the one a governor, the other a legislator, said: "Progress continues to be made on unity of effort, but it is far from complete. In order to ensure unity of effort, there must be comprehensive planning across federal agencies and with state and local authorities. . . . Regular joint training at all levels is . . . essential to ensuring close coordination during an actual incident."[36]

As we shall discuss in the following chapters, horizontal and vertical unity of effort for preparedness and execution is most likely to seed and mature via regional-level networks for planning, staffed by homeland security professionals drawn from the broadest of interagency, intergovernmental, private-sector, and NGO backgrounds.

# CHAPTER ELEVEN

# The Case for a Regionally Based National Preparedness System

Throughout the American Century, national security policy formulation and execution was the exclusive domain of the federal government. In the strategic environment of the post-industrial twenty-first century, however, states have a co-equal role in strategy and policy development, resourcing, and operational execution in steady-state or crises to supplement and in certain cases perform primary missions to support federal security and resilience priorities. Beyond inclusion of declaratory statements about a Homeland Security Enterprise, national security and homeland security policies have yet to redefine the roles, responsibilities, and authorities of the federal government, state, tribal, territorial, and local governments, the private sector, and non-governmental organizations. As previously noted, the *Quadrennial Homeland Security Review* did not meet the mandate of the Homeland Security Act of 2002 to provide detailed descriptions of federal, state, and local roles and responsibilities.

An intergovernmental Homeland Security Enterprise will not come into being via declaratory federal statements that lack substance. In language that repeated HSPD-8, PPD-8 provided for DHS[1] to *coordinate* with other executive branch entities and *consult* with state, tribal, territorial, and local governments, associations, nonprofit organizations, and the private sector to develop the National Preparedness Goal. By distinguishing consultation from coordination, PPD-8 only reinforced the federal predisposition to regard non-federal homeland security stakeholders as unequal. In the National Preparedness System as currently configured, non-federal stakeholders serve only in an advisory capacity. The time has come to reconfigure the system into structures and processes that reflect a truly co-equal and collaborative federal partnership.

The Homeland Security Enterprise will only grow into a reality through development of a preparedness culture of collaboration in venues charged by statute or directive with the authority and responsibility to build and sustain the National Preparedness System. The most politically feasible place to start this "maturing-by-doing" process is at the working level, where homeland security professionals can best resolve the three core and interrelated intergovernmental problem areas that bedevil the National Preparedness System:

- Risk assessment
- Operational planning and exercise validation
- Use of homeland security preparedness grants to target, develop and sustain state and local capabilities

The National Preparedness System is the foundational process undergirding the intergovernmental and interagency partnerships for the Homeland Security Enterprise. The 2006 Post-Katrina Emergency Reform Act provided a statutory definition of the National Preparedness System in various sections of Subtitle C, Chapter 1. Section 644(b) lists eight components: target capabilities and preparedness priorities; equipment and training standards; training and exercises; the comprehensive assessment system; remedial action management program; federal response inventory; reporting requirements; and federal preparedness. Among the sections particularly relevant are §645 National Planning Scenarios, §646 Target Capabilities and Preparedness Priorities, §648 Training and Exercises, §649 Comprehensive Assessment System, §650 Remedial Action Management Program, and §652(c) Reporting Requirements, State Preparedness Report. In November 2011, FEMA released its *National Preparedness System Description* required under PPD-8 that identified it as the "instrument" for building, sustaining, and delivering the core capabilities within the National Preparedness Goal for a secure and resilient nation.[2] According to the *Description*, the National Preparedness System has six components for improving national preparedness for threats and hazards:

- Identifying and assessing risks
- Estimating capability requirements

- Building or sustaining capabilities
- Developing and implementing plans to deliver those capabilities
- Validating and monitoring progress made toward achieving the National Preparedness Goal
- Reviewing and updating efforts to promote continuous improvement

From the foregoing, we can state that the Homeland Security Enterprise seeks to assess risks, define roles and responsibilities, develop and sustain plans with associated tasks, identify capabilities and capability gaps, and determine resource requirements for operational execution of homeland security missions—most crucially with regard to catastrophic emergencies. As defined in National Security Presidential Directive-51/Homeland Security Presidential Directive-20 (NSPD-51/HSPD-20), catastrophic emergency means "any incident, regardless of location, that results in extraordinary levels of mass casualties, damage or disruption severely affecting the U.S. population, infrastructure, environment, economy or government functions."

Catastrophic operational planning is the crux of the National Preparedness System. Federal, state, tribal, territorial, and local governments and their mission partners must agree to and promulgate a uniform, standard, and synchronized deliberative planning effort. They should base homeland security investment decisions on plans that emerge from such a national planning effort—that is, not on generic lists of capabilities that exist in a vacuum without appreciation for risk or geography. FEMA and its mission partners increasingly realize that integration of the components of the National Preparedness System is best accomplished through collaborative and deliberative catastrophic planning at the local, state, and national levels, with an emphasis on regional coordination. It is in the regions that the planning processes of federal and local entities converge.[3] Federal regions must therefore play a central role in facilitating collaboration among *co-equal* sovereigns to drive and tailor their specific catastrophic planning and determine collaboratively established requirements.

In April 2011, FEMA started a rollout through all ten regional offices (expected to complete in 2015) of a direct collaborative planning process, with states and in some cases local jurisdictions. That includes development of planning documents for national security special events and major incidents requiring significant medical countermeasures and regional all-hazards base plans and annexes for specific hazard risks, such as a mass casualty earthquake, tsunami, and detonation of an improvised nuclear device (IND). In these FEMA-facilitated collaborative planning efforts, states are participating in planning sessions and course-of-action development meetings. At the end of the day, the FEMA regions are the plan holders, yet the process is driving direct linkages to development of state plans.

Notwithstanding these types of worthy efforts, two specific and related areas still need attention:

- Unresolved conflict over all-hazards risk in national preparedness
- Inadequate capabilities for state/local-level catastrophic operational planning

### Unresolved Conflict over All-Hazards Risk

Determination and assessment of risks directly drive the identification of preparedness capabilities—and any gaps in capabilities—to meet those risks.[4] Capabilities, and more specifically the identification of inadequate capabilities, in turn drive investment decisions. The key issue is how the federal government, states, localities, and other mission partners agree on prioritizing risks: where and how that agreement will occur and who should facilitate the consensus-building process.

Notwithstanding ongoing risk analysis under the PPD-8-mandated Strategic National Risk Assessment (SNRA) and its continuing refinements with the steady integration of whole-of-community information, the three levels of government do not yet have a structure and process to facilitate effective collaboration for reaching agreement on risk prioritization. The DHS National Protection and Programs Directorate's Office of Risk Management and Analysis, with its SNRA, prioritizes preparedness activities at the national level and is supposed to inform risk assessment efforts at every level of government to identify capability development. However, to date, the SNRA and the assessment efforts that follow do not clearly factor into the analysis of the economic vulnerability caused by a priority risk, nor the interdependency of local, state, and regional infrastructures. The flaw in the SNRA process is the notion that risk is event-driven and reducible to a single formula. Risk is in fact a system issue that must be entered bottom-up. For example, what is the systemic risk of an IND on a city, intrastate region, state, and interstate region? And finally, what are the national implications? By so doing, jurisdictions are accountable at every level for acknowledging what level of risk they are willing to accept. Thus, they will not waste resources on trying to address it through avoidance or mitigation strategies—given that no level of government can afford to mitigate all risk.

However, state, tribal, territorial, and local governments typically do not develop capabilities for resourcing preparedness beyond the high-probability risks they identify. The officials at these jurisdictional levels find it difficult to justify to their constituents funding preparedness efforts for low-probability, high-consequence events or situations, despite federal requirements. This difference in perspective thwarts effective intergovernmental catastrophic operational planning, which is a prerequisite for clarifying roles and responsibilities, accurately assessing capabilities, and establishing resource requirements that contribute to driving grant applications and awards and resource decisions generally.

Federal assistance, grants, or other forms of assistance should be reserved for planning and operational efforts that require federal involvement. Federal law supports the premise that the federal government will provide assistance when disasters in the United States are of such severity and magnitude that effective response is beyond the capabilities of the state and affected local governments. The entire nation, therefore, assumes some degree of shared risk. Since the states assume varying degrees of responsibility and risk, the federal government must either plan to support the least prepared state (the least common denominator)—which is a race to the bottom that could ultimately lead to state and local overdependence on the federal government—or start engaging with state and local governments to articulate clearly: what is expected of them; what the federal government will provide; and what level of preparedness is unacceptable for events that will require federal participation.

Risk is an expression and prioritization of threats, vulnerabilities, and consequences. Determination and assessment of risks directly drive the identification of preparedness capabilities to meet those risks. These assessments of risk drive determination of capability gaps and ultimately formulation of grant guidance and requirements for jurisdictions applying for and receiving grant funding. At issue is the need to make clear how the federal government, states, tribes, territories, localities, and other mission partners arrive at a consensus on prioritization of risk informed by the Threat and Hazard

Identification and Risk Assessment (THIRA),[5] SNRA, and specialized risk assessment processes. Restating what by now is the recurring theme: Where and how will that prioritization occur, and who should facilitate the consensus-building process?

Since 9/11, the federal government's grant programs and their related analyses of risk for the most part have focused on *high-consequence* terrorist threats to urban areas, with their concentration of populations and critical infrastructure/key resources. This approach had been supported in the potential events outlined in the fifteen National Planning Scenarios in the 2007 DHS National Preparedness Guidelines. The intent behind the scenarios was specifically to support the development of the Target Capabilities List—not to serve as a proxy for planning and resourcing decisions, a use for which they are wholly inadequate.

However, states must view prioritization of risks differently, given the demands of providing routine essential services, particularly in times of extreme budget pressures and deficits. State and local jurisdictions resource baseline operational planning for *high-probability* incidents based on their formal or informal Hazard Identification and Risk Assessment (HIRA)[6] processes. For the most part, state, tribal, territorial, and local governments thus do not choose to develop capabilities for resourcing preparedness beyond the high-probability risks they have identified. At these jurisdictional levels, governments find it harder to justify preparedness expenditures to their constituents for low-probability, high-consequence events or situations as federal risk-based scenarios might require.

To restate: despite noteworthy improvements, the three levels of government still do not yet have an effective structure and process to facilitate effective collaboration for agreement on the prioritization of risk. More precisely, the issue is about how to gain collaborative agreement on what constitutes actionable risk and what strategies each level of government will use to address it.

This failure to agree on prioritization of all-hazards risk remains a fundamental problem for the National Preparedness System. This difference in perspective thwarts development of meaningful intergovernmental catastrophic operational planning. Only through effective, collaborative, intergovernmental/interagency, operational planning can the National Preparedness System clarify roles, responsibilities, accurate assessment of capabilities and focused targeting of resource requirements, which contribute to driving grant applications and awards.

### Inadequate Capabilities for Catastrophic Operational Planning

In order to provide accelerated operational support for catastrophic events and situations, all levels of government should conduct detailed, pre-incident planning. State and local officials should do such planning but lack the required resources. They direct their limited resources at preparing for higher-probability events that might occur within their jurisdiction and that are generally the sole responsibility of the state and local governments. Conversely, the federal government has the resources to engage in catastrophic planning efforts—and for the time being has dedicated some of those resources to that effort—but is unable to proceed without state and local partnership. The federal government must rely on state and local planning efforts, capabilities, and leadership. However, from the perspective of state and local authorities, the federal government in many cases focuses on high-consequence, low-probability scenarios that state and local officials do not consider high priorities, given their limited financial resources. As far back as 2004, the National Association of Public Administration stated forcefully, "Planning is the Achilles heel of homeland security."[7] Two years later, Corey Gruber conducted the DHS Nationwide Plan Review, claiming to be "the most comprehensive assessment of catastrophic planning yet undertaken in this country." Among its initial conclusions, the DHS Nationwide Plan Review Phase II Report addressed that Achilles' heel, saying, "The federal government should provide the leadership, doctrine, policies, guidance, standards, and resources necessary to build a shared national homeland security planning system."[8] PPD-8 provided for a set of the five coordinated National Planning Frameworks, each supported by a Federal Interagency Operational Plan, that are compatible with CPG-101. This integrated approach to planning is to ensure the plans are synchronized in purpose, place, and time. Yet again the question remains: At what level of government does this integration and synchronization take place and who does the integrating and synchronizing?

From the state and local perspectives, the cause of an incident or situation may not be as important as the capability to manage it. Practically speaking, consideration of capabilities,[9] informed to a lesser extent by risk, is better for planning at the state level, where the *effects* of an incident or situation are more important than its cause. However, from a *national preparedness* perspective, it is indeed necessary to focus on causes to enable state and local jurisdictions to do the detailed operational planning that better anticipates effects. Moreover, from the federal perspective, given the size and complexity of the federal government, it is not possible to move entirely toward capabilities-based planning to the exclusion of risk-based elements.

In order to provide accelerated operational support for national or regional high-consequence catastrophic events and situations, the federal government must do detailed, pre-incident planning. At the federal level, high-consequence, threat-based risk must inform much of scenario-based planning.[10] As part of the intergovernmental and interagency review of the National Response Framework, the HSC's Domestic Readiness Group in 2007 consolidated the NPG's fifteen National Planning Scenarios—the scenario-based approaches to operational planning—into eight key scenario sets. These eight detailed, time-sequenced operational plans and pre-scripted mission assignments were supposed to determine federal, regional, state, and local capabilities and capability gaps.

In so doing, the federal government in effect determined scenario sets that some states did not deem high priorities requiring expenditure of their limited resources. These resource constraints compel state and local governments to develop operational plans based on their own all-hazards risk assessments— that is, their own HIRAs. Unlike the military, a state by itself cannot afford to develop and sustain eight operational plans. Hence, if a state cannot directly relate to the risk, it will not fund a capability. DHS somewhat recognized this truth in 2011 when it disseminated its draft National Preparedness Goal for stakeholder review and offered a single meta-scenario and its set of planning factors for determining core capabilities to inform a jurisdiction's catastrophic planning.

This capability issue has a significant, negative effect at the federal level and creates a fundamental problem for PPD-8's integrated national planning frameworks. Without scenario-based catastrophic planning at the state and local levels, the federal government does not have assurance that state- and local-level capabilities and operational readiness will achieve the federally assumed level of preparedness. While the federal government expects all states to do catastrophic operational planning, many states do not have the capability to do so.

The direction in which DHS/FEMA is already going to address this problem points to an ultimate solution. It is the "effects-based" planning approach, which offers a middle position—that is, between scenario-based and capabilities-based. Many states embraced FEMA's March 2009 Comprehensive Preparedness Guide 101 as their planning tool. CPG-101 suggested that states can do catastrophic planning any way they want, for example, by employing "hybrids."

Hybrid catastrophic planning incorporates: (1) scenario-based planning through hazard-specific or threat-specific annexes; (2) function-based planning to identify common tasks; and (3) capabilities-based planning to determine the capability for taking a course of action.

Using hybrid effects-based planning, the federal government would have to adjust its own capability requirements accordingly rather than determining additional catastrophic requirements for the states beyond their own all-hazards risk determinations. Nevertheless, to perform operational catastrophic planning, the intergovernmental and interagency preparedness partners must have mutually agreed-upon risk and threat analyses to inform scenarios.[11] CPG-101 suggested this collaboration best occurs at the regional level—that is at neither the federal nor the state level. PPD-8 reinforced the regional point saying, "[T]he national preparedness goal shall be informed by the risk of specific threats and vulnerabilities—taking into account regional variations."

Following agreement at a series of national summits in the summer of 2008, FEMA regions—working with their regional mission partners—were supposed to be integrating state plans within their regions to create operational regional plans for the eight key scenario sets. These plans were to identify shared regional capabilities and capability gaps. Regional catastrophic planning proposes to translate capability gaps into regional requirements for the federal government as well as for state and local governments.

Hybrid effects-based planning is beginning to work via regional planning efforts currently under way. In March 2010, Don Daigler and Brian Appleby of the Response Directorate's National Planning Division issued the FEMA Regional Planning Guide that put forth a systematic and phased planning process whose five key steps are plan preparation, research and analysis, course of action development, writing and plan approval, and exercising and plan implementation. Federal and state representatives sit in the same

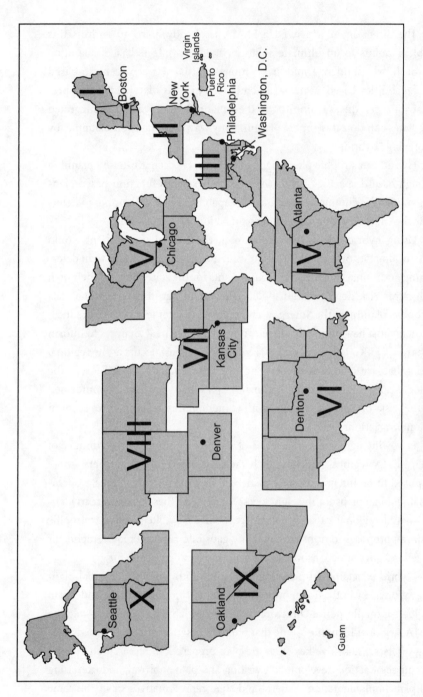

The Ten FEMA Regions and
Their Regional Headquarters

room, look at regional risks and the capabilities needed to address them, and develop courses of action—pointing the way for truly collaborative regional planning. The federal government pays to support plan development. The states pay costs for their representatives to attend the meetings. In return, states get a crash course in planning-by-doing as opposed to online training. This maturing regional planning process has the potential to transform the FEMA regions into fully functional network nodes for aligning federal preparedness with preparedness at the state and local levels.

### Operational Planning and Exercises Validate Determination of Capabilities

Congress, the Office of Management and Budget, and federal departments and agencies with grant-making responsibilities must be able to justify resource expenditures for preparedness. They must also have credible measures for outcomes to determine whether grant monies are well spent. Notwithstanding all the efforts to capture and record capability data, capability only has meaning such as it is validated—or not—operationally. The most efficient and effective validation comes via operational planning, exercises, and execution in an actual event or situation.[12] Absent a developed and sustained capability for states and localities to perform catastrophic operational planning—detailed, time-sequenced operational plans with logistical requirements, pre-scripted mission assignments, and communications processes—credible measurement of capabilities and capability gaps will remain unsatisfactory and continue to frustrate effective intergovernmental collaboration.

The components of the National Incident Management System doctrine deal largely with preparedness, resource management, and mutual aid. Preparedness is an integrated component of NIMS, with NIMS components tying directly to the capabilities required during an incident. The establishment of the FEMA National Preparedness Directorate's Assessment Division may be the answer to address the reconciliation of NIMS assessment requirements with capability gaps. NPD's NIMS Compliance Assistance Support Tool (NIMSCAST) was an attempt to integrate measurement. (NIMSCAST is a self-assessment instrument for federal, state, tribal, and local governments to evaluate and report a jurisdiction's implementation of NIMS.) FEMA has attempted to simplify the assessment of operational capability gaps and NIMS compliance requirements through PPD-8 core capabilities. NPD is still developing the metrics.

In the post-Katrina environment, FEMA's Disaster Operations Directorate created the Gap Analysis Tool for use in the hurricane states to identify capability gaps that would require federal assistance. After two years of testing this approach, the FEMA leadership considered applying this Gap Analysis Tool to other scenarios in other regions. To the detriment of national planning efforts, FEMA disposed of the Gap Analysis Tool in 2009 without developing a successor methodology for reviewing capability gaps. Nonetheless, implicit in PKEMRA, the FEMA regions have the responsibility for reconciling capability gaps in their regions using techniques such as the Gap Analysis Tool. To date, DHS/FEMA has not reconciled this capability analysis with the Target Capabilities List requirements for the grant programs.[13]

The bitter truth is that homeland security stakeholders have yet to establish agreed-to measures or metrics for assessing the level of required capability. The TCL merely indicates what a capability should be able to do. It does not provide a community or state with guidance for determining how much capability is actually necessary to address a given risk. The nation has thus invested in blanket capability development with no measurable outcome that can be tied to a risk or need—except in the most general terms. It has pursued a mistaken attempt to put the cart before the horse. In the correct approach, the analysis of risk precedes planning for what is required to address risk. Planning drives decisions on resourcing to build capability. What follows is a cycle of training and exercising, revision, further training and exercising, and so on to maintain the capability.

Since the beginning of the homeland security grant program, attention and resources have focused on exercises as a way to build capabilities. Systems like the Lessons Learned Information Sharing (LLIS.gov) disseminate lessons learned from the exercise program and establish a strong communication platform for state and local agencies nationally. Unfortunately, well-developed operational plans do not routinely drive the exercise planning process. To the contrary, exercises drive planning—the reverse of intent and good practice. Development of the National Exercise Program (NEP) and Homeland Security Exercise and Evaluation Program (HSEEP) doctrine provided more rigorous evaluation criteria into the exercise planning process. While HSEEP doctrine did not specifically require operational planning as a precursor to exercise plans, it certainly encouraged it. CPG-101 was more direct. It required exercises to serve as an evaluation tool for measuring planning effectiveness. The FEMA National Preparedness Directorate took the position that all national- and regional-level exercises should validate plans, citing the 2006 requirement for the urban area tactical interoperable communications exercises conducted in 2007. This validation requirement applied to the 2010 national-level exercise on an improvised nuclear device (NLE-10) and the 2011 national-level exercise on a catastrophic earthquake (NLE-11).

While these best efforts are progressing, ultimate reconciliation must fully address the underlying intergovernmental challenge to national preparedness: *the complexities of shared sovereignty.*

Herein lies the rub. If the federal government recognizes shared sovereignty, then it must establish preparedness programs with a shared governing structure and process. Today, they are top-down driven, and they work neither efficiently nor effectively. The federal government must move beyond seeing itself as the drafter of homeland security and resilience policy that only asks for input during a comment period. In this network-centric information era, it has to become the national and regional facilitator, the convener for policy and program development and execution.

### Are Grants the Right Tool for Resourcing State and Local Catastrophic Planning and Assessments?

The federal government has strong interest in supporting states to ensure catastrophic operational planning is done effectively. Because all levels of government share a responsibility for resourcing preparedness, they well understand that the levels of shared resources are unequal and finite. Since 2001, the federal government has appropriated billions of dollars in homeland security preparedness grants[14] to state, tribal, territorial, and local governments and nonprofit organizations. Although the homeland security grant programs have made a positive impact on national preparedness, effective performance measurements of preparedness outcomes thus far have been difficult to produce. Indeed, agreement is not universal on how to measure preparedness outcomes or how to identify a preparedness end state.[15] Least effective have been performance assessments that measure training and exercise activities or equipment acquisitions rather than capability outcomes. And so, questions remain.

Several years ago, FEMA's Grant Programs Directorate (GPD) had two working groups conduct a pilot using a FEMA investment perspective to apply a cost/capability analysis to preparedness outcomes via the Cost-to-Capability (C2C) Initiative.

GPD asked the following illustrative questions:

- What is the desired outcome for a grant and preparedness?
- What are the desired capabilities?
- Are they the right capabilities?
- Is it possible to standardize capability requirements across communities with differing risks and threats?
- Are capabilities measured in terms of:
  - How many more communities can be protected?
  - Against how many more types of events/situations can communities be protected?
  - How much more collaboration has been achieved?
- How do the preparedness partners achieve a balance between utilizing limited resources for measuring capabilities versus building those capabilities?

Unfortunately, C2C was a very limited attempt to gauge grant effectiveness and was discontinued by FEMA's Tim Manning and Elizabeth Harmon, the head of GPD. No such successor effort is currently under way. While the expectation was that C2C would measure preparedness, its scope only went as far as doing the analysis of the federal grant portion and did not extend to measuring what a state and localities resourced in terms of training, equipping, and mitigation efforts beyond the federal dollar.

Some homeland security grants to be sure are FEMA legacy programs. Yet the homeland security grant program we have today came of age in fear and haste as a reaction to 9/11. After a decade, it is now possible to do a thoughtful analysis on the effectiveness and efficiency of grant programs as the resource mechanism for state and local catastrophic planning and assessments.

Grants are only one tool to serve national preparedness. State and local government resource contributions—for example, via EMACs—are already very robust.[16] The federal interagency and DHS components to include FEMA provide additional resources such as:

- FEMA's Technical Assistance program
- Lessons Learned Information Sharing
- Responder Knowledge Base
- Radiological Emergency Preparedness Program
- Comprehensive Preparedness Guide 101
- Homeland Security Exercise and Evaluation Program
- National Guard Civil Support Teams
- Doctrine development activities for the National Response Framework and the National Incident Management System
- Education and training activities at the National Domestic Preparedness Consortium, Emergency Management Institute, Center for Domestic Preparedness, and Naval Postgraduate School

Most of these preparedness activities take place without grant funding. The use of grant funds must be assessed in the context of the entire structure and associated processes of the National Preparedness System. At all governmental levels and where appropriate across the private sector and NGO communities, the National Preparedness System requires consistent levels of resourcing for both capability development and sustainment. Two questions must then be asked:

- How can the federal government minimize and integrate the fragmented grant requirements it has determined for the states, as documented by the 2008 Analysis of Federal Preparedness Requirements (AFPR) study—an effort that received broad state-level input?[17]
- In terms of pure funding, is the federal homeland security preparedness grant program by itself the most effective and efficient mechanism to achieve meaningful national preparedness, or is some structural or process improvement required to make it so?

Grants are expensive to manage in terms of time, talent, and treasure, both for the recipients and the federal government.[18] Smaller and poorer jurisdictions have to dual-hat staff. The federal government—for example, FEMA's GPD and National Preparedness Directorate, OMB, and congressional staff—has to dedicate resources to oversight and monitoring. At the state level, state administrative agencies must manage both the grants' interface with the federal government but also do the oversight and monitoring of sub-grantees at the local level, which in turn usually have to dual-hat officials to undertake additional grant reporting and management duties. Resourcing primarily via grants with their oversight and reporting requirements fosters intergovernmental relationships that can be more adversarial than collabora-tive and thus not optimal for unity of purpose.

Grant management requires states to perform voluminous data collec-tion drills in the application and reporting processes. In the past with regard to applications, FEMA advised grant applicants to incorporate references to national-level programs and doctrine like the Gap Analysis Tool, State Preparedness Report, TCL, National Priorities, National Planning Scenarios, and Integrated Planning System. States were supposed to show how they would use these programs to drive their planning while specifying other regional working groups that would participate in the planning process to close gaps, while tying deliverables back to these programs and demonstrating improve-ments in capabilities. On top of that, states needed to meet statutory and pol-icy match requirements for preparedness grants. Budgetary strains are forcing states to forfeit grant monies because they cannot make either an in-kind or cash match. Some would even argue that risk management is too focused on grants rather than pure threat and vulnerability.[19]

The net effect is that most states and local jurisdictions don't have the capability or resources to manage the complexity of the National Preparedness System efficiently and effectively and grow that capability through the grant programs. Some states may indeed have existing state administrative agen-cies—for example, those states receiving Department of Justice criminal jus-tice grants. Others had to establish and staff entirely new SAAs to administer homeland security preparedness grants and do the budget worksheets and post-award sub-jurisdiction monitoring and servicing. They need help from regional structures to collect and manage data both to apply for and do the reporting on grants.

On the other hand, all levels of government can and have become signif-icantly dependent on grants. The annual provision of more than $17 billion is still unobligated at the state and local levels. Grant funds have created and reinforced the temptation especially among elected officials to build infra-structures around obtaining and administering monies without regard to tan-gible need or results. In such instances, grants provide little national benefit and only promote changed behavior that is not in keeping with the best interests of the grantee.

## The Federal Responsibility for Resourcing Preparedness

In our interconnected society and globalized economy of the twenty-first century, our federal system of government increasingly functions according to a network governance model, as opposed to the traditional hierarchical model. It is a familiar and reasonable expectation, therefore, that complex, multisite, catastrophic incidents or situations require management by temporary, hierarchical networks according to principles of unified command at the lowest feasible jurisdictional level.[20] As discussed in the previous chapter, adjacent jurisdictions or state and federal governments provide temporary excess capabilities under mutual aid agreements such as the state-to-state Emergency Management Assistance Compacts. Mutual aid agreements play a supporting role to fill operational capability gaps. This supporting role applies not only to crisis-state mission support in an incident or situation. It also applies to the federal government's steady-state support for preparedness, of which grants are but one tool.

That being said, a local government's determination of its high-probability risks informs its operational planning. Through planning, that locality determines its requirements for resourcing preparedness to meet those risks. As the number and type of jurisdictions that could be affected by the scale of a potential event or situation expands beyond a locality, it becomes the responsibility of those jurisdictions, collaborating intrastate or interstate as regions, to determine requirements for resourcing preparedness to meet those high-probability risks. Historically and by NIMS doctrine, mutual aid is the first layer of resource support beyond the local jurisdiction. Indeed, NIMS is essentially about managing resources via mutual aid, which is fundamental to incident management and is national in scope through EMACs. It is worth noting as well that CPG-101 acknowledges the need for states to factor consideration of private-sector and NGO protection and response capabilities into preparedness requirements.

Inevitably, high-consequence risks and events that are national in scope—regardless of whether they are high- or low-probability—create inherent capability gaps for local and state jurisdictions and regions. These capability gaps for dealing effectively with catastrophic incidents—those regional or national in scope—create a requirements identification problem. State and local governments indeed have a degree of responsibility to support high-consequence events of national significance. Yet by themselves, they do not have the capability or responsibility to support catastrophic national preparedness.

As stated above, the skills and bandwidth of the full- or part-time state and local administrative staff are extremely limited. State and local governments do not have the organic capability to perform low-probability, high-consequence risk assessment, although some may be able to outsource to the private sector to do the assessments for them. Neither do state governments have the resources to develop detailed, time-sequenced catastrophic operational plans. It would be impractical for states and localities to grow their own organic capability for such planning, and once achieved it would have to be sustained in order to maintain personnel resources that are trained and have continuity.

It is, therefore, important to underline two aspects of preparedness relative to resourcing decisions:

- Preparedness is a means to an end and not a core mission.
- The level of preparedness reflects a jurisdiction's risk tolerance for low-probability, high-consequence events.

As a result, when budget-constrained state, tribal, territorial, and local governments consider resource trade-offs, their priority goes to support near-term, operational *mission essential* activities for routine and high-probability events. These jurisdictions will not necessarily support longer-term preparedness capability requirements—especially when viewed as federally determined according to federal assessments of risk.

Despite the progress being made, FEMA has not yet been able to facilitate meaningful definition and assignment of preparedness roles and responsibilities for low-probability, high-consequence catastrophic events and situations among the localities, states, territories, intrastate regions, tribal governments, interstate regions, and the federal government. Only through a fully resourced, federally subsidized, ongoing process for operational planning—properly informed by risk assessment—can capability development and sustainment and capability gaps be determined.

Therefore, given the intergovernmental budget realities, the federal government must assume the financial burden of shared responsibility for resourcing risk assessment and operational planning for catastrophic incidents and situations that require regional preparedness capabilities.

Planning and assessments are critical components of a truly integrated National Preparedness System. To inform a solution to facilitate and resource such integration, the following conclusions can be drawn:

1. Catastrophic operational planning and exercise validation confirm determination of capabilities within regions.
2. The federal government has the financial burden for resourcing national catastrophic planning and assessments.
3. Grants are not the most effective and efficient tools for resourcing state and local catastrophic planning and assessments.

A more comprehensive approach would—by statute or directive— give responsibility and authority to the FEMA region, as the instrument of the DHS executive agent for preparedness, to provide the good offices and resources to serve as the nation's regionally based preparedness facilitator and convener. This action would establish the legal basis for regional homeland security empowerment—that is, where the department and agency have declared in numerous statements that they are already going with the National Preparedness System and Homeland Security Enterprise.

# CHAPTER TWELVE

# The Fulcrum of Network Federal Security Governance:

## The Regional Preparedness Staff

FEMA is the DHS executive agent for preparedness. The Post-Katrina Emergency Management Reform Act assigned "unprecedented responsibilities" to the agency to develop the National Preparedness System and lead in its implementation.[1] The legislation mandated that FEMA regions serve as the decentralized, distributed capability for DHS to integrate preparedness programs and engage states. Implicit in the Comprehensive Preparedness Guide 101 was the understanding that the FEMA regions are closer to the states and localities than FEMA or DHS headquarters and therefore should be the translators of capabilities and requirements. Explicit was FEMA's February 2008 *Regional-National Preparedness Concept of Operations:* "The Region is the principal conduit for delivery of all preparedness programs and activities to state, tribal, and local partners, non-governmental organizations, the private sector, and citizens. Such preparedness activities include, among other things, stakeholder/partner coordination and information sharing, consulting, planning support, capability assessments and reporting, exercise performance and evaluation, internal and external training."[2]

The regional CONOPS sought to accomplish then-administrator Dave Paulison's December 2006 "Vision for New FEMA." It was principally authored by Josh Dozor, at the time Marko Bourne's branch chief for preparedness policy, planning, and analysis. Although the CONOPS was a document of the Paulison era, it remains as a structural and process framework for Craig Fugate's FEMA. Most tellingly, Fugate advanced Dozor to the position of FEMA deputy director for regional operations. In mid-2009, FEMA acted as the federal government's executive agent for updating the National Planning Scenarios; Fugate assigned Dozor to lead the review.

Dozor's regional CONOPS empowers the regional administrator and federal preparedness coordinator as the regional leads for achieving the National Preparedness Goal. It gives the FPC direct supervisory responsibility for national preparedness missions and programs in the region and provides for a network of FPCs and robust region offices to transform Paulison's vision into a reality.[3] In the exercise of this responsibility, the FPC serves as a DHS official to further PKEMRA intent: the CONOPS requires FPCs to implement the FEMA Headquarters' annual planning guidance in their regions. Regional FPCs and their staffs are "the nation's focal points for national preparedness through expanded networks."[4]

If the CONOPS provides the organizational framework for leveraging the Homeland Security Enterprise into twenty-first-century network federal security governance, the fulcrum is potentially the regional office's National Preparedness Division. Headed by the FPC, the division includes the Regional Integration Branch, the preparedness analysis and planning officer (PAPO), and the Office of Plans and Assessments. Thus, this study makes its pivotal recommendation:

> To maintain and develop further regional, state and local preparedness capabilities—in particular those for catastrophic preparedness—FEMA should transform in each region the National Preparedness Division into a standing, intergovernmental/interagency Regional Preparedness Staff (RPS). FEMA should directly and fully resource this staff via:
>
> 1.  Reprogramming funds into its FEMA Management and Administration and State and Local Programs budget lines
> 2.  Augmenting Federal Intergovernmental Personnel Act (IPA) assignments.

Direct resourcing to deliver an intergovernmental capability is a proven means, most notably with respect to Joint Terrorism Task Forces. JTTFs are model collaborative entities, where federal personnel have accounted for nearly half of the task force detailees. In addition, the federal government has assumed, for example, overtime costs and provided vehicles for state and local IPA detailees. Other examples of direct resourcing are assignment of DHS and

FBI personnel to state fusion centers as analysts, the now well-established state assignments of protective security advisors (PSAs) by the DHS Office of Infrastructure Protection, and regional assignments of defense coordinating officers (DCOs) and defense coordinating elements (DCEs) by NorthCom.

The Regional Preparedness Staff would be a standing intergovernmental and interagency coordinating body, as opposed to yet another task force or advisory council. The RPS would integrate inputs from existing regional mechanisms to perform statutorily defined missions. As a full-time staff, it would serve as the interface for de-confliction and collaborative agreement on regional preparedness policy and doctrine, principally with regard to prioritization of actionable risk, catastrophic planning, and assessment. It would not have decision-making authority, however. States would continue to decide on issues affecting the states; the federal government would continue to decide on issues affecting the federal government.

The RPS would leverage the intent of the Regional Interagency Steering Committee (RISC) process to coordinate federal agency participation in regional planning, training and exercises, and current and evolving efforts by FEMA and its mission partners. On behalf of the regional administrator, FPC, and RISC, the staff would manage the regional preparedness interfaces with the Regional Advisory Council, DHS protective security advisors and Sector Coordinating Councils (SCCs), JTTFs, Coast Guard Area Maritime Security Committees (AMSCs), Regional Emergency Communications Coordination Working Groups, HHS regional emergency coordinators (RECs), state and local fusion centers, emergency operations centers and their emergency support function structures and processes, and so forth. In UASI regions that received funding from the now eliminated Regional Catastrophic Preparedness Grant Program, the RPS would supplant and continue the work of the Regional Catastrophic Planning Teams.

The regional CONOPS noted the New FEMA's "broadened preparedness mission" that includes prevention and protection. This staff would thus ensure close coordination with law enforcement, intelligence, and the eighteen CI/KR sector communities. The RPS would engage with state administrative agencies and regional COOP personnel and support the regional office's regional investment officer (RIO), assistance to firefighters grant (AFG) personnel, and grants management specialist (GMS). The CONOPS gave responsibility to the FPC for development of regional action plans and to the region for the evaluation of preparedness program activities. To that end, the RPS would provide the FPC with staff support for development of the region's budget requests and spend plan development as pertains to catastrophic preparedness.

The core function of the RPS, however, would be to facilitate joint inter-agency/intergovernmental collaboration for developing and sustaining capabilities to conduct:

- Catastrophic risk assessment
- Catastrophic operational planning and exercise validation
- Inventories of catastrophic capabilities and negotiated processes to identify gaps and target grants
- Regional evaluations and self-assessments informed by regionally determined performance metrics

The regional CONOPS looked to the regions to provide FEMA Headquarters with the "field perspective." As the consensus expression of the region, the RPS would translate and develop Threat and Hazard Identification Risk Analysis (THIRA) guidance for priorities the federal government wants to support, and would have the latitude to prioritize and focus on regional risk. Taking input from DHS' Homeland Infrastructure Threat and Risk Analysis Center (HITRAC), the Department of Justice, state fusion centers, and other regional and state organizations, the RPS would have the responsibility to conduct the regional THIRA and a catastrophic risk assessment.

Says FEMA:

THIRAs are intended to be tools that allow organizations at all levels of government to identify, assess, and prioritize their natural and man-made risks. These assessments are meant to facilitate the identification of capability and resource gaps, and allow organizations to track their year-to-year progress to address those gaps. THIRAs should leverage existing hazard mitigation processes, but be conducted in a reasonably standard manner so that results may be incorporated into Federal-level assessments. FEMA will use these assessments to develop regional planning assumptions and, working with its partners, identify and implement priority actions to address assumptions identified.[5]

The 2008–9 Task Force Emergency Response program was an interim and worthy attempt to seed a catastrophic planning capability at the state level. However, such efforts by FEMA or NorthCom to provide states with planners is not a substitute for states and their mission partners' developing an organic regional operational planning capability. The better way forward is for the RPS to serve as the means for baselining development and sustainment of the organic regional capability. States and local jurisdictions would be responsible for sustaining and developing an operational planning capability for what they determine as high-probability events or situations. However, the staff would ensure operational plans are in place for low-probability/high-consequence catastrophic events for jurisdictions without the resources for catastrophic planning. Working with existing planning, training, and exercise units in the states and at the local level, the RPS would collaboratively conduct catastrophic operational planning and exercise validation. It would *not* attempt to create yet more exercises to validate these operational plans. Rather, it would strengthen Homeland Security Exercise and Evaluation Program (HSEEP) doctrine by mandating that established exercise programs meet an explicit requirement to validate them.

An RPS would also drive development and sustainment of private-sector and NGO operational planning to advance EMAC and NIMS toward a more robust regional, mutual aid system. Especially critical is empowerment of small and medium businesses who cannot afford the costs of engaging in preparedness and developing private-sector operational frameworks. The RPS has the potential for providing the good offices for a collaborative public-private operational structure to serve as an interface with EOCs at the local, state, and regional levels. It could also facilitate cooperative agreements for a regional catastrophic operational planning that incorporates out-of-region states with their capabilities and their capability gaps into the planning process.

The regional CONOPS provided for the region to give FEMA Headquarters in Washington a field perspective on regional risks, the status of regional capabilities, and how DOJ, HHS, the Department of Agriculture (USDA), and EPA are meeting regional capability needs.[6] The RPS would perform regional inventories of catastrophic capabilities and serve as the venue for negotiated processes to identify gaps and target grants and other resources.

The national debt crisis and inevitable constriction of federal budgets will continue to bite into preparedness grants generally and in particular State

Homeland Security Program (SHSP) and UASI funding. The 2011 elimination of over half of the UASI regions altogether, along with the Regional Catastrophic Preparedness Grant Program and funding for Regional Catastrophic Preparedness Teams, is justification alone for a reprogramming to maintain a regional capability to improve the effectiveness of grant investments and the efficiency of grant program management. The RPS would help target annual grant priorities to develop and sustain broad collaboration for undergirding operational catastrophic capabilities. This process could apply to all preparedness grants for the respective department/agency region. This regional coordination mechanism could serve as a template for a FEMA-facilitated federal-level interagency grant coordination mechanism that would build upon the DHS-HHS Grant Oversight Steering Committee and expand to include DOJ, USDA, EPA, and other grant-providing departments and agencies in the homeland security space.

The RPS would develop and sustain regional operational catastrophic preparedness capabilities with states and other non-federal mission partners and, where applicable, leverage a state's Emergency Management Assistance Program (EMAP) accreditation. Where the regional mission partners through the RPS determine regional and national catastrophic capability gaps, this collaborative determination would inform regional and state applications for preparedness grants to go toward filling those gaps. The most important programs are those that involve personnel—for example, readiness certification, education, planning, training, and exercise priorities. In some states, it may be necessary to use grants to augment the state and local planning capability. Where grants target equipment acquisitions, the RPS should determine a jurisdiction's need based on the mutual aid requirements of the region. Local capabilities do not need to be consistent or the same throughout a state, given the local jurisdictions' determination of their own risk profiles. Priority at all levels will go to those programs most critical to catastrophic preparedness— for example, programs addressing capability gaps in interoperable communications, logistics, and knowledge management (including the use of social networking processes to facilitate network nodes). In general, the positive outcome for a preparedness grant should be increased relationship-building among jurisdictions.

Distribution of grants that are specific to a collaboratively identified requirement is less prone to rely on population-based grant guidance. Because of their emphasis on effects-based criteria, grants that address specific capability gaps are not as likely to generate contention as the region struggles with prioritizing states' needs. FEMA's Radiological Emergency Preparedness Program (REPP) for nuclear power plants provides such a model. Gaps identified in the capability gap inventory for low-probability/high-consequence events involving land- or water-based search and rescue, medical surge, or chemical, biological, radiological, nuclear, and explosives (CBRNE) detection, for example, would be appropriate targets for grants.

Achievement of effective and efficient intergovernmental collaboration requires a feedback loop and metrics which best occur at the regional level. FEMA would not provide federally determined metrics—only the standard format for metrics to allow Headquarters to compile national evaluations and assessments. The RPS would serve as the vehicle for regional evaluations and self-assessments informed by regionally determined performance metrics. Providing the venue for state and local input to determine the regional performance metrics, the staff would base evaluations and assessments on these metrics in accord with nationally determined objectives and planning assumptions.

In its oversight of regional training and exercise programs, the RPS would enable peer-to-peer performance-based evaluations as the basis for regional self-assessments. To perform these assessments, the staff would rely on FEMA's Simulation Cell (SimCell),[7] if necessary, to replicate federal participation and would use the National Exercise Simulation Center (NESC) to include HHS and any other federal departments or agencies. The RPS would thus manage the *collaborative* definition of performance, capabilities, and outcomes and effectively structure them to provide the local, tribal, territorial, state, intrastate regional, and interstate regional feedback to enhance further regional collaboration.

By its own example, the RPS would incentivize the regional jurisdictions to leverage regional assets—for example, universities, national labs, FFRDCs, or contractors, for any required analytical support. With respect to contract support services generally, the RPS would make recommendations to the regional administrator and the FPC, who will be authorized to order—if necessary—contractor support off the General Services Administration (GSA) Schedule. Regional analytical support would come from the region's higher education partners—for example, universities and related research centers/

labs that perform research and projects for the states and federal government. Examples are Region III's partner academic entities of the Mid-Atlantic All Hazards Consortium that are involved in regional information sharing, provide research, development, testing, and evaluation services to states, and partner on regional projects and grant requests. These bodies are: the University of Maryland, Towson University, Johns Hopkins University Applied Physics Lab, Penn State University, Fairleigh Dickinson University, Monmouth University, Rutgers University, Delaware State University, George Mason University, Virginia Commonwealth University, James Madison University, Manhattan Institute, George Washington University, Virginia Tech, West Virginia University, and Temple University.

Finally, the RPS would have the responsibility to develop a strategy for regional NIMS implementation—the working, resourcing, and facilitation of NIMS compliance. While NIMS has wide acceptance in the field, its compliance criteria have added a layer of complexity to the process, given the budgetary pressures on some state and local jurisdictions to meet the costs of compliance. As opposed to determination of compliance standards, which state and local jurisdictions could construe as unfunded mandates, federal guidance should be in the form of best practices. The RPS would be best positioned to arrive at a strategy to implement and evaluate NIMS implementation.

### IPAs as the Vanguard of the Network Federal Security Workforce

The regional CONOPS outlined a number of professional development objectives for the regional office preparedness staff. Two objectives were to:

1. Prepare regional staff to expand the regional network, build preparedness program management capabilities, and manage the integration of preparedness programs consistent with this CONOPS.
2. Build an esprit de corps that promotes collaboration and consistent application of the preparedness mission across the regions.[8]

The Regional Preparedness Staff would serve as the vanguard for developing a collaborative culture across the network federal security and resilience workforce in the Homeland Security Enterprise. This culture would be analogous to that of the "purple-suiters" on joint duty assignments to the Department of Defense's Joint Staff and the joint staffs of the combatant commanders. The military services, especially the Navy, were adverse to the joint duty requirement, imposed by the Goldwater-Nichols Department of Defense Reorganization Act of 1986. However, Goldwater-Nichols made joint duty mandatory for an officer's eligibility for promotion to flag and general officer rank. Similar opposition can be expected for any such homeland security professional workforce requirement for interagency/intergovernment assignment. Nevertheless, anticipated resistance is not an argument against the merits of the requirement.

The regional staff would be composed of positions for federal, state, local, tribal, territorial IPAs, and private-sector and NGO special government employees (SGEs) to serve in rotational assignments. (SGEs are temporary personnel, compensated or uncompensated, who are either appointed, under contract, or serving in an advisory capacity under the Federal Advisory Committee Act.) Federal personnel would serve in a temporary duty (TDY) status up to three years. As is likely, state and local authorities would only be able to provide personnel for one-year TDY rotations at a maximum.

The staff would secure non-federal representatives for positions under the IPA Mobility Program. State and local IPAs would serve in this collaborative body as *co-equals* with federal officials to determine regional policies and priorities. FEMA would incentivize their parent agencies and other mission partner organizations to exchange their employees with federal employees while providing them with the option of receiving straight reimbursements as an alternative. The IPA program would thus enable them to maintain their own full-time employee (FTE) levels while advancing a two-way, intergovernmental culture of collaboration. Rotational assignments would continually refresh and enhance collaborative expertise among state and local personnel in their professional development. As an additional benefit, service on the RPS would provide state and local representatives with exposure to skills related to program management and acquisition strategies.

The RPS structure would conform to a common template adapted by regional partners. Each region would right-size and configure its RPS according to its specific regional assets, needs, character, and set of priorities. The staff composition could reflect such priorities where public-private networks have already embraced interstate regionalization. A representative example is in FEMA Region III, where the RPS could leverage the efforts of the All Hazards Consortium and the National Capital Region (NCR), whose

NCR Homeland Security Strategic Plan was cited by the regional CONOPS as a good model for cross-jurisdictional coordination. Other regions previously mentioned as advancing regionalization networks are Region X, with the Pacific Northwest Economic Region and its Pacific Northwest Center for Regional Disaster Resilience, Region V with ChicagoFIRST, and Region IV and the Community and Regional Resilience Institute.

The FEMA baseline charter for its Regional Advisory Councils providing guidance for membership composition is one benchmark from which a region could determine IPA staffing. The charter says the RAC shall consist of up to thirty-six members. "To the extent practicable, the members shall be drawn from a geographic (including urban and rural) and a substantive cross section of officials, providing diversity to the membership, to include emergency managers, and emergency response providers from State, territorial, local, and tribal governments."[9] The guidance calls for:

- three members representing the interests of the emergency management field and three from related emergency response providers
- one from public health departments
- one from emergency medical services
- three drawn from among governmental law enforcement, fire service, and medical first responders/providers
- one from each state and territorial government within the region, expressly including, but not limited to, adjutants general
- one from local government from each state within the region
- three from tribal governments
- three from executives of state and territorial governments
- three from executives of local governments
- three from executives of tribal governments

Region III in its charter, for example, applied this guidance saying, "The RAC brings together subject matter experts that represent each domain of the emergency management lifecycle: protection, preparedness, response, recovery, and mitigation. To the extent practicable, the membership will be geographically and professionally diverse. RAC members should develop and maintain a professional network in order to communicate and obtain feedback on the activities of the RAC."[10] The Region III charter reads that the RAC will consist of "approximately thirty members" and will extend to include representatives from the private sector and NGOs. The types of individuals Region III envisaged for its RAC were:

- state emergency management directors
- UASI core city designees
- rural area representative
- fire services representative
- emergency medical services representative
- local law enforcement representative
- state law enforcement representative
- public works representative
- IAEM Region III representative
- education representative
- volunteer groups representative
- hospital representative
- university research representative
- the adjutant general representative
- public health representative
- local/county government representative
- elected official
- members of the Chamber of Commerce or other appropriate business associations (by invitation)[11]

By itself, this RAC example with only two law enforcement representatives is insufficient for meeting the broadened preparedness mission that includes prevention and protection. To reflect the law enforcement and intelligence functions necessary to support steady-state regional preparedness and ongoing investigations, a properly considered Regional Preparedness Staff would also have regional representation from:

- Coast Guard districts
- FBI Special Agents in Charge (SACs)
- U.S. Attorneys

Under the regional CONOPS, the FEMA regional administrator has the responsibility for hiring and evaluating regional office personnel. The RPS would act as the federal lead to work with state, local, tribal, territorial, private-sector, and NGO partners to draft and execute for that region a professional development plan that would clearly identify requirements for personnel who should be considered members of the Homeland Security Enterprise cadre. The law enforcement and intelligence component of this cadre would need to be trained and cleared to the top secret/sensitive compartmented information (TS/SCI) level in order to provide liaison to such regional entities as state fusion centers, JTTFs, Area Maritime Security Committees, and critical infrastructure/key resources stakeholders.

In advance of the rollout of the Regional Preparedness Staffs, FEMA could engage the National Academy of Public Administration and the Naval Postgraduate School's Center for Homeland Defense and Security and its regional educational partners to conduct a survey to collect quantitative and qualitative data to inform drafting and execution of a regional professional development implementation plan. This plan would contain regional priorities and leverage and create regional assets, including for training, education, exercising, rotational assignment, and career paths. Though this plan would conform to national guidelines, the RPS will tailor it to the region. With respect to law enforcement and intelligence professionals, it will give significant weight to the regional assessment of national security threats to determine the level of need for personnel to be cleared and trained.

While the RPS would be a preparedness and not an operational staff, personnel may be required in a crisis to staff the region's Joint Operations Center (JOC) and Joint Field Office (JFO) and serve as GS-13/14-level liaison officers in and to both. As the regional CONOPS provided for the FPC, the salaries and expenses of the RPS would be supported through the FEMA Management and Administration appropriation. Travel costs associated with the coordination of exercises may be reimbursed with funding obtained through the State and Local Programs appropriation. Whenever RPS members engage in disaster response or recovery efforts, their salary and travel expenses would be charged against the applicable disaster's funding code.[12]

If not by statute, DHS and FEMA could establish these Regional Preparedness Staffs under existing authorities. They should do so by reprogramming FEMA program funds to develop the concept, program estimate, and implementation plan. The Government Accountability Office (GAO) could undertake a comparative cost analysis to assess current program management costs at all three levels of government relative to the costs of the proposed RPSs. Ultimately, FEMA would insert into its annual budget submission a line for a program appropriation for a standing Regional Preparedness Staff in each region.

As the nation's regionally based preparedness facilitators and conveners, the ten Regional Preparedness Staffs would serve as the nodes of a decentralized Network Federal National Preparedness System. Configured with an intergovernmental and interdisciplinary Homeland Security Enterprise cadre linked both to the federal government and the regional communities and jurisdictions that it serves, this network of Regional Preparedness Staffs would be agile and resilient, optimally able to pulse the system to anticipate and respond to the threats and opportunities posed by a very dynamic twenty-first-century strategic environment.

# CHAPTER THIRTEEN

# Moving Toward an Intergovernmental Homeland Security Professional Cadre

In this increasingly complex twenty-first-century strategic environment, homeland security professionals have become used to the idea that they will routinely be representing their departments and agencies in interagency, intergovernmental policy development and planning. To be sure, sustained interagency, intergovernmental operations may not be the norm. Yet when they occur, they are often unanticipated and require collaboration among stakeholders unique to the incident or situation, as evidenced by the 2010 BP oil spill in the Gulf of Mexico. In these types of operations, top-down, federal-level workforce cultures can impede optimal collaboration. They are social expressions of department and agency national security structures honed in the industrial era with their command and control processes for managing both total and cold war. These workforce cultures predispose senior representatives in particular to defend their department and agency equities, while unintentionally putting at risk effective and efficient execution of the mission.

In the milestone effort to improve military service coordination and defense management, the National Security Act of 1947 led to establishment of the Department of Defense (DoD). Four decades into the Cold War, the U.S. military was still incapable of planning and operating in a unified, multiservice manner.[1] With the Goldwater-Nichols DoD Reorganization Act of 1986, Congress supplied a number of structural and process correctives, among which was the "joint duty requirement" for professional advancement in the military officer corps. This requirement was the key to transforming workforce cultures in the services and was aimed at those wanting to remain eligible for promotion to flag and general officers.

Addressing structure and process in response to 9/11, legislation established the Department of Homeland Security in 2003 and the Office of the

Director of National Intelligence (ODNI) in 2004. Assessments of operational lessons learned in the Hurricane Katrina response and the Iraq and Afghanistan wars gave impetus to the idea of a Goldwater-Nichols for the federal government and development of an "interagency cadre" of national security professionals for "more effective application of all the elements of national power."[2]

In early 2006, the White House released *The Federal Response to Hurricane Katrina: Lessons Learned* report and the Pentagon issued its third *Quadrennial Defense Review (QDR)*. These documents gave additional weight to a "convergence of thinking" on interagency reform. They also introduced "a fundamental tension concerning the relative importance of national and homeland security considerations in shaping future interagency coordination initiatives."[3] Not fully appreciated is the fact that it was Hurricane Katrina—a borders-in event—that prompted establishment of what would be a Goldwater-Nichols-inspired professional development program. Fran Townsend's Katrina report broadened the professional development focus to include the intergovernmental: "Over the long term, our professional development and education programs must break down interagency barriers to build a unified team across the Federal government. Just as the Department of Defense succeeded in building a joint leadership cadre, so the rest of the Federal government must make familiarity with other departments and agencies a requirement for career advancement. Where practicable, interagency and intergovernmental assignments for Federal personnel must build trust and familiarity among diverse homeland security professionals."[4]

Moreover, the report recommended that DHS specifically have the responsibility to: "develop a comprehensive program for the professional development and education of the nation's homeland security personnel,[5] including Federal, state, and local employees as well as emergency management persons within the private sector, non-governmental organizations, as well as faith-based and community groups. This program should foster a 'joint' Federal interagency, state, local, and civilian team."[6]

Townsend's report directly led to Bush's May 17, 2007, Executive Order 13434, National Security Professional Development. The drafters of this EO included Pat Newman, a career civil servant with the Coast Guard's Office of Strategic Analysis detailed to the DHS Chief Learning Officer to work on various approaches for establishing a Homeland Security University, as was being mooted at the time. Newman thus provided input to the executive order that was very attuned to the intergovernmental and the emergency management equities—vice the purely interagency and national security—that it was to reflect. EO 13434 called for establishment of a National Security Professional Development (NSPD) program for seventeen federal agencies resting on three pillars: education, training, and professional experience. The NSPD program proposed to encompass professional development fellowship opportunities, guidelines for career advancement and, most significantly, a plan for interagency and intergovernmental assignments. The DHS secretary had the tasking to develop for federal, state, local, and tribal government officials an education program in disaster preparedness/response/recovery plans and authorities, and a training program in crisis decision-making skills.

For NSPD oversight, EO 13434 established a senior-level Executive Steering Committee (ESC), chaired by the director of the Office of Personnel Management (OPM), Linda Springer, which reported to Townsend and National Security Advisor Stephen Hadley. An interagency body, the ESC coordinated cross-agency integration and implementation of the program. In July, the ESC released the National Strategy for the Development of National Security Professionals. Expanding on the EO, the NSPD Strategy decentralized implementation of the program to the seventeen agencies, reflecting OPM's reluctance to move beyond guidance into oversight of personnel policies within federal departments. While the NSPD system included homeland security and national security personnel, it did not apply to uniformed military and foreign-service officers, both of whom have established professional development systems. Early in the implementation process, the ESC identified some 14,000 Senior Executive Service (SES) and GS 13–15-level NSP positions, of which some 1,200 were SES. In addition, ODNI identified classified totals for positions in the Intelligence Community (IC).

In late 2007, shortly after OPM released an interim NSPD implementation plan, Clay Johnson, OMB deputy director for management, became chairman of the ESC. A longtime friend of the president, Johnson was George Bush's college roommate, his chief of staff as Texas governor, and manager of his presidential transition team. Throughout most of 2008 until the end of Bush's second term, Johnson influenced the NSPD effort in accord with the president's thinking.

EO 13434 provided for a National Security Professional Development Integration Office (NSPD-IO) to coordinate activities for the ESC. Commencing work in early 2008, NSPD-IO was led by Maj. Gen. William A. Navas Jr., a retired Army Guardsman who had been director of the Washington, D.C., National Guard. A professional engineer from Puerto Rico, Major General Navas came to his post from the Navy Department where he had been assistant secretary for manpower and reserve affairs. NSPD-IO had no oversight responsibilities nor could it set interagency NSPD policy. Its role was to support the ESC and coordinate and monitor NSPD implementation. Its funding came from DoD, which served as the NSPD-IO executive agent.

As the apparent impetus behind an NSPD system seemed to be building into 2008, DoD and State participation became more pronounced, as did the national security aspects to the program, to the detriment of the intergovernmental considerations. The NSPD leadership now focused the program on the federal level, as indicated in some of the wording of the NSPD Strategy. With regard to education and training, the strategy document said that the federal government would focus first on identifying "federal programs, facilities, and institutions, followed thereafter by the identification of such programs at the State, local, territorial, tribal, academic, non-governmental, and private-sector levels."[7] According to a number of federal officials, the attitude behind the strategy was that, in the words of one, "the Federal government needed to get its own house in order before bringing in the states and locals."

Given the threat picture in 2008, an election year with all the continuity sensitivities associated with a presidential transition, the federal focus may have been the prudent course of action. In the autumn of 2008, the ESC's final NSPD Implementation Plan proceeded top-down. SES-level NSPs in federal positions with National Response Framework responsibilities took FEMA's online NRF training module, developed earlier in the year by the Emergency Management Institute, along with instruction via other performance tools. In addition, all NSPs took an online training and orientation course on national security.

With the change of administration in January 2009, NSPD implementation went into what NSP development participants called a "strategic pause." As a program with no legislative mandate, the incoming administration understandably viewed NSPD as its predecessor's initiative. In 2010, NSPD-IO transferred from DoD to the Executive Office of the President. As well, the new administration established under the NSC an Interagency Policy Committee with an overlapping NSPD mandate, chaired by Ambassador Mary

Yates, the NSC senior advisor on strategic planning. Despite interagency efforts in 2009 and 2010, the NSPD program remained in strategic pause until early 2011 when Yates became the NSC's senior director for African affairs.

In February 2011, NSPD leadership went to Richard Reed, the senior director of the NSC's Resilience Directorate. The move jump-started the program and led to "NSPD 2.0" with a new NSPD Executive Steering Committee charter. NSPD 2.0 refocused on accomplishing specific missions and achieving tangible professional development outcomes. In June, NSPD-IO returned to life when the office transferred to the Office of Personnel Management and a DOE senior executive at the National Nuclear Security Administration, submariner Rear Adm. Gerald Talbot, USN (Ret.), assumed the helm. Reporting to Reed, Talbot had the responsibility for executive branch implementation of the NSPD program via a reconvened NSPD ESC. The NSPD 2.0 charter specified that the program would focus on a DHS-led pilot effort focused on the emergency management discipline and interagency activities under way in the National Capital Region. To further the NSPD effort, Talbot facilitated a sixteen-member interagency working group (WG) representing the federal agencies working on PPD-8 national preparedness integration. The WG represents what he calls an emergency management community of practice comprised of some 150 members whose agencies voluntarily participate in the pilot. By drawing the WG membership from agencies involved in both the NSPD program and PPD-8 implementation, Talbot and NSPD-IO have been able to leverage the same working group participation lists. Moreover, the focus on emergency management benefits from FEMA's well-established education and training programs, for example, at the Emergency Management Institute.

In face of the multitude of fiscal and security challenges with which the Obama administration has been contending, NSPD implementation enjoys scant political horsepower in the executive branch. Absent the legislative mandate, the NSPD enterprise for the federal homeland security professional workforce lacks teeth. Its bite can only come with sustained structure, management, and funding. To adapt a phrase from American film culture: if Congress forces the federal government to build a homeland security professional cadre for itself, state and local governments, the private sector, and NGOs "will come." One approach could be to amend the Homeland Security Act of 2002 to provide for the establishment of a program office with a mission-essential program line for strategic human capital investment in any department or agency with primary or secondary/collateral homeland security missions or functions.[8] The amendment must include a requirement that all such human capital program offices employ a homeland security professional training, education, and professional development Planning, Programs, and Budget (PPB) cycle that reflects and demonstrates resourcing of homeland security enterprise cadre policy priorities.

These empowered program offices would have authority to develop and execute training, education, and professional development plans for their department/agency homeland security enterprise cadres. Headquarters DHS, its intergovernmental response/recovery mission partners, and ODNI should jointly develop policy guidance to serve as the bases for those plans for the homeland security community[9] and Intelligence Community. These offices would liaise with their counterpart offices in other departments/agencies as well as with relevant state and local jurisdiction, private-sector, and NGO human-capital program offices to fulfill the end-state objectives of the homeland security enterprise in the development and execution of their plans.

### NIMS and the NRF as Two Bases to Inform Structure/Management of the Homeland Security Enterprise Cadre

The NSPD Implementation Plan specified that the initial orientation training for NSPs would focus on the National Response Framework—the national interagency and intergovernmental framework for management of domestic incidents rising to the level of a coordinated national response.[10]

The intergovernmental dimension of an NSPD system must be seen not only in terms of federal, state, and local governments, the vertical dimension. A tenet of emergency management is, "All disasters are local." NRF response doctrine holds: "Incidents must be managed at the lowest possible jurisdictional level and supported by additional capabilities when needed."[11] From the state and local perspectives, the *horizontal* intergovernmental dimension intrastate and interstate is equally—if not more directly—important in terms of developing homeland security professionals. More the norm, complex, multi-site, multi-jurisdictional catastrophic events and situations rise to the level of intrastate or interstate regional crises—vice national—that is, when federal supporting assets are employed. Nevertheless, they still require interagency and intergovernmental management under mutual aid agreements or compacts governing collaborative use of personnel outside of their parent jurisdictions—for example, when Emergency Mutual Assistance Compacts come into play state-to-state.

As stressed throughout our discourse, in the United States, three levels of government share sovereignty over a common people and common territory. Presidentially delegated authority covers the executive branch departments and agencies, their positions and personnel, but it does *not* extend to intergovernmental organizations and personnel. Federal, state, local, tribal, and territorial chains of command are separate. On top of these constitutional and sovereignty aspects, the homeland security space includes a multitude of disciplines whose certification processes are governed and administered by state-level professional boards. States and professions are thus resistant to the idea of national standards. Thus, both intergovernmental dimensions of an NSPD system will not be seamless and are well beyond any national setting of mandatory workforce development requirements.

The NSPD Strategy and other documents on NSPs that reference the private-sector and NGO communities further indicate that conceptually an NSPD system would be more than "whole-of-government." It would be "whole-of-society," "whole-of-nation." When and where appropriate, private-sector and NGO personnel are or may be performing critical homeland security functions—for example, in steady-state, with regard to national critical infrastructure/key resources, or in crisis-state, in a catastrophic event or situation, most especially if that event or situation should rise to a level of threatening continuity of operations, continuity of government, or enduring constitutional government.

In its February 2010 *Quadrennial Homeland Security Review*, DHS defines and frames homeland security as "a widely distributed and diverse—but unmistakable—national enterprise."[12] The department's use of the term "enterprise" refers to "the collective efforts and shared responsibilities of Federal, State, local, tribal, territorial, non-governmental, and private-sector partners—as well as individuals, families, and communities—to maintain critical homeland security capabilities."[13] This whole-of-nation enterprise approach has been reflected in the April 2011 release by the Obama administration of PPD-8, National Preparedness, the rewrite of the Bush administration's HSPD-8 of the same name. PPD-8 reinforces the "shared responsibility" and "integrated, all-of-nation" approach "necessary for preparedness and a national preparedness system." Hence, when the federal government, DHS, as its executive agent, and their homeland security mission partners analyze options for including *all* non-federal stakeholder organizations and personnel in an NSPD system, they must arrive at consensus solutions and not dismiss the problems by putting them into the "too-hard box." For these reasons, the elements of the NSPD system in its current state are better characterized as an "enterprise" and not as a "system." Non-federal homeland security professionals would constitute qualified "enterprise cadres" that may—but not in every case—move in and out of the NSPD system.

The *QHSR* speaks of maturing and strengthening the homeland security enterprise by fostering a unity of effort across a broad national culture of cooperation and mutual aid. First among its unity-of-effort objectives is the requirement to "build a homeland security professional discipline" by developing "the homeland security community of interest at all levels of government as part of a cadre of national security professionals."[14] The *QHSR* specifically refers to EO 13434 and its effort to initiate a program to develop NSPs "through access to an integrated framework of training, education, and professional experience opportunities.[15] . . . As part of that effort, we must take steps to create a homeland security community of interest across the enterprise."[16] Experience is "experience via developmental assignments," and the *QHSR* speaks of "enterprise-wide approaches to enhancing homeland security professional development."[17]

The *QHSR* uses the term "enterprise" for good reason. As stated above, from the non-federal perspective, no federal department, agency, or interagency entity can be "in charge" of the homeland security enterprise cadre. Headquarters DHS is more sensitive to the limitations of federalism than other federal departments and agencies. Its documents frequently use the terms "foster," "facilitate," "coordinate," and so forth. With respect to homeland security professionals, Headquarters DHS thus speaks of "fostering" a collaborative intergovernmental homeland security professional workforce enterprise, which can link into a federal-centric NSPD system. It is, therefore, helpful to pay attention to the *QHSR*'s identification of a "homeland security community of interest" as an "enterprise cadre" within and beyond the NSPD system. This homeland security community of interest, or rather community of practice (CoP), includes *national security* and emergency management, public health, public safety, and so forth. These CoPs—each with their own professional cultures—include private-sector and NGO organizations and personnel. Any NSPD implementation must therefore recognize and distinguish the homeland security enterprise cadre as a CoP both within and beyond the National Security Professional Development system.

The foundational interagency and intergovernmental unity-of-effort framework structures and processes upon which most of the homeland security enterprise has been based include NIMS, the National Response Framework, National Infrastructure Protection Plan, Information Sharing Enterprise (ISE), and the various scenario- and domain-specific plans—for example, the Maritime Operational Threat Response (MOTR) plan. NIMS and the NRF, for example, characterize the response area in which homeland security professionals execute their missions and perform their functions. The Critical Infrastructure and Key Resources Support Annex to the NRF bridges steady-state and crisis-state coordination and execution. At the same time, the national security community, while sensitive to and cognizant of the NIMS and NRF policies and procedures, is bound by laws, guidelines, regulations, executive orders, and findings that are both unclassified and highly classified in nature. Thus, as articulated above, the homeland security workforce as an enterprise is a combination of personnel from the national security and emergency management, public health, public safety, CI/KR, and other communities.

The National Response Framework is "a guide to how the Nation conducts all-hazards response. It is built upon scalable, flexible, and adaptable coordinating structures to align key roles and responsibilities across the Nation, linking all levels of government, non-governmental organizations, and the private sector. It is intended to capture specific authorities and best practices for managing incidents that range from the serious to purely local, to large-scale terrorist attacks or catastrophic natural disasters."[18]

The NRF builds on NIMS and provides a common playbook with NIMS standard command and management structures for response. With respect to the scope of the NRF, "The Framework provides structures for implementing nationwide response policy and operational coordination for all types of domestic incidents."[19]

The NIMS document says, "The NRF is a guide to how the nation conducts all-hazards incident management."[20] NIMS provides "a consistent nationwide template"; it "is not an operational incident management or resource allocation plan. NIMS represents a core set of doctrine, concepts, principles, terminology, and organizational processes that enables effective, efficient, and collaborative incident management."[21] The National Incident Management System:

> provides a systematic, proactive approach guiding departments and agencies at all levels of government, the private sector, and nongovernmental organizations to work seamlessly to prepare for, prevent, respond to, recover from, and mitigate the effects of incidents, regardless of cause, size, location or complexity, in order to reduce the loss of life, property and harm to the environment.[22]
>
> HSPD-5 [Homeland Security Presidential Directive 5, Management of Domestic Incidents] requires all Federal departments and agencies to adopt NIMS and use it in their individual incident management programs and activities, as well as in support of all actions taken to assist State, tribal, and local governments. The directive requires Federal departments and agencies to make adoption of NIMS by State, tribal, and local organizations a condition for Federal preparedness assistance (through grants, contracts, and other activities).[23]

The decision to begin execution of the NSPD Implementation Plan using the DHS Transition Incident Management Training with FEMA's three-hour NRF training module and other such tools to train the federal SES level during the 2008 presidential transition illustrates the foundational—though short of comprehensive—importance of the NRF and by extension NIMS for the homeland security enterprise cadre.

Homeland security personnel from states and jurisdictions in Urban Area Security Initiative regions—so designated by virtue of their population densities and economic importance—should be fully included in the homeland security enterprise cadre.[24] However, not all jurisdictions or communities of practice will have the capacity or will want to participate equally. Rural jurisdictions prioritize risk differently than do UASIs, states, and the federal government. A rural jurisdiction with a small population and no meaningful CI/KR assets will not see the same cost-benefit as a UASI jurisdiction with regard to identifying personnel for homeland security professional development. Facing significant capacity limitations with respect to participation in training, education, exercise, and operational activities, many such local jurisdictions may elect to opt out of some or most aspects of the NSPD program.

To account for the varied assessments by local jurisdictions on the capacity, need, and level of their participation in homeland security professional development, the homeland security enterprise may have to function with a decentralized structure with bottom-up processes, more appropriately facilitated at the regional level. The non-federal quarters of the homeland security enterprise will not necessarily consist of a permanent cadre of homeland security professionals.

More workable might be a designation—for example, analogous to a firefighter's Red Card.[25] Professional qualification may need to entail some sort of renewal regime—for example, as with the widely familiar certification for cardio-pulmonary resuscitation (CPR). For example, those law enforcement, emergency management, public health, and other personnel who reassign from a homeland security professional to a non–homeland security professional position—for example, in an organization having only secondary/collateral homeland security missions or functions—might not retain their homeland security professional designation. This approach would align with the state and local jurisdiction predisposition to see homeland security professionals in terms of positions rather than personnel. As such, the intergovernmental dimension of the homeland security enterprise would be a hybrid—person- and position-based.

Homeland security professional development must also account for different certification, credentialing, professional qualification, and accreditation regimes by state and by discipline. As such, the federal government will not be able to "mandate" homeland security professional requirements. The homeland security enterprise will thus have to include a means for establishing, where necessary, professional boards to benchmark the setting of professional standards for homeland security professional qualifications.

### Factoring Intelligence into the Homeland Security Enterprise Cadre

The events of 9/11 were the "trigger" for the Homeland Security Act of 2002 that established the Department of Homeland Security and the Intelligence Reform and Terrorism Prevention Act (IRTPA) of 2004 that reconfigured the Intelligence Community. The Hurricane Katrina preparedness and response was the trigger for PKEMRA and EO 13434 with its charge to develop an NSP system. The thrust of post-Katrina homeland security reconfigurations was the elevation of emergency management priorities relative to the post-9/11 emphasis on national security and specifically counterterrorism.

Many parallel career-path tracks lead to development of a homeland security professional, including those, on the one hand, for emergency management, public health, and so forth, and on the other, law enforcement, intelligence, and the military, to name a few. Where emergency management, public health professional development, and national security professional development may be seen as parallel tracks, at some point in a person's career they conjoin as *homeland security*, where the individual will be required to have access to classified information and knowledge of the IC and its processes.

Addressing the question of intelligence and reorganization was a main focus of the National Commission on Terrorist Attacks upon the United States. Created by Congress in late 2002, the 9/11 Commission reported in July 2004 with a core recommendation to establish a director of national intelligence to coordinate information sharing. Congress had begun offering legislative proposals to reorganize the intelligence community in June 2002. IRTPA was the final version, which established the DNI, the Office of the Director of National Intelligence, and the National Counterterrorism Center. IRTPA also provided for implementation of an Information Sharing Environment Plan across federal, state, and local jurisdictions. The Department of Justice's Law Enforcement Information Sharing Program (LEISP), for example, is its strategy to implement ISE information sharing to non-federal law enforcement (LE) partners. IRTPA also addressed the need to provide improved education for the IC and its mission partners. Again in DOJ, among the Federal Bureau of Investigation's training initiatives to state and local law enforcement are the offerings at the Combating Terrorism Center at the U.S. Military Academy.

While NIMS and the NRF are the bases for the structure and management of the homeland security enterprise cadre, the NRF is heavily weighted toward response and recovery. While it may be well articulated for emergency management, the NRF does not account for the fact that the prevention and protection missions are at the intersection between national security and homeland security. FEMA is not an intelligence or public-safety agency.

Under Sections 642-54 of Chapter 1, Sub-title C, PKEMRA tasks FEMA with significant responsibility for designing and implementing the National Preparedness System. Certainly in crisis-state, the NRF Emergency Support

Function Annexes apply to law enforcement and its specific role in ESF-13, Public Safety and Security, where the Department of Justice serves as the ESF-13 lead during a natural or man-made catastrophic incident. Man-made disasters (international terrorist attacks on U.S. soil, for example) that result in a large-scale law enforcement and intelligence community response will require a capability to engage quickly state, local, or tribal law enforcement assets with sufficient training and experience to support classified missions that result from such disasters. While some capability currently exists within JTTFs and other established entities for a large-scale response and resulting investigation, an extensive cadre of trained and cleared state, local, and tribal law enforcement officers may be necessary for participation in information-sharing and classified intelligence activities. Depending on the extent of the disaster, this cadre may be needed across the nation in order to assist federal law enforcement in resolving the incident and protecting other possible targets that may be discovered during the course of investigative and intelligence operations.

Since the launch of the DHS/Justice fusion center initiative, both federal and non-federal LE recognize the mutual need for improved collaboration and dramatically enhanced development of "personal relationships." Federal law enforcement recognizes that in many cases state and local law enforcement have better on-the-ground situational awareness; state and local law enforcement recognize the vital importance of access to information held by IC agencies. According to one local-level law enforcement official, "Everybody wants to get more involved with the IC. The IC is a closed system. LE intel is also closed. In the last two or three years, both have recognized there was a gap and want to bridge it to make one system."

# CHAPTER FOURTEEN

# Homeland Security Professional Development

The Federal Civil Service has its GS/SES levels; the military has its pay grades. For federal-level homeland security professionals, the Department of Homeland Security has been approaching its professional development in a fashion similar to the Department of Defense effort two decades ago with its Defense Acquisition Workforce Improvement Act (DAWIA) implementation. DAWIA provided for three levels of qualification prior to an individual's entry into a fourth, the senior Acquisition Corps.

DHS is following this four-level model with what it calls Interagency National Security Professional (INSP) qualification. In their August 30, 2010, presentation to Ambassador Yates' EO 13434 Interagency Policy Committee, Dr. George Tanner, DHS chief learning officer, and Alan Cohn, DHS deputy assistant secretary of policy for strategic planning, referenced the DHS INSP Workforce Development Plan of September 1, 2008. The plan has a matrix of four levels:

- Level 1 (Awareness)—GS 1–9
  - Threshold/baseline knowledge, skills, and abilities (KSA)
- Level 2 (Basic & Intermediate)—GS 9–12
  - 3–10 years' experience for planning and interagency exposure via training and education[1]
- Level 3 (Advanced)—GS 12–15
  - 10–20 years' experience for strategic thinking and critical analysis to attain and maintain "INSP Qualification"
- Level 4 (Executive)—GS 14–SES
  - 20–30+ years of experience for DHS INSP Executive—for example, principal federal official (PFO)

For DoD's acquisition workforce, DAWIA consolidated professional education into a Defense Acquisition University (DAU) comprising existing military institutions as well as civilian universities offering acquisition curricula. By adopting the DAU example, DHS could facilitate and empower a Homeland Security University Network of existing institutions that could provide homeland security professional education for all governmental levels, the private sector, and NGOs. Representative institutions are the Naval Postgraduate School Center for Homeland Defense and Security (CHDS), the Emergency Management Institute, the Federal Law Enforcement Training Center (FLETC), the U.S. Coast Guard Academy, the National Defense University (NDU), the National Domestic Preparedness Consortium (NDPC),[2] the FBI National Academy and National Executive Institute (NEI), the West Point Combating Terrorism Center, ODNI's National Intelligence University/ Centers of Academic Excellence (CAE) Program, and the Memorial Institute for the Prevention of Terrorism (MIPT).

Of particular importance is the capability to track graduates of such programs and to facilitate their networking. Alumni bodies can serve to maintain and deepen personal relationships formed during instruction and foster a collaborative homeland security professional culture. Noteworthy examples are the alumni associations for the FBI's National Executive Institute and the Center for Homeland Defense and Security.

Tracking graduates of the DHS Planners Qualification Program with its National Planning Courses began in August 2010 when the DHS Office of Operations and Coordination established a registrar function to track personnel. These National Planning Courses meet a core capability for homeland security professionals at the GS 13–15 levels, with funding from DoD, DHS OPS, and the DHS Office of the Chief Human Capital Officer (OCHCO). The courses consist of:

- Introduction to Homeland Security/Homeland Defense Planning Course (three-day)
  - ° DoD funded
- National Planner's Course (five-day)
- Train the Trainer National Planner's Course (four-day)
- Planning Team Leader Course (TBD)
- Homeland Security/Homeland Defense Executive Planner's Course (four-hour)

Since 2006, the program has trained over 1,200 federal, state, and local government and NGO planners. These planning courses will advance with and adhere to PPD-8, NRF, NIMS, Comprehensive Preparedness Guide 101, and related DHS directives concerning the planning function. By integrating the courses into the offerings at the Emergency Management Institute, national-level planner qualifications will be available to state and local emergency managers.

The 2007 Strategy made clear that the three pillars of NSPD career development—education, training, and experience—should rest on a networked foundation extending well beyond programs resident in the federal government: "The national security professional will need access to education, training, and opportunities to work in coordination with other Federal departments and agencies, State, local, territorial, and tribal governments, the private sector, non-governmental organizations, foreign governments, and international organizations."[3]

The Strategy proposed an "Interagency Education System" comprised of a broad sweep of existing education and training programs relating to national security mission areas: federal, state, local, territorial, and tribal government; academic; non-governmental; and private sector. While it may have put initial priority on identifying federal program efforts, it made clear that identification of such programs at the "state, local, territorial, tribal, academic, non-governmental, and private-sector levels" should follow thereafter.[4]

The mutually accepted federal law enforcement, IC, and state and local law enforcement need requires its own professional development "track set" for state and local LE within the homeland security enterprise cadre, given the complicating issues associated with clearances and access. This track set would be distinct from the various tracks for emergency management, public health, and such response/recovery-oriented disciplines.[5]

A professional development plan for law enforcement, intelligence analysts, and others on a national security track must include a Web-based block of instruction that clearly defines and describes the national security community, its roles and responsibilities, and the unclassified laws, regulations, and executive orders that govern the IC. At the awareness level, the national security professional development plan would provide for unclassified, certificate

"101 courses" on counterterrorism (CT) and counterintelligence (CI). At the basic and intermediate level, secret-level courses must provide training on basic analysis and on national security targets as may be relevant to specific positions. Provision must be made for classified information to be delivered via a secure system to the student at a sensitive compartmented information facility (SCIF). At the advanced and SES levels, homeland security professionals who are trained and cleared to the TS/SCI level for service in federal regions will participate in annual scenario-driven tabletop exercises that, under the NRF, stand up a Joint Operations Center and Joint Field Office with liaison officers embedded in both.

The public health and medical sector also has unique professional development requirements, driven by public-sector, cross-jurisdictional complexities and the reality that the private sector holds and operates 85 percent of the medical assets in the United States. As an additional consideration, this sector has a high degree of dependency on other sectors (e.g., transportation, energy, and mass sheltering) to complete the mission. Lastly, in addition to specific subject-matter expertise in public health and medicine, homeland security professional requirements include those for training and experience in security matters.

The Department of Health and Human Services has initiated professional development programs and activities as a security enterprise through its regional cross-jurisdictional planning and regional- and federal-level cross-sector planning. While the HHS focus has been mainly on disaster response, man-made or terrorist activities are part of the scenario planning and exercise activities. Advances in public health and medical sector NSP professional development have been happening as a by-product of these recognized cross-sector, interagency, and intergovernmental aspects of operational planning and execution, in exercises real or virtual. Forward-leaning developments at the state and local levels have emanated from regional planning and coordination through HHS regional emergency coordinators and partnerships with state and local jurisdictions and professional groups.

Professional development for public health and medical homeland security professionals begins with professional degree education—for example, MD (doctor of medicine)/MPH (master of public health) programs. Beyond education, development of public health and medical homeland security professionals must start with training at the local level and horizontally

reach across both public- and private-sector professionals, requiring extensive work with private-sector organizations. Simultaneously, vertical training must link local capacities to state, tribal, and federal assets and efforts.
The program should transcend, but not ignore, the subject matter requirements of emergency medicine, trauma care, emergency medical services, and
so forth. It should focus the development of homeland security professionals
on the enterprise functions necessary for adequate preparedness and effective
response and recovery.

Optimal development of the Homeland Security Enterprise cadre for
public health and medical homeland security professionals would benefit
from active engagement of such bodies as the National Association of City and
County Health Organizations (NACCHO), Association of State and Territorial
Health Officers (ASTHO), the American Medical Association's Committee on
Disaster Medicine, American Osteopathic Association, American College of
Emergency Physicians, and American Hospital Association. These organizations have actively developed curricula and criteria for training and qualifications for public- and private-sector homeland security professionals active in
preparedness and the response and recovery missions.

Training efforts can leverage near-term public health and medical homeland security professional development initiatives. For example, the conduct
of cross-jurisdictional and cross-sector operational planning could include
the formal articulation of learning objectives for participants, assessment
of whether they have met those objectives, and a final award of a certificate
of completion. Formalized training curricula should include the principles
and techniques of operational planning and execution, logistics, forensics,
and the functions of other sector operations—for example, transportation,
supply, and energy, to facilitate joint planning and execution with those sectors upon which the health sector critically depends.

NGO homeland security professional development is under way with the
American Red Cross (ARC). The ARC and FEMA are moving toward "common sector training" in mass care and sheltering. The challenge is to broaden
the training to encompass sector-wide mass care training and professional
development under a partnering arrangement for resourcing. Senior ARC
leadership is going to the Harvard Kennedy School's National Preparedness
Leadership Initiative (NPLI) program for "meta-leadership"—the exercise of
leadership across organizational stovepipes by influence rather than via direct

lines of authority. NPLI is a three-week program taken over the course of a year. The program is expanding with regional offerings where the NPLI faculty conducts one-and-a-half day seminars across the country to develop meta-leadership capabilities. The ARC is also conducting an initiative with FEMA for a mid-level, disaster leadership professional development program for certifying local nonprofits. The ARC is training its chapter leaders in all of its 160 Red Cross regions and will expand the effort to offer training to any nonprofit leadership active in disasters.

The scope of private-sector homeland security professional development includes personnel serving owners and operators in critical infrastructure/key resources sectors, homeland security technology and service providers, other homeland security business stakeholders operating at the UASI and state levels, and regional academic and research innovation centers.

The National Guard's requirements for homeland security professional development differ from those for the DoD military departments and their active component (AC) and reserve component (RC). Under the auspices of the U.S. Northern Command, both the AC and RC will respond in crisis to perform Homeland Defense and Defense Support of Civil Authorities (DSCA) missions. State sovereignty, local mutual aid compacts, and the Posse Comitatus Act, for example, give rise to distinct differences between the roles of the Guard and Title 10 forces, active-duty military (precluded from conducting law enforcement activities on U.S. soil per the Posse Comitatus Act, Section 1385 of Title 18, United States Code). National Guard forces operating under Title 32 on state active duty can conduct law enforcement operations at the direction of the governor.

National Guard professional development must account for these differences and optimize any means available for training and exercises. The *NSPD Strategy* included "access to education, training, and opportunities to work in coordination" with foreign governments and international organizations.[6] The Guard affords opportunities for professional development abroad, as the *Strategy* envisioned. The National Guard State Partnership Program (SPP), established in 1993, fosters long-term relationships between states and their partnered nations to share best practices and expert knowledge across a range of areas. The National Guard Bureau's International Affairs Division (J5-IA) administers the program. Currently, fifty states, two territories, and the District of Columbia have partnered with fifty-nine countries worldwide.

The SPP facilitates economic, commercial, social, and cultural government interactions in addition to military-to-military expert exchanges. Multilevel army and air force familiarization exercises provide a platform to share effective practices and techniques. Areas of concentration include military support to civilian authorities, emergency management, disaster planning, port security, HAZMAT/WMD response initiatives, and airport security.

Exercises provide an opportunity to enhance further networked homeland security professional development. The *NSPD Strategy* spoke of integrating the National Exercise Program, "as well as existing national, Federal, State, regional, and local exercises, into professional development programs."[7] As a component of an Interagency Education System for NSPs, the *Strategy* called for utilizing "advances in technology to enable connectivity of multiple education systems in a virtual environment; and [incorporating] full-time and part-time programs, short-term and long-term programs, and distance-learning programs, or a combination of those programs, as appropriate."[8]

Homeland security enterprise leaders must continue to find creative network solutions to incorporate the entire enterprise to include education, training, and exercising. They need to link the enterprise via networks across what Superintendent Todd Jones of the FEMA Center for Domestic Preparedness calls the "loosely coupled systems" to do "learning around the seams." One example would be to network the capabilities of all forty DHS institutions of learning to achieve strategic objectives—for example, the FEMA National Domestic Preparedness Consortium and the Naval Postgraduate School's Center for Homeland Defense and Security to:

- Use the NDPC's Center for Domestic Preparedness in Anniston, Alabama, and Nevada Test Site capabilities to host cohort-team exercises involving several separate states or local jurisdictions to replicate EMAC and federal response to an incident
- Link the exercises to emergency operations centers back in cohort home jurisdictions to engage elected officials
- Provide those EOCs and elected officials with simultaneous instruction (at the policy and strategy level) afforded by the NPS/CHDS Mobile Education Team (MET)

## The Center for Homeland Defense and Security Model and a Regional Approach to Regional Homeland Security Professional Education

In its *QHSR*, the lead federal agency for homeland security, DHS, spoke of a broad homeland security enterprise with "collective efforts and shared responsibilities." Included in this enterprise are the private sector and CI/KR community representatives who have already accessed and are graduates of the full range of FEMA emergency management and planning courses offered online. As has been stressed, implementation of the homeland security enterprise professional development must be an intergovernmental collective effort and shared responsibility along with the private-sector and NGO community as a whole-of-society, whole-of-nation undertaking.

As said before, the thrust of NSPD implementation in 2007–8 had been top-down with a near-term focus of certifying NSPs at the SES and senior GS 14–15 levels. Yet, to foster a truly transformed NSP culture requires professional development from the entry level and even pre-employment. The homeland security professional culture required for the future should leverage the up-and-coming generational culture replete with its orientation to social media and flat, network organizations, team learning, and evidence-based education. DHS does recognize this imperative, as reflected by DHS Chief Learning Officer George Tanner's use of the phrase "a continuum of learning from GS-1" to describe his vision of homeland security professional development.

The Naval Postgraduate School's Center for Homeland Defense and Security (CHDS) provides a network-enterprise model for Tanner's continuum of learning approach. To be sure, we must accept some caveats. CHDS initially proposed only to develop a national cadre of co-equal local, state, tribal, and federal *leaders*. Distinguishing education from training, its intent was to fill the education gap, again with a focus on *senior* professional development. The school does not currently have the capacity, nor did it intend for its curriculum, to undertake the building of a homeland security culture of collaboration at entry level. Yet, CHDS is moving in a direction that holds promise for the basis of a regionally centric, Homeland Security University Network, analogous to the DAU model, which realizes Dr. Tanner's goal of a continuum of learning from GS-1.

The origin of CHDS was in a pre-9/11, August 2001 study conducted by the Justice Department's Office for Domestic Preparedness. This study "determined that key gaps existed in training programs associated with the more complex upper-level leadership challenges requiring critical thinking and problem-solving approaches; filling these gaps would require an educational, vice training, approach."[9] Until that time, state and local training programs in domestic preparedness (the precursor term for homeland security) were at the operational "boots on the ground" levels.[10] After 9/11 in April 2002, Congress, DOJ, and DoD established the Center for Homeland Defense and Security at the Naval Postgraduate School in Monterey, California. Justice's Office of Justice Programs/Office for Domestic Preparedness was the initial sponsor of the Center.[11] Since FY08, however, funding has come from FEMA.

First among its mandates was the education and preparation of "a national cadre of local, state, tribal, and federal leaders to collaborate across professional disciplines and levels of government to secure the nation's homeland by developing new policies, strategies, and organizational arrangements to prevent and respond to future attacks."[12] Among its key offerings are the master's degree program, Mobile Education Team (MET) outreach to governors and urban areas, Homeland Security Executive Leaders Program (ELP), a secure Web-based Alumni Network, and CHDS Alumni Association. For several years, CHDS has offered an East Coast location for the master's degree program at the National Capital Region campus in Shepherdstown, West Virginia.

The CHDS homeland security leadership development curriculum is evidence-based, an education approach that relies on the "use of empirical evidence to make informed decisions about policies, practices, and programs."[13] The master's degree program is an eighteen-month program of six two-week, in-residence sessions. The program has eleven courses, two research-methods, courses, and a thesis. Accreditation comes from the Western Association of Schools and Colleges. Two cohorts per year attend CHDS; NCR hosts one per year. Each campus takes thirty-two students per cohort. At CHDS, twenty-six are from state and local organizations; six are from federal. At NCR, twenty students are from DHS; six are from other departments and agencies; another six are from state and local organizations. DHS fully funds student tuition and expenses.

The outreach MET program delivers policy and strategic-level educational seminars to governors and their cabinets, as well as to community leaders and their homeland security teams in large urban areas. In addition, "topical" METs can focus on a single issue or for delivery to a non-jurisdictional entity like a national association. The Homeland Security ELP provides senior homeland security leaders with a better understanding of the local, state, federal, and private-sector issues and opportunities associated with securing the nation against threats and responding to acts of terrorism. ELP is a nine-month certificate program that includes four one-week in-residence modules.

CHDS created the University and Agency Partnership Initiative (UAPI) to improve national access to homeland security education. As of 2009, UAPI included 155 university and agency members who receive assistance for developing homeland security curricula further to establishing the academic discipline. Elsewhere that year, CHDS listed 271 homeland security–related degree and certificate programs as partner institutions.[14]

A May 2010 *Homeland Security Affairs* article pointed to CHDS capacity limitations. "Despite the success of the CHDS programs, they still only serve a small segment of the homeland security profession. Because of congressional prohibitions, the CHDS [master's degree] program is not available to private-sector attendees—an education gap that must be served by other institutions."[15] The authors make the case for a regionally focused approach. They cite two particular educational institutions, Kansas State University and the U.S. Army Command and General Staff College (CGSC), that "have sought to fill a niche need for homeland security graduate education in order to better serve homeland security professionals regionally."[16] Other programs and institutions noted are Penn State's Master of Homeland Security in Public Health Preparedness Program, Long Island University's Homeland Security Management Institute (HSMI), San Diego State University's Graduate Program in Homeland Security, Tulane University's Master of Professional Studies Homeland Security Program, and Cal Poly's partnership with the California Emergency Management Agency for the Master's of Professional Studies Program in Disaster Management and Homeland Security.

NorthCom J7's Homeland Security/Defense Education Consortium (HSDEC) has attempted to find common ground and propose standardized educational outcomes. The HSDEC-sponsored 2007 Homeland Security Education Survey Project found "little standardization existed from one program to the next in course design, content, or delivery system. . . . Further exacerbating the problem of standardization, no uniform program requirements or overarching program outcomes have been established to serve as guidelines for curriculum development."[17]

While this observation may have intended to be a criticism, one should not rush to embrace a federally driven process toward defining standards, requirements, and outcomes for the homeland security educational enterprise, or indeed homeland security professional development generally. The authors note that "definitions of homeland security often align with jurisdictional perspectives," and further quote CHDS' Chris Bellavita: "In my [Bellavita's] experience, the emergency management 'community of interest' and the fire services tend to constellate around the *All Hazards* definition, law enforcement tends to cohere around *Homeland Security as Preventing Terrorism*, people who work for a federal agency tend toward *Terrorism and Major Catastrophes*, and the Department of Defense sees homeland security as what civilians do"[18] (emphasis in original).

The authors finish the point by citing CHDS' Stan Supinski on an institution-specific approach to development of homeland security graduate educational programs: "The programs and curricula we develop will take many shapes and certainly the quality and applicability to certain sectors of the workforce will vary."[19] Returning to driving education toward the evidence-based verities, they speak of the HSDEC consensus that stresses the importance of including practical applications and exercises. Kansas State and the CGSC, they write, began their designs on "the needs of the regional homeland security professionals and the correlation of those expressed needs with the established HSDEC and DoD recommendations"—that is, *bottom-up, regional*. Not surprisingly given its regional location, Kansas State has a capability in the food-animal disease area. Leveraging its focus, DHS has selected the university as a Center of Excellence for Emerging and Zoonotic Animal Diseases. Also, the Department of Agriculture is relocating its Arthropod-Borne Animal Diseases Research Unit to K-State, and DHS is in the process of siting its National Bio and Agro-Defense Facility near the campus. Thus, with regard to CHDS capacity limitations and the need to improve the accessibility and quality of homeland security graduate educational offerings, the authors support the embrace by the DHS, CHDS, and NorthCom's HSDEC, now the Homeland Security and Defense Education Consortium Association (HSDECA),[20] to strengthen the education pillar by focusing on regional programs responsive to regional needs and input. To some degree, HSDECA- and DoD-determined competences can work as a framework for program analysis and design to help reduce concerns for accreditation, standardization, instructional quality, and competency measurement.[21]

CHDS is thus strengthening the education pillar of homeland security professional development by leveraging its model for regional applications informed by regional needs and inputs. Over three hundred institutions of higher education offer homeland security courses nationwide. Impetus is coming from states and local jurisdictions for developing their own homeland security professional education and training programs. In Texas, the Governor's Office has an executive-level program partnered with the University of Texas that provides senior executive leadership training. In addition, the Texas Department of Public Safety is in the early stages of researching for future development of its own equivalent of the U.S. Army's Command and General Staff College to be sited at the state police headquarters. Courses on executive management will be available for the captain level up. Mississippi offers a graduate-level course at the University of Mississippi for homeland security analysts; the University of Southern Mississippi hosts another graduate-level program at its National Center for Spectator Sports Security. A third master's-level homeland security program is available at satellite campuses for New Orleans' Tulane University in Biloxi and Jackson. Finally, Maryland's Anne Arundel County hosts the Criminal Justice Advisory Consortium, Homeland Security and Criminal Justice Institute at Anne Arundel Community College.

The DHS Office of the Chief Human Capital Officer, Enterprise Learning and Development (OCHCO-ELD), in collaboration with the Homeland Security Studies & Analysis Institute, has developed a curricula alignment tool (framework) to assist institutions of higher learning in ensuring that their curricula are aligned to DHS mission requirements.

In sum, a nationwide homeland security university network with regionally focused nodes can best provide homeland security professional development tailored to regional requirements. Moreover, these network nodes serve as education and training destinations that foster regional personal relationships. Lastly, these nodes have the potential to provide sustained, present, and regionally focused analytical support and technical assistance as an alternative to the often more costly, less regionally attuned Washington-oriented think tanks and federally funded research and development corporations.

# CHAPTER FIFTEEN

# IPA Rotational Assignments:
## The Means for a Network Federal Homeland Security Workforce

Experience is the third pillar of the national security professional development program. Whatever the level to which national security professionals have been educated and trained, a successful career assignment history is the single strongest predictor of their capability to perform in NSP roles. Increasingly challenging rotational assignments are critical to long-term success in creating a national cadre of NSPs and fully capable SES-level NSPs.

In 2008, the Office of Personnel Management recommended that a technical qualification for SES-level NSP positions should be a "demonstrated ability to lead interagency, interdepartmental, intergovernmental activities, or comparable cross-organizational activities."[1] In addition to assignment to federal departments and agencies other than their own, the memo said that NSPs could serve in state and local government entities, nonprofit or nongovernmental organizations, private organizations, and academic institutions. Service could be "on a temporary or permanent assignment, on a multi-agency task force, in an interagency liaison capacity and/or as a volunteer."

The 2007 *NSPD Strategy* explicitly stated that rotational assignments are to have an intergovernmental dimension. It tasked departments and agencies to "make available Federal national security assignments to personnel from State, local, and tribal governments, the public safety community, nongovernmental organizations, and the private sector, as appropriate, and encourage State, local, and tribal governments to create similar opportunities for Federal employees."[2] Significantly, the NSPD Executive Steering Committee phrased this charge first in terms of non-federal personnel rotating into federal NSP positions and then adding the tasking for federal NSPs to go into non-federal positions. Rotational assignments would thus foster a national NSP workforce culture.

Notwithstanding this strategic guidance, departments and agencies with a national security mission have had the latitude to tailor their professional experience programs to fit their specific needs. DHS initially chose to focus on forging an intradepartmental DHS workforce. A 2007 department directive stated that "rotational assignments between the various DHS Components [is] a key goal."[3] Among several examples of such assignments, the directive offered no specific example of an intergovernmental rotational assignment to or from state or local organizations or jurisdictions. The *NSPD Implementation Plan* subsequently put heat under DHS to focus beyond itself—to determine where the assignment opportunities are in the intergovernmental and private-sector space. The Plan charged DHS to "identify state and local government professional experience for NSPs" and all departments and agencies participating in the NSPD system to "identify (within legal parameters) potential private-sector professional experiences for NSPs in the future."[4]

The intergovernmental thrust has survived the change of administration. The 2010 DHS *Bottom-Up Review Report* stated that "FEMA will implement personnel exchanges between headquarters and regional offices to enhance employee understanding of headquarters and regional perspectives, as well as personnel exchanges between FEMA and State governments through the Intergovernmental Personnel Act [IPA]."[5]

Use of the IPA Mobility Program has a tremendous potential to facilitate a network culture of homeland security professional rotational assignments. IPA assignments are not simply a FEMA mechanism but also apply to other DHS agencies, the Department of Health and Human Services, Justice, Transportation, and components of any other departments or agencies that have primary or supporting homeland security functions—for example, Emergency Support Functions. Other activities would include functions associated with the National Infrastructure Protection Plan or in any steady-state, multi-jurisdictional, multi-discipline, interagency, and intergovernmental entities like Area Maritime Security Committees, Joint Terrorism Task Forces, and state fusion centers.

PKEMRA gave additional FEMA authorities to facilitate interagency collaboration at the federal level. However, the agency has not been able to exercise those authorities fully. While coordinating mechanisms such as the National Response Coordination Center (NRCC) were designed to play that role, the other cabinet-level departments do not ascribe to FEMA the gravitas to execute the mission. FEMA—as the DHS lead agency for national preparedness—needs to exercise stronger governance by mandating that assignments to such bodies as the NRCC are career-enhancing. In turn, senior officials elsewhere in the federal department and agency space must exercise their own right level of oversight to ensure that they detail their high performers, like the Coast Guard, to serve in these mechanisms. For example, the ESF Leadership Group has devolved to a "junior group." The ESF Leadership Group must be what its title suggests: a "senior group." Only via strong governance can FEMA fully execute on behalf of DHS its collaborative responsibilities as a convener for other DHS agencies, Justice, HHS, DoD, the Department of Transportation (DoT), and other federal departments and agencies with homeland security missions.

To be sure, at all three levels of government, civilian agency workforce cultures—unlike the military—are generally "expeditionary-averse." Government and in most cases private-sector employees are not usually inclined to relocate themselves or their families. The federal government, at least, could set a condition-of-employment requirement for its homeland security professionals as a willingness to relocate—that is, for assignment to federal regional offices or state levels and, where appropriate, to local jurisdictions such as Urban Area Security Initiative jurisdictions or major metropolitan areas. It would be up to state and local jurisdictions, the private sector, and NGOs to determine for themselves whether they would want to set a similar requirement.

State and local jurisdictions recognize that IPA rotations provide a benefit as opportunities for developing leadership. These assignments should come fairly early in a career as a qualification for service in the homeland security enterprise. The states' and major cities' law enforcement communities say that IPA assignments should occur at the senior lieutenant and captain levels. Other state and local homeland security professionals indicate that rotations should take place when personnel are at the mid-level GS-11/13 equivalent—that is, those with ten years of career left. Observed one state-level official, "Anything later than that only trains people to be consultants."

Assignment duration is particularly thorny for state and local government personnel. The *NSPD Implementation Plan* offered three categories:

- Short-term temporary detail of less than a six-month duration
- Mid-term temporary or semi-permanent detail of six to twelve months
- Long-term of a year or more[6]

Length of time for a rotational assignment would vary for state and local personnel, with geography a key factor for a jurisdiction's homeland security professional development plan. State and local officials feel strongly that plans should only provide for short-term rotations—that is, no more than six months. Short rotations accommodate the aversion to an expeditionary culture. They also allow personnel to return to their parent agencies before they are deemed "not-to-have-been-missed," a fear common to service at all government levels.

Some local jurisdictions may accept longer-term rotations, however. Personnel in UASIs and major metropolitan areas near to state and federal regional organizations may not require a "family move" or long commute. In such instances, local officials recognize a clear value-add returned to the parent agency in terms of the personal relationships and understandings gleaned in a longer-term rotation. Rotating homeland security professionals to nearby state or regional entities would enhance their personnel leadership development and further their eligibility for promotion.

Service on a Joint Terrorism Task Force presents an exceptional case. Because of the nature of the work, JTTF personnel tend to work on cases that take time to develop and thus do not neatly fit into a criterion for shorter-term rotations. Some jurisdictions accept even a long-term engagement extending into a full career choice. For example, the New York City JTTF has at least one New York Police Department officer who has been assigned for some twenty years.

Since 9/11, the homeland security culture at all governmental levels has generally advanced to accepting how rotational assignments add value and build trust through enhanced personal relationships. Said one state-level law enforcement official, "People are no longer 'punished' when they return to their parent organizations." Nevertheless, all parties to the homeland security enterprise agree that a rotational assignment should not be just a "check-the-box" for federal-level national security professionals, a point consistently made by OPM. A rotation must support strategic objectives and outcomes for homeland security professional development, and should only occur when mutual value can be demonstrated as a win-win with benefit and meaning to both parties to the exchange. IPA rotations are not just for exchanges between governmental levels—federal-to-state, state-to-local, federal-to-local. Institution of a network federal homeland security workforce culture requires rotations that are state-to-state, county-to-county, city-to-city as well. Rotations for local jurisdictions still need to be calibrated according to mutually determined needs and practicalities. State and local organizations generally feel that IPA assignments should more frequently be to federal positions at the regional level versus positions in Washington.

IPAs do present additional costs, as state and local governments struggle through these times of deficits. In addition to salaries, IPA rotations must of course make provision for per diems and allowances. Some jurisdictions have laws requiring them to operate under balanced budgets. The IPA program must allow for flexibility. States and local jurisdictions could have the option to exchange personnel or receive IPA reimbursement for the temporary rotational assignment of their employees. The jurisdiction would then have the option to use the reimbursement to cover the cost of "fleeting up" another employee or paying for a short-term contractor.

The *NSPD Implementation Strategy* spoke of creating "opportunities" for IPA rotations. A number of NSPD developers have critiqued their own work and concluded that implementation has only resulted in "catalogs" of rotation opportunities without a specific professional development plan.

The foremost strategic objective and outcome for the NSPD plan must be to serve resilience and sustainability by establishing a network federal homeland security workforce whose primary nodes are in the federal regions. The president has delegated authority over the NSP workforce in the executive branch. The federal government, therefore, can be more directive over its organizations and personnel to effect homeland security enterprise implementation of rotational assignments and the structured and optional supplemental learning activities to support the strategic objective and outcome. The president may not have directive authority over state or local organizations and personnel. The federal government can only lead by example. It must be: "Do as I do," not "Do as I say."

Federal departments and agencies with homeland security missions and functions must seed headquarters-level federal homeland security professionals in identified or created homeland security enterprise cadre positions for rotational assignments in the federal regions as part of a strategic and systematic process that supports workforce/community objectives. Federal personnel would be best served to go to the regional level, states, UASIs, and major metropolitan areas rather than rural jurisdictions. Rotational assignments to and with rural jurisdictions should only occur in response to a specific and compelling need—for example, in the case of southwestern border jurisdictions having to deal with the activities of the Mexican drug cartels.

Further, these departments and agencies must similarly identify or create positions at headquarters level and in the regions for state, local, tribal, territorial, private-sector, and NGO homeland security enterprise cadres. Only states and larger local jurisdictions—for example, UASIs—would derive benefit from IPA assignments to Washington, whereas rural local officials would not.

As said above, state and local organizations generally deem that the maximum benefit from IPA exchanges with federal entities would occur at the regional level. Even then, some local organizations believe that IPA assignment to a state-level position would have greater value in terms of building personnel relationships. For jurisdictions that are particularly resource-constrained, even those assignments may be too onerous. In such instances, a work-around could be establishment of an intrastate homeland security professional pool for rural regional jurisdictions, whereby assignments to state or federal regional-level positions would rotate among personnel from participating jurisdictions. Such a program is under way among sheriff departments in some five rural jurisdictions in western North Dakota.

State and local homeland security professionals should not regard IPA assignments as exclusively rotations into federal positions. IPA exchanges could also be county-to-county, city-to-city, county-to-state, city-to-state, and so forth, according to mutually identified needs and benefits—for example, to develop or deepen Emergency Management Assistance Compact relationships. Such non-federal intergovernmental rotations could be either intrastate or interstate as identified by jurisdictions and region(s) in question. Such rotations, however, are not without difficulties. While agencies may operate under similar sets of policies and procedures, they are not *exactly* the same. As one state law enforcement official offered by example, "The software used by the same agency in different jurisdictions is often different—even the vehicles operated by different municipal police departments have their differences."

position and not the person. Once such health department personnel return to their parent agencies, their clearances would shift to inactive status.

As a whole-of-society construct, the NSP enterprise is thus potentially inclusive of all levels of government as well as the private-sector and NGO communities. Career paths for state and local government, private sector, and NGO enterprise NSPs will follow these track sets. For the track set leading to the JFO level and the other set of national security tracks leading to the JOC level, when the NSP reaches GS-13/15-SES-level equivalent, both track sets would merge and provide for clearances to the TS/SCI level. As may be required, state, local, tribal, territorial, private-sector, and NGO homeland security NSPs will be trained and cleared to the TS/SCI level for assignment to federal positions identified as those based on "need to know." These identified non-federal TS/SCI NSPs will be trained in blocks of instruction that will give them a firm grounding in the IC and how it functions within established law, regulations, executive orders, and guidelines.

# CHAPTER SIXTEEN

# Credentialing

Headquarters DHS and FEMA established the National Incident Management System certification[1] regime that state and local organizations have adopted. The federal carrot and stick has been the requirement for NIMS compliance as a precondition for homeland security grants. FEMA's National Integration Center housed in the National Preparedness Directorate administers NIMS certification, principally via courses offered online by the Emergency Management Institute, in Emmitsburg, Maryland. The NIMS effort serves to professionalize further the national homeland security workforce.

The National Security Professional Development Implementation Plan identified the critical importance of establishing a system for "national security certification" for national security professionals and "a least administratively burdensome method" for database tracking of those NSPs.[2] This identified requirement overlaps with the nation's operational need for real-time, cross-jurisdictional, cross-discipline identification of personnel from the field to the national level—that is, something approaching a national credentialing system. An information-sharing environment that includes a database tracking system for NSP certification and a national credentialing system could satisfy both requirements efficiently and effectively.

As applied narrowly to the response mission, credentialing is a process of establishing an individual's background, authorization, and qualification for performing a specific task. In that context, credentialing is key for the interstate deployment and interoperability of trusted human capital resources in disaster response. A national credentialing system must be able to function within existing jurisdictional protocols, if feasible. Deployment cannot impose an undue burden on the numerous jurisdictions at various levels of government. Such a system must conform to NIMS and its basis on Incident

Command System protocols, principles, and guidelines. It must use or integrate current emergency responder credentialing systems with the national system whenever possible.[3]

To that end, Tim Manning, FEMA's deputy administrator for protection and national preparedness, issued a 2010 memo on "Establishment of a National Credentialing Program."

> The National Credentialing Program will coordinate activities, incorporate policies, and recommend guidance and standards for credentialing all Federal Emergency Management Agency personnel and State, Tribal, and local officials who require access to disaster areas or FEMA facilities during an emergency. This will not be a FEMA-only effort; we will work closely with our partners at all levels of government and with the private sector to develop the program.[4]

The August 2004 HSPD-12, Policy for a Common Identification Standard for Federal Employees and Contractors, mandated a government-wide standard for secure and reliable forms of identification issued by the federal government to its employees and contractors (including contractor employees) for access to secure facilities. HSPD-12 led to the establishment of the Federal Information Processing Standards 201 (FIPS 201). FIPS 201-compliant cards include the Transportation Workers Identification Card (TWIC) and the First Responder Authentication Credential (FRAC). Where the intent of a FIPS 201–compliant card is to ensure operational security at an incident scene, it has significant potential to facilitate coordination and cooperation in response and recovery operations.[5]

FRACs have proved useful for use in after-action reports and assessments and other inventorying and recordkeeping, and are now performance measures in National Capital Region exercises. States are now adopting their own FRAC credentialing systems, notably in Virginia through the Governor's Office of Commonwealth Preparedness and in Colorado with its COFRAC and COFRAC Bridge, which aggregates in an interoperable form all the state's first responder personal attributes, qualifications, and access privileges.[6]

The FEMA National Capital Region Coordination Office led development of a "smart" identity card system for emergency responder access to secure facilities in time of disaster. In February 2006, the NCR coordinated the Winter

Fox Interoperability Demonstration with the FIPS 201-compliant FRAC. Winter Fox also validated the ability of participating agencies to use the FIPS 201 architecture for electronic validation of NIMS or National Infrastructure Protection Plan personnel qualification information, which are needed to facilitate the incident management capabilities of human resource assets.[7]

Development of a national credentialing system is a fundamental underpinning of NIMS, for which the National Integration Center in FEMA's National Preparedness Directorate has the responsibility. As per the November 21, 2008, draft of *NIMS Guidelines for the Credentialing of Personnel*, the NIC and its Incident Management Systems Integration (IMSI) office have the tasking. The National Integration Center is working with other organizations— for example, the Association of Public-Safety Communications Officials (APCO) International's Telecommunicator Emergency Response Taskforce (TERT) and Citizen Corps—as part of its credentialing effort. The NIC has developed several working groups that are designating not only the positions that should be credentialed but also the qualifications, certification, training, and educational requirements for each position—illustrating the potential for NSP tracking for non-federal personnel. The functional areas are:

- Incident management
- Emergency medical services
- Firefighting and hazardous materials response
- Law enforcement
- Public health/medical needs
- Public works
- Search and rescue (SAR) operations[8]

NIMS is a system that can now identify the minimal need for professional qualifications, certification, training, and educational requirements to meet the baseline criteria of a homeland security professional's capabilities.[9] It is important to note that given the nature of a loosely coupled homeland security enterprise personnel system, as opposed to a centralized federal personnel system, the term "capabilities" (vice "competencies") is necessary to avoid condition-of-hire/merit-based issues, which would require formal validation. This concern is of particular importance to the Office of Personnel Management and its sensitivity toward the government employee unions as relates to federal homeland security professionals. Nevertheless, NIMS can and should be extended to include a means to track a homeland security professional's experience level, including assignment history.

Employing existing databases, including or building on FEMA's National Credentialing Program (in development), the federal government is funding a program—and designating Headquarters DHS to serve as executive agent—to convene all public- and private-sector mission partners in an effort to build an affordable, comprehensive national system based on a FIPS 201–compliant architecture for electronic validation of NIMS and NIPP personnel qualification information. This program will enable tracking and inventorying of training, education, exercise, and rotational assignment information for all homeland security enterprise cadre personnel.

The homeland security enterprise will benefit from a national registry based on NIMS resource typing for the Emergency Management Assistance Compacts and EMAP, the Emergency Management Assistance Program.[10] Still needed is an enhanced, multi-discipline, multi-jurisdiction registry for credentialing and human capital management particularly in crisis-state—for example, for EMAC mission assignment numbers, but also for steady-state human capital application.

The American National Standards Institute (ANSI) is also using systems similar to FIPS 201 as it works to incorporate the private sector into a credentialing process.[11] Leveraging FIPS 201 for state and local personnel and extending it to private-sector and NGO personnel,[12] as appropriate, would make for a registry that is simple and cost-effective. The private sector and critical infrastructure/key resources communities have a requirement for their personnel to be included in NSP credentialing, most obviously as regard to access to incident impact areas. The re-entry of CI/KR restoration workers is essential for effective response and recovery and has been a major issue documented in virtually all national-level exercise and real-world event after action and lessons learned reports over the past decade.

DHS has engaged the private sector and CI/KR communities in the Voluntary Private Sector Preparedness Accreditation and Certification (PS-Prep) program, mandated by the PKEMRA legislation and recommended by the 9/11 Commission to improve private-sector preparedness for disasters and emergencies. PS-Prep is a partnership between DHS and the private sector that enables private entities to receive emergency preparedness certification from a DHS accreditation system created in coordination with the private sector.

## Credentialing for Law Enforcement

Federal, state, tribal, and local law enforcement have a need for real-time verification and validation of security clearances and permissions. This need could be met by a classified credentialing database housed in FBI Headquarters that could (a) be modeled on and (b) provide reciprocity guidance and a secure bridge to other similar classified databases such as DoD's Joint Personnel Adjudication System (JPAS) and the Intelligence Community's Scattered Castles, for the purpose only of coordinating policy and passing clearance information when necessary. This database could include data on state, local, and tribal law enforcement personnel who (1) are homeland security professionals or candidate homeland security professionals, (2) have begun to progress along a homeland security professional education and training track, and (3) hold security clearances. State, local, or tribal law enforcement homeland security professionals and candidates would permit their clearance information to be housed, managed, and maintained in this classified database at FBI Headquarters. All FBI Field Divisions would be able to access this database electronically to identify cleared state, local, or tribal law enforcement officers when they need them to assist or support federal law enforcement agencies who are conducting sensitive counterterrorism, criminal, or intelligence investigations. Such assistance could be employed either to prevent or respond to acts of domestic or international terrorism within the United States.

With respect to a domestic credentialing database for law enforcement personnel, the executive branch and Congress could establish a program with an annual appropriation for an independent authority to manage a stand-alone, classified database for real-time verification and validation of homeland security professional law enforcement personnel qualification information, clearances, and permissions. Further, legislation could designate the FBI as the agency to manage, operate, and maintain this database.

Every state should have a law enforcement program manager to interface with the FBI regarding the above clearances. State police or similar state law enforcement agencies should be vested with this responsibility, and federal funds should be allocated to ensure that each state has the capability to work with the FBI in this program. The office of the state law enforcement program manager would best serve as the entity responsible for working with the FBI's homeland security professional credentialing program office as it relates to state-, local-, and tribal-level clearances.

### Benchmarking Guidelines for Voluntary National Standards

The challenge inherent in the development and use of any national standard is in the voluntary nature of the process. For credentialing standards, we can only expect stakeholders to participate voluntarily in their development and in their use as finalized standards. More to the point in terms of federalism, professional standards-setting bodies as a rule are state-level entities. They are neither national nor federal. As long as credentialing remains undefined, homeland security professional standards will still be in need of some level of consistency. However, by leveraging existing credentialing bodies, the federal government could canvass its mission partners to determine where it could establish a process for benchmarking guidelines for voluntary national certification standards by discipline.

The best working model of such a benchmarking program is that provided by the National Wildfire Coordinating Group (NWCG)[13] with its Red Card system. The NWCG is a self-funding credentialing entity independent of federal control, although many of its user/member organizations are federal land management agencies. More formally known as the Incident Qualifications System (IQS), the Red Card system is being expanded to the Incident Qualifications Credentialing System (IQCS). When linked with another existing NWCG software known as the Resource Ordering and Status System (ROSS),[14] IQS enables the wildland fire community to (a) know what personnel are qualified within that system; (b) monitor their qualifications and whether they are current; and (c) actually track personnel assigned to operational theaters.

NWCG is not a quick-fix solution that can be accommodated for all potential users or needs. While an effort was under way to expand its purview to credential a broad representation from the emergency management community, the NWCG chose to remain focused on wildfires. Not only was the size of the task a factor in the decision, but also cost. NWCG is largely funded by its user/member organizations. In the case of federal land management agency members, NWCG management and functions are only a small part of those agencies' budgets.[15]

NWCG is rather unique in its ability to enforce standards for personnel and agencies using its system. Its process is largely driven by funding and the legal authorizations held by the member organizations/agencies. Although NWCG members' standards are very close to identical, members have identified and accepted some internal differences.

Even with the best of intentions, the federal government and mission partners would face difficulties in trying to integrate existing standards systems into one expeditiously functional national system. Most credentialing is a voluntary or consensus standard, including those standards set by the International Fire Service Accreditation Congress (IFSAC), the National Fire Protection Association (NFPA), and the National Board on Fire Service Professional Qualifications (Pro Board). IFSAC is a peer-driven, self-governing system that accredits both public fire service certification programs and higher education fire-related degree programs. The administrative staff consists of the IFSAC manager, a unit assistant, and student staff technicians. NFPA has an elaborate system and process for developing and maintaining a wide variety of national consensus standards—for example, Firefighter and Fire Officer Standards, as well as some model "codes," such as the Life Safety Code and National Gas Code. These codes, however, are neither mandated nor universally accepted. The Pro Board is an independent third-party accreditation organization to verify fire-training entities, which deliver training that conforms to NFPA standards. It does not provide validation of an individual's experience as a connotation of capability or competency.

The NFPA and Pro Board processes differ from the NWCG's. The NWCG system requires detailed documentation of an individual's experience as captured in a Position Task Book (PTB). An already experienced/qualified practitioner must sign the PTB for each position before that candidate individual can be registered as qualified—a critical consideration. Potentially thousands or even millions of individuals have certifications or certificates for completing training (some with varying degrees of testing), but very little validation of skills, abilities, and competencies. Moreover, any national system must allow for differences across disciplines and states for training/qualification requirements. For example, while PTBs may be vehicles best suited for the fire services as the path to ICS qualification, law enforcement will use state-determined Peace Officer Standards and Training (POST) for certification and tracking.

With respect to using ICS from NIMS, for the vast majority of individuals, training incorporated in the NIMS doctrine largely does not provide any actual skills training or development. Short of the recently published ICS Position-Specific training, all of the ICS courses from DHS are instructional training—not practical. Hence, in NWCG the ICS training is categorized as "I" courses for "instructional" and "S" courses for "skills." I-100 through I-400 courses are all classroom instruction. Not until an individual has completed extensive positional training and practice (with PTBs) are they eligible to attend the first "ICS skills" training—that is, S-420, principally a practical evolution over a week or more in which students execute their positional tasks under a graded system. According to one NIMS trainer, "That's one reason I am so 'frothy' about all this stuff. When my life is on the line, and I ask for help, I want someone who has and *can* do the job, not someone who took some classes and got certificates for their time in a chair in a classroom." In the opinion of one municipal law enforcement official, "A rigorous system of exercising is *critical* to build proficiency if this experience gap for national ICS is ever to improve." With regard to designing any "national ICS systems," he cautions: "Keep the systems simple and flexible, recognizing the dynamics of the churn with the organizations that they seek to benefit [state and local jurisdictions with scarce resources]. The KISS [keep it simple, stupid] principle must always be in the forefront of system design."

Third-party benchmarking will ensure that every mission partner discipline has appropriate national guidance upon which to base training, education, and exercise curricula and set professional qualification standards. Among the bodies that can administer this trusted third-party process are the American National Standards Institute, as well as ANSI-accredited organizations like the NFPA, Pro Board, APCO International, and so forth.

# Postscript:
## America's East of Suez Moment and a Thousand Points of Light

**W**hen we began many pages ago, we got under way talking about history, charting the course American expansionism had followed in Britain's hegemonic wake. While navigating our way through the post–Cold War strategic environment, we found ourselves reassessing security governance, finally absorbing ourselves with a deckplate human capital issue—credentialing. We are now at journey's end, dockside, tying up.

The events of 9/11 horribly awakened the American people with the specter of terrorist use of WMD on domestic soil. Since that day, they have witnessed or experienced other frighteningly momentous twenty-first-century events of a different nature—the 2004 Indian Ocean Tsunami, Hurricane Katrina, the 2010 Haitian Earthquake and BP Oil Spill, and most especially the 2011 Great Tohoku Earthquake and Tsunami and radioactive meltdown at the Fukushima Daiichi nuclear power plant.[1] These events are portents of future catastrophes whose cascading system failures could threaten America's ability to maintain regional or national continuity.

In March 2008, the collapse of the U.S. investment bank Bear Stearns was the first shock of successive waves of a worldwide financial crisis that engulfs us all today. That month, the British government issued its first published single overarching national security strategy. Like our *National Security Strategy* of 2010 that restated the U.S. commitment to serve as a comprehensively engaged guarantor of a "just and sustainable international order" and its "rules-based international system," the 2008 *National Strategy of the United Kingdom* similarly supported "a rules-based approach to international affairs."[2] The document characterized the international landscape as increasingly complex and unpredictable with a diverse but interconnected set of threats and risks that directly threaten states and have the potential to undermine wider international stability. This set includes international terrorism, WMD, conflicts, failed states, pandemics, and finally transnational organized crime. All were driven by "a diverse and interconnected set of underlying factors, including climate change, competition for energy, poverty and poor governance, demographic changes, and globalisation."[3]

The American left-of-the-boom/right-of-the-boom approach presupposes that the National Preparedness System is event-driven. But what is an event? Is it a moment in time? How long is a moment? At what point in the homeland security continuum is the boom in a pandemic, for example? The boom for the recovering Gulf Coast region and communities was Hurricane Katrina. But for those Rust Belt communities like Detroit or Gary, Indiana, similarly "recovering" in this post-industrial age, when was the boom? And how does this last question inform our thinking about the Homeland Security Enterprise and security and resilience?

Consider the remarks of two four-star admirals. Adm. Dennis C. Blair, USN (Ret.), went straight from his position as deputy director of the Project on National Security Reform to become director of national intelligence in 2009. In his first congressional appearance as DNI, Denny told lawmakers his "focus on extremist groups that use terrorism" was only item two of his security concerns. "The primary near-term security concern of the United States," he said, "is the global economic crisis and its geopolitical implications. . . . It already has increased questioning of U.S. stewardship of the global economy and the international financial structure." Similarly in his widely reported series of "Conversation with the Country" speeches during the summer of 2010, Adm. Mike Mullen, the chairman of the Joint Chiefs of Staff, told audiences, "The greatest danger to American security comes from the national debt."

Following World War II and into the late 1960s, Great Britain experienced a number of "East of Suez" moments. America is now confronting her own East of Suez moment. Addressing the National Defense University in the summer of 2010, former U.S. Comptroller General David M. Walker forcefully told it like it is:

We have rested on our past success too long. We have rampant myopia, tunnel vision, and self-interest. It has reached epidemic proportions in the halls of Congress and in Washington, D.C. We need policy, operational, and political reforms, and we need them soon because we have a dysfunctional constitutional republic. If we do not take steps to keep our economy strong for both today and tomorrow, our national security, international standing, standard of living, and even our domestic tranquility will suffer over time. That is the bottom line.[4]

Identifying what he called a "neat paradox," British resilience expert Charlie Edwards wrote in 2009, "As *individuals* we have never been safer, wealthier (in spite of the current recession) or healthier. We have never had so many tools to help us live our lives, but as a *society* our complicated lives, individual fears and increasingly high expectations have led us to believe that we are more at risk than ever."[5] Our "consumerist society," he wrote, is afflicted with "affluenza," which he defined as "a painful, contagious, socially transmitted condition of overload, debt, anxiety, and waste resulting from the dogged pursuit of more."[6]

Charlie's thinking aligns with an American private-sector resilience thought-leader, Debra van Opstal, who has written that "the increasing race for competitiveness and economies of scale pushes firms to develop ever-larger systems, with larger potential associated risks.[7] . . . The quest for economies of scale induced by a highly competitive market economy," she wrote, "has the potential to amplify the consequences of a catastrophic failure in an infrastructure system."[8] Addressing the financial services sector specifically, Debbie observed, "With financial instruments, new risks are almost invariably explored before anyone has developed a good way to measure them."[9]

Van Opstal thus shares with Edwards a concern about the unintended and unanticipated consequences of selfish personal or corporate behaviors. "Complex interdependencies in the post-industrial age," she wrote, "have exposed a different set of vulnerabilities throughout the civil societies of today.[10] . . . Risks are just as likely to emanate from disruptions in global networks—for energy, communication, information, transportation—that are interlocked, allowing failures to cascade across networks, borders, and societies."[11] Referring specifically to "the major shock of the sub-prime fallout in the [United States]" in 2008, Edwards wrote how we must accept that contemporary systems will incur shocks, disruptions, and stresses. But significantly, he added that these interruptions of continuity make "not an argument for disconnecting from the global system [but rather] an argument for ensuring that our complex social system, our way of life, is more resilient."[12]

Similarly advising that we must to learn to live with the threat of cascading failures, John Robb tags the threat "system disruption."[13] An American theorist on resilience and networks who comes from an Air Force spec ops background, Robb has more of a classical view of security—that is, in terms of responses to adversaries. He says that al Qaeda, for example, is not a proxy, but rather one network among a number of "global guerrillas." Not wanting to govern territory or a population after a national liberation, such terrorist groups are merely "spoilers of order" that use system disruption as a tactic.[14] By attacking the systems that keep a nation intact, they seek to drive people toward their primary loyalties, thus causing states to withdraw from their spaces and fail.[15] Another network theorist, Albert-László Barabási, agrees, writing, "Today the world's most dangerous aggressors, ranging from al Qaeda to the Columbian drug cartels, are not military organizations with divisions but self-organized networks of terror."[16] This line of thought has prompted Debbie van Opstal to observe, "At the start of the 21st century, the very notion of security defined in terms of 'perimeter defense' or 'threat containment' has become all but obsolete. Today's threats are too ubiquitous to be isolated and too nimble to be contained."[17] For John Robb, the nation-state hasn't yet conceptualized a strategy to fight this threat, and thus it must discard the idea of state-versus-state conflict.[18]

The alternate idea of inter-communal conflict in failed or failing states is generally associated with the lesser-developed world. Yet absent effective and efficient structures and processes for post-industrial governance, system failure is now a risk in the developed world. *Persistent* system failure in developed states could lead to their disengagement as international political actors, perverting the positives—such as may be—proffered by Anne-Marie Slaughter in her conception of an international political-economic system of disaggregated states relating to each other by means of transgovernmental networks.

To summarize, the cause of a system disruption can thus be:

- Intentional—action by state, state-sponsored, or non-state adversaries
- Unintentional—a by-product of accidental or selfish public-sector, private-sector, or criminal activity
- An Act of God or Mother Nature

Regardless of cause, instead of thinking about security and resilience in terms of some kind of twenty-first-century Maginot Line under the command and control of a single-point-of-failure Washington, we should mirror our asymmetric adversaries somewhat by adopting Network Federal governance. If Anne-Marie Slaughter's conception of a transgovernmental network of disaggregated states—albeit far from rigorously developed—characterizes the borders-out political-economic system of today, the same disaggregation conceit can equally apply borders-in along the intergovernmental dimension of our federal system.

Albert-László Barabási can help us in this regard when he distinguishes between random networks that, when plotted, are akin to simple road maps and directed, scale-free networks that render like airline route maps. "A scale-free network is a web without a spider. In the absence of a spider, there is no meticulous design behind these networks." Self-organized, directed networks have a hierarchy of hubs that are not as centralized as a "star network." These networks are fault-tolerant, having no single node whose removal could break the web.[19] Barabási's thinking is consonant with Bob Agranoff's conception of action networks, a subset of what he calls "public management networks" that formally adopt collaborative courses of action and deliver services. *The defining characteristic of an effective and resilient network is that it is self-organized.*

In the same vein, Charlie Edwards speaks of "governance networks" and applies the term to characterize a complex system of self-organized community resilience networks visible only at a node.[20] As opposed to implementing specific plans, he wrote, central government develops resilience frameworks for a "uniformity of approach" and then "lets go."[21] Emergency planning officers "actively seek out communities that are able to play a role in their own resilience. They are comfortable with letting go—giving communities the tools and support they need for planning and preparing for risks."[22] In effect, what Charlie was describing was the system provided by the UK's Civil Contingencies Act of 2004. This "partnership approach" between Whitehall and parish-level communities instituted a nationwide network for resilience coordinated by the Cabinet Office, in some respects the British equivalent to our FEMA. The responsibilities for assessing local risk, preparing plans, and promoting business continuity lie not with the central government: they are with the frontline responders.[23]

The theme of the World Economic Forum's 2009 annual meeting at Davos was "Shaping the Post-Crisis World." Global leaders acknowledged the ongoing world economic crisis as the "most serious global recession since the 1930s." Putting forth for Davos her take on the resilience imperative in her *Innovations* piece, Debbie van Opstal wrote:

> Resilience is the quality that enables enterprises and societies to cope with those unexpected events that have potentially catastrophic consequences. . . . [A] sustained strategic focus on resilience—one as intense as that ordinarily placed on growth—is an urgent priority for business and government at all levels worldwide. . . . Where sustainability (a more familiar term as applied to policy) is about managing a level of resource consumption, resilience is about managing disruptions to critical systems—physical, virtual, health, and economic. . . . It is also about being poised to seize suddenly available opportunities to create value.[24]

Elsewhere Debbie has addressed resilience in the borders-in security context, writing that the homeland security challenge "is less about security and more about economic resilience: the capacity to minimize disruption and recover quickly."[25] In her Davos article, she stated that "a critical new skill is required for effective policy and governance: an ability to adapt to the unexpected. But that adaptability is rarely spontaneous."[26] Debbie van Opstal is talking about Anticipatory Governance.

This anticipatory process, to her mind, is bottom-up and largely private-sector driven. "Businesses cannot be resilient if the communities in which they operate and the citizens they employ are not also resilient.[27] . . . Governor Tom Ridge famously noted that homeland security is based on hometown security. Community risk management really comes together at the grassroots, where companies come together with infrastructure providers, universities['] research centers and training programs, emergency responders, and government executives. It is at the grassroots where the fusion of interests and responsibilities creates the potential for fruitful exchanges of information and best practices."[28]

As if she were anticipating our call for Network Federalism, Debbie makes the case for collaborative regional centers to exchange information, explore new crisis management options, and serve as test beds for exercising current crisis plans.[29] She wants government resilience policies to (1) encourage regional information-sharing networks for support of disaster-resistant communities and (2) make investments in new computational models, "analytic tools that improve risk assessment capabilities."[30]

"Next generation resilience," reads the caption on the cover of Charlie Edwards' *Resilient Nation*, "relies on citizens and communities, not the institutions of the state." "Resilience," he wrote, is the "capacity of an individual, community or system to adapt in order to sustain an acceptable level of function, structure, and identity."[31] Charlie acknowledges that the concept of a community is subjective and elastic. In this post-industrial era, identity is the key driver of a community. "Communities, like our individual identities, are made up of variations of categories to which we can simultaneously belong. . . . A community might be drawn from a local area (a village), share common interests (virtual, sporting, intellectual), or take part in similar activities (shopping, walking and travelling)."[32]

Information Age community is thus not geographically bounded, as the social sciences recognize in their use of the terms community of interest, community of practice, and social networks. Advances in social media, for example, have resulted in collaborative emergency response communities that form via the phenomenon of crowdsourcing—the positive flipside of the otherwise dystopian flash mob. Social media are scalable, user-friendly, accessible, and instantaneous, says Edwards, and government agencies and emergency services in the United Kingdom are already leveraging their potential for disaster management and emergency planning.[33]

In 2011, the year after he served as the national incident commander of the response to the BP Oil Spill, Thad Allen addressed the challenge that leaders must face in the midst of a national crisis. "The combination of seven-by-twenty-four social media, the different uses of spectrum bandwidth and computation, including increased computation through cloud computing, the ability of people to gather and aggregate virtually to produce social behaviors has created the sociological equivalent of climate change. And we don't get it."[34]

The next generation does.

The e-publication *DomesticPreparedness.com* addressed the potential of social networking in emergency response by hosting a September 25, 2010, webinar in Washington titled "Crisis Communications: Does Social Media Work?" There we were introduced to the transformative next-generation thinking exemplified by the use of crowdsourcing and collaborative crisis mapping during the Haitian Earthquake response earlier that year. This use of social media was pioneered by the brilliant thirty-something Patrick Meier, of the Fletcher School of Law and Diplomacy at Tufts University, and Ushahidi, the nonprofit tech company that develops free and open-source software for information collection, visualization, and interactive mapping. Patrick is now director of crisis mapping at Ushahidi. The *MIT Technology Review* has voted Ushahidi as one of the fifty most innovative companies in the world, alongside Facebook, Google, and Twitter. Its software platform continues to be refined and has been applied in numerous major disasters worldwide since 2010.[35] Meier and Ushahidi's work is truly revolutionary and network-empowering.

And Admiral Allen does get it.

As he finished his work as national incident commander for the spill response, he hinted how his own thinking was moving toward this kind of bottom-up-driven network solution that Ushahidi epitomizes. "We have got to better integrate all those resources, passion, and commitment that exist out there," he told listeners as he concluded a radio interview. "Because if we don't, they're going to be disaffected and you're going to break down that unity of effort you're trying to achieve. . . . I like to steal President [George H. W.] Bush's line in reverse: We need to take a thousand points of light sometimes and make it a laser beam."[36]

This journey we have shared has been one considered foray into the matter of governance and the Homeland Security Enterprise. The intent was to amplify, direct, and inspire a thousand points of next-generation passion and commitment in search of coherent solutions to the problems of security and resilience that beset our federal republic in her fourth century. Now is the moment for those who follow to study the charts, take the helm, and proceed.

# Acknowledgments

As this work has been very much a collaborative effort, I want to make a point of acknowledging the many folks who either directly or indirectly contributed.

My involvement in homeland security began before the term existed. I got into the field in 1998 following a suggestion of Phil Odeen, who the year before had served as the chairman of the National Defense Panel, the independent response to the Pentagon's first Quadrennial Defense Review. In late 1997, he was giving a keynote address to a gathering I had assembled at the Army and Navy Club in Washington. We were looking at planning for defense modernization from very much a big-ticket, systems perspective. Over lunch, Phil leaned toward me and said, "Don't overlook the asymmetric threat." I am grateful to Phil for that brief utterance of inside wisdom, for it led to a calling.

Within a year, I was finding myself in the same orbit as Lisa Gordon-Hagerty, George Foresman, Al Goodbary, Bob Fitton, Rini Campana, Myra Sochar, and others who have remained colleagues and friends to this day. Under their tutelage, I became a quick study. By the time Gen. Chuck Boyd started work in mid-1998 on his U.S. Commission on National Security for the 21st Century, I had already come to the conclusion that the post–Cold War strategic environment required this nation to legislate a national security reorganization to update the structures and processes of the National Security Act of 1947.

My thanks go to former defense publishers Llewellyn King, *Armed Forces Journal*'s Don Fruehling, and the Memorial Institute for the Prevention of Terrorism's Denny Reimer and Jim Gass. These men assisted in providing me with a platform for what was then called the domestic preparedness community to interact and exchange insights on the challenges and the way forward for things like WMD consequence management, protection of national critical infrastructure, and military support to civil authorities. My work prompted me to encourage and assist Marty Masiuk in starting his *DomesticPreparedness.com* in an effort to deliver via the Web cross-disciplinary information to this new community whose front lines were in the American heartland. In turn, Marty and his *DomPrep* team, especially Editor-in-Chief Jim Hessman, Susan Collins, and all *DomPrep's* partner technology providers, enabled me to continue that work in an effort to help build this community nationwide. All during this time and into the first decade of this century, I was able to forge a network of operationally experienced homeland security professionals from all levels of government and across the broadest of disciplines. These men and women are perhaps the most committed public servants with whom I have had the honor to serve, and it is entirely their wisdom that I have endeavored to reflect in my work.

In mid-2007, I started preparing the idea for this book. I must thank Tom Wilkerson of the U.S. Naval Institute for surprising me with his and the Institute's interest in publishing a work on homeland security—a topic somewhat different than their traditional "wet" fare of and for the sea-service professionals. Thanks as well go to Rick Russell, the director of the Naval Institute Press, and especially to my editor, Adam Kane, who was unfailingly supportive and tolerant of my need to extend my deadlines as new work assignments at the Project on National Security Reform generated additional material to build the case behind our recommendations. Thanks also to my copy editor, Jehanne Moharram, my designer, David Alcorn, and my indexer, Heidi Blough, for their important contribution to making the book user-friendly for students and general readers alike.

I'd like also to acknowledge and thank Jim Woolsey for his kind introduction to the folks at the Smith Richardson Foundation, whose cheerful assistance and patient encouragement throughout has been a blessing. I should give specific mention to Dr. Marin Strmecki and his program staff, in particular Nadia Schadlow and her colleagues Paula Landesberg and Dale Stewart, who provided oversight of what transpired to be a rather lengthier effort than we first imagined. Thanks as well to my colleagues Asha George and Peter Roman for their introduction to Dr. Tom Kirlin of Ambassador David Abshire's Center for the Study of the Presidency and Congress, and to Dr. Abshire himself for his enormous interest in what the Homeland Security Team of Project on National Security Reform was trying to achieve in our efforts, much of which is reflected in this book. Tom and later Elizabeth Perch served as the administrators for my Smith Richardson grant to do this study. At the time, the Center was helping sponsor Jim Locher and PNSR. Tom assigned me to provide Jim with homeland security input. Jim and his research director, Chris Lamb of the Institute for National Strategic Studies at the National Defense University, asked me to serve as the homeland security lead and assemble a team of my own choosing. Thanks to both for their example and support and for allowing me to bring members of my network on board. I was humbled that everybody I asked to join me "roger'd" enthusiastically, a testimony to how important they regarded the work of continued homeland security structural and process reform.

The bedrock upon which the analysis and recommendations in Part Two of this book rest comes from the work of our PNSR Homeland Security Team in 2008–9. That team included: Adm. James Loy, USCG (Ret.), former DHS deputy secretary; the Hon. John O. Marsh, former secretary of the Army and former congressman from Virginia; George Foresman, former DHS undersecretary for preparedness; Col. John Brinkerhoff, USA (Ret.), former FEMA acting associate director of national preparedness; Steve Grainer, chief of IMS Programs, Virginia Department of Fire Programs; Lisa Gordon-Hagerty, former director for combating terrorism at the NSC Staff; Joel Bagnal, former deputy assistant to the president for homeland security; David Trulio, former special assistant to the president and executive secretary of the HSC; Josh Filler, former DHS director for state and local government coordination; Vice Adm. Harvey E. Johnson Jr., USCG (Ret.), former FEMA deputy administrator and chief operating officer; Dennis Schrader, former FEMA deputy administrator for national preparedness; Cindy Williams, former assistant director of the Congressional Budget Office; Bill Helming, vice president of the public health and biodefense practice at PRTM's Global Public Sector Group; Dan McKinnon, a commissioner on the Commission on the National Guard and Reserves; Col. Bob Fitton, USA (Ret.), former Army Director of Military Support (DOMS); Vice Adm. James Hull, USCG (Ret.), former commander, Atlantic Area; the late Tom Steele, former CIO, Delaware Department of Safety and Homeland Security; Capt. Joe Watson, operations chief, Culpepper County (Virginia) Sheriff's Office, and former incident commander in Alexandria during the Moussaoui Trial NSSE; Joe Trindal, former director, National Capital Region for the Federal Protective Service and Immigration and Customs Enforcement (ICE); Jerry Mothershead, physician advisor to the medical readiness and response group, Battelle Memorial

Institute; Steve Harrison, assistant director, emergency operations, logistics, and planning, Virginia Department of Health; Tim Beres, former DHS director of preparedness programs; Sam Clovis, professor, Morningside College and fellow, Homeland Security Institute; John Contestabile, former director, engineering and emergency services, Maryland Department of Transportation; Fire Chief Lynn Miller, emergency management coordinator, Winchester (Virginia) Emergency Management; Charlie Lathram, Business Executives for National Security (BENS); Joe Becker, senior vice president, preparedness, American Red Cross; Matt Deane, director, homeland security standards, American National Standards Institute; Greg Rothwell, former DHS chief of procurement; Capt. David Hill, USCG (Ret.), DHS Office of the Chief Learning Officer; and Stan Soloway, president and CEO, Professional Services Council. In 2008, we got additional academic input from Paul Posner, director of the master's in public administration program at George Mason University. Input also came from Judge William Webster, the co-chair of the DHS Homeland Security Advisory Council, and former FEMA director James Lee Witt.

At various times in 2009, external input came from many officials and experts in and out of government. Particular thanks should go to: Josh DeLong, senior policy analyst at the DHS Office of Policy (Strategic Plans); Eric Fagerholm, director of doctrine and concept development, DHS Office of Coordination and Planning; Don Grant, director of FEMA NPD's Incident Management Systems Integration Division; Neal Anderson, senior NORAD and NorthCom representative to DHS; Col. Ron Salazar, ARNG, Joint Staff representative to DHS; Maj. Gen. Warren Edwards, USA (Ret.), director of the Community and Regional Resilience Institute (CARRI); William H. Austin, chief of the West Hartford (Connecticut) Fire Department; Washington State Rep. John McCoy, chairman of the National Caucus of Native American State Legislators; J. B. Pennington, senior police officer at the Houston Police Department and liaison officer for the Harris County District Attorney's Office; Col. Bob Stephan, USAF (Ret.), former DHS assistant secretary for infrastructure protection; Ann Beauchesne, vice president for national security and emergency preparedness, U.S. Chamber of Commerce; and Trina Sheets, executive director of the National Emergency Management Association.

My invaluable and able research assistants were in 2008 Creighton Vilsack from the Elliott School of George Washington University and in 2009

Mike Klingle of George Mason University. Also thanks to Joel Bagnal and BAE Systems for loaning me to PNSR for much of 2009 to enable us to continue our important work and for providing me with additional research support in the form of the very capable and committed BriAnnan Jones.

As I was finishing Part One in 2011, I received particular support from a number of public servants who were part of this history. I'd like to thank especially: Dennis Schrader; Marko Bourne, former director of policy and program analysis at FEMA; and the hugely knowledgeable Bill Cumming, who served in a variety of positions in the FEMA Office of General Counsel since its establishment in 1979. With them came additional vetting by Lisa Gordon-Hagerty; Jim Loy; Bob Stephan; Maj. Gen. Bruce Lawlor, ARNG (Ret.), chief of staff to Secretary Ridge; John Brinkerhoff; Bob Blitzer, former chief of the FBI's domestic terrorism/counterterrorism planning section and former deputy assistant secretary for emergency operations and security programs at HHS; Tom Bossert, former deputy assistant to the president for homeland security; Duncan Campbell, managing director of operations for Ridge Global; and his colleague, Chris Furlow, Ridge Global's principal for the U.S. sector; Dan Kaniewski, assistant vice president for homeland security and deputy director at the Homeland Security Policy Institute of George Washington University; and Kay Goss, then senior principal and senior advisor for emergency management and continuity programs at SRA International.

Chapters 11 and 12 are largely based on the work my Homeland Security Team did for PNSR in 2009. (*Recalibrating the System: Toward Efficient and Effective Resourcing of National Preparedness*, Project on National Security Reform, 2009, http://www.pnsr.org/data/files/pnsr_national_preparedness_system.pdf, accessed January 24, 2012.) The core team was led by Dennis Schrader with assists from Josh Filler and Tim Beres. Key input came from Nancy Dragani, executive director of the Ohio Emergency Management Agency, and also at the time president of NEMA; Al Berman, president, DRI International; Fire Chief Bill Austin; Jim Loy; Harvey Johnson; Mike Koroluk of BAE Systems; and Tom Bossert. Thanks in part to the assistance of Trina Sheets of NEMA and the NEMA-administered National Homeland Security Consortium, and Chris Logan, program director for homeland security and technology at the National Governors Association, field input came from Matt Bettenhausen, secretary, California Emergency Management Agency; Don Macsparran, homeland security manager of the Washington State Emergency

Management Division; Dave Maxwell, director of the Arkansas Emergency Management Department; Jim McMahon, executive director and chief of staff, International Association of Chiefs of Police; and John Thompson, chief of staff and deputy executive director, National Sheriffs' Association. Additional input came from the National Institute of Justice; George Tillery, associate deputy director of the Office of Science and Technology; John Morgan, deputy director for science and technology; and Thomas Sexton. HHS input was provided by Matt Payne, deputy director, Office of the Secretary; Lara Lamprecht, program analyst, and Matthew Minson, both in the Office of the Assistant Secretary for Preparedness and Response; Gregg Pane, director in the Division of National Healthcare Preparedness Program; and Michael Latham, communications officer, Strategic National Stockpile. Congressional professional staff comments came from Drenan Dudley, Adam Killian, and Ty McKeiver.

Unofficial comments were provided by Tracey Trautman, acting assistant administrator of the FEMA Grant Programs Directorate; David Kaufman, director of the FEMA Office of Program and Policy Analysis; Tina Gabbrielli, director of the DHS Office of Risk Management and Analysis in the DHS National Protection and Programs Directorate; Bob Kolasky, assistant director of the Office of Risk Management and Analysis in NPPD's Risk Governance and Support Division; Josh Dozor, branch chief, preparedness policy, planning, and analysis at FEMA; Jim Mullikin, FEMA director, evaluations and assessments; Dan Catlett, national program manager of FEMA's National Hurricane Program; Doug Ham, senior policy advisor, DHS Office of Policy Development; Ken Rapuano, director of advanced systems and policy analysis at MITRE; and Mike French, MITRE department head for preparedness and infrastructure protection.

Chapters 13 through 16 are based on the work my team did in the second half of 2010 for PNSR's Myra Shiplett and Nancy Berg on a study mandated by Section 1054 of the FY10 National Defense Authorization Act (*The Power of People: Building an Integrated National Security Professional System for the 21st Century*, Project on National Security Reform, http://www.pnsr. org/data/images/pnsr_the_power_of_people_report.pdf, accessed January 24, 2012). Special thanks go to my leads Dennis Schrader and Bob Blitzer and to those who provided assists: Dave Hill; Pat Newman, senior consultant to the DHS Office of the Chief Learning Officer; Craig Vanderwagen, the founding assistant secretary for preparedness and response (ASPR) at HHS; Bob Stephan; Ellen Gordon, associate director and faculty for the Naval Postgraduate School Center for Homeland Defense and Security; and Lisa Gordon-Hagerty. Thanks as well go to our DHS liaisons: John Kiecana, program manager for national security professional development, and John Bartleson, manager for strategy and homeland security professional development, Office of the Chief Human Capital Officer, Department of Homeland Security. Thanks to those who provided field input, again in part due to the assistance of Trina Sheets of NEMA and this time Carmen Ferro of the NGA: Robert J. Bodisch, deputy director, Texas homeland security, Texas Department of Public Safety; Capt. Richard Cashdollar, USCG (Ret.), former public safety director, City of Mobile (Alabama); Randall C. Duncan, MPA, CEM(R), chairman, U.S. Government Affairs Committee, International Association of Emergency Managers; Dr. Christopher T. Jones, superintendent of FEMA's Center for Domestic Preparedness; Tom Gilboy, chief, Preparedness Branch, Emergency Management Institute; Maj. Gen. Timothy J. Lowenberg, ANG, Adjutant General, State of Washington; Frederick W. Piechota Jr., the Proboard; Robert Smith, director of strategic development, Association of Public-Safety Communications Officials International; Byron E. Thompson Jr., deputy director, Mississippi Office of Homeland Security; John Thompson, deputy executive director, National Sheriffs' Association; and Joseph E. Wainscott Jr., executive director, Indiana Department of Homeland Security. DHS input came from Dr. George L. Tanner, chief learning officer, Office of the Chief Human Capital Officer; Alan D. Cohn, deputy assistant secretary for policy (strategic plans); and Josh DeLong, deputy director of strategic studies, Office of Policy. Research assistants were Cezar A. B. Lopez, law and policy analyst at the University of Maryland Center for Health and Homeland Security, and Lisa M. Connor from the Integrated Homeland Security Management Program at Towson University.

The closing thoughts on resilience in the postscript owe much to British thinking, specifically the work of two officials in Her Majesty's Government whom I met through PNSR and with whom I have continued to maintain contact: Charlie Edwards, former deputy director for strategy and planning in the Office for Security and Counter Terrorism at the Home Office, and Bruce Mann, the former director of civil contingencies at the Cabinet Office, more or less the UK's equivalent to FEMA. Charlie's and Bruce's conceptions of resilience align well with another colleague here in America, Debra van Opstal, currently a senior advisor at the Center for the Study of the Presidency and Congress. My first interaction with Debbie was in the early nineties when we were both working on defense industrial base and science and technology policy issues.

The PNSR Homeland Security Team was engaged in further work that did not make it into this book but supports the bottom-up Network Federal paradigm and is certainly worthy of further development and implementation. I should be remiss if I did not mention the participants in the Net-enabled Information Sharing Environment (N-ISE) Operational Proof-of-Concept Working Group: Joe Trindal, Joe Watson, Lisa Gordon-Hagerty, John Contestabile, Tom Steele, George Foresman, and Tim Beres. The working group got solid support from PNSR's Patti Benner, who was TDY from the Office of the Secretary of Defense where she was the director of strategic planning for the Office of the DCIO, ASD/Networks, and Information Integration/CIO. Patti brought to us an extremely talented team: Marian Cherry, special assistant to the vice chairman of the Joint Chiefs of Staff; Margaret E. Myers, assistant director of the Information Technology and Systems Division, IDA Studies and Analyses Center; William E. DePuy Jr., former president and CEO, Calibre Systems; and one of PNSR's most able research assistants, Elaine Banner.

I myself had also wanted to include a discussion on medical preparedness and response, but I exhausted both time and resources. This topic and others will have to await other opportunities. A great story awaits the proper recording on the 2006–7 reorganization of HHS, the establishment of the Office of the Assistant Secretary for Preparedness and Response (ASPR), and the roles played by Dr. Bob Kadlec, special assistant to the president and the HSC's senior director for biodefense policy, and Dr. Craig Vanderwagen, the first ASPR. These two men are indeed two national treasures and among very few public servants who can testify how bureaucrats can still make a positive difference to the way things get done in government.

Finally, acknowledgments would not be complete without a heartfelt thanks to my wife, Gail Bradshaw Morton. Gail's insights drawn from her years of service at the state and local government levels in Maryland have been invaluable.

John Fass Morton
Annapolis, Maryland
St. Valentine's Day, 2012

# Abbreviations

| | |
|---|---|
| **2SR** | Second Stage Review |
| **AC** | active component |
| **AFG** | assistance to firefighters grant |
| **AFPR** | Analysis of Federal Preparedness Requirements |
| **AHC** | All Hazards Consortium |
| **AMIO** | alien migrant interdiction operations |
| **AMSC** | Area Maritime Security Committee (Coast Guard) |
| **ANG** | Air National Guard |
| **APCO** | Association of Public-Safety Communications Officials |
| **ARC** | Appalachian Regional Commission or American Red Cross |
| **ASP** | Advanced Spectroscopic Portal |
| **ASPR** | assistant secretary for preparedness and response (HHS) |
| **ASTHO** | Association of State and Territorial Health Officials |
| **ATAC** | Anti-Terrorism Advisory Council |
| **ATS** | Automated Targeting System |
| **BUR** | Bottom-Up Review (DHS) |
| **C²** | command and control |
| **C2C** | Cost-to-Capability Initiative |
| **CAARS** | Cargo Advanced Automated Radiography System |
| **CAE** | Centers of Academic Excellence (ODNI) |
| **CAP** | Corrective Action Program |
| **CARRI** | Community and Regional Resilience Institute |
| **CBP** | Customs and Border Protection |
| **CBRNE** | chemical, biological, radiological, nuclear, and high-yield explosive |
| **CDP** | Center for Domestic Preparedness |
| **CDRG** | Catastrophic Disaster Response Group |
| **CEM** | Comprehensive Emergency Management |
| **CFIA** | Center for International Affairs (Harvard University) |

| | |
|---|---|
| **CFIUS** | Committee of Foreign Investment in the United States |
| **CFSI** | Congressional Fire Service Institute |
| **CFT** | cross-functional team |
| **CHDS** | Center for Homeland Defense and Security |
| **CICG** | Critical Infrastructure Coordination Group |
| **CI/KR** | critical infrastructure/key resources |
| **CIP** | critical infrastructure protection |
| **CIWG** | Critical Infrastructure Working Group |
| **COG** | continuity of government |
| **CONOPS** | concept of operations |
| **CONPLAN** | Concept of Operations Plan |
| **COOP** | continuity of operations |
| **CoP** | community of practice |
| **COPS** | Community Oriented Policing Services |
| **CPA** | certified public accountant |
| **CPG** | Comprehensive Preparedness Guidelines |
| **CPPG** | Crisis Pre-Planning Group |
| **CPT** | Center for Policing Terrorism |
| **CRCOG** | Capitol Region Council of Governments |
| **CS&C** | Office of Cyber Security and Communications |
| **CSEPP** | Chemical Stockpile Emergency Preparedness Program |
| **CSG** | Coordination Sub-Group (under Reagan), later Counterterrorism Security Group (under Clinton) |
| **CST** | civil support team |
| **CTC** | Counterterrorism Center |
| **DAU** | Defense Acquisition University |
| **DAWIA** | Defense Acquisition Workforce Improvement Act |
| **DCE** | defense coordinating element |
| **DCIO** | deputy chief information officer |
| **DCO** | defense coordinating officer |
| **DCPA** | Defense Civil Preparedness Agency |
| **DFCO** | deputy federal coordinating officer |
| **DNDO** | Domestic Nuclear Detection Office |
| **DO** | Directorate of Operations (CIA) |
| **DOMS** | Directorate of Military Support (U.S. Army) |

| | |
|---|---|
| **DRF** | Disaster Relief Fund |
| **DRG** | Domestic Resilience (formerly Readiness) Group |
| **DSCA** | Defense Support of Civil Authorities |
| **DTRIM** | Domestic Threat Reduction and Incident Management |
| **EBS** | Emergency Broadcast System |
| **ECG** | enduring constitutional government |
| **ELP** | Executive Leaders Program |
| **EMAC** | Emergency Management Assistance Compact |
| **EMAP** | Emergency Management Accreditation Program |
| **EMI** | Emergency Management Institute |
| **EMP** | electromagnetic pulse (weapons) |
| **EOC** | emergency operations center |
| **EOP** | Executive Office of the President |
| **ESAR-VP** | Emergency System for Advance Registration of Volunteer Health Professionals (HHS) |
| **ESC** | Executive Steering Committee (OPM) |
| **ESF** | Emergency Support Function |
| **FCDA** | Federal Civil Defense Administration |
| **FCO** | federal coordinating officer |
| **FDAA** | Federal Disaster Assistance Administration |
| **FDEM** | Florida Division of Emergency Management |
| **FDRC** | federal disaster recovery coordinator |
| **FFRDC** | Federally Funded Research and Development Center |
| **FIA** | Federal Insurance Administration |
| **FIMA** | Federal Insurance and Mitigation Administration |
| **FIPS** | Federal Information Processing Standard |
| **FIRESCOPE** | FIrefighting RESources of California Organized for Potential Emergencies |
| **FISA** | Foreign Intelligence Surveillance Act |
| **FLETC** | Federal Law Enforcement Training Center |
| **FPA** | Federal Preparedness Agency |
| **FPC** | federal preparedness coordinator |
| **FRAC** | First Responder Authentication Credential |
| **FRP** | Federal Response Plan |
| **GMS** | grants management specialist |

| | |
|---|---|
| **GOCO** | government-owned, contractor-operated |
| **GPD** | Grant Programs Directorate (FEMA) |
| **GSA** | General Services Administration |
| **HIRA** | Hazard Identification and Risk Assessment |
| **HITRAC** | Homeland Infrastructure Threat and Risk Analysis Center |
| **HMGP** | Hazard Mitigation Grant Program |
| **HSAC** | Homeland Security Advisory Council |
| **HSC** | Homeland Security Council |
| **HSDEC** | Homeland Security/Defense Education Consortium |
| **HSDECA** | Homeland Security and Defense Education Consortium Association |
| **HSEEP** | Homeland Security Exercise and Evaluation Program |
| **HSMI** | Homeland Security Management Institute |
| **HSOC** | Homeland Security Operations Center |
| **HSPD** | Homeland Security Presidential Directive |
| **HSPI** | Homeland Security Policy Institute |
| **HSTF-SE** | Homeland Security Task Force-Southeast |
| **HUD** | Department of Housing and Urban Development |
| **I&A** | Office of Intelligence and Analysis |
| **IAEM** | International Association of Emergency Managers |
| **IAIP** | Directorate of Information Analysis and Infrastructure Protection |
| **IC** | U.S. Intelligence Community or incident commander |
| **ICE** | Immigration and Customs Enforcement |
| **ICP** | Incident Command Post |
| **ICS** | Incident Command System |
| **ICS/UC** | Incident Command System/Unified Command |
| **IEMS** | Integrated Emergency Management System |
| **IFSAC** | International Fire Service Accreditation Congress |
| **IG/T** | Interdepartmental Group on Terrorism |
| **IIMG** | Interagency Incident Management Group |
| **ILP** | intelligence-led policing |
| **IMPT** | Incident Management Planning Team |
| **IMSI** | Incident Management Systems Integration |
| **IMT** | incident management team |

| | |
|---|---|
| IND | improvised nuclear device |
| INR | Bureau of Intelligence and Research |
| INS | Immigration and Naturalization Service |
| INSP | Interagency National Security Professional |
| IPA | Intergovernmental Personnel Act |
| IPS | Integrated Planning System |
| IQCS | Incident Qualifications Credentialing System |
| IQS | Incident Qualifications System |
| IRTPA | Intelligence Reform and Terrorism Prevention Act |
| ISAC | Information Sharing and Analysis Center |
| ISE | Information Sharing Environment |
| I-Staff | Integration Staff (DHS) |
| JFO | Joint Field Office |
| JIC | Joint Information Center |
| JOC | Joint Operations Center |
| JOPES | Joint Operational Planning and Execution System |
| JTF | Joint Task Force |
| JTF-CS | Joint Task Force-Civil Support |
| JTTF | Joint Terrorism Task Force |
| KSA | knowledge, skills, and abilities |
| LE | law enforcement |
| LEDET | law-enforcement detachment |
| LEISP | Law Enforcement Information Sharing Program (DOJ) |
| MAC | multi-agency coordination |
| MACS | multi-agency coordination system |
| MCAC | Maryland Coordination and Analysis Center |
| MET | Mobile Education Team |
| MOTR | Maritime Operational Threat Response |
| MTOE | modification table for organization and equipment |
| NACCHO | National Association of County and City Health Officials |
| NADO | National Association of Development Organizations |
| NAFPC | National Academy of Fire Prevention and Control |
| NAPA | National Academy of Public Administration |
| NARC | National Association of Regional Councils |
| NBC | nuclear, biological, and chemical |

| | |
|---|---|
| **NCP** | National Oil and Hazardous Substances Pollution Contingency Plan |
| **NCR** | National Capital Region |
| **NCS** | National Communications System |
| **NCTC** | National Counterterrorism Center |
| **NDPC** | National Domestic Preparedness Consortium (DHS) |
| **NDPO** | National Domestic Preparedness Office |
| **NDPTC** | National Disaster Preparedness Training Center |
| **NDRF** | National Disaster Recovery Framework |
| **NEF** | National Essential Function |
| **NEI** | National Executive Institute (FBI) |
| **NEMA** | National Emergency Management Association |
| **NEP** | National Exercise Program |
| **NESC** | National Exercise Simulation Center |
| **NETC** | National Emergency Training Center |
| **NFA** | National Fire Academy |
| **NFIP** | National Flood Insurance Program |
| **NFPA** | National Fire Protection Association |
| **NFPCA** | National Fire Prevention and Control Administration |
| **NHSU** | National Homeland Security University |
| **NIC** | National Integration Center |
| **NICC** | National Infrastructure Coordinating Center |
| **NIMS** | National Incident Management System |
| **NIMSCAST** | NIMS Compliance Assistance Support Tool |
| **NIPC** | National Infrastructure Protection Center |
| **NIPP** | National Infrastructure Protection Plan |
| **NIP-WOT** | National Implementation Plan for the War on Terrorism |
| **N-ISE** | Net-enabled Information Sharing Environment |
| **NJTTF** | National Joint Terrorism Task Force |
| **NLC** | National League of Cities |
| **NLE** | national-level exercise |
| **NMCC** | National Military Command Center |
| **NNSA** | National Nuclear Security Administration |
| **NOC** | National Operations Center |
| **NorthCom** | Northern Command |

| | |
|---|---|
| **NPA** | National Production Authority |
| **NPD** | National Preparedness Directorate |
| **NPES** | National Planning and Execution System |
| **NPG** | National Preparedness Goal |
| **NPLI** | National Preparedness Leadership Initiative |
| **NPPD** | National Protection and Programs Directorate |
| **NPRA** | National Preparedness and Response Agency |
| **NPS** | National Planning Scenarios |
| **NRC** | Nuclear Regulatory Commission |
| **NRCC** | National Response Coordination Center |
| **NRF** | National Response Framework |
| **NRP** | National Response Plan |
| **NSDD** | National Security Decision Directive |
| **NSPD** | National Security Presidential Directive or National Security Professional Development |
| **NSPD-IO** | National Security Professional Development Integration Office |
| **NSRB** | National Security Resources Board |
| **NTS** | Nevada Test Site (DOE) |
| **NWCG** | National Wildfire Coordinating Group |
| **NWWARN** | Northwest Warning, Alert, and Response Network |
| **OCD** | Office of Civil Defense |
| **OCDM** | Office of Civil and Defense Mobilization |
| **OCDP** | Office of Civil Defense Planning |
| **OCHCO** | Office of the Chief Human Capital Officer (DHS) |
| **OCHCO-ELD** | Office of the Chief Human Capital Officer, Enterprise Learning and Development |
| **ODM** | Office of Defense Mobilization |
| **ODNI** | Office of the Director of National Intelligence |
| **ODP** | Office of Domestic Preparedness |
| **OECD** | Organization for Economic Cooperation and Development |
| **OEM** | Office of Emergency Management |
| **OEP** | Office of Emergency Planning (later Preparedness) |
| **OHS** | Office of Homeland Security |
| **OIG** | Office of the Inspector General (DHS) |
| **OIP** | Office of Infrastructure Protection |

| | |
|---|---|
| **OMB** | Office of Management and Budget |
| **ONDCP** | Office of the National Drug Control Policy |
| **ONP** | Office of National Preparedness |
| **OPB** | Operational Planning Branch (FEMA) |
| **OPLAN** | operational plan |
| **OPM** | Office of Personnel Management |
| **OPS** | Office of Operations and Coordination (DHS) |
| **OPU** | Operational Planning Unit (FEMA) |
| **ORAU** | Oak Ridge Associated Universities |
| **OSG** | Operations Sub-Group |
| **OSS** | Office of Strategic Services |
| **OTP** | Office of Telecommunications Policy |
| **PACIC** | Pennsylvania Criminal Intelligence Center |
| **PAPO** | preparedness analysis and planning officer |
| **PCC** | policy coordination committee |
| **PDD** | Presidential Decision Directive |
| **PDM** | Pre-Disaster Mitigation |
| **PEMA** | Pennsylvania Emergency Management Association |
| **PFO** | principal federal official |
| **PKEMRA** | Post-Katrina Emergency Management Reform Act |
| **PNR** | passenger name record |
| **PNSR** | Project on National Security Reform |
| **PNWER** | Pacific NorthWest Economic Region |
| **P&O** | Peninsula and Oriental Steam Navigation Company |
| **POETE** | plan, organize, equip, train, and exercise |
| **POG** | planning oversight group |
| **POST** | Peace Officer Standards and Training |
| **PSA** | protective security advisor |
| **PSD** | Presidential Study Directive |
| **PSM** | Presidential Security Memorandum |
| **PTB** | Position Task Book |
| **RAC** | regional advisory council |
| **RC** | reserve component |
| **RCPGP** | Regional Catastrophic Preparedness Grant Program |
| **RDD** | radiological dispersal device |

| | |
|---|---|
| **REC** | regional emergency coordinator (HHS) |
| **REPP** | Radiological Emergency Preparedness Program |
| **RFC** | Reconstruction Finance Corporation |
| **RICO** | Racketeer Influenced and Corrupt Organizations Act |
| **RIO** | regional investment officer |
| **RISC** | Regional Interagency Steering Committee |
| **RoI** | return on investment |
| **ROSS** | Resource Ordering and Status System |
| **RPP** | Readiness, Prevention, and Planning Division (NPD) |
| **RPS** | Regional Preparedness Staff |
| **RRCC** | Regional Response Coordination Center |
| **SAA** | state administrative agency |
| **SAC** | special agent in charge (FBI) |
| **SAD** | state active duty |
| **SBA** | Small Business Administration |
| **SBI** | Smart Border Initiative |
| **SCC** | Sector Coordinating Council |
| **SCIF** | sensitive compartmented information facility |
| **SCO** | state coordinating officer |
| **SES** | senior executive service |
| **SGE** | special government employee |
| **SHSP** | State Homeland Security Program |
| **SIG** | Senior Interagency Group |
| **SIOC** | Strategic Intelligence and Operations Center |
| **SLG** | State and Local Guide |
| **SLGCP** | Office of State and Local Government Coordination and Preparedness |
| **SNRA** | Strategic National Risk Assessment |
| **SOG** | senior oversight group |
| **SO/LIC** | special operations/low intensity conflict |
| **SSG** | Special Situation Group |
| **SSP** | sector-specific plan |
| **SSTP** | Streamlined Sales Tax Project |
| **S&T** | Science and Technology (Directorate) |
| **START** | Strategic Arms Reduction Treaty |

| | |
|---|---|
| **TAG** | adjutant general (National Guard) |
| **TCL** | Target Capabilities List |
| **TEEX** | Texas A&M University National Emergency Response and Rescue Training Center |
| **TEMCO** | Territorial Emergency Management Coordination Office |
| **TERT** | Telecommunicator Emergency Response Taskforce |
| **TFER** | Task Force for Emergency Response |
| **THIRA** | Threat and Hazard Identification and Risk Assessment |
| **TIWG** | Terrorist Incident Working Group |
| **TopOff** | Top Officials national counterterrorism exercise |
| **TPO** | Transition Planning Office |
| **TS/SCI** | top secret/sensitive compartmented information |
| **TSWG** | Technical Support Working Group |
| **TTCI** | Transportation Technology Center, Inc. |
| **TTIC** | Terrorist Threat Information Center |
| **TWIC** | Transportation Workers Identification Card |
| **UAPI** | University and Agency Partnership Initiative |
| **UARC** | University Affiliated Research Center |
| **UASI** | Urban Area Security Initiative |
| **UC** | Unified Command |
| **UCG** | Unified Coordination Group |
| **USCIS** | U.S. Citizenship and Immigration Services |
| **US-VISIT** | United States Visitor and Immigrant Status Indicator Technology |
| **UTL** | Universal Task List |
| **WHMO** | White House Military Office |
| **WMD-CST** | Weapons of Mass Destruction-Civil Support Teams |
| **YOYO** | "You're on Your Own" |

# Notes

## Introduction

1. This line of thought derives from a longer treatment found in John F. Morton, "Toward a Premise for Grand Strategy," ch. 2 in *Economic Security: Neglected Dimension of National Security?* ed. Sheila R. Ronis (Washington, DC: Institute for National Strategic Studies, National Defense University Press, 2011), pp. 13–61, http://www.ndu.edu/press/lib/pdf/books/economic-security.pdf (accessed 26 April 2012).
2. See Anne-Marie Slaughter, *A New World Order: Government Networks and the Disaggregated State* (Princeton, NJ: Princeton University Press, 2004).
3. See Project on National Security Reform, *Forging a New Shield* (Washington, DC: November 2008), http://www.pnsr.org/data/files/pnsr_forging_a_new_shield_report.pdf.
4. Four key sources support this contention with regard to devolution of homeland security functions: Albert-László Barabási, *Linked: The New Science of Networks* (Cambridge, MA: Perseus Publishing, 2002) for network theory and the ramifications of the Internet on socio-political structure; John Robb, *Brave New War: The Next Stage of Terrorism and the End of Global Civilization* (Hoboken, NJ: John Wiley & Sons, 2007) for leveraging network approaches to achieve national resilience; Donald P. Moynihan, *Leveraging Collaborative Networks in Infrequent Emergency Situations* (Washington, DC: IBM Center for The Business of Government, June 2005) for the applicability of network structures for managing emergency governance; and Donald P. Moynihan, *From Forest Fires to Hurricane Katrina: Case Studies of Incident Command Systems* (Washington, DC: IBM Center for The Business of Government, 2007) for the incident command system (ICS) model as a temporary hierarchical-network model for managing catastrophic events.
5. Barabási, *Linked*, p. 118.
6. Robb, *Brave New War*, p. 164.
7. See ibid., p. 185.
8. Ashton B. Carter, Michael M. May, and William J. Perry, *The Day After: Action in the 24 Hours Following a Nuclear Blast in an American City* (Harvard and Stanford Universities, The Preventive Defense Project, April 2007), pp. 10–11.

### Chapter 1:.The Evolution of Emergency Management and Preparedness

1. Federal Emergency Management Agency (FEMA), "FEMA History," http://www. fema.gov/about/history.shtm (accessed 19 January 2011).
2. The War Finance Corporation gave loans to industries deemed essential to the war effort. Its chairman was the Wall Street financier Eugene Meyer Jr. who also led Hoover's RFC. Meyer would serve as Federal Reserve chairman and is best remembered as the publisher of the *Washington Post*.
3. EO 12127, Federal Emergency Management Agency, 31 March 1979, and EO 12148, Federal Emergency Management,' 20 July 1979.
4. In the 1990s, the escalating consequences of terrorist attacks on the homeland prompted inclusion of prevention as a fifth phase to precede the other four in the emergency management mission continuum. In an August 2006 monograph, *Introduction to Modern Emergency Management*, Col. John R. Brinkerhoff, USA (Ret.), FEMA's acting associate director for national preparedness in the 1980s, defines prevention as "a set of actions taken to avert an incident that would cause an emergency" to include deterrence, protection, and defense.
5. Brinkerhoff, *Introduction to Modern Emergency Management*.
6. NETC has two tenants, the National Fire Academy (NFA) and the Emergency Management Institute (EMI). The latter activity began operations in 1981 when the former Defense Civil Preparedness Staff College relocated from Battle Creek, Michigan, and reopened as EMI.
7. Pittman came from an entirely different professional background. He held various consultancies: one with the Eisenhower-era Second Hoover Commission on Organization of the Executive Branch of the Government, for which he authored a report on international investment and lending; another with the State Department, negotiating investment guaranty agreements in seven Latin American countries; and a third with the Development Loan Fund, establishing precedents for mixed public and private financing methods for Third World projects.

### Chapter 2. Counterterrorism

1. Many accounts cite the Marxist Popular Front for the Liberation of Palestine 22 July 1968, hijacking of El Al Flight 426, Rome to Tel Aviv, as the beginning of modern terrorism. See, for example, Steve Coll, *Ghost Wars: The Secret History of the CIA, Afghanistan, and Bin Laden, from the Soviet Invasion to September 10, 2001* (New York: The Penguin Press, 2004), p. 138.
2. On 29 December 1979, the Department of State established its first list of state sponsors of terrorism. This was statutorily mandated by the Export Administration Act of 1979. The initial four on what became an annually announced list were: Libya, Iraq, South Yemen, and Syria. The designation provides for the United States to impose: restrictions on foreign assistance; a ban on defense exports and sales; certain controls over exports of dual-use items; and miscellaneous financial and other restrictions.

3. Timothy Naftali, *Blind Spot: The Secret History of American Counterterrorism* (New York: Basic Books, 2005), p. 101.

4. The numbering of these two NSDDs was deliberately not in order of their chronological release dates.

5. In September 1982 the domestic case of the Tylenol poisoning raised the specter of terrorism and the food supply.

6. Cold War tensions were still high. In September 1983 they peaked when a Soviet pilot downed the Korean KAL 007 airliner, which had strayed into restricted airspace over Kamchatka. Among the 269 fatalities was Congressman Lawrence McDonald (D-GA).

7. Terrorist violence, such as it was gaining ground as a tactic of choice, still seemed to occur overseas. With the exception of civilian airlines and Beirut hostage-taking, the assumption was that terrorism was more likely directed at diplomatic and military targets. A domestic exception came in 1984 when members of the Rajneesh cult in Oregon used salmonella in a bioterror attack on a local restaurant salad bar.

8. Naftali, *Blind Spot*, p. 178.

9. Ibid., pp. 178–79.

10. Harvey W. Kushner, *Encyclopedia of Terrorism* (Thousand Oaks, CA: Sage Publications, 2003), p. 90.

11. Joseph T. Stanik, *El Dorado Canyon: Reagan's Undeclared War with Qaddafi* (Annapolis, MD: U.S. Naval Institute Press, 2003), p. 119.

12. Among the key CSG team members during this period were the FBI's Bill Baker, Buck Revell, John O'Neill, Bob Blitzer, Mike Rollins, and Dale Watson; Justice's Jim Reynolds, chief of the Terrorism and Violent Crime Section; the CIA's Steve Richter and Winston Wiley from the Counterterrorism Center; DoD's Allen Holmes, assistant secretary of defense for special operations and low-intensity conflict (SO/LIC); State's Philip C. Wilcox Jr., ambassador-at-large for counterterrorism; Peggy Hamburg, HHS assistant secretary for policy and evaluation; Rear Adm. Frank Young Jr., U.S. Public Health Service; and FEMA's Bruce Baughman and Lacy Suiter.

13. See Coll, *Ghost Wars*, pp. 274–78.

14. Preparations for a possible Year 2000 (Y2K) failure of computers and computer networks benefited from a lot of the structures and activity generated by the Marsh Commission and PDD-63. Opinions differ, however, on whether those preparations actually prevented a cyber meltdown or whether in fact the Y2K scenario was overblown in the first place.

15. Richard A. Clarke, *Against All Enemies: Inside America's War on Terror* (New York: Free Press, 2004), p. 196.

16. These "train the trainer" programs included those run by DoD, FEMA, HHS, Department of Energy, and the Environmental Protection Agency.

17. The most notable counterterrorism restructuring studies of the latter years of the Clinton administration were generated by three successive commissions led

by Ambassador Paul Bremmer, who served as ambassador-at-large for counter-terrorism in the mid-eighties, former Virginia Governor Jim Gilmore, and former Senators Gary Hart and Warren Rudman. The last, the U.S. Commission on National Security/21st Century—the Hart-Rudman Commission—would present its final report a month after the George W. Bush team took office. Among other things, this report would recommend a cabinet-level National Homeland Security Agency, chartered in law to provide a focal point for federal response in "all natural and man-made crisis and emergency planning scenarios."

18. Anthony H. Cordesman, "Redefining the Conceptual Boundaries of Homeland Defense," revised 12 December 2000 (Washington, DC: Center for Strategic and International Studies, 2000), p. 5, http://edocs.nps.edu/AR/org/CSIS/budgetoverview.pdf (accessed 22 January 2012).

19. Ibid., p. 11.

20. Clarke, *Against All Enemies*, p. 234.

21. See John Robb, *Brave New War: The Next Stage of Terrorism and the End of Global Civilization* (Hoboken, NJ: John Wiley & Sons, 2007), p. 31.

22. Tom Ridge, *The Test of Our Times: America under Siege . . . And How We Can Be Safe Again* (New York: Thomas Dunne Books, 2009), p. 272.

**Chapter 3. The Political Dynamics behind the Creation of the Department of Homeland Security**

1. Quoted in Lynn F. Rusten, "U.S. Withdrawal from the Antiballistic Missile Treaty," Center for the Study of Weapons of Mass Destruction Case Study 2 (Washington, DC: National Defense University Press, January 2010), p. 1.

2. Ibid., p. 2.

3. David J. Rothkopf, *Running the World: The Inside Story of the National Security Council and the Architects of American Power* (New York: Public Affairs, 2005), p. 404.

4. See Staff Statement No. 8, "National Policy Coordination," http://www.9-11commission.gov/hearings/hearing8.htm, p. 8.

5. Donald Rumsfeld, "Submitted Testimony," http://www.9-11commission.gov/hearings/hearing8.htm, p. 7.

6. See Naftali, *Blind Spot*, p. 293.

7. Tom Ridge, *The Test of Our Times: America under Siege . . . And How We Can Be Safe Again* (New York: Thomas Dunne Books, 2009), p. 57.

8. Ibid., p. 72.

9. Other such officials on Ridge's staff included Barbara Chaffee, who oversaw private-sector outreach; Ashley Davis, who came from the White House to serve as a special assistant; Heather Musser, a Texan who assisted Mark Holman; and Carl Buchholz, a Philadelphia attorney, who served as the OHS executive secretary.

10. Another key loyalist at the top was Clay Johnson. George Bush's prep school roommate at Phillips Andover and fraternity brother at Yale, Johnson served as

his chief of staff when Bush was Texas governor, managed his presidential transition, and was his first director of personnel.

11. Among Goldman's clients was the oil firm British Petroleum (BP). In June 2010, BP hired Bolten to assist in its efforts to defend its interests and mount a public relations campaign to restore its reputation in the wake of the catastrophic Macondo oil spill.

12. Robert Belfer and his family were Poles who escaped the Nazis early in the war. Arthur Belfer, his entrepreneurial father, became a successful oil man through his company, Belco Petroleum Corporation, established in the mid-fifties. Belco operations were in exploration and development, mainly in Wyoming and Peru. In the early eighties the Belfers merged Belco with InterNorth, Inc. In two years, their new firm, BelNorth Petroleum Corp., merged with Houston Natural Gas to become Enron Corp. Belfer remained a major stockholder in Enron and a board member.

13. Ridge, *The Test of Our Times*, p. 58.

14. Ibid., p. 94. Unfortunately, by this time O'Neill was already straying off the reservation. In February 2001, just prior to a G-7 finance ministers meeting in Palermo, Italy, O'Neill told a German newspaper, "We are not pursuing, as is often said, a policy of a strong dollar. In my opinion, a strong dollar is the result of a strong economy." International financial markets went into a mini-crisis; the value of the dollar dropped while the euro rose. An angry White House forced O'Neill to retreat from his words. The next day, he reassured markets that the Bush administration would not abandon the strong-dollar policies of Clinton and the elder Bush that undergirded the international financial system. From the beginning, he had put himself at odds with Bush-Cheney policies through his opposition to the NSC's planning for regime change and intervention in Iraq, his desire to pursue terrorist financing more aggressively in the wake of 9/11, and his vocal questioning of the administration's decisions to cut taxes and run deficits. At the end of 2002, Cheney asked for his resignation, and he was gone. Unlike his predecessors, Robert Rubin and Larry Summers, O'Neill was a corporation man, not a Wall Streeter. A former chairman and CEO of Pittsburgh's Alcoa and chairman of RAND, he was one who owed his position more by virtue of his longtime association with the elder Bush than by his allegiance to the Bush-Cheney team.

15. True, the Navy Department, ever seeing itself as the exception, chose to keep its offices in the temporary World War I–era Main Navy and Munitions Buildings when the War Department vacated for the Pentagon in 1943. Main Navy occupied several blocks of Constitution Avenue along the National Mall overlooking the Reflecting Pool. There it would remain until President Nixon decreed it be demolished in 1969.

## Chapter 4. DHS and the Politics of National Preparedness

1. The White House, National Strategy for Homeland Security, 16 July 2002, p. 3.
2. Ibid., p. 5.
3. See Valerie Bailey Grasso, "Defense Acquisition: Use of Lead Systems Integrators (LSIs)—Background, Oversight Issues, and Options for Congress," Congressional Research Service, 8 October 2010, http://www.fas.org/sgp/crs/natsec/RS22631.pdf (accessed 13 June 2011).
4. Michael Grunwald and Susan B. Glasser, "Brown's Turf Wars Sapped FEMA's Strength," *Washington Post*, 23 December 2005.
5. FEMA, Press Release, "FEMA Hails 2000 as Year of Major Gains in Disaster Prevention," 22 December 2000, http://www.fema.gov/news/newsrelease.fema?id=9993 (accessed 2 June 2011).
6. Pre-Disaster Mitigation is FEMA's own left-of-the-boom program, where mitigation is arguably an emergency management mission comparable to homeland security's protection. For a discussion of Pre-Disaster Mitigation, see Francis X. McCarthy and Natalie Keegan, "FEMA's Pre-Disaster Mitigation Program: Overview and Issues," Congressional Research Service, 10 July 2009, http://www.fas.org/sgp/crs/homesec/RL34537.pdf (accessed 4 June 2011).
7. The law enforcement lobby worked both ends of Pennsylvania Avenue in the crafting of DHS in 2002–3. On the one hand, it was able to induce lawmakers to overturn the administration's provision in the original 2002 legislation to transfer the Department of Energy–managed Nuclear Emergency Support Team (NEST) to DHS. Established in 1975 in response to concerns over nuclear terrorism, NEST has collaborative relationships with the FBI and DoD, and the decision reflected law enforcement concerns over command and control issues, among others. On the other hand, the intent of Congress in the 2002 legislation was for DHS to integrate terrorist threat information, law enforcement and intelligence communities; hence, the law enforcement lobby worked on the executive branch to pressure the administration to stand up in the spring of 2003 its interagency Terrorist Threat Information Center (TTIC) under the CIA.
8. The White House, Homeland Security Presidential Directive, Management of Domestic Incidents (HSPD-5), 28 February 2003, http://www.dhs.gov/xabout/laws/gc_1214592333605.shtm (accessed 3 June 2011).
9. The system was initially called FIRESCOPE (FIrefighting RESources of California Organized for Potential Emergencies). Its developers were the U.S. Forest Service, the California Department of Forestry and Fire Protection, the Governor's Office of Emergency Services, the Los Angeles City Fire Department, and the Los Angeles, Ventura, and Santa Barbara County Fire Departments—a genuine intergovernmental collaboration of equals.
10. U.S. Department of Homeland Security, Initial National Response Plan, Memo from Tom Ridge, 30 September 2003, http://www.crcpd.org/Homeland_Security/Initial_NRP_100903.pdf (accessed 3 June 2011).

11. For a discussion of the development and release of the NRP and NIMS, see James M. Loy, "Adm. James M. Loy, USCG (Ret.), Acting Secretary of Homeland Security," audio interview by John F. Morton, *Domestic Preparedness*, 9 February 2005, http://www.domesticpreparedness.com/pub/docs/DomPrepTIPSFeb9.pdf (accessed 14 June 2011).

12. In an incident, the NRCC and RRCC expand with their ESF staffs. At the regional level, in an ongoing RRCC operation rising to the level of an incident of national significance, federal coordination shifts to the JFO, the primary federal incident management field structure.

13. Ridge memo, p. 3.

14. Ridge memo, p. 4.

15. For a discussion of the development and release of the NPG, see Matt Mayer, "Matt Mayer, Acting Executive Director, Office of State and Local Government Coordination and Preparedness, Department of Homeland Security," audio interview by John F. Morton, *Domestic Preparedness*, 4 May 2005, http://www.domesticpreparedness.com/pub/docs/DomPrepTIPSMay4.pdf (accessed 14 June 2011).

16. See the work of Samuel H. Clovis Jr., a retired Air Force colonel who is a member of the faculty at the Center for Homeland Defense and Security at the Naval Postgraduate School in Monterey, California: "Federalism, Homeland Security, and National Preparedness: A Case Study in the Development of Public Policy," *Homeland Security Affairs* 2, no. 3 (October 2006), http://www.hsaj.org/?article=2.3.4 (accessed 7 June 2011); "Promises Unfulfilled: The Suboptimization of Homeland Security National Preparedness," *Homeland Security Affairs* 4, no. 3 (October 2008), http://www.hsaj.org/?article=4.3.3 (accessed 7 June 2011); "The Cost of Compliance: Preparedness and the Target Capabilities List," paper delivered at the Midwest Political Science Association Annual Conference, April 2008, http://convention2.allacademic.com/meta/p269039_index.html?phpsessid=5d41c533cc339abf3341d3f9bdb0281 (accessed 7 June 2011); and "Normalized Jurisdictional Traits for Homeland Security Grant Allocations: Exposing Governance Vulnerability in Large Urban Settings," paper delivered at the Midwest Political Science Association Annual Conference, April 2008, http://www.allacademic.com/pages/p268584-1.php (accessed 7 June 2011).

17. See Paul Posner, "The Politics of Coercive Federalism in the Bush Era," *Publius* 37, no. 3 (May 2007), http://publius.oxfordjournals.org/content/37/3/390.full (accessed 8 June 2011). Posner is director of the public administration program at George Mason University. A fellow of the National Academy of Public Administration, he chairs its Federal Systems Panel. A recent president of the American Society for Public Administration, he led the budget and public finance work of the Government Accountability Office (GAO) for over a decade.

18. Christine E. Wormuth, *Managing the Next Domestic Catastrophe: Ready (or Not)? A Beyond Goldwater-Nichols Phase 4 Report* (Washington, DC: CSIS Press, June 2008), p. 60.

19. Ibid., p. 58.
20. Ibid., p. 59.
21. Ibid., p. 62.
22. Ridge, *The Test of Our Times*, p. 213.
23. Ibid., p. 261.
24. Ridge was referring to a paper by Dwight Ink and Alan L. Dean, "Modernizing Field Operations," in *Making Government Manageable: Executive Organization and Management in the Twenty-First Century*, ed. Thomas H. Stanton and Benjamin Ginsberg (Baltimore and London: The Johns Hopkins University Press, 2004), pp. 175–203. The book was a joint product of NAPA's Standing Panel on Executive Organization and Management and the Johns Hopkins Center for the Study of American Government.
25. Ridge, *The Test of Our Times*, p. 212.
26. Ibid., p. 261.
27. Ibid., p. 213.
28. Richard J. Webster, "Learning from Operation Able Manner," U.S. Naval Institute *Proceedings* 137, no. 8 (August 2011), p. 34.
29. DHS updated Operation Plan Able Sentry in 2007 to reflect the PKEMRA organizational changes to the department. Subsequent changes have come through inputs from over a dozen operational or tabletop exercises. The plan now provides for a senior oversight group (SOG) at the assistant secretary level for resolving any major DHS policy issues. The SOG chairman is the DHS director of operations coordination and planning. A planning oversight group (POG) includes key action officers who facilitate interagency coordination and assist the SOG with policy. These two groups identify issues and contribute to issue papers and talking points for decision in the national security system at the deputies level.
30. Ridge memo, p. 9.
31. Ridge, *The Test of Our Times*, p. 217.
32. Ibid., p. 224.
33. Ibid.
34. Ibid., p. 220.

### Chapter 5. DHS Pre-Katrina

1. The link was Rove staffer Chris Henick, who left the White House in 2003 to join Giuliani Partners. Henick was a deputy assistant to the president and deputy to Rove for overseeing strategic planning, political affairs, intergovernmental relations, and public liaison. During the 2000 campaign, he was deputy director of strategy. The executive director of the Republican Governors Association in the early nineties, Henick was closely aligned with high-power Mississippi Republican lobbyist Haley Barbour, then chairman of the Republican National Committee and one of the architects of the Republican electoral victory of 1994 when the party captured both houses of Congress.

2. For background on how the regional political establishment transformed at the end of the century, see Daniel Gross, *Bull Run: Wall Street, the Democrats, and the New Politics of Personal Finance* (New York: PublicAffairs, 2000). In 2004, scandals had rocked the Democratic governor of New Jersey (extramarital homosexual affair) and Republican governor of Connecticut (corruption) resulting in resignations. Republican operatives deemed that the region was in flux politically and potentially ripe for a GOP restoration.

3. As components from other departments and agencies were transferring to DHS in late January 2003, President Bush modified the department's original organization plan. The new plan reconfigured the functions of the border security agencies going to the DHS Border and Transportation Security Directorate into two new components—the Bureau of Customs and Border Protection and the Bureau of Immigration and Customs Enforcement. Critics felt the dividing of CBP, with its inspection and border patrol functions, and ICE, with its detention and removal functions, made little sense. With respect to investigations into terrorist financing, a 13 May 2003 memorandum of agreement between DHS Secretary Tom Ridge and Attorney General John Ashcroft gave the FBI the lead role.

4. Liza Porteus, "Bush Names Homeland Security Chief," Fox News, 12 January 2005, http://www.foxnews.com/story/0,2933,143997,00.html (accessed 23 June 2011).

5. Ibid.

6. Ibid.

7. Michael Chertoff, "Remarks for Secretary Michael Chertoff, U.S. Department of Homeland Security, George Washington University Homeland Security Policy Institute," 16 March 2005, http://www.dhs.gov/xnews/speeches/speech_0245.shtm (accessed 23 June 2011).

8. Michael Chertoff, *Homeland Security: Assessing the First Five Years* (Philadelphia: University of Pennsylvania Press, 2009), p. 125.

9. Ibid.

10. Commission on the Intelligence Capabilities of the United States Regarding Weapons of Mass Destruction, *Report to the President of the United States*, 31 March 2005, p. 30.

11. Ibid., pp. 31–32.

12. Ibid., p. 32.

13. Ibid., p. 33.

14. Ibid.

15. National Response Framework, January 2008, pp. 55–57.

16. Johnson is notorious as the Navy's nemesis in 1949 for provoking the tumultuous Revolt of the Admirals with his cancellation of the postwar supercarrier in favor of the Air Force's B-36 strategic bomber. The Navy's public insubordination challenged the Truman administration's decision to favor the upstart Air Force and its Strategic Air Command over carrier aviation for conducting attacks on the Soviet Union that would include the use of atomic bombs.

17. U.S. Department of Justice, Office of Justice Programs, Bureau of Justice Assistance, "Intelligence-Led Policing: The New Intelligence Architecture," September 2005, p. 9.

18. Col. Joseph R. Fuentes, "New Jersey State Police Practical Guide to Intelligence-Led Policing," Center for Policing Terrorism (CPT) at the Manhattan Institute and Harbinger/ICx Technologies, September 2006, p. 3.

19. Chertoff, *Homeland Security*, p. 156.

20. These proposed exemptions were finalized in February 2010.

21. The Tenth Amendment to the U.S. Constitution states: "The powers not delegated to the United States by the Constitution, nor prohibited by it to the States, are reserved to the States respectively, or to the people."

22. Myers was an especially sensitive appointment politically. She had no experience in immigration matters and was not a law enforcement professional. Foremost in her political résumé, she had been Independent Counsel Kenneth Starr's lead prosecutor in the 1998 case against Susan McDougal, the wife of a Clinton associate, during the Whitewater scandal. She was also the niece of Gen. Richard Myers, USAF, chairman of the Joint Chiefs of Staff during Bush's first term, and the wife of Chertoff's first chief of staff at DHS, John F. Wood.

23. Senator Joseph Lieberman, "Statement on the Nominations of George Foresman as Under Secretary for Preparedness and Tracy Henke as Assistant Secretary for Grants and Training," 8 December 2005, http://hsgac.senate.gov/public/index. cfm?FuseAction=Press.MajorityNews&ContentRecord_id=35111e54-3735-447a-98ab-e2c5aee88b79 (accessed 29 June 2011).

24. U.S. Senate, "Nominations of George W. Foresman and Tracy A. Henke Hearing before the Committee on Homeland Security and Governmental Affairs," 8 December 2005, p. 19.

25. Ibid.

26. Department of Homeland Security, "Press Briefing by Secretary for Homeland Security Michael Chertoff and Under Secretary for Preparedness George Foresman," 25 September 2006, http://www.dhs.gov/xnews/releases/pr_1159903739058.shtm (accessed 29 June 2011).

27. Lieberman, "Statement on the Nominations."

28. Ibid.

### Chapter 6. Right of the Boom

1. Rove, *Courage and Consequence*, p. 449.

2. George W. Bush, *Decision Points* (New York: Crown Publishers, 2010), p. 310.

3. "America Humbled," *Los Angeles Times*, 8 September 2005, http://articles.latimes.com/2005/sep/04/opinion/ed-levees4 (accessed 30 July 2011).

4. White House, "Press Briefing by Homeland Security and Counterterrorism Advisor Fran Townsend," 21 October 2005, http://georgewbush-whitehouse.archives.gov/news/releases/2005/10/20051021.html (accessed 8 August 2011).

5. Morton, "Toward a Premise for Grand Strategy," p. 18. Note especially the reference to Hoover and footnote 10.

6. Bush, *Decision Points*, p. 319.

7. Prepositioned Coast Guard rescue helicopters were in Shreveport, Louisiana, and other staging areas including Mobile, Alabama. The hurricane wrecked stations in Gulfport and Pascagoula, Mississippi, and looters vandalized part of its base in New Orleans. While the Coast Guard on August 28 relocated its regional command from New Orleans to St. Louis, in advance of the storm, it had established a unified command with states and local industries. Of the 60,000 storm victims stranded in New Orleans, the Coast Guard rescued over 33,500.

8. Critics would note that Brown's proactive stance in Florida and FEMA's generous assistance reflected the administration's recognition of the importance of the state in a presidential election year, especially given its sensitivities over the recount crisis in the 2000 election that colored the Bush mandate throughout the first term.

9. The worst example was a reckless statement in the 29 August morning exchange between Matt Lauer and Brian Williams on the *NBC Today Show* that "New Orleans dodged the big bullet." Reporters then repeated this heedless headline-grabbing phrase all over the media, giving the impression to city residents that the threat to their safety had passed with the hurricane, whereas the second-order catastrophe came with the failure of the levee system and consequent flooding of the city. For its part, DHS did not establish its Federal Joint Information Center (JIC) until September 6—over a week after Hurricane Katrina made landfall. This fateful DHS failure to coordinate messages to the media left news presenters with no guidance.

10. Rove, *Courage and Consequence*, pp. 446–47.

11. Bush, *Decision Points*, p. 321.

12. Ibid., p. 326.

13. White House, "Press Briefing by Scott McClellan," 29 June 2005, http://georgewbush-whitehouse.archives.gov/news/releases/2005/06/20050629-4.html (accessed 8 August 2011).

14. The senior DHS representatives for the review were Stuart Baker, the assistant secretary for policy, and the deputy administrator of the U.S. Fire Administration, Michael O. Forgy. Since March 2001, Forgy had been the branch chief of the Homeland Security Exercise and Evaluation Program (HSEEP). At the time he was participating in the White House review, he was the DHS director of training and exercise policy.

15. White House, "Press Briefing by Homeland Security and Counterterrorism Advisor Fran Townsend," 21 October 2005.

16. In addition, Townsend was able to draw upon a number of part-time detailees for specific issues.

17. Rapuano had been serving as deputy assistant to the president and deputy homeland security advisor since June 2004, following deployment as a Marine Corps

Reserve intelligence officer in Afghanistan targeting high-value terrorist leaders for the Joint Special Operations Task Force. Originally an infantry officer, he had worked in a number of agencies to develop and implement counterterrorism and WMD policies. Previously, he had been DOE deputy undersecretary for counterterrorism, where he coordinated counterterrorism policy for its National Nuclear Security Agency and served as the department's senior point of contact with DHS. Earlier at DOE, he had been senior national security policy advisor to Secretary Spencer Abraham. In 2003, Rapuano deployed on voluntary active duty to Iraq, having served in the Pentagon with the Joint Chiefs and OSD on nonproliferation and WMD policy.

18. White House, "Press Briefing by Homeland Security and Counterterrorism Advisor Fran Townsend," 21 October 2005.

19. Ibid.

20. Ibid.

21. Ibid.

22. White House, *The Federal Response to Hurricane Katrina: Lessons Learned*, 23 February 2006, p. 2. For the purposes of this discussion, the most significant section of the report is ch. 6, "Transforming National Preparedness," pp. 65–82. In it, the review team detailed the case for transformation, as evidenced by the flawed Katrina response, and defined the elements of the National Preparedness System that its recommendations were to serve. In effect, the team grounded this vision on administration strategy documents, directives, and doctrine further to codify them by statute—as was to happen via PKEMRA.

23. Ibid., p. 68; U.S. Government Printing Office, *The National Preparedness System: What Are We Preparing For?* Hearing before the Subcommittee on Economic Development, Public Buildings, and Emergency Management of the Committee on Transportation and Infrastructure, House of Representatives, 14 April 2005, p. 2; Keith Bea, *The National Preparedness System: Issues in the 109th Congress*, CRS Report for Congress, 10 March 2005, summary page.

In an April 2005 hearing, Rep. Bill Shuster (R-PA), chairman of the Economic Development, Public Buildings, and Emergency Management Subcommittee of the House Committee on Transportation and Infrastructure, characterized the National Preparedness System saying, "In releasing Homeland Security Presidential Directives 5, 7, and 8, the President established the framework for such a system and a roadmap for achieving it. Collectively, these directives require the creation of a National Preparedness System, one that establishes a national preparedness goal, outlines the targeted capabilities required to meet that goal, lays out the tasks necessary to reach the targeted capabilities, establishes a common incident command system to utilize these capabilities to the greatest potential, and then puts together an operational plan for how all of these parts come together when they are needed, the National Response Plan."

A month before, the Congressional Research Service listed six foundational documents. "Work on the NPS [National Preparedness System] stems from authority set out in the Homeland Security Act of 2002 (P.L. 107-296), the DHS appropriations legislation for FY2005 (P.L. 108-334), and executive directives issued by President Bush. Six basic documents comprise the NPS. First, the draft National Preparedness Goal (NPG) sets a general goal for national preparedness, identifies the means of measuring such preparedness, and establishes national preparedness priorities. Second, 15 planning scenarios set forth examples of catastrophic situations to which non-federal agencies are expected to be able to respond. Third, the Universal Task List (UTL) identifies specific tasks that federal agencies, and non-federal agencies as appropriate, would be expected to undertake. Fourth, the Target Capabilities List identifies 36 areas in which responding agencies are expected to be proficient in order to meet the expectations set out in the UTL. Fifth, the National Response Plan (NRP) sets out the framework through which federal agencies (and voluntary agencies) operate when a catastrophe occurs. Sixth, the National Incident Management System (NIMS) identifies standard operating procedures and approaches to be used by respondent agencies as they work to manage the consequences of a catastrophe. These documents (and other ancillary agreements) are intended to establish a national system to ensure that the response to a catastrophe will be as efficient and effective as possible."

24. White House, "Press Briefing by Homeland Security and Counterterrorism Advisor Fran Townsend," p. 66.

25. Ibid., p. 67.

26. Ibid., p. 52.

27. Ibid., p. 70.

28. Ibid., p. 68.

29. Ibid., p. 79.

30. Ibid., p. 69.

31. Ibid., p. 67.

32. Ibid., p. 54.

33. Ibid., p. 70.

34. Ibid., p. 53.

35. Ibid., p. 72.

36. Ibid., p. 73.

37. U.S. House of Representatives, *A Failure of Initiative: The Final Report of the Select Bipartisan Committee to Investigate the Preparations for and Response to Hurricane Katrina*, 15 February 2006.

38. "Fixing FEMA," *PBS News Hour*, 13 February 2006, http://www.pbs.org/newshour/bb/fedagencies/jan-june06/fema_2-13.html (accessed 7 August 2011).

39. Lamont is the great-grandson of the influential Progressive financier Thomas W. Lamont, partner of J. P. Morgan, who was instrumental in drafting the Dawes and Young Plans, the two post–World War I mechanisms for settling German

reparations and which led to the establishment of the International Bank of Settlements. His father was an economist who worked on the Marshall Plan.

40. In November, Lieberman would win re-election with 70 percent of Republicans supporting him. He thereupon struck a deal with the Democratic leadership allowing him to keep his seniority and the chair of the Homeland Security and Governmental Affairs Committee, given that the 2006 elections gave Democrats the majority in the Senate.

### Chapter 7. The New FEMA

1. The initial language of the legislation put some DHS offices with homeland security protection functions into FEMA as well, i.e., the Office of Infrastructure Protection, the National Communications System, and the Office of National Capital Region Coordination. DHS and the law enforcement community lobbied hard to keep those offices in DHS. Some language was removed, largely due to the efforts of the Republican senator from New Hampshire, Judd Gregg, who sat on the Senate Judiciary Committee and was very tight with law enforcement. In the end, only the Office of National Capital Region Coordination transferred to FEMA and its National Preparedness Directorate.

2. In May, Robert Jamison relieved him as acting undersecretary for the national protection and programs. A transportation security official, Jamison had been deputy administrator at TSA, the agency's chief operating officer, and had served for over three years as the deputy administrator of the Department of Transportation's Federal Transit Administration. During that time, he led TSA's transit security program and its $4.5 billion Lower Manhattan transportation recovery operation, established following 9/11. In 2005, he had the title acting administrator of the Federal Railroad Administration. He had also served as manager of the National Communications System when it transferred from DoD to the DHS Information Analysis and Infrastructure Protection Directorate. Earlier in his career, Jamison was the senior operations officer for the American Red Cross.

3. Eileen Sullivan, "Foresman Resignation Follows DHS Decision to Eliminate New Preparedness," *CQ Homeland Security*, 30 March 2007, http://www.voicesofseptember11.org/dev/content.php?idtocitems=ForesmanResignation (accessed 12 August 2011.)

4. As per HSPD-8, "The term 'preparedness' refers to the existence of plans, procedures, policies, training, and equipment necessary at the Federal, State, and local level to maximize the ability to prevent, respond to, and recover from major events. The term 'readiness' is used interchangeably with preparedness."

5. The battle of the badges continues to frustrate NIMS implementation within law enforcement, which sees the ICS culture as better suited to the fire service, which tends to operate more collaboratively whereas police officers tend to function independently from the patrol car.

6. With the Kennedy administration, the military additionally prepared for counterinsurgency, which by the time of the 1986 Goldwater-Nichols legislation had transmuted to what was called special operations/low intensity conflict (SO/LIC).

7. U.S. Coast Guard, *U.S. Coast Guard: America's Maritime Guardian*, Coast Guard Publication 1, 1 January 2002, p. 1.

8. Ibid., p. 52.

9. U.S. Coast Guard Press Release, "Success through Preparation, Teamwork, Prevention: First-of-Its-Kind Task Force Prevents Exodus, Saves Lives," n.d., http://www.d7publicaffairs.com/external/?fuseaction=external.docview&cid= 586&pressID=43272 (accessed 15 September 2011).

10. The U.S. policy was to exercise operational force in a repatriation that would be highly visible in order to send a strong message to potential migrants that a transit to Florida by sea was not achievable. HSTF-SE completed the first interdictions and repatriations on February 27 that resulted in the rescue and return of 531 migrants to Haiti. Two other boats ferrying 336 migrants were also stopped that day. By mid-March, DHS had repatriated 905 Haitians. When it concluded, Able Sentry had rescued and repatriated some 1,500 Haitians with no loss of life at sea, thus successfully preventing the mass migration.

11. This arrangement, though successful in Able Sentry, led to the bureaucratic backlash among DHS legacy law enforcement components that sank the Ridge/ Lawlor/Stephan regional empowerment plan in late 2004.

12. Dennis Schrader, "Unfinished Business at FEMA: A National Preparedness Perspective," Heritage Lectures, Number 1125, 26 June 2009, p. 2, http://www. heritage.org/research/lecture/unfinished-business-at-fema-a-national-preparedness-perspective (accessed 14 September 2011).

13. The FBI would pay for their overtime and provide vehicles.

14. By February 2009, Oberstar would have twenty-nine co-sponsors, yet having neither the support of the Obama administration nor the Senate, his measure never made it to the House floor.

15. *The Federal Response to Hurricane Katrina: Lessons Learned*, p. 92.

16. To the extent he succeeded, the NRF references Pub 1 in a footnote. See footnote 10, *National Response Framework*, p. 9.

17. Department of Homeland Security, *Nationwide Plan Review Phase 2 Report*, 16 June 2006, p. viii.

18. Ibid., p. 79.

19. U.S. Government Printing Office, *The Stafford Act: A Plan for the Nation's Emergency Preparedness and Response System*, Hearing before the Committee on Environment and Public Works, U.S. Senate, 27 July 2006.

20. *National Response Framework*, pp. 2–3.

21. Ibid., p. 8.

22. Ibid.

**Chapter 8. DHS OPS, FEMA, and the Mandate for Operational Planning**

1. *National Response Framework*, p. 72.
2. *The Federal Response to Hurricane Katrina: Lessons Learned*, p. 69.
3. Ibid., p. 89.
4. Ibid., p. 46.
5. When published in January 2009, the Integrated Planning System document stated that IPS replaced NPES. See Department of Homeland Security, *The Integrated Planning System*, January 2009, p. iiin3.
6. As per NSPD-51/HSPD-20, National Essential Functions are a subset of Government Functions that are necessary to lead and sustain the Nation during a catastrophic emergency and must be supported through COOP and COG capabilities. The eight NEFs are: (1) Ensuring the continued functioning of our form of government under the Constitution, including the functioning of the three separate branches of government; (2) Providing leadership visible to the Nation and the world and maintaining the trust and confidence of the American people; (3) Defending the Constitution of the United States against all enemies, foreign and domestic, and preventing or interdicting attacks against the United States or its people, property, or interests; (4) Maintaining and fostering effective relationships with foreign nations; (5) Protecting against threats to the homeland and bringing to justice perpetrators of crimes or attacks against the United States or its people, property, or interests; (6) Providing rapid and effective response to and recovery from the domestic consequences of an attack or other incident; (7) Protecting and stabilizing the Nation's economy and ensuring public confidence in its financial systems; and (8) Providing for critical Federal Government services that address the national health, safety, and welfare needs of the United States.
7. National Strategy for Homeland Security, p. 3.
8. OPS was only able to generate a short, pre-decisional paper outlining the National Homeland Security Plan that did not get any traction in the transition to the Obama administration.
9. Christine E. Wormuth, *Managing the Next Domestic Catastrophe: Ready (or Not)? A Beyond Goldwater-Nichols Phase 4 Report* (Washington, DC: CSIS Press, June 2008), p. 48.
10. FEMA provides a technical assistance software tool for game planning called the Synchronization Matrix to support emergency plan development.
11. U.S. Government Printing Office, *The National Preparedness System: What Are We Preparing For?* Hearing before the Subcommittee on Economic Development, Public Buildings, and Emergency Management of the Committee on Transportation and Infrastructure, House of Representatives, 14 April 2005, pp. 9–10.
12. Vice Adm. Thad Allen, the second principal federal official for the Katrina response, told Congress that the National Response Plan as written did not contemplate an event on such a massive scale. See *A Nation Still Unprepared*, p. 554.

13. Larry Gispert, "The Federal Emergency Management Agency: Is the Agency on the Right Track?" Testimony before the Subcommittee on Homeland Security Committee on Appropriations, U.S. House of Representatives, 13 March 2008, http://www.iaem.com/publications/news/documents/IAEM LarryGispert031308.pdf (accessed 29 October 2011).

14. Larry J. Gispert, "From the President—Remain Vigilant Concerning New U.S. Integrated Planning System," *Bulletin of the International Association of Emergency Managers* (June 2008).

15. Gispert, "The Federal Emergency Management Agency: Is the Agency on the Right Track?"

16. Prior to IPS implementation, the federal interagency community developed incident response plans between September 2006 and December 2007 for the Improvised Nuclear Device, Terrorist Use of Explosives, Pandemic Influenza, Radiological Dispersal Device, Major Hurricane, and Cyber Attack scenarios. Some departments and agencies thus already had operational plans for certain scenarios. IPS did not require redrafting of these operational plans, only that such plans be compatible with the strategic and concept of operations plans developed using IPS.

17. *The Integrated Planning System*, pp. iii–iv.

18. Ibid., pp. 1–2.

19. Ibid., pp. 4–8.

20. Regional Catastrophic Preparedness Grant Program (RCPGP), http://www.fema.gov/government/grant/rcp/index08.shtm.

21. See Wormuth, *Managing the Next Domestic Catastrophe: Ready (or Not)?* p. 81.

22. *The Integrated Planning System*, pp. 4–6.

**Chapter 9:.The Homeland Security Enterprise**

1. As referenced in Chapter 7, Corey Gruber, then the lead for the DHS Preparedness Directorate's National Preparedness Task Force, first used the term "homeland security enterprise" publicly in a 2006 Senate hearing on the Stafford Act and HSPD-8.

2. White House Office of the Press Secretary, "Statement by the President on the White House Organization for Homeland Security and Counterterrorism," 26 May 2009.

3. The 13 February 2009 Presidential Policy Directive 1 (PPD-1), Organization of the National Security Council System, maintained the Principals Committee and Deputies Committee but replaced the system of assistant secretary–level Policy Coordinating Committees with Interagency Policy Committees (IPCs) to serve as "the main day-to-day fora for interagency coordination of national security policy."

4. White House, *National Security Strategy*, May 2010, p. 12.

5. Ibid., p. 15.

6. Ibid., pp. 18–19.
7. Department of Homeland Security, *Quadrennial Homeland Security Review Report: A Strategic Framework for a Secure Homeland (QHSR)*, 1 February 2010, p. viin1.
8. Ibid., p. viii.
9. Ibid.
10. Ibid., p. ix.
11. Department of Homeland Security, *Bottom-Up Review Report*, July 2010, p. viii.
12. Ibid., p. 31.
13. *QHSR*, p. 71.
14. Ibid., p. 72.
15. BUR, p. 32.
16. See Local, State, Tribal, and Federal Preparedness Task Force, *Perspective on Preparedness: Taking Stock since 9/11*, September 2010, p. 1.
17. Subject matter expertise came from such thought leaders as Matt Bettenhausen, secretary of the California Emergency Management Agency; Ann Beauchesne, vice president of the U.S. Chamber of Commerce's National Security and Emergency Preparedness Department; Jim Caverly of the DHS Office of Infrastructure Protection; and Ellen Gordon, associate director of the Naval Postgraduate School's Center for Homeland Defense and Security and former president of the National Emergency Management Association. Gordon was in the running to succeed Dave Paulison as FEMA administrator, the post that went to Craig Fugate.
18. The first was a task-force-defined area of cross-cutting and foundational emphasis it called "strategic investments" to provide outstanding outcomes for minimal investment.
19. *Perspective on Preparedness: Taking Stock Since 9/11*, p. ix.
20. Ibid., p. 31.
21. Ibid., p. x.
22. Ibid.
23. Ibid., p. 33.
24. Ibid., p. 34.
25. See ibid., pp. 21, 49.
26. See ibid., pp. x, 28.
27. Ibid., pp. 29, 31.
28. Ibid., pp. x, 27.
29. Ibid., p. 29.
30. Ibid., pp. 34–35. It could be argued that these broad issues are more appropriately regionally determined, as opposed to federal-centric, where the RACs serve as the regional focal points that the FEMA Headquarters NAC supports, as opposed to vice versa. The report's example of a futures analysis working group was actually a state-level body, Alaska's Climate Change Sub-Cabinet, a broad-based

collaborative approach to addressing the challenge of climate change using long-range assessment and analysis for development of an intergovernmental and collaborative strategy to manage the short- and long-term risks of climate change.

31. Ibid., pp. 36, 49. With respect to typing and inventorying assets, the task force said, "More uniform usage of common capability types and visibility into a national resource inventory, coupled with improved assessment methods, will ease the challenge of aggregating the complex landscape of nationwide preparedness data into authoritative conclusions about progress made, and at what cost in time and resources. Through proposed enhancements to the high-level policy and guidance process, those conclusions can be integrated with global intelligence, including futures analysis, in order to determine new preparedness priorities."

32. Ibid., p. 38. EMAP is an independent nonprofit entity providing a standard-based voluntary assessment and peer review accreditation process for government programs that coordinate prevention, mitigation, preparedness, response, and recovery activities for natural and human-caused disasters. EMAP accreditation is based on program compliance with collaboratively developed national standards, the EMAP-facilitated Emergency Management Standard.

33. Although FEMA had the lead for preparedness, DHS Policy was able to argue for PPD-8 language that directs the secretary of homeland security to develop the National Preparedness Goal. In any case, the White House is not normally willing to issue a directive to the head of a component agency in a department. Rather the directive is to the cabinet level where the responsibility to execute gets delegated, in this case from Janet Napolitano to Craig Fugate to Tim Manning as the head of FEMA's National Preparedness Directorate.

34. FEMA's National Preparedness Directorate is not responsible for preparedness of the mitigation mission. That responsibility lies with FEMA's Federal Insurance and Mitigation Administration (FIMA). FIMA manages the National Flood Insurance Program (NFIP) and a range of programs designed to reduce future losses to homes, businesses, schools, public buildings, and critical facilities from floods, earthquakes, tornadoes, and other natural disasters.

35. Jared T. Brown, *Presidential Policy Directive 8 and the National Preparedness System: Background and Issues for Congress*, Congressional Research Service Report for Congress, 21 October 2011, p. 19.

36. Ibid.

37. The National Infrastructure Protection Plan was a baseline document for this framework.

38. Brown, *Presidential Policy Directive 8*, p. 17.

39. The six RSFs and their lead federal coordinating agencies are: Community Planning and Capacity Building Recovery Support Function (FEMA), Economic Recovery Support Function (Commerce), Health and Social Services Recovery Support Function (HHS), Housing Recovery Support Function (HUD), Infrastructure Systems Recovery Support Function (U.S. Army Corps of Engineers),

and Natural and Cultural Resources Recovery Support Function (Interior). Just as the National Response Framework provided for an FCO, a federal coordinating officer, the NDRF established a federal disaster recovery coordinator (FDRC).

40. See *QHSR*, p. ix.
41. PPD-8, p. 2.
42. Presidential Policy Directive/PPD-8 Draft—National Preparedness Goal Review Package, accessible via the International Association of Emergency Managers (IAEM) Web site, http://www.iaem.com/committees/governmentaffairs/docu ments/NPG_DRAFT_20110822_for_review.pdf (accessed 25 November 2011), p. 6; Brown, *Presidential Policy Directive 8*, p. 19.
43. Brown, *Presidential Policy Directive 8*, p. 9.
44. Department of Homeland Security, *National Preparedness Goal*, 1st ed., September 2011, p. 4.
45. Ibid., pp. 3–4.
46. See the discussion in Brown, *Presidential Policy Directive 8*, pp. 4–5.
47. Craig Fugate, Testimony before the United States House Subcommittee on Homeland Security on FEMA's Fiscal Year 2011 Budget, 10 March 2010, http://www.dhs.gov/ynews/testimony/testimony_1274285305684.shtm (accessed 27 November 2011).

## Chapter 10. The Intergovernmental Dimensions of the Homeland Security Enterprise

1. The same day the Okaloosa commissioners took their vote, elsewhere Governor Bobby Jindal (R-LA) ordered his National Guard to start building barrier islands off the Louisiana coast independent of coordination with Unified Command.
2. Lee Hamilton and Thomas Kean, *Tenth Anniversary Report Card: The Status of the 9/11 Commission Recommendations* (Washington, DC: Bipartisan Policy Center National Security Preparedness Group, September 2011), p. 12. The Bipartisan Policy Center's National Security Preparedness Group was an outgrowth of the 9/11 Commission and was tasked to monitor implementation of its broad policy recommendations. (NB: Admiral Allen served as the national incident commander as the Commandant until his retirement in May 2010. Thereafter, he continued to serve in that role as a DHS official.)
3. Ibid.
4. National League of Cities, "Is the Federal-State-Local Partnership Being Dismantled? Roundtable Proceedings," *Research Report on America's Cities* (Washington, DC: NLC Press, 2003), p. iii. Cited in William H. Austin, "The United States Department of Homeland Security Concept of Regionalization— Will It Survive the Test?" master's thesis for the Center for Homeland Defense and Security, Naval Postgraduate School (September 2006), p. 19.
5. Over 65,000 residential units were damaged, representing over 350,000 units of multifamily housing and almost 65,000 units of single-family housing. The

supplemental HUD appropriation for the Northridge Earthquake was for almost $900 million. Cisneros got authority to waive requirements or specify new ones for any statute or regulation that applied for the use of these funds.

6. Among his many other activities after government service, Cisneros was on the board of the National Smart Growth Council. This bipartisan coalition of some one hundred nonprofit organizations represents the environment, historic preservation, housing affordability, social equity, land conservation, neighborhood redevelopment, farmland protection, business, labor, public health, and town planning and design communities to advance planning alternatives to urban sprawl. A proponent of inner-city revitalization, Cisneros serves on the Partnership for Sustainable Communities Leadership Advisory Council, an urban policy and regional planning initiative launched in 2009 by HUD, the Department of Transportation, and EPA to coordinate federal grant programs for housing, transportation, and energy efficiency.

7. National Academy of Public Administration, *Advancing Management of Homeland Security: Managing Intergovernmental Relations for Homeland Security* (Washington, DC: NAPA, February 2004), p. 10, cited in Austin, "The United States Department of Homeland Security Concept of Regionalization—Will It Survive the Test?" p. 19.

8. Austin, "The United States Department of Homeland Security Concept of Regionalization—Will It Survive the Test?" p. 25.

9. Ibid., quoting Christopher Bellavita, "What Is Preventing Homeland Security," *Homeland Security Affairs*, no. 1 (Summer 2005): p. 9. Writing in 2005, Bellavita expressed rather caustically his view that the federal mind-set in the homeland security policy development process was top-down and controlling: "Most homeland security guidance documents are the product of this hierarchical mentality. . . . Because this is the 21st century, however, it is necessary to get 'input from the locals.' [Hence,] the well-meaning efforts at inclusion are largely unconvincing to those on the front lines of homeland security" (Bellavita, p. 7).

10. Now called the National Civic League, the headquarters are in Denver.

11. PACIC fuses information from the Federal Bureau of Investigation, DHS and its Immigration and Customs Enforcement, Justice's Drug Enforcement Agency and Bureau of Alcohol Tobacco and Firearms, Pennsylvania's Office of the Attorney General and Department of Corrections, and the New York City Police Department.

12. For example, mutual aid in a snow emergency might involve an Emergency Support Function 3 (ESF-3, Public Works and Engineering) request for plow trucks. The NIMS-typed resource definitions succinctly specify four "types" according to minimum capabilities expressed by style and gross vehicle weight (GVW) in pounds: TYPE I: Style—tandem axle, GVW—46,000+; TYPE II: Style—Single Axle; GVW—20,000–33,000; TYPE III: Style—1 Ton Truck; GVW—15,000; TYPE IV: Style—Pickup Truck; GVW—9,500.

13. The Conference Report accompanying the 2006 DHS Appropriations Act states the following with regard to units of local government: "[A]ny county, city, village, town, district, borough, parish, port authority, transit authority, intercity rail provider, commuter rail system, freight rail provider, water district, regional planning commission, council of government, Indian tribe with jurisdiction over Indian country, authorized tribal organization, Alaska Native village, independent authority, special district, or other political subdivision of any state shall constitute a 'local unit of government.'"

14. Oak Ridge National Laboratory, for example, has a collaborative partnership with Oak Ridge Associated Universities (ORAU) to enhance nationwide scientific research and education. ORAU is a 101-member university consortium that brings together university faculty and students to collaborate and partner with other national laboratories, government agencies, and private industry. ORAU's National Security and Emergency Management program provides federal, state, and local governmental agencies with emergency planning and operational support for their all-hazard emergency preparedness and response capabilities. ORAU's Radiation Emergency Medicine program offers hands-on training and deployable teams to emergency personnel responsible for medical management of radiation incidents—from medical advice and specialized continuing education courses to on-site assistance.

15. In 2011, CARRI started piloting its Web-based Community Resilience System assessment tool in seven communities nationwide: Anaheim, California; Anne Arundel County and Annapolis, Maryland; Charleston and the Tri-County Area, South Carolina; Gadsden, Alabama; Greenwich, Connecticut; the Mississippi Gulf Coast; and Mount Juliet, Tennessee.

16. See Jennie M. Temple, "Enhancing Regional Collaboration—Taking the Next Step," master's thesis for the Center for Homeland Defense and Security, Naval Postgraduate School (March 2007), p. 16. For a complete list of theses by participants in the Master's Degree Program at CHDS from 2002 to 2008, see "Master's Degree Program Participants and Thesis Titles," Appendix A in Center for Homeland Defense and Security, *Education: The Key to Homeland Security Leadership, 2002–2008 Report* (Monterey, CA: Naval Postgraduate School, 2009), pp. 43–67.

17. Austin, "The United States Department of Homeland Security Concept of Regionalization—Will It Survive the Test?" p. 3.

18. Ibid., p. 48.

19. Ibid., p. 73: "Under the current ambiguous situation, networks are talked about, but undermined through federal policy that forces relationships based on functional responsibility instead of a natural community of interest."

20. Ibid., p. 31.

21. National Association of Development Organizations, *Regional Approaches to Homeland Security Planning and Preparedness—Survey of the Nation's Regional*

*Development Organizations* (Washington, DC: NADO, August 2005), p. 1, cited in Austin, "The United States Department of Homeland Security Concept of Regionalization—Will It Survive the Test?" p. 71.

22. Ibid., p. 2, cited in Austin, "The United States Department of Homeland Security Concept of Regionalization—Will It Survive the Test?" p. 71.

23. Austin, "The United States Department of Homeland Security Concept of Regionalization—Will It Survive the Test?" p. 26. This approach is consistent with the European Union's subsidiarity principle: the appropriate level for bottom-up governance over a matter is at the smallest, lowest, or least centralized competent unit.

24. Ibid., p. 32.

25. Ibid., p. 33.

26. Ibid., p. 17.

27. Robert Agranoff, "A New Look at the Value-Adding Functions of Intergovernmental Networks," paper prepared for Seventh Annual National Public Management Research Conference at Georgetown University, 9 October 2003 (Bloomington, IN: Indiana University, 2003), p. 7, cited in Austin, "The United States Department of Homeland Security Concept of Regionalization—Will It Survive the Test?" p. 26.

28. Donald P. Moynihan, *From Forest Fires to Hurricane Katrina: Case Studies of Incident Command Systems* (Washington, DC: IBM Center for The Business of Government, 2007), p. 6.

29. NIMS FEMA 501/Draft, August 2007, p. 50.

30. Ibid.

31. Ibid., p. 47.

32. Donald P. Moynihan, *Leveraging Collaborative Networks in Infrequent Emergency Situations* (Washington, DC: IBM Center for The Business of Government, June 2005), p. 7.

33. National Response Framework, January 2008, p. 10.

34. NIMS FEMA 501/Draft, p. 45.

35. Donald F. Kettl, *System under Stress: Homeland Security and American Politics* (Washington, DC: CQ Press, 2004), p. 90.

36. Hamilton and Kean, *Tenth Anniversary Report Card*, pp. 12–13.

**Chapter 11. The Case for a Regionally Based National Preparedness System**

1. While HSPD-8 and PPD-8 speak of DHS, FEMA is the department's executive agent for preparedness policy and doctrine. However, while the agency has statutory responsibility for the National Preparedness System, it does not have directive authority to manage it.

2. FEMA, *National Preparedness System Description* (November 2011), p. 1.

3. See *National Security Strategy* (May 2010), pp. 18–19, and Local, State, Tribal, and Federal Preparedness Task Force, *Perspective on Preparedness: Taking Stock since 9/11* (September 2010), p. 33.

4. FEMA, *National Preparedness System Description*, p. 1. The National Preparedness System now speaks of "threats and hazards, including acts of terrorism, cyber attacks, pandemics, and catastrophic natural disasters" that inform risk.

5. Ibid., p. 2: THIRA "guidance currently under development will provide a common, consistent approach for identifying and assessing risks and associated impacts." The term "THIRA" assumed importance once FEMA included it in the FY11 Homeland Security Grant Program guidance: "In order to qualify for FY 2011 funding, all grantees shall develop and maintain a THIRA." While FEMA is developing a Comprehensive Preparedness Guide supplement to aid in the conduct of THIRAs and other risk assessments, the agency as of 2011 had released no specific guidance on how to do a THIRA to meet the requirements of a grant. The guidance did say, however, that current state Hazard Identification and Risk Assessments developed for the Pre-Disaster Mitigation (PDM) or Hazard Mitigation Grant Program (HMGP) that have a terrorism component would satisfy the FY11 State Homeland Security Program and UASI grant requirements.

6. See *EMAP Standard* (Lexington, KY: Emergency Management Accreditation Program, September 2007), pp. 5–9, 11–12, for a discussion of HIRA as an EMAP voluntary standard for planning. EMAP is a tool for continuous improvement as part of a voluntary accreditation process for local and state emergency management programs. EMAP is an evolving process—thirty-two programs are currently EMAP accredited as of October 2011: twenty-six states, the District of Columbia, three counties, one parish, and the Consolidated City/County of Jacksonville/Duval, Florida. Five programs are on conditional accreditation. The EMAP program began in 2007 and functions under the auspices of the EMAP Commission, whose members are appointed by the National Emergency Management Association and the International Association of Emergency Managers.

7. National Association of Public Administration, *Advancing the Management of Homeland Security: Managing Intergovernmental Relations for Homeland Security* (A NAPA Forum of Homeland Security Executive Report, February 2004), pp. 5, 19.

8. DHS, in cooperation with the Department of Transportation, *Nationwide Plan Review: Phase II Report* (16 June 2006), p. xi.

9. PKEMRA §641(1) defined capability as "the ability to provide the means to accomplish one or more tasks under specific conditions and to specific performance standards. A capability may be achieved with any combination of properly planned, organized, equipped, trained, and exercised personnel that achieves the intended outcome." The *National Preparedness System Description* (p. 1) said, "Capabilities are the means to accomplish a mission, function, or objective based on the performance of related tasks, under specified conditions, to target levels of performance."

10. Another argument can be made, however, with respect to generic categories of events, such as a nuclear detonation/dirty bomb/high-casualty WMD, large-scale

hurricane, earthquake, or pandemic disease outbreak. Where these scenarios might take place in high-density population areas with the likelihood of high casualties and significant impact on the national economy, the federal government would be prudent to look through the lens of capabilities-based planning.

11. These risk and threat analyses are especially difficult when it comes to terrorist scenarios that as yet have no precedent and thus no objective basis for quantifiable measurement.

12. The *National Response Framework* of January 2008 (p. 27) illustrates the so-called Preparedness Cycle for capability-building, which begins with planning. The Preparedness Cycle consists of: Planning → Organizing, Training, and Equipping → Exercising → Evaluating and Improving.

13. The same argument for realistic risk assessment applies to the Gap Analysis Tool, the TCL, and other such federal approaches. If a jurisdiction does not feel that the Gap Analysis reflects realistic preparedness goals for that jurisdiction's risk, then it will put minimal effort into the analysis.

14. The terms homeland security preparedness grants are comprehensive and cover those grants originating in DHS, FEMA, HHS, CDC, Department of Justice, and Department of Agriculture. Of this $35 billion, some $30 billion have been DHS/FEMA monies.

15. Some even question whether outcomes should be measured at all, what level of government should do the measuring, and whether it is ever possible to reach a satisfactory end state agreed on by all levels of government.

16. Expressed in terms of a percentage of state and local homeland security budgets, federal homeland security grants represent a very small fraction of total state and local homeland security expenditures.

17. Nothing significant has changed in the four years since the AFPR study, nor was it ever used effectively to reduce state and local burdens.

18. Traditionally, FEMA preparedness programs have taken the form of cooperative agreements, e.g., the Chemical Stockpile Emergency Preparedness Program. The use of DHS and FEMA preparedness grants for the most part derived from the Justice Department Office of Justice Programs' practice of awarding formula grants, e.g., Community Oriented Policing Services (COPS) grants, to state agencies, which in turn sub-grant funds to various units of state and local government.

19. As is well known, the statutory 80/20 pass-through requirement for grant funds from states to local jurisdictions has fostered more of an adversarial than collaborative relationship. Solid data to support an across-the-board national 80/20 mandate is absent and does not distinguish between those states that need more resourcing of state-level capability from those that don't. States see the rule as counterproductive to state-wide planning. In addition, since 9/11, states may only apply 3 percent of their grants to management and administration of grant programs. The Senate version of the FY10 Homeland Security Appropriations Bill raised that limit to 5 percent, which was resolved in conference.

20. See Donald P. Moynihan, *From Forest Fires to Hurricane Katrina: Case Studies of Incident Command Systems* (Washington, DC: IBM Center for The Business of Government, 2007), p. 6.

### Chapter 12. The Fulcrum of Network Federal Security Governance

1. FEMA, *Regional-National Preparedness Concept of Operations* (8 February 2008), p. 3.
2. Ibid., p. 6.
3. Ibid., p. 23.
4. Ibid., p. 11.
5. FEMA, *FEMA Strategic Plan for FY 2011–2014, Frequently Asked Questions* (15 March 2011), http://www.fema.gov/about/2011_14_strategic_plan_faq.shtm (accessed 28 December 2011).
6. FEMA, *Regional-National Preparedness Concept of Operations*, p. 8.
7. FEMA characterizes SimCell as an exercise area where controllers generate and deliver injects, and receive player responses to non-participating organizations, agencies, and individuals who would likely participate actively in an actual incident. Physically, the SimCell is a working location for a number of qualified professionals who portray representatives of non-participating organizations, agencies, and individuals that would likely participate during an actual incident.
8. FEMA, *Regional-National Preparedness Concept of Operations*, p. 19.
9. DHS/FEMA Regional Advisory Council, http://www.fema.gov/about/regions/regionviii/records/charter_060807.shtm (accessed 16 January 2012).
10. Region III Regional Advisory Council, http://www.fema.gov/txt/about/regions/regioniii/jan_2011_rac_charter.txt (accessed 16 January 2012).
11. Ibid.
12. FEMA, *Regional-National Preparedness Concept of Operations*, p. 27.

### Chapter 13. Moving Toward an Intergovernmental Homeland Security Professional Cadre

1. Some might note that perhaps the development of strategic nuclear policy was an exception. However, this realm was never purely military. Civilian scientists and technology developers in the national labs and their analytical allies in think tanks like RAND had as much to do—if not more so—with strategic policy development as did the military. Moreover, beyond wargaming, those policies—fortunately—were never operationally tested or executed.
2. For a concise overview of interagency workforce reform efforts since World War II, see Catherine Dale, "Building an Interagency Cadre of National Security Professionals: Proposals, Recent Experience, and Issues for Congress" (Congressional Research Service Report for Congress, 8 July 2008, RL34565), pp. 2–5.
3. Ibid., p. 5.

4. White House, "Transforming National Preparedness," ch. 6 in *Federal Response to Hurricane Katrina: Lessons Learned* (Washington, DC: White House, 2006), http://www.globalsecurity.org/security/library/report/2006/katrina-lessons_wh_060223_ch6.htm.

5. Homeland security personnel are a subset of NSPs. Though not necessarily exclusively, their missions and functions are in the realm of "borders-in" national security.

6. White House, "Transforming National Preparedness," ch. 6 in *Federal Response to Hurricane Katrina*.

7. White House, *National Strategy for the Development of National Security Professionals* (July 2007), p. 2.

8. These missions or functions are established by law, regulation, executive order, or policy guidance. Federal departments/agencies that have homeland security missions or functions are those having Emergency Support Function roles or responsibilities for executing the National Infrastructure Protection Plan. In the case of federal law enforcement agencies, these components have well-established primary functions like drug, gun, alcohol, and smuggling enforcement. However, in the post-9/11 climate, they now are attuned to looking beyond their primary missions into secondary/collateral intelligence functions and determining any connection to national security matters including terrorism and the activities of hostile foreign services. Normally, such information—if identified—is provided to FBI Joint Terrorism Task Forces for operational exploitation in an interagency setting of federal, state, local, and tribal representatives.

9. Homeland security broadly encompasses the emergency management, public health, and other professional communities.

10. See NSPD Executive Steering Committee (ESC), *National Security Professional Development Implementation Plan* (1 August 2008), p. 8.

11. *National Response Framework* (January 2008), p. 10.

12. Department of Homeland Security, *Quadrennial Homeland Security Review Report (QHSR)* (February 2010), p. 12.

13. Ibid.

14. Ibid., p. 36.

15. Ibid., p. 71.

16. Ibid., pp. 71–72.

17. Ibid., p. 72.

18. *NRF*, p. 1.

19. Ibid., p. 7.

20. *NIMS*, p. 3.

21. Ibid.

22. Ibid., p. 1.

23. Ibid., p. 3.

24. UASIs are the sixty-four highest-risk major metropolitan areas across the country, which are eligible to receive FEMA grants to support regional preparedness collaboration.

25. Before a wildland firefighter can assume duty, he/she must earn a Red Card, issued by the National Wildfire Coordinating Group. Red Cards offer information about the firefighter and his/her level of training.

### Chapter 14. Homeland Security Professional Development

1. DHS regards the years of experience indicated in its DHS INSP Workforce Development Plan as for illustrative purposes only until such time when the population may be properly analyzed to adjust and record expected experience and time factors.

2. NDPC has seven members, including the Center for Domestic Preparedness (CDP) in Anniston, Alabama, the New Mexico Institute of Mining and Technology (New Mexico Tech), Louisiana State University's Academy of Counter-Terrorist Education (National Center for Biomedical Research and Training), Texas A&M University National Emergency Response and Rescue Training Center (TEEX), the Department of Energy's Nevada Test Site (NTS), the Transportation Technology Center, Inc. (TTCI), and the National Disaster Preparedness Training Center at the University of Hawaii (NDPTC).

3. White House, *National Strategy for the Development of National Security Professionals* (July 2007), p. 2.

4. Ibid., p. 5.

5. Depending on context, the terms "national security" and "emergency management" can have very precise meanings. In the context of career paths and professional development, national security personnel *routinely* require access and permissions, as distinct from other broadly defined homeland security personnel who do not.

6. White House, *National Strategy for the Development of National Security Professionals* (July 2007), p. 2.

7. Ibid., p. 7.

8. Ibid., p. 5.

9. Cheryl J. Polson, John M. Persyn, and O. Shawn Cupp, "Partnership in Progress: A Model for Development of a Homeland Security Graduate Degree Program," *Homeland Security Affairs* 6, no. 2 (May 2010): p. 5, http://www.hsaj.org/pages/volume6/issue2/pdfs/6.2.3.pdf.

10. In 1996, Congress authorized the Nunn-Lugar-Domenici Domestic Preparedness Program as part of the Defense Reauthorization Act. This domestic preparedness program focused on enhancing the ability of local and state governments to respond to a weapon of mass destruction (WMD) incident, with a particular emphasis on terrorism. Elements of the program consisted of advanced training, equipment, and exercises for local first responders. While FEMA was the

lead agency for "consequence management" in response to acts of terrorism, Nunn-Lugar did not assign that agency as the lead agency for managing the program. Instead, Congress gave the DoD that task. Nunn-Lugar was the immediate legacy program of the homeland security preparedness programs of today. While the lead went to DoD, other federal agencies also played a role in the new domestic preparedness program. This included FEMA, the FBI, HHS, DOE, and EPA. At the time, FEMA chaired the Senior Interagency Coordination Group on Terrorism, which was established to facilitate better federal interagency coordination on policy issues and program activities focusing on WMD response. Eventually in the late 1990s, DOJ through the assistant attorney general for the Office of Justice Programs would manage the preparedness program through the Office for State and Local Domestic Preparedness Support, which later became the Office for Domestic Preparedness. The National Domestic Preparedness Office (NDPO), housed in the FBI, inherited oversight of the Nunn-Lugar-Domenici "train-the-trainer" programs for states and localities. At that time, FEMA declined the opportunity to assume the national-preparedness mission.

11. Center for Homeland Defense and Security, *Education: The Key to Homeland Security Leadership, 2002–2008 Report* (Monterey, CA: U.S. Naval Postgraduate School, Center for Homeland Defense and Security, 2009), p. 7.
12. Ibid., p. 5.
13. Ibid., p. 7n2.
14. Polson, Persyn, and Cupp, "Partnership in Progress," p. 1.
15. Ibid., p. 5.
16. Ibid., p. 4.
17. Ibid., p. 8–9.
18. Ibid., p. 9.
19. Ibid., p. 12.
20. The Homeland Security and Defense Education Consortium Association supports educational institutions with educational program development and accreditation. HSDECA is currently pursuing recognition by the Department of Education as the accrediting body for homeland security and homeland defense education programs; https://www.hsdeca.org/.bbb.
21. Polson, Persyn, and Cupp, "Partnership in Progress," p. 20.

### Chapter 15. IPA Rotational Assignments

1. Michael W. Hager, "Memorandum for Chief Human Capital Officers: Recommended National Security Professional Qualification for NSP SES," Office of Personnel Management, 13 November 2008.
2. *NSPD Strategy*, p. 9.
3. Department of Homeland Security, "Rotational Assignments," DHS Directive System, Directive Number: 250-01 (13 November 2007), p. 4, http://www.dhs.gov/xlibrary/assets/foia/mgmt_rotational%20assignments_md%20250-01.pdf.

4. Ibid., p. 15.
5. Department of Homeland Security, *Bottom-Up Review Report* (July 2010), p. 32.
6. *NSPD Implementation Plan*, p. 14.
7. Depending on context, the terms "national security" and "emergency management," for example, can have very precise meanings. In the context of career paths and professional development, national security personnel *routinely* require access and permissions, as distinct from other broadly defined homeland security personnel who do not.
8. FEMA defines a JFO as "the primary Federal incident management field structure. The JFO is a temporary Federal facility that provides a central location for the coordination of Federal, state, tribal, and local governments and private-sector and nongovernmental organizations with primary responsibility for response and recovery. The JFO structure is organized, staffed, and managed in a manner consistent with National Incident Management System principles and is led by the Unified Coordination Group. Although the JFO uses an Incident Command System structure, the JFO does not manage on-scene operations. Instead, the JFO focuses on providing support to on-scene efforts and conducting broader support operations that may extend beyond the incident site."
9. FEMA defines a JOC as "an interagency command post established by the Federal Bureau of Investigation to manage terrorist threats or incidents and investigative and intelligence activities. The JOC coordinates the necessary local, State, and Federal assets required to support the investigation, and to prepare for, respond to, and resolve the threat or incident."

### Chapter 16. Credentialing

1. OPM defines certification programs as those offering a professional designation (certification/credential) certifying qualification to perform a specific task and periodic renewal or recertification (e.g., CPA). It calls certificate programs as those offering attendance or completion of coursework (e.g., not a professional designation). A third category is a career development program.
2. *NSPD Implementation Plan*, pp. 16–17.
3. Diana Hopkins, "The Development of National Standards for Credentialing," in *"C" Is For Credentials, Time Is of the Essence, DomPrep Journal* (27 August 2010), pp. 5–6, http://www.domesticpreparedness.com/pub/docs/DPJournalAug09.pdf.
4. Timothy W. Manning, "Establishment of a National Credentialing Program" (Memo to All FEMA Employees, 24 August 2010).
5. Glen Rudner, "Qualifications, Credentials, and the Need for Speed," in *"C" Is For Credentials, Time Is of the Essence, DomPrep Journal* (27 August 2010), pp. 14–15, http://www.domesticpreparedness.com/pub/docs/DPJournalAug09.pdf.
6. The COFRAC program provides the State of Colorado with a three-tiered level of assurance (FIPS 201–compliant, 2D barcode, or open technology) that runs on the FIPS 201–compliant COFRAC Bridge to allow for secure information

sharing of credentials. See http://www.colofirechiefs.org/CSFCA%20Documents/COFRAC_Standard.pdf.

7. Kay C. Goss, "Emergency Services Credentialing: FEMA Leads the Way," in *"C" Is For Credentials, Time Is of the Essence, DomPrep Journal* (27 August 2010), pp. 10–11, http://www.domesticpreparedness.com/pub/docs/DPJournalAug09.pdf .

8. Rudner, "Qualification, Credentials, and the Need for Speed," pp. 14–15.

9. DHS distinguishes between qualification and certification programs. As per the draft version of the DHS memo on the DHS Planner's Qualification Program (27 August 2010), a qualification program "details the necessary steps an individual must take in order to gain and/or demonstrate the knowledge, skills, abilities, competencies, and required attitudes in a specified functional area." A certification program "reviews evidence submitted by individuals and conveys special permissions or acknowledges achieved standards of performance for functioning at specified levels of service based on proven exhibition of knowledge, skills, abilities, competencies, and required attitudes."

10. EMAP is a standard-based voluntary assessment and peer review accreditation process for state and local government programs responsible for coordinating prevention, mitigation, preparedness, response, and recovery activities for natural and human-caused disasters. Accreditation is based on compliance with collaboratively developed national standards, the Emergency Management Standard by EMAP. Accreditation is open to all states, territories, and local government emergency management programs. The EMAP program began in 2007 and functions under the auspices of the EMAP Commission, whose members are appointed by the National Emergency Management Association and the International Association of Emergency Managers.

11. Goss, "Emergency Services Credentialing: FEMA Leads the Way," p. 11.

12. By example, HHS employs the concept for such as registry under its Emergency System for Volunteer Health Professionals (ESAR-VP) program. Another example is Colorado's COFRAC program.

13. See http://www.nwcg.gov.

14. See http://ross.nwcg.gov/aboutross.html.

15. The four major federal land management agencies are the U.S. Forest Service in the Department of Agriculture and the Bureau of Land Management, U.S. Fish and Wildlife Service, and National Park Service in the Department of the Interior.

## Postscript

1. While they were neither frightening nor catastrophic, I should cite the 2002 West Coast Port Lockout, 2003 Northeast Power Blackout, and 2010 volcanic eruptions in Iceland as representative examples of events that produced major system disruptions. I'm sure others have additional examples to make the point.

2. Cabinet Office, *The National Strategy of the United Kingdom: Security in an Interdependent World* (March 2008), p. 6.

3. Ibid., p. 3.
4. David Walker, "We the People: Keeping the Economy and the Nation Strong," ch. 1 in *Economic Security: Neglected Dimension of National Security?* ed. by Sheila R. Ronis (Washington, DC: Institute for National Strategic Studies, National Defense University Press, 2011), pp. 1–12.
5. Charlie Edwards, *Resilient Nation* (London: Demos, 2009), p. 16. As the deputy director for strategy and planning in the Office for Security and Counter Terrorism at the Home Office, he was responsible for developing the third version of *CONTEST: The United Kingdom's Strategy for Countering Terrorism*, released in July 2011.
6. Edwards, *Resilient Nation*, p. 27.
7. Philip Auerswald and Debra van Opstal, "Coping with Turbulence: The Resilience Imperative," *Innovations Technology/Governance/Globalization: Special Edition for the World Economic Forum Annual Meeting, 2009* (pp. 203–18 Davos-Klosters Cambridge, MA: MIT Press, 2009), p. 208. In the 1980s and 1990s, Debbie van Opstal was a defense industrial base and competitiveness expert who later became senior vice president for programs and policy for the Council on Competitiveness.
8. Ibid., p. 209. Some of Edwards' concern over the vulnerability of Britain's "brittle infrastructure" reflects a post-Thatcher critique of the two-decade privatization of "essential services." See Edwards, *Resilient Nation*, p. 25.
9. Auerswald and van Opstal, "Coping with Turbulence," p. 210. Later in the article, however, van Opstal noted an encouraging development, citing Standard & Poor's integration of enterprise risk management into its ratings assessment (p. 214).
10. Ibid., pp. 207–8.
11. Ibid., pp. 203–4.
12. Edwards, *Resilient Nation*, p. 32.
13. Robb, *Brave New War*, p. 182.
14. Ibid., pp. 5, 50.
15. Ibid., pp. 19, 79–80.
16. Barabási, *Linked*, p. 223.
17. Auerswald and van Opstal, "Coping with Turbulence," p. 217.
18. Robb, *Brave New War*, p. 7. From the standpoint of the homeland security mission continuum, the extreme left-of-the-boom missions beyond borders-in prevention involve disruption and thus overlap with borders-out preemption missions. Such missions do not require divisions, but rather special operations forces and capabilities as provided so famously by Navy SEALs.
19. Barabási, *Linked*, p. 221.
20. Edwards, *Resilient Nation*, p. 27.
21. Ibid., p. 80.
22. Ibid., p. 51.

23. *National Strategy of the United Kingdom*, pp. 8, 41.

24. Auerswald and van Opstal, "Coping with Turbulence," p. 204.

25. Debra Van Opstal, *The Resilient Economy: Integrating Competitiveness and Security* (Washington, DC: Council on Competitiveness, 2007), p. 39.

26. Auerswald and van Opstal, "Coping with Turbulence," p. 207.

27. Ibid. Debbie and John Robb are in sync. His resilience strategy calls for the devolution of power to local government, private companies, and individuals. See Robb, *Brave New War*, p. 185.

28. Van Opstal, *The Resilient Economy*, p. 42.

29. Ibid.

30. Ibid., p. 39.

31. Edwards, *Resilient Nation*, p. 18.

32. Ibid., p. 19.

33. Ibid., pp. 72–73.

34. Thad Allen, "Leadership in Times of National Crisis" (presentation at the Advancing U.S. Resilience to a Nuclear Catastrophe Conference, 19 May 2011, Washington, DC).

35. The webinar is available to members of *DomesticPreparedness.com*. *DomPrep* is a free service to qualified preparedness professionals and students. To become a *DomPrep* member and register for the webinar, go to http://www.domesticpreparedness.com/Member_Registration/ and follow directions for registering. Once registered, type in the Search box "Crisis Communications, Does Social Media Work?" and click Search, which leads to the Crisis Communications, Does Social Media Work? Webinar page. Click on "Crisis Communications, Does Social Media Work? Webinar" to enter the webinar.

Other presentations by Patrick Meier on the Ushahidi platform, crowd sourcing, and collaborative crisis mapping for the Haitian Earthquake response are available on YouTube. Three recommended are: his presentation at *PopTech 2010*, the annual conference of a global community of design and technology innovators, http://www.youtube.com/watch?v=8qjy9LOe5nk; the American Red Cross' Emergency Social Data Summit in Washington, D.C., on 12 August 2010, http://www.youtube.com/watch?v=4ANZd6v9qIc; and *Re:publica 2011*, Germany's largest annual conference on blogs, new media, and the digital society, http://www.youtube.com/watch?v=Hh_PiVqf8BA (all accessed on 1 February 2012).

36. Thad Allen, interview by Steve Inskeep, *Morning Edition*, National Public Radio, 9 September 2010.

# Bibliography

## Books

Barabási, Albert-László. *Linked: The New Science of Networks.* Cambridge, MA: Perseus Publishing, 2002.

Bush, George W. *Decision Points.* New York: Crown Publishers, 2010.

Chertoff, Michael. *Homeland Security: Assessing the First Five Years.* Philadelphia: University of Pennsylvania Press, 2009.

Clarke, Richard A. *Against All Enemies: Inside America's War on Terror.* New York, London, Toronto, Sydney: Free Press, 2004.

Coll, Steve. *Ghost Wars: The Secret History of the CIA, Afghanistan, and Bin Laden, from the Soviet Invasion to September 10, 2001.* New York: The Penguin Press, 2004.

Edwards, Charlie. *Resilient Nation.* London: Demos, 2009.

Gross, Daniel. *Bull Run: Wall Street, the Democrats, and the New Politics of Personal Finance.* New York: PublicAffairs, 2000.

Kettl, Donald F. *System under Stress: Homeland Security and American Politics.* Washington, DC: CQ Press, 2004.

Kushner, Harvey W. *Encyclopedia of Terrorism.* Thousand Oaks, CA: Sage Publications, 2003.

Naftali, Timothy. *Blind Spot: The Secret History of American Counterterrorism.* New York: Basic Books, 2005.

Ridge, Tom. *The Test of Our Times: America under Siege . . . And How We Can Be Safe Again.* New York: Thomas Dunne Books, 2009.

Robb, John. *Brave New War: The Next Stage of Terrorism and the End of Global Civilization.* Hoboken, NJ: John Wiley & Sons, 2007.

Ronis, Sheila R., ed. *Economic Security: Neglected Dimension of National Security?* Washington, DC: Institute for National Strategic Studies, National Defense University Press, 2011.

Rothkopf, David J. *Running the World: The Inside Story of the National Security Council and the Architects of American Power.* New York: Public Affairs, 2005.

Rove, Karl. *Courage and Consequence: My Life as a Conservative in the Fight.*
    New York: Threshold Editions, Simon and Schuster, 2010.
Slaughter, Anne-Marie. *A New World Order: Government Networks and the*
    *Disaggregated State.* Princeton, NJ: Princeton University Press, 2004.
Stanik, Joseph T. *El Dorado Canyon: Reagan's Undeclared War with Qaddafi.*
    Annapolis, MD: U.S. Naval Institute Press, 2003.
Stanton, Thomas H., and Benjamin Ginsberg. *Making Government Manageable:*
    *Executive Organization and Management in the Twenty-First Century.*
    Baltimore and London: The Johns Hopkins University Press, 2004.

## Periodicals, Interviews, and Audiovisual Sources

Allen, Thad. Interview by Steve Inskeep. *Morning Edition*, National Public Radio,
    9 September 2010.
"America Humbled." *Los Angeles Times*, 8 September 2005. http://articles.latimes
    .com/2005/sep/04/opinion/ed-levees4 (accessed 30 July 2011).
Bellavita, Christopher. "What is Preventing Homeland Security?" *Homeland Security*
    *Affairs*, no. 1 (Summer 2005).
Clovis, Samuel H., Jr. "Federalism, Homeland Security, and National Preparedness: A
    Case Study in the Development of Public Policy." *Homeland Security Affairs*
    2, no. 3 (October 2006). http://www.hsaj.org/?article=2.3.4 (accessed 7 June
    2011).
———. "Promises Unfulfilled: The Suboptimization of Homeland Security National
    Preparedness." *Homeland Security Affairs* 4, no. 3 (October 2008). http://
    www.hsaj.org/?article=4.3.3 (accessed 7 June 2011).
"Fixing FEMA." *PBS News Hour*, 13 February 2006. http://www.pbs.org/newshour/
    bb/fedagencies/jan-june06/fema_2-13.html   (accessed 7 August 2011).
Gispert, Larry J. "From the President—Remain Vigilant Concerning New U.S.
    Integrated Planning System." *Bulletin of the International Association of*
    *Emergency Managers* (June 2008).
Goss, Kay C. "Emergency Services Credentialing: FEMA Leads the Way." In *"C" Is*
    *For Credentials: Time Is of the Essence, DomPrep Journal* 5, no. 8 (August
    2009): pp. 10–11. http://www.domesticprepared
    ness.com/pub/docs/DPJournalAug09.pdf .
Grunwald, Michael, and Susan B. Glasser. "Brown's Turf Wars Sapped FEMA's
    Strength." *Washington Post*, 23 December 2005.
Hopkins, Diana. "The Development of National Standards for Credentialing." In
    *"C" Is For Credentials, Time Is of the Essence, DomPrep Journal* 5, no. 8
    (August 2009): pp. 5–6. http://www.domesticpreparedness.com/pub/docs/
    DPJournalAug09.pdf.
Irish, Kerry E. "Apt Pupil: Dwight Eisenhower and the 1930 Mobilization Plan." *The*
    *Journal of Military History* 70 (January 2006): pp. 31–61.

Loy, James M. "Adm. James M. Loy, USCG (Ret.), Acting Secretary of Homeland
    Security." Audio interview by John F. Morton. *Domestic Preparedness*
    (3 February 2005). http://www.domesticpreparedness.com/pub/docs/
    DomPrepTIPSFeb9.pdf (accessed 14 June 2011).

Mayer, Matt. "Matt Mayer, Acting Executive Director, Office of State and Local
    Government Coordination and Preparedness, Department of Homeland
    Security." Audio interview by John F. Morton. *Domestic Preparedness*
    (4 May 2005), http://www.domesticpreparedness.com/pub/docs/
    DomPrepTIPSMay4.pdf (accessed 14 June 2011).

Polson, Cheryl J., John M. Persyn, and O. Shawn Cupp. "Partnership in Progress:
    A Model for Development of a Homeland Security Graduate Degree
    Program." *Homeland Security Affairs* 6, no. 2 (May 2010): p. 5. http://www.
    hsaj.org/pages/volume6/issue2/pdfs/6.2.3.pdf.

Porteus, Liza. "Bush Names Homeland Security Chief." Fox News, 12 January 2005.
    http://www.foxnews.com/story/0,2933,143997,00.html (accessed 23 June
    2011).

Posner, Paul. "The Politics of Coercive Federalism in the Bush Era." *Publius* 37, no.
    3 (May 2007). http://publius.oxfordjournals.org/content/37/3/390.full
    (accessed 8 June 2011).

Rudner, Glen. "Qualifications, Credentials, and the Need for Speed." In *"C" Is For
    Credentials, Time Is of the Essence, DomPrep Journal* 5, no. 8 (August 2009):
    pp. 14–15. http://www.domesticprepared
    ness.com/pub/docs/DPJournalAug09.pdf.

Sullivan, Eileen. "Foresman Resignation Follows DHS Decision to Eliminate New
    Preparedness." *CQ Homeland Security*, 30 March 2007. http://www.
    voicesofseptember11.org/dev/content.php?idtocitems=ForesmanResignat
    ion (accessed 12 August 2011).

Webster, Richard J. "Learning from Operation Able Manner." U.S. Naval Institute
    *Proceedings* 137, no. 8 (August 2011): p. 34.

## Reports, Papers, Studies, and Testimonies

Agranoff, Robert. "A New Look at the Value-Adding Functions of Intergovernmental
    Networks." Paper prepared for Seventh Annual National Public
    Management Research Conference at Georgetown University, 9 October
    2003. Bloomington, IN: Indiana University, 2003.

Allen, Thad. "Leadership in Times of National Crisis." Presentation at the Advancing
    U.S. Resilience to a Nuclear Catastrophe Conference, 19 May 2011,
    Washington, DC.

Auerswald, Philip, and Debra van Opstal. "Coping with Turbulence: The Resilience
    Imperative." *Innovations Technology/Governance/Globalization: Special
    Edition for the World Economic Forum Annual Meeting, 2009.* Paper

presented to the 2009 World Economic Forum Annual Meeting. Cambridge, MA: Davos-Klosters; MIT Press, 2009.

Austin, William H. "The United States Department of Homeland Security Concept of Regionalization—Will It Survive the Test?" Master's thesis, Center for Homeland Defense and Security, Naval Postgraduate School, September 2006.

Bea, Keith. *The National Preparedness System: Issues in the 109th Congress.* Congressional Research Service Report for Congress, 10 March 2005.

Brinkerhoff, Col. John R., USA (Ret.), *Introduction to Modern Emergency Management.* Monograph. August 2006.

Brown, Jared T. *Presidential Policy Directive 8 and the National Preparedness System: Background and Issues for Congress.* Congressional Research Service Report for Congress, 21 October 2011.

Carter, Ashton B., Michael M. May, and William J. Perry. *The Day After: Action in the 24 Hours Following a Nuclear Blast in an American City.* The Preventive Defense Project, Harvard and Stanford Universities, April 2007.

Center for Homeland Defense and Security. *Education: The Key to Homeland Security Leadership, 2002–2008 Report.* Monterey, CA: U.S. Naval Postgraduate School, Center for Homeland Defense and Security, 2009.

Chertoff, Michael. "Remarks of Secretary Michael Chertoff, U.S. Department of Homeland Security, George Washington University Homeland Security Policy Institute." 16 March 2005. http://www.dhs.gov/xnews/speeches/ speech_0245.shtm (accessed 23 June 2011).

Clovis, Samuel H., Jr. "The Cost of Compliance: Preparedness and the Target Capabilities List." Paper delivered at the Midwest Political Science Association Annual Conference, April 2008. http://convention2.allacademic.com/meta/p269039_index.html?phpsessid =5d41c533cc339abf3341d3f9bdb0281 (accessed 7 June 2011).

———. "Normalized Jurisdictional Traits for Homeland Security Grant Allocations: Exposing Governance Vulnerability in Large Urban Settings." Paper delivered at the Midwest Political Science Association Annual Conference, April 2008. http://www.allacademic.com/pages/p268584-1.php (accessed 7 June 2011).

Commission on the Intelligence Capabilities of the United States Regarding Weapons of Mass Destruction. *Report to the President of the United States,* 31 March 2005.

Cordesman, Anthony H. "Redefining the Conceptual Boundaries of Homeland Defense." Center for Strategic and International Studies, revised 12 December 2000. http://edocs.nps.edu/AR/org/CSIS/budgetoverview.pdf (accessed 22 January 2012).

Dale, Catherine. "Building an Interagency Cadre of National Security Professionals: Proposals, Recent Experience, and Issues for Congress." Congressional Research Service Report for Congress, 8 July 2008, RL34565.

Fuentes, Col. Joseph R. "New Jersey State Police Practical Guide to Intelligence-Led Policing." Center for Policing Terrorism (CPT) at the Manhattan Institute and Harbinger/ICx Technologies, September 2006.

Fugate, Craig. *Testimony before the United States House Subcommittee on Homeland Security on FEMA's Fiscal Year 2011 Budget.* 10 March 2010. http://www.dhs.gov/ynews/testimony/testimony _1274285305684.shtm (accessed 27 November 2011).

Gispert, Larry. "The Federal Emergency Management Agency: Is the Agency on the Right Track?" Testimony before the Subcommittee on Homeland Security Committee on Appropriations, U.S. House of Representatives, 13 March 2008. http://www.iaem.com/publications/news/documents/IAEMLarryGispert031308.pdf (accessed 29 October 2011).

Grasso, Valerie Bailey. "Defense Acquisition: Use of Lead Systems Integrators (LSIs)—Background, Oversight Issues, and Options for Congress." Congressional Research Service, 8 October 2010. http://www.fas.org/sgp/crs/natsec/RS22631.pdf (accessed 13 June 2011).

Hamilton, Lee, and Thomas Kean. *Tenth Anniversary Report Card: The Status of the 9/11 Commission Recommendations.* Bipartisan Policy Center National Security Preparedness Group, September 2011.

Lieberman, Senator Joseph. "Statement on the Nominations of George Foresman as Under Secretary for Preparedness and Tracy Henke as Assistant Secretary for Grants and Training." 8 December 2005. http://hsgac.senate.gov/public/index.cfm?FuseAction=Press.MajorityNews&ContentRecord_id=35111e54-3735-447a-98ab-e2c5aee88b79 (accessed 29 June 2011).

Local, State, Tribal, and Federal Preparedness Task Force. *Perspective on Preparedness: Taking Stock since 9/11*, September 2010.

McCarthy, Francis X., and Natalie Keegan. "FEMA's Pre-Disaster Mitigation Program: Overview and Issues." Congressional Research Service, 10 July 2009 http://www.fas.org/sgp/crs/homesec/RL34537.pdf (accessed 4 June 2011).

Moynihan, Donald P. *From Forest Fires to Hurricane Katrina: Case Studies of Incident Command Systems.* IBM Center for The Business of Government, 2007.

———. *Leveraging Collaborative Networks in Infrequent Emergency Situations.* IBM Center for The Business of Government, June 2005.

National Academy of Public Administration (NAPA). *Advancing Management of Homeland Security: Managing Intergovernmental Relations for Homeland Security.* Washington, DC, February 2004.

National Association of Development Organizations (NADO). *Regional Approaches to Homeland Security Planning and Preparedness—Survey of the Nation's Regional Development Organizations.* Washington, DC, August 2005.

National League of Cities (NLC). "Is the Federal-State-Local Partnership Being Dismantled? Roundtable Proceedings." *Research Report on America's Cities*, National League of Cities. Washington, DC: NLC Press, 2003.

Project on National Security Reform. *Forging a New Shield*. Washington, DC: PNSR, November 2008. http://www.pnsr.org/data/files/pnsr_forging_a_new_ shield_report.pdf.

———. *The Power of People: Building an Integrated National Security Professional System for the 21st Century*. Washington, DC: PNSR, November 2010. http://www.pnsr.org/data/images/pnsr_the_power_of_people_report.pdf.

———. *Recalibrating the System: Toward Efficient and Effective Resourcing of National Preparedness*. Washington, DC: PNSR, 2009. http://www.pnsr.org/data/ files/pnsr_national_preparedness_system.pdf.

Rumsfeld, Donald. "Submitted Testimony." Hearings of the 9/11 Commission. 23 March 2004. http://www.9-11commission.gov/hearings/hearing8.htm.

Rusten, Lynn F. "U.S. Withdrawal from the Antiballistic Missile Treaty." Center for the Study of Weapons of Mass Destruction, Case Study 2. Washington, DC: National Defense University Press, January 2010.

Schrader, Dennis. "Unfinished Business at FEMA: A National Preparedness Perspective." Heritage Lectures, Number 1125, 26 June 2009. http://www. heritage.org/research/lecture/unfinished-business-at-fema-a-national-pre paredness-perspective (accessed 14 September 2011).

Staff Statement No. 8. "National Policy Coordination." Hearings of the 9/11 Commission. http://www.9-11commission.gov/hearings/hearing8.htm, p. 8.

Temple, Jennie M. "Enhancing Regional Collaboration—Taking the Next Step." Master's thesis, Center for Homeland Defense and Security, Naval Postgraduate School, March 2007.

United Kingdom Cabinet Office. *The National Strategy of the United Kingdom: Security in an Interdependent World*. March 2008.

Van Opstal, Debra. *The Resilient Economy: Integrating Competitiveness and Security*. Washington, DC: Council on Competitiveness, 2007.

Wormuth, Christine E. *Managing the Next Domestic Catastrophe: Ready (or Not)?* A Beyond Goldwater-Nichols Phase 4 Report. Washington, DC: CSIS Press, June 2008.

### Executive Branch Documents

Department of Homeland Security. *Bottom-Up Review Report*. July 2010.

———. *Initial National Response Plan*. Memo from Tom Ridge, 30 September 2003. http://www.crcpd.org/Homeland_Security/Initial_NRP_100903.pdf (accessed 3 June 2011).

———. *The Integrated Planning System*. January 2009.

———. *National Preparedness Goal*. 1st ed. September 2011.

———. *National Response Framework*. January 2008.

———. *Nationwide Plan Review Phase 2 Report*. 16 June 2006.

———. *NIMS FEMA 501/Draft*. August 2007.

———. *Press Briefing by Secretary for Homeland Security Michael Chertoff and Under Secretary for Preparedness George Foresman.* 25 September 2006. http://www.dhs.gov/xnews/releases/pr_1159903739058.shtm (accessed 29 June 2011).

———. *Quadrennial Homeland Security Review Report: A Strategic Framework for a Secure Homeland.* 1 February 2010.

———. "Rotational Assignments." DHS Directive System, Directive Number: 250-01, 13 November 2007, http://www.dhs.gov/xlibrary/assets/foia/mgmt_rotational%20assignments_md%20250-01.pdf.

Department of Homeland Security in cooperation with the Department of Transportation. *Nationwide Plan Review: Phase II Report.* 16 June 2006.

Department of Justice, Office of Justice Programs, Bureau of Justice Assistance. "Intelligence-Led Policing: The New Intelligence Architecture." September 2005.

Department of the Treasury. "Fact Sheets: Taxes—History of the U.S. Tax System." https://ustreas.gov/education/fact-sheets/taxes/ustax.shtml (accessed 17 January 2011).

FEMA. "FEMA History." http://www.fema.gov/about/history.shtm (accessed 19 January 2011).

———. *National Preparedness System Description.* November 2011.

———. Press Release, "FEMA Hails 2000 as Year of Major Gains in Disaster Prevention." 22 December 2000. http://www.fema.gov/news/newsrelease.fema?id=9993 (accessed 2 June 2011).

———. *Regional-National Preparedness Concept of Operations.* 8 February 2008.

———. *FEMA Strategic Plan for FY 2011–2014, Frequently Asked Questions.* 15 March 2011. http://www.fema.gov/about/2011_14_strategic_plan_faq.shtm (accessed 28 December 2011).

Government Printing Office. *The National Preparedness System: What Are We Preparing For?* Hearing before the Subcommittee on Economic Development, Public Buildings, and Emergency Management of the Committee on Transportation and Infrastructure, House of Representatives, 14 April 2005.

———. *The Stafford Act: A Plan for the Nation's Emergency Preparedness and Response System.* Hearing before the Committee on Environment and Public Works, U.S. Senate, 27 July 2006.

Hager, Michael W. "Memorandum for Chief Human Capital Officers: Recommended National Security Professional Qualification for NSP SES." 13 November 2008.

Manning, Timothy W. "Establishment of a National Credentialing Program." Memo to All FEMA Employees, 24 August 2010.

U.S. Coast Guard. *U.S. Coast Guard: America's Maritime Guardian,* Coast Guard Publication 1, 1 January 2002.

————. Press Release, "Success through Preparation, Teamwork, Prevention: First-of-Its-Kind Task Force Prevents Exodus, Saves Lives." n. d. http://www.d7publicaffairs.com/external/?fuseaction=external. docview&cid=586&pressID=43272 (accessed 15 September 2011).

White House. *Federal Response to Hurricane Katrina: Lessons Learned*. Washington, DC: White House, 2006.

————. Homeland Security Presidential Directive, Management of Domestic Incidents (HSPD-5). 28 February 2003. http://www.dhs.gov/xabout/laws/gc_1214592333605.shtm (accessed 3 June 2011).

————. *National Security Strategy*. May 2010.

————. *National Strategy for Homeland Security*. 16 July 2002.

————. *National Strategy for the Development of National Security Professionals*. July 2007.

————. NSPD Executive Steering Committee (ESC). *National Security Professional Development Implementation Plan*. 1 August 2008.

————. Office of the Press Secretary. *Statement by the President on the White House Organization for Homeland Security and Counterterrorism*. 26 May 2009.

————. Presidential Policy Directive 1 (PPD-1). Organization of the National Security Council System. 13 February 2009.

————. Presidential Policy Directive/PPD-8 Draft—National Preparedness Goal Review Package, accessible via the International Association of Emergency Managers (IAEM) Web site, http://www.iaem.com/committees/governmentaffairs/documents/NPG_DRAFT_20110822_for_review.pdf, p. 6 (accessed 25 November 2011).

————. "Press Briefing by Homeland Security and Counterterrorism Advisor Fran Townsend," 21 October 2005, http://georgewbush-whitehouse.archives. gov/news/releases/2005/10/20051021.html (accessed 8 August 2011).

————. "Press Briefing by Scott McClellan." 29 June 2005. http://georgewbush-white-house.archives.gov/news/releases/2005/06/20050629-4.html (accessed 8 August 2011).

### Legislative Branch Documents

Government Printing Office. *The National Preparedness System: What Are We Preparing For?* Hearing before the Subcommittee on Economic Development, Public Buildings, and Emergency Management of the Committee on Transportation and Infrastructure, House of Representatives, 14 April 2005.

U.S. House of Representatives. *A Failure of Initiative: The Final Report of the Select Bipartisan Committee to Investigate the Preparations for and Response to Hurricane Katrina*. 15 February 2006.

U.S. Senate. "Nominations of George W. Foresman and Tracy A. Henke, Hearing before the Committee on Homeland Security and Governmental Affairs." 8 December 2005.

# Index

# About the Author

John Fass Morton recently served as a distinguished fellow and the homeland security lead for the Project on National Security Reform. With over twenty-five years' analytical experience in homeland and national security, he has supported government, industry, associations, and think tanks. Extensively published, he has written for virtually every major defense publication, including *Proceedings*.

The **Naval Institute Press** is the book-publishing arm of the U.S. Naval Institute, a private, nonprofit, membership society for sea service professionals and others who share an interest in naval and maritime affairs. Established in 1873 at the U.S. Naval Academy in Annapolis, Maryland, where its offices remain today, the Naval Institute has members worldwide.

Members of the Naval Institute support the education programs of the society and receive the influential monthly magazine *Proceedings* or the colorful bimonthly magazine *Naval History* and discounts on fine nautical prints and on ship and aircraft photos. They also have access to the transcripts of the Institute's Oral History Program and get discounted admission to any of the Institute-sponsored seminars offered around the country.

The Naval Institute's book-publishing program, begun in 1898 with basic guides to naval practices, has broadened its scope to include books of more general interest. Now the Naval Institute Press publishes about seventy titles each year, ranging from how-to books on boating and navigation to battle histories, biographies, ship and aircraft guides, and novels. Institute members receive significant discounts on the Press's more than eight hundred books in print.

Full-time students are eligible for special half-price membership rates. Life memberships are also available.

For a free catalog describing Naval Institute Press books currently available, and for further information about joining the U.S. Naval Institute, please write to:

Member Services
**U.S. Naval Institute**
291 Wood Road
Annapolis, MD 21402-5034
Telephone: (800) 233-8764
Fax: (410) 571-1703
Web address: www.usni.org